JAMES AGEE

A Life

ALSO BY LAURENCE BERGREEN

Look Now, Pay Later: The Rise of Network Broadcasting

JAMES AGEE

A Life

Laurence Bergreen

E. P. DUTTON, INC. | NEW YORK

Copyright © 1984 by Laurence Bergreen
All rights reserved. Printed in the U.S.A.

No part of this publication may be reproduced or transmitted in any form or by any means, electronic or mechanical, including photocopy, recording or any information storage and retrieval system now known or to be invented, without permission in writing from the publisher, except by a reviewer who wishes to quote brief passages in connection with a review written for inclusion in a magazine, newspaper or broadcast.

Published in the United States by
E.P. Dutton, Inc., 2 Park Avenue, New York, N.Y. 10016

Library of Congress Cataloging in Publication Data
Bergreen, Laurence.
James Agee: a life.
1. Agee, James, 1909–1955—Biography. 2. Authors,
American—20th century—Biography. I. Title.
PS3501.G35Z59 1984   818'.5209[B]   83-25496
ISBN 0-525-24253-8

Published simultaneously in Canada
by Fitzhenry & Whiteside Limited, Toronto

COBE

Designed by Nancy Etheredge

10 9 8 7 6 5 4 3 2 1

First Edition

To Betsy and Nicky

CONTENTS

vii

CONTENTS

ACKNOWLEDGMENTS

I am grateful to David McDowell, Trustee of the James Agee Trust, for granting me unrestricted access to and permission to quote from Agee's writing, both published and unpublished.

Rarely has there been a more autobiographical writer than Agee. He was, if anything, even more objective and factual in his "fiction" than in his journalism and made little or no attempt to disguise events about which he wrote. Both his letters and my interviews with those who knew him have confirmed the accuracy of his novels and stories, which I have treated accordingly. Comprehensive notes on my sources can be found at the end of the book.

Agee loved to write letters, but only the celebrated letters to Father Flye and a handful of others have been published. In writing this biography I consulted and quoted from hundreds more; they have shed much light on previously ignored aspects of Agee's varied life and career. The mother lode of unpublished letters—as well as stories, screenplays, notebooks, and poetry—is located at the Humanities Research Center of the University of Texas at Austin. I have drawn heavily on this large and rich collection, and I wish to express my appreciation to the HRC staff, especially Cathy Henderson, for unfailing assistance, courtesy, and patience.

Other unpublished Agee material, primarily letters, is scattered across the country in various libraries and archives. Much of it has only recently come to light, and in many instances I have had the privilege of being the first to make use of it. I thank Sam Gill of the Academy of Motion Picture Arts and Science's Margaret Herrick Library for guiding me to the John Huston papers; the Colonial Williamsburg Foundation, where Peter Brown and Bland Blackford located Agee's last screenplay; the Columbia University Oral History Collection and Rare Book and Manuscript Library; the Hamilton College Library and especially Frank Lorenz, who placed at my disposal a wealth of Agee letters and manuscripts included in the Saunders family papers; Harvard University's Alumni Records Office and the assistance of Mrs. Wu; the Houghton Library of Harvard University, where Susan Halpert and Rodney Dennis helped me; Lilly Library, Indiana University, Bloomington, Indiana, where Saundra Taylor gave me access to the Frank Taylor papers; the Calvin M. McClung Historical Collection of the Public Library in Knoxville, Tennessee, where I absorbed much local history and color; the Library of Congress, Washington, D.C., where Paul T. Heffron obligingly unearthed uncatalogued letters and notes from Agee to Archibald MacLeish; Peter Galassi of the Museum of Modern Art's Department of Photography; the Berg Collection of the New York Public Library and in particular Walter Zervas of Special Collections, who cut through the red tape binding Agee's uncatalogued letters to Robert Fitzgerald; the Phillips Exeter Academy Library, where archivist Ed Desrochers facilitated my research; Princeton University's Firestone Library; the James Agee Memorial Library at St. Andrew's-Sewanee; the Time Inc. archives, where Elaine Felsher and Cheryl Wacher found no request of mine too large or small to fill; Twentieth Century-Fox Pictures and Les Gerber, who directed me to several unpublished screenplays and treatments by Agee; Wesleyan University's Saudek-Omnibus Collection and the assistance of Elizabeth Swaim and Jeanette Basinger; and last but not least, Yale University's Sterling Library, where Judith Schiff expedited my inquiries into the Agee correspondence in the Dwight Macdonald papers.

Some of Agee's letters remain in private hands. My thanks to Tamara Comstock, Mrs. Howard Doughty, Alma Mailman Neuman, and James Stern for sharing theirs with me.

This biography owes much to my interviews with numerous friends, relatives, and colleagues of Agee. I am particularly grateful to Alma Mailman Neuman and to Mia Agee for answering my questions about their marriages. No less helpful in their interviews were Nan Abell, who was unstinting with both her hospitality in Greenwich and her photographic memory; Jay Grayson Agee; Dr. Oliver Agee, who furnished me with the invaluable *Record of the Agee Family;* Mary Ahern; Esther Bear; Paul Brooks; Tamara Comstock; Marguerite Courtney; Brad Darrach; Mrs. F. W. Dupee; Robert Fitzgerald; Father James Harold Flye, now nearly a century old and still flourishing; W. M. Frohock; Clement Greenberg; Paul Gregory; Eunice Jessup; Richard E. Harrison; John Huston, who took time out of an exceedingly busy schedule to talk; Christopher Isherwood; Alfred Kazin; Ilse Lahn; Jay Leyda; Helen Levitt; Katherine Ling-Mullins, Agee's niece; the late Dwight Macdonald, who in his zeal to help paid no heed to his failing health; Ivan Moffat; Alice S. Morris; Osgood Nichols; Mary O'Gorman; William Phillips; Selden Rodman; Edith Phillips Russell; Terry Sanders; Robert Saudek, who long ago said he could tell me some interesting stories about his friend and college roommate James Agee and kept his promise; B. F. Skinner; Perrin Stryker; Howard Taubman; Frank Taylor; Diana Trilling; Archer Winsten; and Dwight Whitney.

Still others were kind enough to answer my inquiries by letter: Malcolm Cowley; John Goodbody; the late Archibald MacLeish; Bernard Schoenfeld; James Stern; and, last, Irvine Upham, who responded with extraordinary thoroughness and insight.

I am also indebted to the following: Jeffrey Apter; Mary Barno; Christopher Caldwell; Mell Cohen, who ably assisted in the search for photographs; James Laughlin; the Reverend Franklin Martin; Jim Menick; the Museum of Broadcasting; the National Council on Alcoholism; Mary Newman, for her transcription of

Scientists and Tramp, one of Agee's unpublished screenplays; Elisa Petrini, for coming up with the right word at the right time; Gerard Reedy, S. J., and Patrick Ryan, S. J., both of whom illuminated aspects of Agee's religious background for me; David Schoonover; Mr. and Mrs. Jack Skirball, for their kind hospitality; Linda Spencer, for several perceptive remarks about Agee's poetry; Kevin and Sheila Starr, for hospitality, encouragement, and shrewd insights into my subject; James Thompson; George Wead, for supplying me with a transcript of an interview with Irvine Upham about Agee; Leslie Wells; Richard Wilbur; and, for help in ways too numerous to mention, my parents.

Once again it was a pleasure to work with my literary agent, Peter Lampack, and his capable assistants Tony Gardner and Vanessa Futrell.

I am especially grateful to Joseph Kanon, my editor and publisher. Joe believed in this book when it was scarcely more than a gleam in my eye, and he backed his belief with generous logistic support and superb editorial advice.

PART ONE

Photograph courtesy of Phillips Exeter Academy

I

A DEATH
IN THE FAMILY

*We are talking now of summer evenings in Knoxville, Tennessee
in the time that I lived there so successfully disguised to myself
as a child.*

—"KNOXVILLE: SUMMER 1915"

At the turn of the century, Knoxville, Tennessee, was a grimy little
city strewn along the banks of the Tennessee River. The city offered
commercial opportunity rather than Southern charm and demanded grit, not breeding. It was a resolutely industrial city, a
workingman's city, where a farmer from the surrounding hill country might come to make something more of himself than his ances-

3

tors had been; the pride of Knoxville lay not in its mansions but in its factories.

In the outlying hamlets, where many of James Agee's paternal ancestors had lived for nearly two centuries, life had changed little since the death of the Confederacy. Amid the gently rolling hills of Eastern Tennessee, farmers worked the rich clay soil in unevenly shaped small fields planted with blue-green grass. In the fall, trees flamed into intense yellows and reds. On cold mornings the Tennessee River coughed up cottony mist, the cattle snorted steam, and low-lying fog wrapped the hills and hamlets in a cocoon of obscurity. Overshadowed by Memphis and Nashville and miles from any significant body of water, the region remained irrevocably isolated and provincial.

There is a Tennessee saying that it is but three generations from the plow handle to the silk hat, but the Agees perpetually hovered between the two extremes. Never again, it seemed, would one attain the eminence enjoyed by the first Agee in the New World, Mathieu Agee (sometimes called Agé), a French nobleman. Born near Nantes, Mathieu had espoused the Huguenot faith, and he was consequently forced to give up land and title. Along with thousands of other Protestants, Mathieu left France in 1688, at the age of eighteen, and joined soldiers led by William of Orange, who, in the so-called Glorious Revolution, captured the English throne. As William III, he offered free passage to the New World and land grants to those who had helped his campaign. Accepting the offer, Mathieu arrived in Virginia in 1690, where, much later in life, he married one Ann Godwin. Of their four children, two, James and Anthony, each had a dozen offspring, and it was from these twenty-four grandchildren of old Mathieu that nearly all Agees claim ancestry.

Succeeding generations of Agees were predominantly farmers but claimed a number of country doctors, lawyers, and teachers in their number. Like most of their neighbors, they were staunchly Republican, not that they paid much attention to politics, and Unitarian or Baptist, not that they paid much attention to religion, either. James Agee's great-grandfather, James Harris Agee, a descendant of Anthony, achieved local renown as a doctor, and his son, the writer's grandfather, Henry Clay Agee, reared his children on a farm near the small town of La Follette, forty miles north of

Knoxville. There were four children in all; the eldest, Hugh James Agee, born April 15, 1878, was James Agee's father.

Hugh James Agee—or Jay, as he was known to all—was tall and lanky, with sandy hair, a long, sloping nose, and a casual, relaxed manner. He had completed school through the fourth grade, enough to allow him to try his hand at teaching, but he soon gave it up in favor of making a new beginning in Knoxville. In 1902 he found a position with the post office, a good, steady job, but not the kind a man of his quiet ambition was content to hold for very long.

Shortly after joining the post office, Jay attended a dance in Knoxville. There he met the woman who was to become his wife and the writer's mother, Laura Tyler. She was an attractive young woman still in her teens. She had a full head of dark hair, large brown eyes, an overgenerous nose, and a perfectly formed little mouth. She was a serious, intense young lady, a student at the University of Tennessee, and, in her spare time, an aspiring poet. But she was six years younger than Jay, a mere child, much too young for marriage. Nonetheless, a courtship ensued, during which Jay came to learn about her family, one much more highfalutin than his own.

Laura's father, Joel Tyler, was an unusual amalgam of businessman and progressive thinker. He had spent his youth in Michigan, where he had attended the state university, but since he was prone to respiratory ailments, had moved to a warmer climate. He bought a large tract of land in Eastern Tennessee in the hope of making a killing when the railroad came through, but he grew tired of waiting and sold out just before the tracks were laid. He went on to the construction field, forming a small company, Ty-Sa-Man Construction, named after its founders, Tyler, Savage, and Manning.

Joel Tyler was even-tempered, but his wife Emma was highstrung, intelligent, and discontented with her place in society. As one of the first women to receive an undergraduate degree from the University of Michigan, she was determined to make her mark. She maintained an interest in literature, in part because family lore had it that Walt Whitman was one of her ancestors. (She made Whitman Laura's middle name.) Failing to find a satisfactory outlet for her energies, Emma fell back on sheltering "wayward girls" in her home, presumably prostitutes and unwed mothers, from whom it is said she contracted syphilis. In later life she grew deaf and weak from its effects and resorted to using a cumbersome ear trumpet.

With the notable exception of Joel Tyler, religion dominated this side of the writer's family. Emma's sister Jessie was an Episcopalian nun and founded a contemplative order in Chattanooga. Later, Emma herself became an Anglo-Catholic. This movement, which was to exert a formidable influence on James Agee, was the American version of the Oxford Movement in England. While regretting the divisiveness of the Reformation, Anglo-Catholics were, in the last analysis, Protestants, even though they maintained such Roman Catholic trappings as confession. Although priests were encouraged to remain celibate, they were permitted to marry.

Steeped in Anglo-Catholicism from her childhood, Agee's mother became ever more serious about religion as she approached maturity. She had little of her mother's brilliance but much of her fanaticism when it came to matters of the church. Agee's father, in contrast, was a positive infidel. He had never been baptized and had little interest in the Kingdom of Heaven or the niceties of Anglo-Catholic theology. Joel would have welcomed this relative unbeliever into the family, but Emma opposed the match on the grounds that Jay Agee was simply beneath her daughter. She feared he would turn out to be just another hard-drinking mountain man with no desire to advance himself in this world or the next. Jay's younger brother Frank, an undertaker in La Follette, was already showing a disconcerting fondness for drink.

In despair at his inability to win Laura's hand, Jay accepted an offer to join the United States Post Office in Cristobal, Panama, shortly after President Theodore Roosevelt opened the Canal in 1904. In self-imposed exile made all the more oppressive by heat, humidity, and the threat of malaria, Jay Agee labored for two years. A photograph of him taken during this period shows an elegantly attired, lithe young man reclining on a bed of grass, impudently chewing on a stalk and, beneath the rakish tilt of his hat, squinting pensively. It was on this image that the lovesick Laura Tyler gazed during her lonely days and nights back in Knoxville.

Finally, in 1906, Laura persuaded her brother to chaperon her on the long journey south. She had made up her mind to marry Jay Agee in the Canal Zone and face the consequences later. That she was willing to make such a hazardous and unpleasant journey against her family's wishes revealed a streak of impetuousness and passion simmering beneath her prim facade.

Shortly after arriving in Panama, she and Jay Agee wed, and the couple spent their first year together in the Canal Zone until an epidemic of yellow fever forced Laura to return to the United States. Jay followed as soon as his term with the post office ended. Laura found it a great relief to be home, for life in the tropics had been harsh and threatening. Panama, she told friends, "didn't have a white man's climate."

The Agees settled in Corbin, Kentucky, where Jay found employment with the rapidly expanding Louisville & Nashville Railroad. It was in Corbin that he fell prey to a mysterious "health problem," either malaria or drinking or a combination of the two. He was also in search of a more promising career than the L&N had to offer when his father-in-law proposed a job with Ty-Sa-Man. Jay eagerly accepted. Joel Tyler did not mind in the least his son-in-law's lack of formal education, claiming that Jay needed college less than any man he knew.

The promise of secure employment in the family business brought the couple back to Knoxville, where they bought a modest home only a few blocks from the imposing Tyler residence. By then they were expecting their first child. The Agees' new address, 1505 Highland Avenue, was located on a snug little suburban street only a few blocks from downtown Knoxville and within walking distance of the university. The two-story dwelling, in which James Agee would spend the first years of his life, featured a porch and an ample backyard. It was a bit finer than the other houses on the block, which was populated mostly with the families of minor executives or small businessmen. It seemed to Jay Agee that at the age of thirty-one he had come into his own. If he was not living as grandly as the Tylers, neither had he become the rural ne'er-do-well his mother-in-law had expected. And he was soon to be a family man.

On November 27, 1909, Laura Agee gave birth to a healthy baby boy, the first son of a first son. The proud father quickly gave him his own middle name, James, as a first name, followed by the distinctly rural Rufus. To distinguish the boy from his father, everyone called the child Rufus, a name he came to despise as awkward and undignified. Years later he recalled how older boys in the neighborhood taunted him with that name.

Uh-Rufus, Uh-Rastus, Uh-Johnston, Uh-Brown,
Uh-What ya gonna do when the rent comes roun?

To make matters worse, they pronounced his name "Roofe-ass." He much preferred to be called James or Jim—anything but Rufus.

At the insistence of his mother's family, James Rufus Agee was baptized on Palm Sunday, March 10, 1910, by a family friend, Dr. Walter C. Whitaker, rector of St. John Episcopal Church in Knoxville. James would always remember Dr. Whitaker fondly, as a man who "gave his words and phrases special emphasis and personal coloring, as though they were matters which required argument and persuasion." And although Dr. Whitaker was not an Anglo-Catholic, James's mother insisted that her son be brought up as one. Two years later, she gave birth to another child, this time a girl, on whom she bestowed her mother's maiden name, Emma Ferrand.

James's parents ran a strict household. Prayers were said before meals; liquor, feared as the ruination of family life, was all but banished. Indeed, the entire city was "dry" by law, though when James's father had to have a drink, he found a ready supply of alcohol at bars thinly disguised as all-night cafés. As a small child, James found life cozy but never intimate, comfortable but never secure. His mother was a scold and, when aroused, quick to become holier than thou. Although his parents loved one another, he lived in a house divided.

Though his mother was distant, his father, as James never forgot, was a warm, virile, outgoing man who, despite the outwardly comfortable circumstances of his life, felt isolated and unfulfilled. He was caught between the faith of the Tylers and the dissoluteness of the Agees. This sense of conflict gave him a special poignance in his son's eyes, for even as a boy James saw that his father lacked a true home. He was neither of the mountains nor of the town. The closest he came to having a home was in his children, for through them he recaptured his own lost youth with all its promise.

With each passing year, James developed a stronger physical resemblance to his father. Though he had his mother's thick, dark hair, which fell in bangs to the top of his eyebrows, he had his father's quizzical expression and sloping nose. His mother often dressed him in a Russian-style belted tunic that set off his large features and cold blue eyes, but so far as he was concerned, clothes were a nuisance barely to be tolerated.

To escape the repressive atmosphere at home, he often wandered over to the Tylers, his grandparents, on nearby West Clinch Street, where he could watch his Uncle Hugh, a portrait painter, hard at work in his studio, or his Aunt Paula, a musician, practicing the piano. Each of these art forms made a lifelong impression on young James. Although he identified intensely with his loving father, the Tylers' artistic pursuits fascinated him. When the time came for his father to teach him the rudiments of a more manly art, boxing, the boy was unable to raise his fists in self-defense and considered himself a coward. He was just "too trusting" to fight, even for fun, and so gullible that Grandfather Joel once persuaded him that whistling at cheese would make it jump.

One of the most exciting events of his young life occurred when his father bought a shiny new black Ford, against his mother's strenuous protests. She had a premonition that something terrible would happen in that car, but his father would not be deterred. The car made a vivid impression on James, who long remembered how his father struggled to crank it up. *"Ughgh-Ughgh*—yuhyuh *Ugh* wheek yuh yuh,"* the engine seemed to say. *"Ughgh* yuh wheek wheek yuh yuh: wheek wheek: uh."* It reminded the boy of a "hideous, horribly constipated great brute of a beast" or a "lunatic sobbing" or a "mouse being tortured."

The car incarnated for James his father's obscurely perceived destructive impulses, and in the boy's mind it came to be linked with the masculine sensations of a stiff wool coat, celluloid collar, beard stubble, "dry grass, leather, and tobacco, and sometimes a different kind of smell, full of great energy and a fierce kind of fun, but also a feeling that things might go wrong: whiskey." When his father drank, James imagined, "images of stealthiness and deceit, of openness, anger and pride, immediately possessed him." He would fight them off, declaring, "If I ever get drunk again, I'll kill myself. And there are plenty of good reasons why I won't kill myself. So I won't ever get drunk again."

All these homely details made an enormous impression on

James, as they would on any small child. He was mesmerized by the sight of men such as his father watering their lawns at dusk, "tasting the mean goodness of their lives" as the rasps of locusts swelled in the distance. It seemed to him that the world consisted of a "great order of noises": streetcars, insects, dogs, cars, mothers calling to their children—all of them "shivering in your flesh and teasing your eardrums." As if to count his blessings, he would enumerate the chief figures in this idyllic landscape, his family. "All my people are larger bodies than mine, quiet with voices gentle and meaningless like the voices of sleeping birds. One is an artist, he is living at home. One is a musician, she is living at home. One is my mother who is good to me. One is my father who is good to me. By some chance, here they are, all on this earth."

As James approached his sixth year, he occasionally went on brief expeditions into Knoxville with his father. Together they noted the local landmarks James considered wonderful to behold: the depot of the L&N Railroad with its stained-glass windows that "smoldered like an exhausted butterfly"; the drugstore window display featuring a replica of the Venus de Milo, "her golden body laced in elastic straps"; and, not far from that, bustling Market Square, focal point of the city's commercial life. Here, on nocturnal walks with his father, he came across horse-drawn wagons containing entire mountain families.

Of even greater interest than these sights was the Majestic Theatre on Gay Street, where father and son engaged in the thoroughly disreputable activity of watching silent movies flicker across the silver screen amid the "exhilarating smell of stale tobacco, rank sweat, perfume, and dirty drawers," not to mention the incessant pounding of a honky-tonk piano. Above them, the ghostly image of "William S. Hart with both guns blazing and his long, horse face and his long, hard lip." But Hart was faintly ludicrous compared with the boy's real cinematic hero, Charlie Chaplin, whose balletic routines he could re-create gesture by gesture years after he first saw them. In one, the Little Tramp, while trying to catch the attention of a pretty girl, inadvertently sat on a bag of eggs, and his sickly smile, James recalled, "made you feel just the way those broken eggs must feel against your seat." Meanwhile, his father all but "tore his head off laughing."

On the way home from the picture shows, his father thought

nothing of taking him to one of the all-night cafés serving liquor. James liked the ambience of the exclusively male preserve, where he sat on the bar, watching his father drinking the forbidden whiskey. After bending backward to toss off one jolt after another "in a lordly manner," he would pause to introduce his son to the strange men ranged along the bar. "That's my boy," he would say. "Six years old, and he can already read like I couldn't read when I was twice his age." The boast only served to remind James of his inability to box. "You don't brag about smartness if your son is brave," he told himself.

The boy's anxiety, so strong at this early age, stemmed from the conflict between his mismatched parents. His father was the nurturing one, his mother the disciplinarian. If James awoke in the middle of the night with a nightmare, it was his father who sang him back to sleep with the sort of mountain melody his mother despised almost as much as she did Charlie Chaplin.

> I got a gallon an a sugarbabe too, my honey, my baby,
> I got a gallon an a sugarbabe too, my honey, my sweet thing.
> I got a gallon an a sugarbabe too,
> Gal don't love me but my sugarbabe do
> > This mornin,
> > This evenin,
> > > So soon.

Other little boys cried for their mothers; James cried for his father. He associated his father's love and warmth with sin and destruction, his mother's goodness and religiosity with a cold, punitive remoteness. It seemed to him there was no way to be both loving and good at the same time. Of course, he yearned to ally himself with both his parents, but the impossibility of reconciling their divergent temperaments left him in a continual state of unease and hypersensitivity to every undercurrent of tension in the household.

By the spring of 1916, the Agee family had attained a comfortable plateau. At thirty-eight, Jay had established himself at Ty-Sa-Man and seemed destined to inherit the company one day from his father-in-law. James, now six, attended the local public school, and his mother busied herself with church activities and her poetry. Life might well have gone on this way indefinitely, had not an event of singular importance taken place, one with drastic and irreversible consequences for them all.

In May of that year, James's paternal grandfather, a tall, proud man with a beak nose and a thick mustache, suffered a serious stroke and took to his bed at home in La Follette, where James's uncle Frank, the undertaker, maintained a vigil. On the night of May 17, James's father came home late from work and went straight to bed. He had not been asleep long when the phone rang; it was Frank, calling from La Follette, drunk and blubbering. He barely managed to say that their father had taken a turn for the worse. "But O Lord God, it looks like the end, Jay!" he exclaimed.

Jay was thrown into a state of confusion and anxiety. He knew Frank was prone to exaggerate, especially under the influence of alcohol, but at the same time Jay Agee would never forgive himself if his father died alone. Too wrought up to go back to sleep, he decided to drive out to La Follette in the big, black Ford, if for no other reason than to put his mind at ease. He figured he would be home by daybreak.

When James's mother learned of his intent, she dutifully prepared her husband's favorite breakfast: strong coffee, hot milk, eggs, and pancakes. She thought that if his stomach was full, he would resist the temptation to stop at one of those all-night cafés serving liquor. After eating, he laboriously cranked the Ford to life, no doubt waking half the neighborhood in the process. Under way, he turned off Highland Avenue onto Forest Street, followed Forest past the L&N viaduct, passed the railway yards on his left that were but "faint skeins of steel, blocked shadows, little spumes of steam" —or so James later wrote. "Along his right were dark vacant lots, pale billboards, the darker blocks of small sleeping buildings, an occasional light." Already the trip had taken longer than anticipated. It was nearly dawn, and his father had yet to reach the farm.

Early on the morning of May 18, his father reached a river crossing where he rapped on the window of a shanty to wake the ferryman, the local Charon. He paid double to cross, the full nighttime rate. To pass the time, he probably smoked his pipe, and when he arrived on the opposite shore, he drove faster than was absolutely safe through the dark hills toward La Follette. Years after, James re-created his father's thoughts on the last leg of the journey.

This was the real, old, deep country now. Home country. The cabins looked different to him, a little older and poorer and simpler, a little more homelike; the trees and rocks seemed to come differently out of the ground; the air smelled different. Before long now, he would know the worst; if it was the worst. Quite unconsciously he felt much more deeply at leisure as he watched the flowing, freshly lighted country; and quite unconsciously he drove a little faster than before.

All the while, James's mother tried to go back to sleep, but portents loomed and kept her awake. Soon the children were up, and she had to get them off to school.

James's father arrived at the family farm expecting to witness a deathbed scene, but he was both relieved and irritated to discover that Frank had, predictably, exaggerated the seriousness of the problem. Jay Agee spent most of the day at the farm, observing the unpleasant sight of his brother Frank drinking himself into a stupor. After supper, Jay decided to head back to Knoxville. In all probability he had something to drink on the way, not enough to get drunk, but enough to take away the pathetic sight of his father rendered helpless by a stroke.

This time he drove too fast for safety. By the time he came to an intersection known as Powell's station, a driver going in the opposite direction assumed that whoever was at the wheel of the Ford was "crazy drunk." Seconds later, the observer, S. H. Tinsley, heard a "terrifying noise" followed by deathly silence. Tinsley drove back slowly along Clinton Pike for a quarter of a mile, seeing nothing on either side of the road, until he came on the overturned Ford lying at the foot of a steep embankment. One of the wheels was still spinning. The driver, Jay Agee, lay face down about a foot from the car, his clothes scarcely rumpled. Tinsley assumed the man was dead, but he lit matches to make a closer inspection, listened for a heartbeat, felt for a pulse, and even used a piece of the shattered windshield to detect the man's breath, but there were no signs of life.

The odd thing was that there was no evidence of physical trauma except for a small cut on the point of the dead man's chin. Tinsley sent for help, which arrived in the form of two doctors, William Cochrane and William Delpeuch, who determined that the victim had died either of a broken neck or a concussion received from a blow to the chin. Several others gathered at the scene, including a blacksmith named Brannick, who lived nearby. The body was taken to his shop.

About ten that evening, two hours after the accident, Tinsley called James's mother and in a calm, countrified voice told her that her husband had been involved in a "serious accident"; she had better send someone immediately to the scene. She dispatched her brother Hugh and remained at home with James and Emma, anxiously awaiting news.

Several hours later, Hugh returned to the Agee home, where the Tylers—Joel, his wife Emma, and Jessie—had joined James, his mother, and his sister. He entered without bothering to knock, and as soon as the family saw his "tight, set" way of walking, they knew the worst. They broke out whiskey, water, and ice, which they drank as they slowly absorbed the overwhelming fact of Jay Agee's death. Even James's mother drank, but she felt nothing. All she had feared about her husband's dangerous tendencies had come to pass. The car she had never wanted him to buy, the liquor she had never wanted him to drink, and the family she had never wanted him to see had conspired to bring about his death.

As if the fact of her husband's death were not tragedy enough, the manner in which he died added to her misery, for, as Hugh insisted, the man had died instantly. Hugh imparted the information as a way of comforting his sister, but her religious training would not allow her to forget that he had therefore died without making his peace with God, without even so much as a prayer. Hugh took exception to her religious scruples, impulsively blurting out, "He wasn't a *Christian,* you know," a reference to Jay's never having been baptized, but the attempt to ease Laura's pain had just the opposite of its intended effect. Hugh went on to insist, "He didn't have to make his peace with God. He was a man, with a wife and two children." Laura could only think ahead to the complications her husband's irreligiousness would cause at the time of the funeral.

And then there was the awesome question of why the accident had occurred. No one dared to discuss the possibility that Jay had been drinking, fell asleep at the wheel, and driven off the road. Hugh offered a plausible theory that a cotter pin in the steering mechanism had worked loose, causing the driver to lose control through no fault of his own. The family clung to the theory to avoid contemplating other, less pleasant circumstances.

In the midst of this animated discussion, Laura suddenly heard footsteps upstairs. At first she thought it was the children, but when she realized the sound came from the bedroom she shared with Jay, she decided his spirit or presence had come to pay them all a last visit. She was not alone in her belief that Jay had returned; the others felt his presence as well. He had come to say goodbye.

The next day, an account of the accident in the Knoxville *Journal and Tribune* hinted that the driver, not the steering mechanism, had been responsible for the accident. The headline read:

FOUND DEAD ON
CLINTON PIKE

James Agee, of the City
Pinned Under Automobile

When Car Struck Embankment
and Overturned was
Returning from La Follette

Farther down came disconcerting details that the surviving family members could hardly have wished to be made public.

> Tracks of the car, a 5-passenger Ford, show that just before turning over, it had been run up a slight embankment at the side of the road, and this was probably responsible for the accident. The stretch of road in the vicinity is unusually good, and it is probable that Mr. Agee was going at a fast speed. An examination failed to disclose any defect in the steering apparatus of the machine.

Turning a blind eye to the real cause of the accident, the family fastened obsessively on the single, small wound the victim had received. It was so neat, so perfectly aimed, the chances of its occurring so remote, that it suggested to James's mother that her husband's death had been divinely ordained. But why? As a warning, a test of faith? For once she could not fathom the ways of the Lord.

In the morning, when James awoke, he immediately began

searching for signs of his father's presence, but there was none to be found. Summoning her last reserves of strength, his mother called him and his sister and broke the news as best she could.

"Daddy didn't come home," she explained in terms James would remember the rest of his life.

"Why not?" the boy asked.

"Because God wanted him," his mother replied. "Daddy was on his way home last night—and he was—he—got hurt and—so God let him go to sleep and took him straight to heaven."

But his mother could not have believed in the business about heaven. As she knew, her husband had not died in a state of grace; he had gone to hell.

James reacted to the loss not with rage or tears, but with a slowly developing sense of awe and wonder. At six, he was barely able to comprehend the idea of death. All he knew for certain was that his father would not be coming home anymore. He puzzled over the details his mother fed him. "What's an eightfoot embackmut?" he asked her. And what did it mean to be instantly killed? "Like snapping off an electric light," she replied. What was it that had actually killed his father? Aunt Jessie, who had stayed the night, explained that James's father had suffered a "concus-sion of the brain. That's the doctor's name for what happened. It means, it's as if the brain were hit very hard and suddenly, and jogged loose. The instant that happens, your father was—he . . ."

"Instantly killed," James said, and Aunt Jessie agreed. "Then it was that, that put him to sleep."

"Hyess," Aunt Jessie conceded.

"*Not* God."

Thus James joined the ranks of the skeptics, despite the best efforts of his mother and aunt to soothe him with theological fairy tales. A sense of terrible, endless deprivation settled over him. He wandered the house in search of evidence of his father's existence. He smelled the chair where his father had sat and smoked his pipe, ran his finger along the inside of the ashtray. If only there were enough ashes to save. He hungered for a keepsake. He studied his finger for a moment and licked it. As he remembered, his tongue "tasted of darkness."

Although he persisted in seeing his father's death in a more realistic light than his mother thought best, he nonetheless endowed it with a special glamour. Seeing the body at rest in the living room, James noted a sculptural perfection that his father had lacked in life. The sight of his father's corpse made such a strong impression on him that he later re-created it in the novel he would write about his father's death. He would call the novel (actually a memoir in its fidelity to fact) *A Death in the Family,* and its hero would be this flawless corpse:

> The arm was bent. Out of the dark suit, the starched cuff, sprang the hairy wrist.
>
> The wrist was angled; the hand was arched; none of the fingers touched each other.
>
> The hand was so composed that it seemed at once casual and majestic. It stood exactly above the center of the body.
>
> The fingers looked unusually clean and dry, as if they had been scrubbed with great care.
>
> The hand looked very strong, and the veins were strong in it.
>
> The nostrils were very very dark, yet he thought he could see, in one of them, something which looked like cotton.
>
> On the lower lip, a trifle to the left of the middle, there was a small blue line which ran also a little below the lip. At the exact point of the chin, there was another small blue mark, as straight and neat as might be drawn with a pencil, and scarcely wider.

The funeral took place on Saturday, May 20, a harrowing day for all concerned. It began with the *Journal and Tribune's* running another account of the accident, this time playing up the mawkish details of Jay Agee's errand of mercy. Later that morning, Frank showed up roaring drunk. As an undertaker, he had assumed he would prepare his brother's body, but Joel Tyler dismissed the idea as "downright incestuous," and another mortician was called in. In reaction to this supposed insult, Frank succumbed to a poisonous mixture of sorrow, guilt, and envy. And the thought that he had inadvertently contributed to his brother's death by summoning him to La Follette that fateful night was too much to bear. Frank started drinking, and he arrived at the Tyler home, scene of the funeral, in a "stumbling, sobbing rush," as James remembered, "heavily drunk with whiskey strong and sour on his breath." Frank bellowed that he would never forgive himself for what he had done. The mark of Cain was upon his brow. Only his mother was able to console him.

The funeral service itself became another bone of contention. Reflecting the religious divisions within the family, there were two clergymen present. The first was the familiar and popular Dr. Whitaker, of whom Jay Agee would have approved. The second was a stranger from Chattanooga, Father W. C. Robertson, an Anglo-Catholic priest with a reputation for a stern, High Church manner. He arrived impressively turned out in a tall silk hat, purple vest, and shiny briefcase. He treated James and Emma with a coolness bordering on cruelty and unwittingly committed the sacrilege of sitting in James's father's favorite chair. Father Robertson spoke "almost wholly without emphasis and with only the subtlest coloring, as if the personal emotion, the coloring, were cast against the words from a distance, like echoes." In such tones he lectured the children to mind their manners and refrain from staring at their elders.

Even more than Father Robertson's treatment of him, James resented the priest's mysterious hold on his mother. In horror he listened at her bedroom door while the strange man tried to calm her. The boy "repeatedly saw himself flinging open the door and striding in, a big stone in his hand, and saying, 'You stop hurting my mother.' " It seemed his mother was religious not from strong conviction but from weakness. He had felt stunned by his father's death; now the priest made them all feel ashamed as well. At least the calamity of death belonged to the natural order of things. But this man-made cruelty in the name of God was, in its own way, a far greater evil.

After the funeral, the mourners proceeded to Greenwood Cemetery in Knoxville, where Father Robertson completed his humiliation of the family by refusing to read the entire burial service, since the deceased had not been baptized. Prayers were said, flowers thrown, tears shed over the coffin. At the head of the dark grave stood a modest tombstone inscribed with an epigram his mother had chosen: "In His Strength." With this choice of phrase, she hoped to reassure herself and the world that her husband had died sober and ready to meet his Maker.

At the last moment, what seemed a minor miracle took place. James was not there to see it himself, but later his uncle Hugh told him how just as the coffin was being lowered into the ground "a perfectly magnificent butterfly alighted on it and just stood there for several seconds while they kept on lowering the coffin." Since the butterfly was a time-honored symbol of resurrection, even the skeptical Hugh took heart. "If I ever believe in God," he said to James, "it will be because I remember what I saw today." But Father Robertson's gratuitous snub continued to rankle Uncle Hugh, who ranted, "Bury a man who's a hundred times the man *he'll* ever be, in his stinking, swishing black petticoats, and a hundred times as good a man too."

Three weeks later, James's paternal grandfather died of another stroke, this one brought on by the strain of his son's premature death. Several days before the end, James's mother went to see him in La Follette. The enfeebled old man whom she could barely tolerate pointed to himself and whispered, "My fault, my fault."

STRANGE RITES

Following the unfathomable death of her husband, James's mother sank into the arms of the church. Adopting a course of piety and duty, she was unable to recover her former charm and high spirits. She felt wholly inadequate to the task of rearing two small children by herself but too attached to her late husband to contemplate remarriage. For all their differences, the marriage had been a love match, and she despaired of finding a man to take Jay's place. Every corner of the house on Highland Avenue, every odor and shaft of light evoked memories of her life with him. To free herself of these oppressive reminders, she sold the house and moved to a similar dwelling nearby, on Laurel Avenue, where for the next three years she existed on family charity. James and Emma, meanwhile, attended the nearby Van Gilder School.

For James it was a lonely, empty period. He resented his mother's piety and remoteness, especially at Christmastime. Several years later, in one of his earliest poems, "Widow," he portrayed her unhappiness and inability to cope with her children. In the poem, his mother tries to trim the tree, but one fragile ornament crashes to her feet, sending splinters flying. The sound of carolers outside only serves to increase her aggravation. She warns herself "to take things quietly" or risk going "raving crazy." Yet with every strand of tinsel she arranges on the tree she sees her husband's coffin being lowered into the ground. In the end, her wretchedness reaches a hysteric pitch.

> That branch is thick—it spoils the symmetry.
> I'll get the hatchet now, and lop it off . . .
> How sharp and bright it is; how cold the blade!
> I draw my thumb along the edge; and think
> What it could do! Oh, God forgive me that.

She forces herself to take refuge in her bedroom, where she lies on the bed awaiting a "comforting caress" but finds only "emptiness."

Throughout this period James matured rapidly. At eight he looked two years older than his classmates. The smooth circle of his boyhood face stretched into the unmistakably lean-jawed proportions of his father, and he had the same relaxed stance, sympathetic expression, and soft Southern accent.

At the same time he demonstrated a new and to his mother disturbing tendency to act aggressively. He came home from school streaked with blood from fighting with other boys in the neighborhood. When his mother asked about the origin of the blood, he replied, "Don't keer, it ain't mine." He took to killing small animals such as birds and snakes and for amusement placed toads on trolley tracks and waited for passing cars to crush the ugly little beasts. His mother tried to make him behave by stressing the importance of God's will. "Why does God let us do bad things," he would ask of her.

"Because he wants us to make up our own minds."

"Even to do bad things, right under His nose?"

"He doesn't *want us* to do bad things, but to know good from bad and be good of our own free choice," she insisted, adding, "You can't love to do what you are *made* to do, and you couldn't love God if He *made* you."

It was all so sensible, yet it made no sense. "Why *doesn't* He want us to?" James demanded. "It would be so much easier for him."

"God—doesn't—believe—in—the—easy—way."

The boy's proclivity for cruelty coexisted with an astonishingly precocious capacity for compassion. He became fascinated by the sight of the rural poor, about whom he questioned his mother endlessly. "Why do they have to stay in such a place? What are they there for?" he asked when he saw several small children working in a mill. She was similarly moved and pointed out that some of them did not have even shoes or stockings. The boy's eyes filled with tears of pity. He immediately took off his shoes and socks and offered them to the barefoot children.

Despite his mother's efforts to reform him, he remained a problem child. His emerging sexual feelings gave rise to a constant self-loathing. Left to his own devices, he roamed the Tyler home, where he would be "taken at the pit of the stomach with a most bitter, criminal gliding and cold serpent restiveness." To stave off the shameful act he knew he would sooner or later commit, he tried reading and playing the piano. In the library he yielded to temptation by studying the volumes of "soft-painted nudes." He stared "hungrily and hatefully" into mirrors, as if searching for the answer to the riddle he had become. His senses were starved. To satisfy them he stealthily went through closets, drawers, and boxes "for the mere touch at the lips and odor of fabrics, pelts, jewels, switches of hair, smoking cigars." He went up the attic to plunder piles of old letters with their "piteous enthusiasms." When he could no longer stand the internal pressure, he later forced himself to recall, "I took off all my clothes, lay along the cold counterpanes of every bed, planted my obscenities in the cold hearts of every mirror ... before the innocent fixtures of a lady's hair: I permitted nothing to escape the fingering of my senses nor the insulting of the cold reptilian fury of the terror of lone desire which was upon me." But the furtive masturbation provided no relief, merely an intensification of his inexplicable anger. He saw himself as a "half-shaped child, pressing between the sharp hip bone and the floor my erection." When he finished, he would lie, "nearly crying, striking over and over again the heel of my bruised hand against the sooty floor and sweating and shaking my head in a sexual and murderous anger and despair."

His mother could not even begin to understand his overpowering anger. She failed to sense that Jay's death had unleashed a torrent of guilt in the boy, who held himself responsible for the tragedy in some mysterious way. Her constant emphasis on right and wrong fed the fires of his inner turmoil and reinforced his unconscious guilt. As a result, the shy and sensitive lad of six had metamorphosed into the savage of eight.

Matters went from bad to worse when she insisted he be circumcised, despite his advanced age. James understandably resisted the idea and considered the operation as punishment for his masturbating. But his mother maintained that the circumcision was necessary for reasons of "health," and James was forced to submit.

Throughout his life he bitterly resented the humiliation his mother inflicted on him at that time. In a sad, satirical poem, he assessed the effects of her repressiveness on his personality.

> *Mumsy you were so genteel*
> *That you made your son a heel.*
> *Sunnybunch must now reclaim*
> *From the sewerpipe of his shame*
> *Any little coin he can*
> *To reassure him he's a man.*

Recognizing that she needed help with James, she turned to the church. In the summer of 1918, she decided to retreat with her children to a monastic setting where James could enjoy the benefits of masculine guidance and counsel. As a mother of two, she could not take holy orders herself, but she did the next best thing by renting a small cottage on the grounds of an Episcopalian boarding school for boys.

The school she selected, St. Andrew's, was administered by the Monastic Order of the Holy Cross and was beautifully situated on the remote Cumberland Plateau in south-central Tennessee, 2,100 refreshing feet above sea level. The air was dryer, cooler, and cleaner than in Knoxville, fairly vibrant with holiness. Located on the site of an old farm, the grounds covered two hundred acres. Tall pines sheltered the tiny campus and perfumed the air with their clean fragrance. Only twelve years old at the time, the school consisted of a few simple structures, the most impressive of which was the chapel, and a small monastery to house the monks who taught the hundred or so students. Not far from the tiny campus were several swimming holes brimming with frigid water.

To reach this idyllic retreat the family made a daylong journey by rail, disembarking at an all but invisible stop known as Gipson Switch. Once at the school they quickly fell in step with the monks' strict routine. They rose before the sun each morning and faithfully worshiped at Mass. As James recalled, "I used as a child in the innocence of faith to bring myself out of bed through the cold lucid water of the Cumberland morning and to serve at the altar at earliest lonely Mass, whose words were thrilling brooks of music and whose motions, a grave dance." James's fascination with worship pleased his mother greatly. With each morning's observance the purifying powers of religion seeped into his festering soul, affording him relief from his inner torment. As his mother wished, he gradually came to conceive of faith in God as the primary escape from personal hell. For a few minutes each day, at least, he did not feel guilty.

The summer at St. Andrew's went so well that his mother decided to return the following year. On the second visit she made the crucial decision to leave Knoxville and her family altogether and live at St. Andrew's permanently. Although the school accepted only the sons of farmers, she persuaded the administration to make an exception in her son's case and take him on as a student in the fall of 1919. By then she had become a deaconess in the order, serving God in such humble ways as doing the school's laundry and supplying Lady Chapel with a lavish assortment of fresh flowers. These flowers evoked in James a sense of wonder and a relatively innocent sensuality. Their brilliance and fragrance, intensified by rows of burning candles, "all one wall of dizzying dazzle, were such that it was at first almost as difficult to breathe the freighted air as to breathe water." That blossoming did not extend to his mother, who took to wearing a severe, long black dress with a high, white, starched collar, reminiscent of a nun's habit.

With her daughter Emma, now seven, she took up residence in a cottage separated from the rest of the school by an imposing fence. James was forced to live under a separate roof for the first time in his life, exchanging the privacy and comforts of home for a barrackslike dormitory swarming with foulmouthed farmers' sons. Fully a fifth of the students were orphans, and in a sense James considered himself one as well, for he had lost his father and grandfather, and his mother had little use for him, even forbidding him access to her house.

The students' life at St. Andrew's followed a monastic routine. The daily schedule consisted of worship, meals, classes, and exercise. Every hour of the day had its appointed task, each day its significance in the religious calendar. Free time did not exist; idle hands were the devil's playground. Even Saturdays were reserved for confessions and penance. One of the priests routinely practiced corporal punishment by striking the backs of students' hands with a ruler. Most students worked at farming tasks, but a favored few, including James, who were considered intellectually advanced pursued a traditional academic curriculum that included history, languages, mathematics, and of course Bible study. James became imbued with the Bible and the Book of Common Prayer, whose substantial, repetitive cadences later influenced much of his writing.

It soon became apparent to the monks that James possessed an extraordinary aptitude for language. They extended permission for him to use the modest school library, a rare privilege. In a short time he was reading and analyzing poems by John Keats, especially "The Eve of St. Agnes," whose medieval, religious aura reminded him of his surroundings. Keats's sensual images went a long way toward satisfying the boy's hunger for stimulation. He realized that in literature, unlike life, he could give way to his wildest impulses without coming to actual harm. Indeed, he might even earn the approval of others, rather than their censure.

At the time of this intellectual awakening he formed a close friendship with one of the teachers at St. Andrew's, the Reverend James Harold Flye. One of the first questions the boy asked the Anglo-Catholic priest was, "Father, have you read *Penrod?*" Quickly they fell into discussions of books and music, the lonely student's two main passions. "I was immediately impressed by this boy who was all of nine years old at the time," Father Flye remembered. "His people were intelligent, people of books." In short order, Father Flye and his wife, Grace, became James's substitute parents. Nonetheless, the priest did not predict a literary career for his young friend: "There were no signs that I observed then or for some time afterward of his being of the quality of a well-known and professional writer."

The friendship drew strength from the fact that each offered something the other lacked. The boy had no father; the Flyes had no children. Father Flye played the role of substitute parent in a gentle, nonthreatening manner. He was far more tolerant of James's behavioral excesses than his mother, and James responded by being at his best in the priest's company. As a result, Father Flye did not perceive James as having been "traumatized" by the death of a parent but rather possessed of a levelheaded appreciation of the "magnitude of the loss." Part of the priest's sensitivity to such matters stemmed from his own father's having died young.

At the time they met, Father Flye was a tall, powerfully built man of thirty-three. His family, originally from Maine, had moved to Florida when he was a boy, but he had gone back north to attend Yale. After graduation, while teaching in Orlando, Florida, he became so fascinated by the local Episcopalian church that within a few weeks he decided to become a priest even though he had been raised as a Congregationalist. He attended General Theological Seminary in New York, married, and came to St. Andrew's thinking he would stay a year or two before moving on; he would remain for thirty-seven years.

In time James became a frequent guest at the Flyes' cottage, where they talked endlessly about fossils, foreign lands, Indians, scout lore, and survival in the wilderness—all subjects of intense interest to the boy. They fashioned a simple bow and arrow; later James requested a .22 rifle for use, he said, in target practice, though he might have hunted small animals with the weapon. They studied French, but after learning several hundred words, James abruptly became "ashamed of himself" and resolved to switch to German, a more virile tongue. Though he tried to mask his sensitivity, Father Flye thought him "very tender-hearted, touched to quick sympathy and pity at the sight or thought of suffering, human or other, and incapable of willingly causing it."

Occasionally their conversation turned to religion. James expressed confusion over the phrase "Blood of Christ, inebriate me" because it seemed to advocate drunkenness. The priest patiently explained that it was possible to be "amused" by the word without feeling irreverent. But the merest suggestion of alcohol caused James to brood on his father's death. Even the word *God* reminded him of death, and he would suddenly see his father's "prostrate head and, through the efforts to hide it, the mortal blue dent on the chin."

Even while enjoying Father Flye's companionship, James yearned for his mother's attention. He would stare at her cottage by the hour, for it was "the one place he was almost never allowed to go." He relished the knowledge that others saw him keeping vigil and hoped the sight would embarrass her into inviting him in, but when she did acknowledge his presence, it was only to tell him to go away. To his frustration, she provided a series of lame explanations why her "senseless cruelty had to be law." She said it was best that he not go near her precisely because he missed her so much, "because your father isn't—with us," and "because Mother thinks you need to be among other boys." When he was older, she said he would thank her for these stern measures. As she had often said, God did not believe in the easy way.

Homesick and lonely, James recoiled from the empty homilies. In his anger he wet his bed, welcoming the humiliation the lapse entailed. On the mornings he awoke in a dry bed he even felt regret, for by now he had come to the conclusion that it was a "secret kind of good to be punished, especially if the punishment was exorbitant or unjust; better to be ignored by others, than accepted; better still to be humiliated, than ignored." He was a masochist in the making; if he could not get the love and attention he craved by behaving, he would do his level best to misbehave in a desperate bid for someone to notice his plight.

Nor did he limit himself to self-punishment; he displayed a sadistic streak as well. He resumed hunting small animals in an effort to prove his masculinity. He knocked baby robins out of their nests and stoned them while their mothers screamed. After killing the birds disgust overwhelmed him and he vomited. He forced himself to eat worms and, unsuccessfully, to taste his own excrement.

After these bouts of extreme behavior he would calm down and resolve to maintain a "vigil over his thoughts and his language and over his sensuous actions upon himself." In a penitent mood he sought God's forgiveness by kneeling for unnecessarily long periods of time on the hard floor of the chapel, where he meditated on the ultimate justification for his self-inflicted suffering, the Crucifixion. At first he thought he was merely imitating Jesus; later he imagined himself taking Jesus' place on the cross, "a solemn and rewarding moment," he dared to feel, "but almost within the next breath he recognized that he had no such cause or right as Jesus to die upon the Cross." Nonetheless, he considered the likelihood of building one in the school's manual training shop. His inflamed imagination gave rise to a bizarre fantasy in which he hung, crucified, on the grounds of St. Andrew's. People would come from all around to gaze at the strange sight, a photographer would snap his photograph, and a newspaper would run an article with this headline:

STRANGE RITES AT MOUNTAIN SCHOOL

But, he knew, it was "out of the question that in a deep part of Middle Tennessee, in nineteen twenty-three, he could actually manage to have himself nailed to a cross." Many a lonely young boy in search of his identity has considered a religious calling, but it was characteristic of James's inordinately passionate and sensitive nature to take this desire to such an extreme. The fantasy was so intense that it bordered on a delusion.

Unaware of the full extent of James's morbid fascination with crucifixion, his mother broke her vow of silence to tell him that she was bothered by the "vanity" tainting his piety, "not that you *mean* it, of course, dear." However, he did mean it, down to the last outlandish detail. He was still trying to work off the accumulated guilt he had felt since his father's death. Only in Father Flye's comforting presence did he find relief from these torments. The priest had become both mother and father to him.

In the spring of 1923, James underwent a spiritual crisis marking the end of his obsessive identification with Jesus, the story of which he related in his autobiographical novel *The Morning Watch*. The event occurred on Maundy Thursday, the day before Good Friday. At St. Andrew's it was the custom for students to keep an all-night vigil or watch in memory of Jesus' asking his disciples,

"What, could ye not watch with me one hour?" On Maundy Thursday morning, James was awakened at quarter to four. He then went to the chapel to pray and fast, but when he took his place he found that he no longer believed in the ritual. Try as he might to concentrate on the death and resurrection of Jesus, he felt overcome by an irresistible urge to cast off the cloak of religion and morality. Burning candles seemed to consume all the air in the tiny chapel; he was suffocating. When his turn in the vigil finally ended, he found it a great relief to walk down the sandstone steps into the cool morning atmosphere and to inhale deeply of the profane world. "Morning had not yet begun," he wrote, "but the night was nearly over." Like Judas, he had betrayed Jesus, but he no longer cared.

With a group of friends he walked to one of the nearby swimming holes. Along the way he "found a locust shell, transparent silver breathed with gold, the whole back split, the hard claws, its only remaining strength, so clenched into the bark that it was only with great care and gentleness that he was able to detach the shell without destroying it." The shell called to mind primitive beasts, dinosaurs, and pterodactyls, in whose ferocious company he now belonged, rather than with gentle, suffering Jesus. Henceforth, Nature would be the only god he would obey. At the swimming hole he came to another realization: his extreme piety had been analogous to holding his breath for too long under water. He had tried to "stay down . . . as an act of devotion," and it was time to come up for air or drown.

He completed his apostasy by killing a snake, discovering a pagan joy and fulfillment in hunting that no religious experience could match. As he attacked with a rock, the little creature "lashed about his fist like summer lightning." And when he had finished the sacrifice, James "looked coldly at his trembling hand: bloody at the knuckles and laced with slime, which seemed to itch and burn as it dried." A student watching the display warned him to wash, but James ignored the advice. He "began to feel brave in a way he had never been brave before." He was proud of himself; he was a man.

By the time Good Friday arrived, James felt "pretty well anaesthetized." He was, as he would later tell a friend, "finally through with religion but still carrying a deep load of it, some of it benign, much of it poisonous." At the same time, he was left with a "gravitation towards death," a "giant set of guilt reflexes," and an "extreme masochism and sense of guilt which that kind of religion—Roman or in that case Anglo-Catholic—is liable to poison you with if you become religiously infected at all." By now some of the young man's principal characteristics were evident: his fascination with death, an oppressive and unfathomable sense of guilt, a tendency toward extreme behavior, an alternation of cruelty with compassion, acute intelligence, and a hopelessly frustrated longing for his mother.

She, meanwhile, began to flourish in her own genteel fashion. In 1922 she published a slim volume of verse—twelve religious poems titled *Songs of the Way*. Later she developed a relationship with the school's bursar, the Reverend Erskine Wright, who hailed from a well-to-do Philadelphia family. In every way Father Wright was the opposite of Jay Agee. He was exceedingly proper, cultivated, and refined. He neither smoked nor drank nor swore, nor would he tolerate others doing so in his presence. He exuded an aura of rectitude that nearly everyone but James's mother found disagreeable. But just as their courtship got under way, her father, Joel Tyler, fell ill; and in early 1924 she decided to return to Knoxville with the children to be closer to him.

James had left Knoxville a confused, bereaved boy. He returned a cocky young man in the throes of adolescence. Everywhere he looked he saw examples of his elders' stupidity and hypocrisy. His mother enrolled him at mid-term in Knoxville High School. To add to his sense of alienation, the students were overwhelmingly Protestant. After years in a structured, monastic setting, he felt wholly out of place in the chaos of a public school.

During that unhappy year he kept in touch with Father Flye, now his closest friend and ally. At the same time his mother kept in touch with Father Wright, and the two were married in the spring of 1924. James's new stepfather made himself instantly unpopular. It was as though she had married Father Robertson, the smug clergyman from Chattanooga. To the Agee side of the family in particular, Father Wright appeared to be the sort of Christian who made one long to be a heathen. And as far as James was concerned, the clergyman could not even begin to fill the void left by the death of his real father. Though his mother now called herself Mrs. Erskine Wright, James and Emma clung to Agee as their last name.

Father Wright's forbidding exterior concealed serious inner conflicts. The demands of married life caused him to suffer a breakdown even before his new life had begun. He became a semi-invalid, unable to cope with more than a minimum of responsibility. The father, breadwinner, and social lion James's mother had been counting on failed to materialize. Instead she was burdened with an even larger family to manage.

To remain in this environment portended disaster for James. Fortunately, Father Wright had a small private income, part of which was set aside to send the boy away to a good school where he could fulfill his obvious intellectual promise. Father Wright desired that the school be more socially esteemed than St. Andrew's, and the family immediately set their sights on the best available, Phillips Exeter Academy in New Hampshire. James applied, was accepted, and planned to enter in the fall of 1925.

As he finished the year at Knoxville High, his mother and Erskine undertook, on doctor's orders, a protracted search for a mild, moist climate conducive to recuperation. They tried various locations in Tennessee, Florida, and South Carolina before deciding to abandon the South altogether in favor of the tiny coastal town of Rockland, Maine, whose proximity to Penobscot Bay promised all the fog, if not the warmth, Father Wright required.

These were severely anxious times for James. His family situation and educational plans had undergone so many drastic alterations in the previous few months that he had no idea what the immediate future held in store. Knowing of his troubles, Father Flye came to the rescue with a proposal James was bound to find irresistible: a trip to France. Because money was a consideration, they would economize by traveling by bicycle and sleeping in inexpensive hostelries or, weather permitting, under the stars. At the same time, they could improve their French and keep James's family at a comfortable distance until the beginning of Exeter's fall term.

Leaving Knoxville early in the summer, they took the train to New York. James's first glimpse of the city, "virgin before me at fifteen" (as he was before it), filled him with rapture. Much later, he recalled, "I first walked in the late brilliant June dusk into the blinding marvel of Times Square, watching the Covered Wagon cross the Platte River in electric lights, over and over and over, my heart nearly breaking for joy when all the shows of every kind on the otherwise rural planet were spread at once before me, a tray of choicest diamonds." He feasted his eyes on sights unknown to Knoxville: high-stepping blacks, prostitutes flagrantly plying their trade, first-run movies, and a brilliant concentration of streetlights capable of turning night into day. For once he had found a place more than equal to his enormous appetite for sensual stimulation.

They sailed for Boulogne, rented bicycles in the quaint town of Amiens, and toured the tranquil Loire Valley with its stately châteaux and air of romantic mystery. Unlike other Americans, who made the Grand Tour in luxury, they put in long hours of pedaling and ate frugal meals. Each morning James awoke to examine the "new crop" of bedbugs that had fastened onto his skin overnight. Because they experienced the country on this humble level, they soon became powerfully aware of the sadness and suffering of ordinary French citizens struggling to overcome the ravages of the Great War. The ruins were so nakedly fresh it seemed as if the conflict had ended only the day before.

James was inspired by the sight. He took pen in hand to record his impressions, as if he were a roving correspondent on assignment for a newspaper. With practice his vignettes deepened into mystical accounts fraught with personal significance. In one, he told how a landlady provided him with directions to the ruin of an ancient church. He set out immediately. Along the way, all that he saw, from the "oddly subdued geese" to the "crumpled shadow of an old man on crutches," drew a deeply emphatic response. After all, he was crossing the soil of his ancestors. Suffering, it seemed, was everywhere, not just in his breast, and the ruin, when he found it, resembled an artifact of a long-lost civilization.

> I stood knee-deep in a profuse tangle of weeds and coarse grasses through which were pushed, here and there, the broken shoulders of rocks. . . . With the flaming rim of the sinking sun for a background, the shattered remains of the mullioned window reared above. . . . At my feet were ancient splintered rails, on which I could still see intricate carving; they had, undoubtedly, been part of the choir stalls.
>
> I retraced my steps and, at the western edge of the church, found the twisted ruin of the organ. The sun had set and the

pale moon became brighter. By its light I saw wraithlike old images, bestowing upon the desolation a deathless, hopeless benediction.

These meditations inevitably led the young man to invoke the theme that would come to dominate his writing over the years: death—the death of his father, of belief, at times (it seemed), of civilization.

Then, for the first time, I noticed that many of the stones at my feet were lettered. They were tombs. In the ghastly brilliance of the moon I saw that the shoulder of a slab had buckled; that beneath it was the dark shadow of an opening. As I stepped to its edge, a great bat rose from its depths and fluttered heavily in the wan weird dusk above me.

The ruin seemed to mirror his chaotic inner life. He had believed in his father; his father had died. He had turned to religion to ease the sorrow and guilt he felt over the death; religion had failed him. Now he was adrift, a willing convert in search of a new faith.

3

FIRST LOVES

In September 1925, James joined the "middle," or sophomore, class of Phillips Exeter, then a rather hidebound institution priding itself on a constitution antedating that of the United States. The school's imposing buildings and sprawling playing fields made a striking first impression, all but overwhelming the town's modest houses. For James, the key landmarks were the forbidding Phillips Church, where he would worship; the lavish gym and swimming pool, where he would exercise; and the comfortable, wood-paneled library and common rooms, which offered the perfect background for elegantly attired tycoons-in-training.

What the catalogue termed the "tough and definite truths of Latin" made up the core of the curriculum, but it was a great stroke of luck for James that the school prided itself on its English department, which excelled that of many colleges. It received strong support from Exeter's principal, Lewis "Doc" Perry, the younger brother of a well-known Harvard English professor. When James arrived, the reigning presence was F. W. Cushwa, who, with his cavernous features, resembled a latter-day Daniel Webster.

The department's liberal, humanistic atmosphere found expression in a surprisingly sophisticated magazine, the Phillips Exeter *Monthly,* in whose pages aspiring young poets, critics, and novelists flaunted their precocious talents. James immediately set his sights on cracking the *Monthly* with poems and accounts of his trip to France. Within two months of his arrival, the first of these began to appear. He also drew a bead on the Lantern Club, the school's literary society, which boasted special quarters and often invited prominent writers of the day, such as Booth Tarkington (Exeter '89), to speak. On such occasions, James discovered, the distinguished guest would often consent to read the manuscripts nervously thrust in his hands by eager young apprentices and admirers.

Soon after entering Exeter, James acquired the nickname Springheel, in honor of the countrified, loping manner in which he walked. By now he was a tall, gangly young man with a shock of thick, dark hair that flopped across his head in unruly clumps and outsized hands and feet that imparted a rawboned quality to his physique. He took to compensating for his size by moving as quietly and gracefully as he could. His manner of speaking, with its gentle Southern inflections and cadences, was just different enough to mark him as an outsider. His voice was low, flat, and seemed filled with thoughtfulness and concern. Rarely did he let loose the anger that seethed within. Beyond a fierce determination to win the approval of Exeter's literary fraternity, routine participation in the choir, and a casual interest in swimming, Springheel kept pretty much to himself.

One of the few friends he did make that first year was Freeman Lewis, nephew of Sinclair, whose novels James promptly bought or checked out of the school's ample library. He was fascinated to hear Freeman talk of wandering through the slums of New York with his famous uncle in search of material about which to write. He had daydreamed about the literary life, and now Freeman made it seem but one step removed from Exeter's musty classrooms.

For his part, Freeman soon found himself caught up in his ambitious young friend's "overwhelming passion for words, which came tumbling out him like a waterfall." When James spoke he unconsciously spread his large hands on either side of his face, bunching his fingers together as if conjuring words out of the air. As his intensity grew, he gnarled and twisted his hands, straining every muscle in his body as he articulated the ideas churning within. Conversation was more than a pastime with James; it was a passionate need.

Throughout the year he underwent an extraordinarily rapid mental unfolding. He undertook an unusually heavy course load: Latin, Math, English, French, History. He muddled through with lackluster Cs and Ds in most, but English was another matter. He quickly earned straight As in third-year-level courses. Throughout this period of intellectual ferment he kept in touch with the one constant in his life, Father Flye, who had resumed his teaching duties at St. Andrew's. "I have been snowed under with work," James wrote on October 19, "and am only now shoveling out after two or three most harrowing weeks. Yes, it's more strenuous even than our sightseeing last summer." Cringing with anxiety, he promised to forward his latest marks to the priest as soon as they were available.

In addition to the heavy course load he carried, James pushed himself to write poetry suitable for the *Monthly,* but from the first his published verse struck a falsely Romantic note. At the same time, his prose displayed remarkable self-assurance and a willingness to grapple with difficult themes. "Minerva Farmer," his earliest story to run in the magazine, tells of a Tennessee farm woman who leaves the fields for a life of scholarship, achieves a measure of success, but in the end finds a disappointingly sterile life stretching before her. Through his heroine, James expressed his doubts about where his scholarly existence would ultimately lead, at the same time indulging in nostalgia for the cloud-wrapped Appalachian Mountains of his boyhood. In Exeter's snobbish atmosphere, other fledgling writers labored to conceal their humble origins, but he publicly reveled in his.

Inevitably, James turned his attention to writing about his father's death, and in April 1926 the *Monthly* ran the resulting story, titled "The Circle." Unlike the masterly novel he would write years later on the same subject, "The Circle" contains little autobiographical material. In it, the father of "Edgar Butler" dies suddenly of "apoplexy." Edgar is valedictorian of his high school class and plans to enter the state university in the fall to study law. He realizes he must now forfeit his plans to stay home and care for his Aunt Selina "week after week, month after month, year after year. . . . She might live to be a hundred." Despite these evasions, the youthful author was determined to demonstrate what his lot would have been had he stayed close to his mother instead of attending Exeter, with all its opportunity and promise.

By publishing some specimen of his writing in nearly every issue of the *Monthly,* the rising star of Exeter's literary scene quickly won admission to the Lantern Club, where he soon expounded on his newest passion: movies. Each week, on the school's movie night, he saw examples of the most advanced motion pictures of the era, especially the products of UFA, the German film studio where such silent film masters as Ernst Lubitsch, F. W. Murnau, and Emil Jannings practiced their art. Unlike his classmates, who went to the movies in search of escapist entertainment, James paid close attention to the emerging language of cinema, the rhythms of editing, and the use of camera angles and movement to tell a story. Within months he began to see in movies possibilities for a universal, all-embracing art form whose reach and sweep far exceeded that of literature's. He came out of his self-imposed shell to discuss his theories with anyone he could manage to buttonhole and campaigned to have the films he most admired on campus, all the while risking ridicule by Exeter's literary standard-bearers, who considered movies an inferior, populist form of entertainment.

To persuade the anti-movie contingent to take their cinema more seriously, James wrote an impassioned pro-movie tract that appeared in the March issue of the *Monthly.* "In the first place, I like the movies," he began. "Despite their obvious defects, despite their gross exaggeration, their commercialism, and their general bad taste, there is, I feel, much to be said for the movies." He defended them on the basis of the advances the Germans had made, especially Murnau in his masterpiece *The Last Laugh,* the disarmingly simple story of a pompous doorman, superbly played by Jannings, who endures a humiliating demotion to the rank of washroom attendant. "This is the perfect moving picture," he declared,

and with considerable eloquence based his judgment on the evidence that the "camera seemed to be human. Every scene was taken
with infinite care that in composition and grouping and movement
of characters, it might leave a definite psychological impression on
the onlooker. . . . The camera was used as an artist uses his brush;
there were actually broad, sweeping strokes and fine lines, and an
infinite variety of shadings." He went on to deplore the American
practice of merely adapting books to movies. As any purist knew,
movies required material "written *especially, originally,* for them."
Caught up in the fervor of his argument and, one suspects, the
sound of his own voice, he concluded:

> In twenty-five years there will be very few scoffers at the mov-
> ies; in fifty years the most cultivated men will be reading movie
> literature; in a hundred years such men as von Stroheim and
> Murnau will be spoken of as reverently as Mozart or Dickens
> are today, and *The Last Laugh* will be as enduring a work of
> Art as *Vanity Fair.*

The work of a talented, enthusiastic proselytizer, the review was
James's way of making himself known to the school at large. He
kept his poetry and fiction largely to himself, rarely, if ever, discussing it and seemingly oblivious to its publication. In contrast, he
actively sought publicity as a champion of the movies, that brand-
new art form that, like no other, satisfied his hunger for human
contact. By this time James had come to consider literature essentially a private endeavor akin to religion, while film elicited the
most extroverted side of his nature.

At the time the movie manifesto appeared, Easter break was
at hand, and with it the gloomy prospect of several weeks in Rockland with his unhappy family. On March 3 he revealed to Father
Flye a novel plan to avoid them. "I'm going to spend my spring
vacation in Cambridge with the Cowley Fathers. Frankly, I look
forward to a dreary holiday. It's been a hard term and I feel like
'cutting loose' rather than staying in a monastery. But it's a fine
place to spend Holy Week. I think it's pretty poor, even in a
non-denominational school, to have the vacation then." Of course,
the weeks in Cambridge were not all that dreary, not with the entire
panoply of Harvard student life at hand as well as Hollywood's

latest releases. The stay at the monastery did not mark a return to religion so much as a sincere desire for refuge from domestic troubles.

A few weeks and much late-night studying for final examinations later, the Exeter school year ended, a year that had seen a remarkable flourishing of James's literary and critical abilities. In recognition of these, Exeter awarded him two academic prizes, the first consisting of four volumes of the works of Rudyard Kipling for Creative Writing, the second, an even more welcome thirty dollars in cash for Composition.

Back in Rockland, James did whatever he could to accommodate his remote and awkward family. He whiled away the long days playing tennis with Father Wright's clerical friends, trying hard to conceal his impatience as they hitched up their robes to chase after the ball. When he tired of exercise, he played Bach, read Sinclair Lewis and Eugene O'Neill, and pondered ways to overcome the shyness he felt around girls. In an unpublished autobiographical sketch written two decades later, he portrayed himself at this time as "pointedly ill at ease with girls and with most people his own age; no girl has ever reciprocated his love with so much as mild, friendly interest. But he comes to this new place [Rockland] with great fear, and with great hope that this will be turning over a new leaf."

Through a friend of his mother he fell in with Rockland's smart set, young men and women on vacation from their preparatory schools. His shyness masked an intense need for their attention, and he judged himself "liable to fall hopelessly in love, no matter, almost, with whom." When their parents were not around, the little group took over one or another seaside cottage, pushed back the jute rugs covering the sandy floors, and danced to records played on a portable phonograph.

Still, James remained too ill at ease to participate in these adolescent mating rituals until a chance encounter on the tennis court, when one of the girls took a special interest in him. They found themselves crowded into a car, and when she sat on his lap, she "forced on him the kinds of physical contact he would never have dared be responsible for." "To his almost fainting excitement," the "shy-deliberate pressures" he exerted were reciprocated.

James and the forward young lady again met at a dance. Unfortunately, he was "execrable" on the dance floor, but the girl promised to teach him. "The teaching gets nowhere, but the interest and the physical contact does wonders for both of them." The next step was a date at the movies, but, as he considered his next move, anxiety overwhelmed him.

> He knows that after the movies, you are supposed to drive and neck. Gritting his teeth, he drives; half-dead with fear, he touches her; trembling, delicate and clumsy; they make love. He has a tremendous rush of confidence to the head; for the first time, with a girl, he feels unafraid of using his intelligence in talk. He talks a blue streak. She is amazed, and interested. . . . They talk about everything under the sun—their childhoods, movies, sexual ethics, religion, popular music, literature, themselves, each other, their future plans. . . . Though neither quite dares to say it directly, neither has any doubt that their lives are now complete.

James clung tightly to their shared pleasure, trying to milk it of every last drop of sweetness, but his intensity caused the girl to withdraw. Within weeks, the romance entered a "slow, sure, complex" decline for which James blamed himself. Sadly, he realized he had been "too inquisitive, too analytical, too capable of (trying to) examine their actions impersonally—above all too talkative and too little able to let their emotions alone." Wounded by the rejection, he carried on a flirtation with a Polish dental assistant, but once the first girl got wind of the affair, both romances collapsed.

James's troubled summer of '26 reached a dismal anticlimax the night before he returned to Exeter. Although it was September 18, well past the end of the season, his mother and stepfather decided to throw their one party of the year. James dreaded the occasion, for, he recognized, they were not the "affable party-giving sort, and should never attempt such a thing." As expected, he found the party "an evening of acute misery for both children and parents" and an "embarrassment for most of the participants," who, unable to smoke, drink, or tell off-color jokes, must have had a devilishly difficult time warming to the enfeebled Father Wright and his pious new wife. The next day James bid farewell to his former girl friend. Perhaps she would come down to Exeter for the Fall Dance. Perhaps they would get together at Christmas, that is, if he could bring himself to ignore the dental assistant. They made no promises they could not keep. Returning home, he was overcome with shame at having neglected his mother all summer. Not until the party had he realized how lonely and isolated she was. In a rare moment of intimacy between them, he tried to strengthen their tie, only to discover that their relationship had irrevocably declined into a "sad and coldhearted confusion."

In the morning, James stole away for a last glimpse of his former girl friend's house, then boarded the train to Exeter. The tracks led past the secluded, seaside nook where they had first "made love," but the tide was so low, the daylight so "harshly cheerful" that he scarcely recognized it.

On his return to Exeter for his "upper middle" year, James cast a cold eye on Knoxville, which served as the setting for a series of satirical stories heavily influenced by Sinclair Lewis. But the points he scored against the conformist citizens of "Jenkinsville," as he renamed his birthplace, were too easy to have an impact, and he put aside satire for another bout with Romantic poetry. If he could not be the Sinclair Lewis of Knoxville, perhaps he might be its Shelley.

At the same time he struggled mightily to improve his grades, but with lackluster results. "This morning I had a French test—a big one," he wrote to Father Flye on October 20. "I tried so desperately to make an A that I made a D+, my poorest mark yet." Still, he tried to convince himself that he was making progress. "Algebra is coming much easier than before. I've had three tests, and have made respectively 100, C, and 100." In History, he found himself more fascinated by the teacher, Dr. Chadwick, than the subject matter. "He has a rather imposing array of dates, time-parallels, and maps which are apparently silly—*but* besides he has a most delightful and lovely way of lecturing." And the antics of his Declamation teacher elicited gales of schoolboy laughter: "He makes use of . . . dope-fiendish gestures with his hands; he has a piano in his classroom, on which he splatters out vile chords; he leans against the mantelpiece and sobs." He found targets for satire wherever he looked.

He felt pressure to improve his grades because Father Wright threatened to cut off the flow of money to Exeter. Since the tuition was onerous—$1,000 a year—James tried to win at least a partial scholarship to ease the burden on his family. Although his marks were below par, most of his teachers recognized in him an intelligence and sensitivity well beyond his years. They began treating him on a man-to-man basis, rarely condescending as they did to his classmates. Acknowledging his promise and effort, if not his actual accomplishment, the faculty awarded two partial scholarships, the Hole and the Sturgis, thus ensuring that he would complete the academic year.

Fits of scholarly labor alternated with nostalgia for his summer-time romance, of which he confided as many details as he dared to Father Flye. "All I did was 'run around' with this crowd. I learned to dance, after a fashion, and I've got over the worst, at any rate, of my bashfulness. I want to keep a certain amount of it; if there's anything that disgusts me, it's what's called a 'smooth line.'" He reproached himself for jilting "a girl whom I fell violently for and loved forever—until I came away to Exeter" and halfheartedly attempted to persuade himself that he had done the right thing. "She is the most interesting egotist I ever ran into. But unalloyed egotism—or is it egoism—is wearing." He might as well have been describing himself.

At the same time, he could not get the dental assistant out of his mind. She, in contrast, was "entirely devoid of the affected squawk and squeals and shiverings which ruin most girls." Only now, from the remove of Exeter, did he appreciate her "unobstreperous intelligence, tinged with limeadish sarcasm."

Girls, he decided, were even more difficult to master than Algebra and less trustworthy than boys his own age. Around them, at least, he could be himself. In the fall he felt drawn to one classmate in particular, Fred Lowenstein, of Brookline, Massachusetts. They spent hours analyzing the events of the day in minute detail, and during the long gray months of late fall their friendship blossomed in Exeter's hothouse social environment.

Enjoying the solace of male camaraderie, James happened to come across a highly relevant story in a back issue of the *Monthly*, written by a former Exeter student named Dwight Macdonald, who was now an undergraduate at Yale. Macdonald's story, "The Wall," explored one of Exeter's more arcane traditions, that of "romantic friendships" between boys. In these, one student would enlist another as a protégé, guarding his charge as jealously as a lover. Macdonald had written out of his own experience tutoring a younger boy in the finer points of literature and eventually suffered a heartbreaking loss when the boy decided to seek out other friendships. Although such liaisons were usually platonic, they could become emotionally charged with envy and bitterness. In "The Wall" James found confirmation that he had set himself a course for disaster, but he nonetheless continued to court his own friend's favor. Back in Rockland for Christmas, he spoke of Lowenstein with such warmth that his mother feared the relationship might become overtly homosexual.

James's new obsession had a deleterious effect on his writing. To escape the unhappiness threatening to engulf him, he wrote more but enjoyed it less. The *Monthly*'s board rejected one story after another. He retreated to less prominently featured book reviews, in one taking his former inspiration Sinclair Lewis to task. Discussing the recently published *Elmer Gantry*, James commented, "Where Lewis should have used a black snake whip he has substituted a slapstick, and into the slapstick he has driven twenty-penny nails." The lambasting he inflicted on the novel contained unmistakable overtones of self-disgust. "It is one gigantic crescendo of walloping filthiness, and I have the feeling that it carried Mr. Lewis before it, and left him stranded where not even himself can work his salvation."

The immediate cause of the hotheaded young critic's discontent was the perilous romantic friendship. By the spring of 1927 he had become pathologically possessive. "I'd become terribly mad if any other fellow was around," he wrote several months later. "It seemed to spoil the whole thing. I wanted him all to myself, and I wanted terribly to feel that I was just as necessary to him." When they were at last alone together, "I was swept completely off my guard, and was perfectly overwhelmed by the idea that this could be an ideal friendship—something Greek in its beauty. For weeks I lived on air." But it anguished him to realize that he always played the role of the pursuer, never the pursued. "My friend has everything in common with me except this peculiarly intense love I have for him. He absolutely can't understand that, and can hardly sympathize with it." James's intense dissatisfaction left him "disgusted at myself, sometimes at the school or at my friends," he noted on March 17. "I was that way this evening—feeling inexplicably like crying or biting into something or beating it with my fists."

At these moments he doggedly tried to relax his body and mind, as Father Flye suggested, but the inward assault resumed all too quickly. He complained of suffering from a "horrible tight feeling as if I were wrapped in mummy cloths," a sensation reflecting the panic he felt. To soothe his inflamed nerves he immersed himself in mammoth tomes of serious fiction: John Dos Passos' *Manhattan Transfer* ("an unalleviatedly filthy book," "a bellyful of sexual filth") and Theodore Dreiser's *An American Tragedy* ("You feel you're reading a rather inadequate translation of a very great foreign novel—Russian probably. He's horribly obvious, and has no humor.").

While James read and suffered, spring plodded gracelessly into New Hampshire. Wet snow yielded to cold, muddy fields, and in the overheated hallways the radiators hissed mercilessly. At Easter, James again took refuge in Cambridge, where he gave free rein to his instincts. Night after night he went to Symphony Hall to hear the Boston Symphony Orchestra perform Beethoven's Sixth, Seventh, Eighth, and Ninth symphonies. So impressed was he by the music's suggestion of vast spaces and emotional conflict that he instantly installed the composer in his private pantheon of artistic gods.

With the triumphant chords of the "Ode to Joy" still ringing in his ears, he spent his days in a wholly different and bizarre manner. Mustering his considerable charm, he befriended an "Irish politician" who gave him access to the Boston morgue and jail. While his Exeter classmates were at home learning about the stock market at their father's knee or making their first fumbling advances with girls, James studied corpses and meditated on the fine line between the quick and the dead. Perhaps he saw himself as another Sinclair Lewis, prowling the lower depths in search of material. Certainly his father's death lay at the root of his curiosity. Afterward he wrote a breezy account of his activities to Father Flye, as though it were the most natural thing in the world to visit a morgue over Easter vacation. James said the place struck him as rather worse than he had expected, "in a clammy, metallic way. I had a taste in my mouth as if I'd been licking an old sardine can."

On his return to Exeter, James was showered with a trio of honors. Having entered a national essay contest on the "frightful" topic "To what extent do the ramifications of International Trade affect the political relations of the U.S. and the British Empire?" he learned to his amazement that he had been awarded the school prize. Of greater moment, he won election as editor of the *Monthly* and president of the Lantern Club, thus ensuring him an unshakable grip on the Exeter literary world. "This last is going to be hard," he joked after the triumph. "I must make twittering, pleasant little introductory speeches." No matter that he was close to flunking most of his courses and in danger of losing his scholarship, he had become a Big Man on Campus.

In the flush of victory, even his troubled romantic friendship took on a special glow. He wrote warmly of its possibilities to Father Flye in a manner calculated to earn the priest's approval, at the same time revealing more than James could have wished about its actual nature.

> There seems to me at best so much possible . . . between two people of the same sex—so much more to encourage friendship. A girl's brain is mysterious, but only in a superficial way —a way very exasperating to me. But this boy and you and I know how our thoughts work, what we are interested in and why—everything—no finessing, no nerve twisting, egg-walking deprecation such as I'd feel you'd have even with a wife. I wish we could all three enjoy this friendship together; I know you'd like each other.

By including Father Flye, James hoped to legitimize, if not sanctify, the friendship, at the same time denying the awkward emotions it stirred.

The roundabout strategy was self-defeating, as well as self-deceptive. Fellowship concealed desire, and desire led to despondency. James "became very unhappy" because "nothing we could say or do could measure up to our friendship." He despaired of ever finding the perfect happiness he had sought in the company of Lowenstein. After a few days' rumination on the problem, James came to a "pretty alarming conclusion":

It was that my love for him was more or less tinged with homosexuality. My line of thought had been this: our relations thus far had been entirely intellectual; this had seemed incomplete. Of late, too, I had been wonderfully happy simply looking at him—chiefly at his head or hands. Finally, . . . we had a roughhouse, and in that physical contact I thought I found the complete fulfillment of the ideal friendship I'd built up. It rather distressed me, however. I was quite sure he didn't feel this at all; and I felt the only thing I could do was to tell him. Before I could, he asked me if I'd made anything more out of my worry the other night [about homosexuality]. I told him, then.

The confession terminated their relationship, much to James's sorrow. Lowenstein disappeared from school over the following weekend, and when he returned and finally spoke to James, it was to announce that they could now be together only at meals.

The rejection sent James into an emotional tailspin. He had expressed his love only to be confronted with an embarrassment verging on scandal. "It really killed at one blow all the happiness which had been carrying me above my schoolwork," he lamented. "I was left with nobody to talk to and such a need of talking as I'd never felt before."

Eventually he went to Dr. Cushwa with his troubles. The English teacher did his best to console the unhappy young man by assuring him that he need not fear a recurrence of his homosexual feelings. "I immensely admire his wisdom in putting me into such an attitude," James gratefully noted, aware that Dr. Cushwa, "by proper manipulation of my introspective twists," could have made the sensitive student into a "desperate homosexualist."

But the relief Dr. Cushwa offered, devoid of true understanding of James's problem, was short-lived, and soon the young man was in deeper despair than he had ever known. "Even if we'd drowned in homosexuality, we'd have been better off than this!" he wailed. "I simply wasn't able to face the fact that all that was gone for good. I got into a terrible state of melancholia, and was a number of times on the verge of suicide."

Within weeks of the agonizing breakup, James, inspired by Macdonald's story, realized he had accumulated considerable creative capital. Like many good writers, he vowed to turn his suffering into art. "Any such kid's affair, written up truly and fully with sympathy, couldn't help but be good," he declared. He poured out his feelings on the subject in a forty-page theme titled "Who Am I?" Then he wondered whether the romantic friendship could serve as the basis for a novel or a movie. "My dabble in homosexuality could make a beautiful vehicle," he decided. But his last word on the subject came in a long, intricate, allusive poem that would cause a minor scandal.

In "Pygmalion," as the work was titled, James promised to "shoot the works" on an extravagant paean to nature heavily influenced by his matrilineal (and homosexual) ancestor Walt Whitman. The poem began conventionally enough with a description of God's rapture in creating the earth, but James went on to describe the process as a form of cosmic lovemaking, fearlessly wringing out his metaphor to explicit extremes.

> *I see thee shrink, thou tattered shroud of snow.*
> *Discovering the body of my world,*
> *Naked, and palpitant with new-found life.*
> *I press my face into thy hot, sweet earth,*
> *And hear the steady singing of the sap—*
> *And feel the pricking grass against my cheeks—*

But Whitman's generosity of spirit eluded the younger poet, in whose hands creations resembled rape.

> *Fear not,*
> *Beloved earth; if I must strain thee close,*
> *'Tis to alleviate the agony*
> *Of such passion as I never knew.*

The poem staggered to a close as the Supreme Being clutched "the bruised and broken form of Earth" to His breast.

The *Monthly* duly accepted the poem; it was set in type. At the last minute the magazine's faculty adviser, Myron Williams, gave James "undeserved hell" for the blasphemous imagery. James threatened to resign, enlisted the board members to go along with him, and Williams retaliated with a threat to hand over the *Monthly* to the Mathematics Department. "Rather than see this happen, I reinstated myself," he remarked. "Pygmalion" never appeared in the *Monthly* (or anywhere else), and the term ended with James's losing his first battle with censorship.

In foggy sedate Rockland for the summer, James endlessly re-hashed the details of the failed romantic friendship and daydreamed of grandiose cinematic epics. Physically he lived with his family on 138 South Main Street; in all other ways he remained at Exeter. Increasingly his thoughts turned to Macdonald as a potential role model and mentor. Months before, Exeter faculty members had endeavored to put the two prodigies in touch, and Macdonald had written James without receiving an answer. Aware that Macdonald roomed with the playwright Thornton Wilder's nephew, Wilder Hobson, and that he wrote for all the important student publications at Yale, James convinced himself they were kindred spirits. On June 16 he wrote a belated reply. So hungry for human contact was he that his most intimate thoughts and experiences came tumbling out on paper. "Last September I first read your story . . . about the rise and decline of a friendship," James wrote. "During the last term almost precisely the same thing happened to me . . . I was almost drowned in psychological meanderings too dreary and far too long for any story."

Having established this rather morbid bond, James went on to second Macdonald's belief in the importance of movies as an art form, "especially from the director's point of view." He cited *The Last Laugh, Potemkin,* and *Variety* as examples of grandly conceived cinema and proposed a regular correspondence devoted to discussing the newest cinematic milestones. In a subsequent missive James brought his by now finely tuned critical powers to bear on his favorites. "As for Potemkin, I think it was pretty messy on the whole, but perfectly marvellous as a study in orchestration of movement. The first shots in the picture—the repeated flashes first of water sousing the rocks, then of the sea lying in a welter on a flat shining place of concrete—gives me just what I've been looking for in the movies—a sort of key-note speech, a topic sentence, as it were." This young man's gift for visual description both impressed and alarmed Macdonald, who would subsequently observe, "Jim could always fill out the botched, meagre, banal outlines of what was actually projected on the screen with his own vision of what, to his sympathetic, imaginative eye, the director had clearly intended to be there—and what, had he been the director, undoubtedly would have been there. . . . His critiques, in short, are usually more interesting than their subjects."

Discussing movies in such an imaginative fashion, James found it natural to launch into a description of the kind of film he would like to make, a story brimming with his by now familiar obsession with death.

> I have a wild desire to direct *Ethan Frome*. . . . I'd begin with the death of Ethan's mother, an oblique shot, from near the ground, of a coffin being lowered into the grave—a lap dissolve—becoming a shot from the coffin lid with rain blurring the lens and the light above telescoping into a small rectangle. The four walls of the grave, rough-dug, slipping slowly upward with cut roots sprawling out. Camera moved upward, out of the grave, swings in behind the ground, catching in profile the heads of Ethan and Zeena. Then the camera swings on up the hill—with the group at the grave crumbling away in the rain and the snow—swerves over a semi-circular sweep of New England country and comes to rest on the Frome farmhouse. . . .

So taken was he with the potential for movies and his own gift for screenwriting that James suddenly contemplated abandoning the prospect of college for an early start in Hollywood. "Have you ever thought of trying to direct in the movies?" he asked Macdonald. "I'd give anything if I had the guts to try it—to go within a year or so, too. I have one or two short stories which I've worked out much more carefully as movies than as writing—and I think they could be told entirely without subtitles." Even at this early date he had exhilarating notions of the kind of film he wanted to make, one that would "portray a state of mind by the method of photographing commonplace things. . . . What couldn't be done with Freud in the movies!" While Macdonald clucked in appreciation, he did not yet thoroughly comprehend the phenomenon calling himself James Agee, but, he realized, "We were lucky to have found each other." In a surge of confidence, Macdonald wrote to a friend, "Our generation is one of great power, I think. There's talent running around like loose quicksilver. A fellow named Jim Agee . . . has the stuff. . . . He is all there is when it comes to creative writing, or rather *will be* all there."

The letter-borne friendship deepened to the point that Macdonald unwittingly became a secular version of Father Flye, a paternal figure to whom James freely confessed his peccadilloes, doubts, and aspirations. That the two had never met made confession all the easier; Macdonald remained as invisible and idealized as the priest on the other side of the screen in a confessional.

This summer-long infatuation with film coincided with a period of emotional fallowness. Scarred by two romances, one heterosexual, one homosexual, he frittered away the warm months watching movies and savoring the splendors of the Maine coastline. "As for my feelings now, they are not," he told Macdonald on July 21. "In fact, I'm unable just now to imagine I'll ever feel any sexual emotion again. Of course, I shall; common sense tells me that. I suppose this [is] the natural reaction to my unnatural nervous condition of last spring. At the same time I feel a great need for some girl or other, not for physical as much as for mental well-being." But the cinematic tastes of the ones he found in Rockland ran more to Ramon Navarro than Sergei Eisenstein: "That's the hell of this lousy town."

Nothing seemed able to shake him out of his listlessness. In conjunction with a local friend, Wilbur "Brick" Frohock, he tried his hand at a Greek tragedy ("one of the most discouraging things on earth"); he tried to start a novel ("I've just introduced a new man, and know I've got him entirely wrong."). When inspiration failed, he adopted Draconian measures—to no avail. "Of course I'll never be able to write on tap, but after a half-hour of desperate mental masturbation, all I produced was some lousy characterization," he complained to Macdonald, adding, "I'd be grateful for a hoe and convenient corn." The sight of a blank page filled him with fear and loathing. Two years had passed since he had found his objective correlative in a ruined church in France, two years of frantic searching for fresh material that would engage his mind and satisfy his heart. At this time of doubt and confusion, movies supplied an artificial inner life when his own became too muddled to manage.

In the fall of his senior year at Exeter, James finally found a girl friend he considered his intellectual equal. Her name was Dorothy

Carr, she was a few years older than he, and she worked at the Exeter Public Library, where they first met. Over the winter, when Dorothy fell ill, he recklessly crept out of his ground-floor window in Hoyt Hall at night to spend hours with her. Meanwhile, news of the romance spread rapidly among his classmates and reached the ears of faculty members, who, impressed if not intimidated by his intellectual stature, conveniently turned a blind eye to nocturnal escapades normally punishable by expulsion.

On the heels of the love affair, James gained confidence in his intellectual abilities, though his grades remained at their previous dismal level, with Ds in Math, Chemistry, even his beloved Music. No A in English brightened the record; he had taken the most advanced course the previous year.

In his new, expansive mood, he undertook to write a dramatic poem on a larger scale than anything he had attempted, a summation of all that he had learned about the art of verse and himself. This time inspiration struck, and the resulting four hundred lines marked a complete departure from the excess of his juvenilia. In simple, straightforward blank verse, heavily but not oppressively influenced by the great Elizabethans, he spun a Tennessee folktale about the harsh life and death of a mountain woman named Ann Garner.

As the story opens, she is giving birth, the lines fairly resounding with her groans.

> *In her agony*
> *Bent like a birch ice-laden, Ann Garner lay:*
> *The silent woman by her in the dimness*
> *Turned to the firelight and said to her husband,*
> *"She's laborin' hard, best set the plow beneath her."*

The child, brought forth according to this mountain custom, is stillborn. Ann Garner chips away a frog from the ice to suckle the unneeded milk from her breasts. She then holds the little lifeless body "in a fleece close-wrapped . . . in a strong oak box" before allowing it to be lowered into the grave while the earth "drums" on the coffin.

No pathos marred the stark scene; it was as grim as reality. Drawing on his memories of the mute dignity of the mountain people and secure in his appropriately plain manner of description,

James endowed events with the force of myth, and his habit of writing visual descriptions for screenplays paid off handsomely.

Deprived of her own child, Ann Garner becomes known as an expert on planting and, eventually, a local fertility goddess who grows increasingly learned "In all the mysteries of the darkened moons." Her very body ripens with each passing year, until she incarnates the natural forces that had victimized her.

Through this transformation she realizes that "Life was in death," to be found, like her child, "locked deep in the sheathing snows." The revelation fills her with joy as she goes about handling farmers' tools as if they were "sacred symbols of fertility." Overcome with her generative powers, she now madly plows furrows and casts grain until she dies of exhaustion on her child's grave. Pondering the "chisellings of lust," her stalwart husband furtively digs her grave before the neighbors, whose livelihood depends on Ann Garner's skills, learn of the tragedy. In a grisly last gesture, he disinters the child's body and sprinkles its crumbled bones in her eyes and mouth before burying them together.

While working on the poem, James avidly read some of the newest arrivals on the American literary scene: Ernest Hemingway, Robert Frost, and Robinson Jeffers. From them he learned the lessons of dry, spare, hard writing, lessons that served as a welcome antidote to his penchant for Romantic excess. Jeffers' 1925 dramatic poem *Roan Stallion,* filled with graphic violence and stark surroundings, in particular pointed the way for "Ann Garner." Nonetheless, the eighteen-year-old Exeter student's poem, despite its obvious excess, was the product of a fiercely independent approach to writing.

On completion of the work, James received his first encouragement from recognized writers. Displaying a knack for literary hustling, he persuaded his friend Brick Frohock, now a student at Brown University, to give the play on which they had collaborated the previous summer to one of Brick's professors, S. Foster Damon, known as an authority on mysticism. On the strength of the play, Damon supplied James with the names and addresses of fifteen prominent American poets who might prove helpful in finding a publisher. The list included Edna St. Vincent Millay, Rockland's other claim to literary fame; Hilda Doolittle, who signed her poems "H.D."; Ezra Pound; and Robert Frost. James fearlessly mailed off several poems to each, including the ungainly "Pygmalion," but collected little more than mild praise for his trouble.

Undaunted, he next tried to turn to his advantage his position as outgoing president of the Lantern Club by inviting Frost to speak at Exeter. Twelve years earlier, Frost had published his first collection of poems, *A Boy's Will,* on the strength of a recommendation from Ezra Pound, and James hoped to establish a line of succession extending to him. Meeting Frost on April 22, James eagerly submitted more examples of his work, but the selection failed to include his chef d'oeuvre, "Ann Garner." Again, Frost had nothing more than kind words to offer. Disheartened, James wrote to Father Flye, "The general verdict is that I can do a lot if I don't give up to write advertisements. . . . If I remain convinced they're right I'll croak before I write ads or sell bonds—or do anything but write."

James's thoughts had suddenly turned to the world at large because he was about to graduate. On the advice of his teachers he had applied to Harvard, and his acceptance hung in the balance. Although his grades fell well below Harvard's standards, Exeter faculty members recommended James Agee as a candidate of unusual promise. "Put him in the English Department and let him do as he pleases," urged one. "He will probably be the joy and despair of his tutor," said another. Dr. Cushwa summed up the faculty's feelings about him: "He was meant for Harvard and Harvard for him."

His mother sounded the single sour note in this chorus of praise. In reply to a query from the Harvard Dean's Office, she wrote, "His one deep enthusiasm is English, and writing, in which he is above the average and will work with zeal. In all else he is careless. . . . He has always been a very high-strung boy, nervously [sic], and tending much to introspection. At present he is intensely modern in all his thinking and theories and in need of better balance." Perhaps Harvard, like some progressive reform school or monastery, would straighten the lad out. Ignoring her reservations, Harvard accepted James as a member of the class of 1932.

Secure in his future, James delivered a straightforward, somber history of his Exeter class on graduation day, June 25. His mother was on hand to hear him stress the accomplishments of the Lantern Club and to compare the school to a mother who would "give to the world not its leaders, but lives, lived steadfastly, sincerely, to the utmost of their own capabilities." He received his diploma, and his Exeter career was at an end.

In private he confessed to Father Flye his sorrow at leaving the school where he had spent three trying but fruitful years. "I'm much fonder than I realized of Exeter," he wrote, "and know I'll never be nearly so much a part of the school again—not even if I give a couple of million for a baseball cage or a boiler plant."

Following the excitement of graduation, with its pomp and circumstance, the prospect of yet another summer in Rockland came as a distinct disappointment. James spent weeks moping around his family's new lodgings at 10 Summer Street. To make matters worse, he was deprived of the companionship of Dorothy, who remained in Exeter, and Brick, who had sailed for France. To fill the empty hours he forced himself to write until he felt, as he later recalled, "so tired that several times he put his forehead down on to the paper and stayed there several minutes, nauseated with chain smoking." Depriving himself even of trips to the bathroom, he labored to compose paragraph after paragraph. Finishing a story, he would experience a fierce desire to read it to his mother, then think better of the idea and resign himself to rereading the manuscript "coldly, correcting and recasting with a feeling of perfect professionalism." After this ordeal of penitence, James would decide he was entitled to a reward, usually in the form of a drink. Though his mother and stepfather permitted him to imbibe in moderation, James preferred to take sizable nips of gin in secret, afterward unwinding with jazz records played on a hand-cranked portable machine.

When not forcing himself to work, the young poet dipped into the chilly gray waters of the Atlantic and passed damp, cloudy afternoons gazing at women clad only in their skimpy bathing costumes. He would stare at these strange women cavorting on the beach and wonder who they were, what their lives were like, and weave fantasies suggested by their appearance. At his most daring, he would sneak around their cottages to observe them smoke or drink on their screened porches or behind windows, his desire increasing as he felt the textures of their bathing suits drying on outdoor lines. One suit "smelled of its own fabric and of the sea, and . . . he remembered the delicate discoloration" of his anonymous love object's thighs. Out of his loneliness he composed an artless tribute to her: "On First Watching a Young Woman Come Out of the Sea." It began

Where I waited, listlessly,
On Summer's unportentous brink,
You stepped up out of the sea
Now I can no longer think.

Of greater interest than the poem itself were notes James made during its composition. Working late at night and no doubt chain-smoking, he endlessly fussed over the language, replacing one word with another, then returning to the original, but the effort left him unsatisfied, and he concluded he had "seldom written a worse poem." Once it was finished he snapped off the light and went to bed, but the poem refused to leave him in peace. He pushed back the covers and altered the title to "Sea Piece," changed more words, and by the time he had completed revising a poem he did not even like it was four o'clock in the morning.

Rarely was he able to compose even the most ephemeral piece of poetry without bringing his extraordinary intensity to bear, but his passion proved at the same time to be his undoing. When the spell was upon him, he lacked the clarity of mind necessary to compose verse. Instead of stimulating and shaping his thoughts, the poetic discipline stifled them. Formal restrictions ran against the grain, and he felt far more at home in relatively formless stories and especially in letters, when he could "talk" to a friend and relieve his sense of isolation. Any one of his letters to Father Flye or Dwight Macdonald contained more beauty, insight, and sense of wonder—more "poetry"—than his stilted verse. Although he was capable of rising above his limitations to write a work of the stature of "Ann Garner," his prose efforts displayed a uniformly higher standard of sensitivity to language and thought. Despite his growing habit of revision, he essentially wrote freely and easily; only in prose could he hope to capture the vagaries of thought and his lightning-quick impressions. Yet he stubbornly persisted in this increasingly futile pursuit of poetry in a misguided attempt to reconcile his wild literary gift with his need for his mother's love and approval. She, too, continued to write poetry, and the art served as a bond between them, one her Harvard-bound son could not bear to sever.

4

OF HARVARD AND
HOBOES

From the outset of his college career, it was apparent to all who came into contact with James Agee that he was unique and refused to be governed by the laws affecting ordinary undergraduates. "The door burst open," remembered his close friend Robert Saudek of their first meeting,

> and in strode the roommate—tall, shy, strong, long arms and legs, a small head, curly dark hair, a spring in his heels as he bounded past with a wicker country suitcase in one hand and an enormous, raw pine box over his shoulder. He turned his head suddenly, squinted his eyes in an apologetic smile, said softly, "Hello, Agee's my name," swept through to an empty

bedroom and deposited his belongings, bounded back through the gabled, maroon and white study, murmured, "See you later," waved an awkward farewell and didn't show up again for several days. Such was the magnetic field that had rushed into the room, that I didn't even think to introduce myself.

In all likelihood, he repaired to the Cowley Fathers monastery to collect himself before beginning the rigors of the year.

The Harvard Agee came to in September 1928 stood midway between the caste-ridden institution it had been during the previous century and the democratic university it would become after the Second World War. Even at this late date the student body consisted of several sharply defined constituencies who rarely mingled outside the classroom. Wealthy students with a trust fund at their disposal were handsomely ensconced on the "Gold Coast" along Mt. Auburn Street, living in private "final" clubs equipped with indoor swimming pools, squash courts, and servants. At the lower end of the economic scale, where Agee found himself, students resided in comfortable but simple rooms maintained by the college and located in tranquil, leafy Harvard Yard, the original center of the university, or near the Charles River. Agee was assigned to thoroughly plebeian accommodations in George Smith Hall, now part of Kirkland House, within sight of the river and a short walk from the Yard. One of his earliest—and most lasting— impressions of the august university was how little money he had compared to the other students, especially those who had come from preparatory schools such as Exeter. Every few weeks he received a small check from his stepfather, grudgingly sent and grudgingly accepted. If he overspent, he had to make up the difference himself.

Given his habitual identification with society's outcasts, Agee naturally recoiled from Harvard's lack of social democracy and rampant elitism. Not long after he arrived in Cambridge he fought his way onto the pages of the *Crimson,* the student newspaper, to denounce the "incredible mirror maze of fake self-perceptions" that was Harvard, insisting that "only a little fool who never questions nor examines can get out without embarrassment or injury." To emphasize his unwillingness to adopt the "smooth line" he had long detested, he remained ill-kempt and unshorn, just a boy from the mountains of Tennessee—anything but an ambitious literary star from Exeter. In a forgetful moment he did purchase a brown suit that would see him through four years of social occasions, and, when it was absolutely necessary, rented evening clothes to attend grander functions in Boston's genteel homes.

Agee was hardly alone in his distaste for the stratification of Harvard society. The university's president, A. Lawrence Lowell, then in the last year of his tenure, was determined to end the more flagrant inequities of student life. "An intellectual aristocrat himself," historian Samuel Eliot Morison has remarked, "Mr. Lowell disliked the social divisions . . . because they were based on wealth, schooling, and Boston society, rather than on intellectual ability. . . . The traditional union of religion, learning, and social life no longer existed." In the fall of 1928, Lowell announced a plan to establish a series of houses for students and tutors that signaled the end of the final clubs' hegemony over undergraduate life, but he acted in the face of student criticism. The *Crimson* condemned the plan because students feared a loss of precious freedom and a return to the restrictions of their prep school days.

Awaiting the results of President Lowell's reforms to trickle down to the lowly ranks of freshmen, Agee determined to conquer these strange new surroundings by proving his literary and intellectual worth. He pored over the thick course catalogue studded with the names of eminent professors—Kittredge, Perry, Hillyer—who had been but distant, lofty figures to him at Exeter. Now he would be able to learn the mysteries of the Metaphysical poets straight from the horse's mouth; yet, in class, he found little of the personal concern for student welfare that had marked his Exeter days. The professors marched into large, ugly lecture halls, often in barely heated buildings antedating the Civil War, to deliver uninspiring lectures before marching out again. It was all as orderly as clockwork, and as perfunctory. Agee found his sophomore-level English course merely a "Cook's tour of English literature very smugly presented." The Geology course, a time-honored freshman ordeal, fell well below St. Andrew's standards, in his estimation. Only European History and Latin, relying heavily on Horace, Plautus, and Terence, satisfied.

In the numerous libraries at his disposal he found greater sustenance. There was, preeminently, the vast Widener Library in the Yard, one of the largest in North America. And the Boston Public Library, which he frequented as well, satisfied his craving for art books and other exotic items he could not locate in Widener. He read all of Dostoevsky, dwelling especially on *The Possessed;* Joyce's *Dubliners;* the works, both visual and literary, of William Blake, whom he installed in the pantheon beside Beethoven; and A. E. Housman's *A Shropshire Lad* and *Last Poems,* whose simplicity he found greatly appealing and soon began to imitate. He burned the midnight oil studying accounts of witchcraft and demonology and contemplated writing an adaptation of Edgar Lee Masters' *Spoon River Anthology* set in an eighteenth-century New England village. After these bouts with the masters he felt thoroughly out-classed and intimidated, aware of the vast distance he had yet to go before he became a writer of distinction rather than the pride of the Exeter English Department.

In contrast to the harsh opinion he held of himself, those around him quickly realized that someone highly unusual had come into their midst. It was not long before the word *genius* was used to describe him. To his compact, stable roommate, Robert Saudek, Agee seemed a fiery shadow requiring little or no sleep. He would stay up until four o'clock in the morning rehearsing his role in a modest Harvard Dramatic Club show, then go directly to the Cowley Fathers monastery to serve early Mass. He would attend a concert given by the Boston Symphony Orchestra, then drive through the night to New Hampshire in a borrowed car to climb a mountain at dawn in waist-high snow. He would see Helen Hayes in *Coquette* not once or twice but seven nights in a row. He thought nothing of swooping down to New York to watch all-night movies in Times Square or traveling north to Exeter to visit Dorothy Carr. No matter what he did, he smoked fiendishly, one Chesterfield after another, until his fingers turned bright orange from the nicotine.

That Prohibition was in full force only made liquor more desirable. Agee found it easy enough to arrange for bootleggers to deliver booze to his room in the dead of night. Two knocks on the door and a bottle of gin would materialize from beneath the coat of a shadowy figure. Like other Harvard students, James sampled the popular drinks of the day: sidecars, Alexanders concocted with gin and chocolate ice cream, and a "fearful and wonderful" mixture of nonalcoholic Benedictine fortified with gin. When the bootleggers ran dry, a nearby Greek restaurant thoughtfully served ouzo to familiar patrons. Agee drank his fill, but not conspicuously more than any other freshman on his own for the first time and willing to try anything that caught his fancy.

The more he drank, the more he talked. These expansive moments revealed a new side of Agee—that of a wickedly effective parodist. Hearing that an actor named Anton Lang, known for portraying Jesus in the Oberammergau Passion Play, had broken his arm sliding down a banister, James repeatedly slid down a banister himself, head first, crying, "Zis iz ze way ve play ze Christ in ze Passion Play!" And then he crashed to the floor. He also liked to mime a liquor-sodden Ulysses S. Grant at Appomattox, accepting the sword of Robert E. Lee while sliding out of a chair.

In addition to his clowning, Agee displayed the anger he had carefully concealed at Exeter, and his penchant for scathing profanity shocked the rather more staid Robert Saudek, who remembered Agee's sudden, violent dislike for their classmate Joseph W. Alsop, later prominent as a newspaper columnist. Saudek recalled, "He went over to the fireplace, turned, and announced that he hated the place and hated a system that would seat 'Agee' next to 'Alsop' since that fat sonofabitch, not yet having bought himself a Latin textbook, picked up Agee's new book, opened it up, and broke its spine." Agee took out his anger not on Alsop but on himself. Had Alsop damaged a valuable book? Agee further desecrated it by spitting on an open page. Still enraged, he "swung his fist against the stucco wall above the fireplace with all his might, abrading his knuckles." Finally anger gave way to shame as he "struck the bleeding fist against his own temple and leaned spent against the wall." Never did he utter a word of his grievance directly to Alsop.

The exasperation of catching streetcars in Boston sent Agee into a rage of similar ferocity. On more than one occasion he drove his fist through the window of a public conveyance that had pulled away before he could climb aboard. As a result of these eruptions, he often went about with his hand sore or bandaged—but never, apparently, broken.

Once the rage subsided, Agee would be overcome with remorse and tenderness. Although no longer a believer, he still considered himself a Christian, and he knew more acutely than anyone else that his outbursts violated the fundamental precept of turning the other cheek. How he wished he could; if only he were able! He vowed he would never willingly cause harm to another—not to his mother, Dorothy, even Joseph W. Alsop—if he could possibly avoid doing so.

In this mood of quiet contrition he was much given to brooding on the example of Abraham Lincoln, whom he considered a figure of moral greatness on a par, almost, with Jesus, Blake, and Beethoven. He told Saudek a story concerning Lincoln's visiting his son at Exeter; supposedly Lincoln had told the boy ribald stories. Saudek took exception, but Agee calmly insisted that the anecdote revealed Lincoln's earthiness and warmth. In 1928, Lincoln still seemed a vivid figure. There were people who had been alive when he was President. Strangely enough, Lincoln was also the darling of the Dadaists in Paris, his rough-hewn quality signifying to them a genuine American elegance. Agee adopted the sweet, fragile lilac, Walt Whitman's symbol of Lincoln's passion, as his favorite flower.

This fascination with Lincoln suggests that Agee saw him as an idealized version of his own father, for he attributed to Lincoln the same qualities he had prized in Jay: warmth, earthiness, and forbearance. And of course they had both died prematurely. When Agee mentioned his father, it was with an awed hush and an unmistakable worshipfulness that even his less sensitive friends noticed. At the same time, Agee betrayed a fear that he was a marked man, owing to his father's death, and often gave the impression that he, too, expected to die prematurely in unexplained circumstances. He laid his premonition to a sense of inescapable fate, of being "bitched" by circumstances over which he had little control.

This premonition very nearly came true over Christmas vacation. Tonsillitis had plagued Agee through the fall semester, and his family arranged for him to have his tonsils removed when he returned to Rockland. At the time, the Wrights lived on the second floor of a former maternity hospital that had been converted into apartments; on the first floor lived, coincidentally, his friend Brick Frohock, whose father was an anesthesiologist. On the morning of the operation, Dr. Frohock administered the ether, the tonsillectomy went off without a hitch, and Agee later went home to recuperate. When Dr. Frohock returned to his apartment that night he smelled a faint odor of blood. He dashed upstairs to find an unconscious Agee hemorrhaging.

The doctor immediately brought the patient back to the hospital, cauterized the wound, injected adrenaline, and watched as Agee gradually came around. That he had happened to be asleep in a room one floor above his anesthesiologist's apartment proved a miraculous stroke of luck. Unattended, he would have bled to death before morning.

Throughout the winter of 1928 and spring of 1929 Agee navigated the difficult straits of the traditional freshman-year identity crisis. Unlike Exeter, Harvard made little pretence of acting *in loco parentis;* thrown back on their own devices in an unfamiliar, competitive situation, students groped frantically for self-definition. Agee withdrew into himself, his state of mind by his own description turning foggy, even comatose. "I've felt rather petrified mentally and spiritually," he wrote Father Flye on April 29. Still, he managed to churn out six "light" poems, an unspecified but "horribly filthy" story, and translations of various odes by Horace.

Near the end of the spring semester Agee's low morale vanished when a truncated version of "Ann Garner" appeared in the *Hound and Horn,* a new "little" magazine devoted to progressive writing and criticism. The occasion marked his first appearance in other than a student publication; indeed, he suddenly found himself in the best of literary company. The *Hound and Horn* was the brainchild of a Harvard senior named Lincoln Kirstein, scion of a prominent merchant family in Boston, who had known Agee when both were students at Exeter. Kirstein had founded the magazine two years earlier, but it had already compiled an impressive record, counting among its contributors T. S. Eliot, Ezra Pound, Edmund Wilson, and E. E. Cummings. Those in the know, like Agee, took to calling the magazine the *Horny Hound* or the *Bitch and Bugle* as a way of deflating its pretensions.

Agee quickly gravitated toward the little group of Harvard aesthetes clustering around the magazine. He befriended a popular young English professor, Theodore Spencer, known for the extravagant gin parties he gave on Shakespeare's birthday; and Robert Hillyer, an English professor in a more conservative, scholarly mold. With Kirstein Agee shared interests in poetry, photography, and Kirstein's namesake, Abraham Lincoln. And like Agee, Kirstein had his dark side. The slightest insult, real or imagined, sent him into paroxysms of rage.

The resurrection of "Ann Garner" prompted Macdonald to resume his correspondence with Agee. Since graduating from Yale the previous spring, Macdonald had been taking a crash course in capitalism. With his father dead and his mother in need of money, Macdonald had temporarily forsaken his literary ambitions to work in Macy's executive training program, which he had recently left— to his great relief. He was now working for a new magazine called *Time,* founded only five years earlier by two other enterprising young Yalies, Britton Hadden and Henry Luce, who had scraped together the money necessary to launch a weekly news summary. After floundering for several anxious years, *Time* had suddenly caught on, recruiting droves of Ivy League graduates, Macdonald included, to its editorial ranks. Always on the lookout for a literary connection, Agee instantly wrote back for more information. "What sort of work do you do?—or does a member of the staff do any and every sort of thing? I'd like to follow your work, if that is possible." Macdonald was glad to comply.

Despite this testing of the waters of journalism, Agee continued to envision a career in Hollywood. Having seen the work of the pioneer documentary filmmaker Robert Flaherty, he revealed to Macdonald plans for making experimental movies in the Boston area.

A fellow in my dormitory owns a movie camera . . . and has done some interesting work with it. He's worked out a good deal, unassisted, about lighting, and has a few test shots for a movie he was thinking of making last summer. At present it's possible we'll make two movies: one a sort of $24 *Island* of Boston. There's no chance for such beautiful stuff as Flaherty got in that, but Boston has a real individuality that may be fun to try to photograph. The idea is, that I'll devise shots, angles, camera work, etc—and stories; he'll take care of the photographing and lighting. The other thing is a story I wrote last fall. I've worked a good bit of it into pictures already. . . . The difficulty is, finding good actors. It wouldn't be very expensive; we intend to make it in 3 reels; it would be necessary to hire 2 tenement rooms for a while.

But the scheme came to nought. Agee was shrewd enough to realize that with the coming of the talkies, the era of the silent film and its magisterial montages was finished. "I'm trying to write a paper on the possibilities of talkies," he informed Macdonald, "which I despise. Nevertheless, great things could be done with them. Both depend on the possibility of fusing pictures, sound, and in one case color into a unity. One is—that they could be a fulfillment of all that Blake wanted to do—great pictures, poetry, color, and music—the other is the chance they offer Joyce and his followers. I should think they'd go wild over the possibilities of it. I wrote a story last spring which I'd give anything to make as a 'test case' —but somehow I feel a traitor to the movies as they should be, even to think of such things."

It is hard to say whether the medium of film or Hollywood itself exerted the stronger fascination. Coming across a photograph of Emil Jannings' Hollywood Christmas party "did my soul good. . . . All Germans & such—Murnau, Munde, Veidt, Mrs. Jannings —. . . and all beautifully soused and enjoying it." The Hollywood expatriate crowd formed another fringe group, albeit a glamorous and highly paid one, to which he felt strongly attracted. If only he could think of a way to catch up with them, to escape Harvard's oppressive influence.

As his Hollywood dream took on substance, he disavowed former literary idols. Whitman: "He seems generally half-assed to me now," only occasionally "more than an ecstatic young gent flexing his thighs and letting the wind tear up his hair." Jeffers: "His hands are too big for the keys." And Frost, if Agee had only had the wisdom to realize it earlier, wrote nothing more than pansified drivel. "I don't like Frost's 'mellowness' at any time, and when it's turned into . . . sweetie-pie channels it's Godawful." Only Housman's verse escaped Agee's new fastidiousness. "Perhaps you haven't heard the real reason for his works," Agee knowingly told Macdonald. "When he was twenty or so he had a homosexual love-affair." The intelligence encouraged Agee to view his own romantic friendship as a rite of passage necessary to the creation of poetry.

Agee's dissatisfaction with the privileged world around him extended to his by now turbulent affair with Dorothy Carr. The young lovers found it difficult to maintain a stable relationship with several hundred miles separating them. James desperately wanted to break out and date other women, but he felt bound by loyalty to the librarian. They communicated in brief notes filled with longing and recrimination. The *Advocate,* Harvard's literary magazine, ran several stories in which Agee obliquely referred to the frustration the affair created for him. "A Walk Before Mass" tells of a man tempted to murder his son and so be free of his wife. While confessing his horrible thoughts to the boy, the father accidentally drowns him. In another, "Near the Tracks," an escaped convict abandons his girl friend, who is in the throes of labor, to find "another wench in a warmer climate." The hapless girl meets her death chasing her boyfriend as he boards a train. Clearly, Agee dreaded entrapment by Dorothy even more than seduction by Harvard.

To make a complete break with all those forces he thought conspired to lure him into submission, he decided to spend the summer as a bindlestiff following the harvest from state to state, until, by season's end, he reached Hollywood. For sheer novelty, his determination to toil as a migrant farm worker outdid even the stay in the Cowley Fathers' monastery. In the devil-may-care summer of 1929, college students—especially Harvard students—were not given to exchanging their evening clothes for fraying work shirts and straw hats. Agee's motivation was not political; he did not consider farm workers oppressed. To his way of thinking, they were better off than conventional bourgeois society. Having been a wanderer since the death of his father twelve years before, he felt a spiritual kinship with the disenfranchised, the outcast, the homeless. In a mood of romantic fervor, he described to Macdonald what he expected to find in their midst.

> I'm going to spend the summer working in the wheatfields, starting in Oklahoma in June. The thing looks good in every way. I've never worked, and greatly prefer such a job; I like to get drunk and will; I like to sing and learn both dirty songs and hobo ones—and will; I like to be on my own—the farther from home the better—and will; and I like the heterogeneous gang that moves north on the job. You get a wonderful mess of bums and lumberjacks, so I'm told. Also, I like bumming, and shall do as much of it as I can. Finally, I like saving money, and this promises from 5 to 11 a day. It will be hellishly bad

work, so for once I won't have a chance to worry and feel like hell all summer. I'm afraid it sounds a little as if I were a lousy bohemian and lover of the Earth Earthy, but I assume I'm nothing so foul, quite, as that.

After confining months at Harvard, where he fretted endlessly over meter and rhyme, the life of a bum, with its freedom and anonymity, held a wondrous appeal. No one would expect anything of him; he could start anew.

But when he struck out on his own, the ecstatic promise fast yielded to the harsh reality of a bindlestiff's life. He hitched rides along hot, dusty roads in search of work. When he found it, he spent twelve hours a day in exhausting physical labor, for which he earned fifty cents an hour. He passed sleepless nights in strange, uncomfortable, dollar-a-night boardinghouses, and when he accumulated excess cash, he quickly spent it on movies and cigarettes. The camaraderie he expected to find among the workers scarcely existed; fear and mistrust ruled their lives. He spoke little of himself to his companions; no one knew exactly who he was or where he had come from, only that he was a young man on the move and willing to work. In midsummer, he paused briefly to send Macdonald a letter fairly reeking of the midwestern fields' heat and dirt.

> Maybe August 1st
> Oshkosh, Nebr.
> c/o Mr. John Hutchinson

Dear Dwight:

If pen and ink and white paper give you trouble, this should rival the Rosetta Stone. To add insult to injury, it's written in a wagon bed —about my only chance to write is between loads.

Am now working at hauling and scooping grain on a "combine" crew. . . . I rammed a pitchfork into my Achilles tendon and it gave me a good deal of trouble when I went on the road again.

Kansas is the most utterly lousy state I've ever seen. Hot as hell and trees ten miles apart. I worked near a town which proudly bore the name "Glade" because of a clump of scrawny, dusty little trees it had somehow managed to assemble.

The first town across the Nebraska line was so different I declared a holiday, sat on bench in the court-house park, and wrote a story. I rather think I've stumbled onto the best possible surroundings, and state of mind, in which to write. I certainly was more at home with it than at Harvard, home, or Exeter. . . .

Have you ever done any bumming? It's a funny business. In 24 hours I made over six hundred miles; in 23, I failed to make 28, was caught simultaneously by night and a cloudburst. I hope the good sort of luck prevails when I try to get home. I'm going to try to make it in 5 or 6 days, on ten dollars.

Have to tackle a load now,

Jim

Meanwhile, back in foggy Rockland, Laura's peaceful enjoyment of the sea air was disturbed by a letter from Harvard announcing that her son had been placed on academic probation for having flunked German and earning mediocre grades in the rest of his subjects, including English. Laura sent an anxious letter to the Dean's Office and dispatched a family friend, Richard Wierum, to visit the dean on her son's behalf. After the visit, Dean Nichols hastened to mollify the poor woman. "The form which was sent to you was far 'more violent' than James deserved," he wrote on July 3. "In addition, the work which he had done outside, notably his poem in the *Hound and Horn,* has attracted considerable attention and marked him as an exceptional student." Laura took little comfort from such reassurance about her son's obvious literary ability; she would have preferred better grades, better behavior. And the painful fact remained that when Agee returned to Harvard in the fall, he would be classified as a freshman again and possibly require five years to earn his degree.

On the road, Agee remained oblivious to this academic setback. As the summer wore on, his adventures took on an increasingly bizarre and threatening aspect. He came to a boardinghouse whose appearance filled him with dread. It was painted a "remote white" and "barrenly fronted the street." His tiny room "contained a bed, a bureau, a shallow closet, a straight chair, and, upon request, a table" and smelled of linoleum baking in the heat. After taking a bath to rid himself of the dirt and rust clinging to his skin and hair, he went down to dinner and felt inexplicably drawn to the landlord, whose hands were "abnormally small and seamless." After dinner, Agee and the landlord smoked cigarettes on the porch. "Across his left cheek," Agee wrote of his companion, "I saw the flutter of some irrelevant sinew and the nicely curled mustache was wry and twitching. At the same time a ticklish, cold weakness rilled through the roots of my spine." They made deceptively casual conversation.

"Is your work pretty heavy?" the landlord asked.

"Digging a ditch and hauling iron, today."

"That must have been hot, on a day like this. Are you used to such work?"

"Not very, but it wasn't bad."

"Not bad, eh? Ah, my boy, when you're young, you can stand up to any sort of work." Agee said nothing. "A fine, strapping fellow like you. You can stand up to anything, can't you?" The landlord reached for Agee's arm. "Let me feel your biceps. Ah, what a fine, strapping young fellow," he repeated, slipping one arm across Agee's shoulder and clenching the young man to his chest. His eyes narrowed and he asked, "Is everything understood?"

No, everything was not understood. Agee freed himself from the man's grasp and fled to his room on the pretext of getting matches. There he fell prey to "exhaustion and self-contempt" so powerful that he wanted to "beat my face to bits."

The next morning the landlord simultaneously put his arms around Agee and another young boarder, "and as he openly fondled me, he said that we were all one big family." Suddenly the other boarder struck the landlord across the mouth. More in sorrow than in anger, Agee struck the assailant behind the ear, only to find himself knocked senseless for his trouble.

He quickly settled up with the landlady: nine dollars, the price of a week's food and lodging. In the midst of his hurried leavetaking, the landlord burst through the door. The man had been shaving; half his mustache was gone, and strips of plaster covered his lips. In this condition he made a speech to Agee emphasizing "kindliness and brotherly love, . . . the Christian virtues." But, "As he became more florid in his praise of me, the whole was tinged with involuntary salaciousness." Now Agee feared the landlord despised him and regretted deeply that lust had ruined the fellowship and sympathy they might have shared.

After leaving the boardinghouse and the provocative encounter behind, Agee decided to keep to himself. He had grown hard from the summer's exertions and had managed to put a little money aside; now he wanted to see such fabled places as California, the

Pacific Ocean, and Mexico before the summer ended. Rides came easily, and he made it all the way to Tijuana, on the Mexican border, within a few days. He debated trying his luck in Hollywood, but apparently his courage failed him and he returned East without even setting foot in the city that had inspired so many of his dreams.

The return trip proved far more trying than the voyage out. After several short hops in the summer heat and one nightlong ride, he found himself at dawn in the small town of St. Johns, Arizona, where he devoured a meal of sauerkraut and bread purchased at an A&P and lolled away the morning in the shadow of a church. He could not bring himself to go inside, dirty and smelly as he was; it was enough to remain in its shade. By this time a boil had developed in his right ear, so painful that his entire jaw swelled and he could barely chew. He had no choice but to press on and hope the problem would take care of itself.

From St. Johns he hitched south to Springerville, Arizona, and from Springerville east to Magdalena, New Mexico, across "one hundred and forty miles of desert so deathly that no sane man will undertake them on foot." To his dismay, he found the highway outside Magdalena jammed with other bums who shared the intention of hitching a ride. While awaiting his turn, he struck up a conversation with a peg-legged man of about sixty, at last savoring the camaraderie he had sought all summer. How much more highly he prized this simple communion with his fellow man than all the pointless carousing at Harvard. The hours passed quickly, and with them a succession of dusty Fords, Pierce-Arrows, and Buicks—all refusing to pick up hitchhikers.

Late in the day, Agee grew desperate. "With my ear in the shape it was, I'd have been willing to travel in a tux or a green gauze chiton for the sake of a good ride." He wondered whether holding up a sign reading "SORE EAR, PLEASE" would do the trick. At last, a "Buick touring car from Oklahoma, five or six years old and in need of paint" slowed to pick him up. "It was funny that even in my present condition I could be snooty about my cars, but I was, and so is every bum. Few bums, however, are snooty enough to refuse a ride." He joined a family of three: a husband, wife, and ten-year-old son. After making small talk, Agee succumbed to the monotony of the trip. "My face was crawling with fatigue, and my nose began to itch unbearably. . . . I gave my ear all possible comfort in my cupped hand, and once more felt the film-thin globe of lead build around my brain." He fell into a fitful sleep in which he dreamed he was back in Tennessee, watching a king snake and a rattler fight to the death. Then he was at Harvard, listening to his professors lecture, until a painful lurch yanked him back to reality.

A shape on the horizon caught his attention. "Far ahead there was a black speck, and as we came nearer it was moving, and was a man, and the man was limping toward us and moving wildly." The driver slowed, but when he realized the stricken hitchhiker was an "exhausted nigger, very tall, and with terrible effort limping toward us," he speeded up. The hitchhiker's "marbled eyes" and "wheezing yells, pleading still and still demanding that God bless us" made an indelible impression on Agee, who was horrified at the driver's cruelty in refusing the hitchhiker a ride.

"Let some of these nigger-loving Yankees pick him up, if they want to," said the man at the wheel.

"You ain't even Christian," his wife countered.

The driver stopped the car, turned around, and glared at her. "I'm pretty damned sick of all this bugling about some filthy nigger that didn't even know enough to stay home and let well enough alone."

All the while, Agee blamed himself for the hitchhiker's plight. "I was the reason why an exhausted Negro remained in the desert near death." He tried to rationalize his guilt. What business had he to tell the driver what to do? The driver's wife had tried, to no avail. Furthermore, Agee told himself, he had exaggerated the situation out of all proportion. What difference did it make what happened to the hitchhiker? And yet, hours before, Agee himself had been in the same predicament, physically afflicted, alone, without a ride. It was only through the grace of God that he rode in a Buick while the black man withered in the desert. If only he could persuade the driver to go back and permit him to trade places with the black man, thought Agee, still the small boy who wanted to give his shoes and socks to the children who had none.

On this occasion he kept his conscience to himself, and the drive resumed. They crossed the Rio Grande, the Oklahoma panhandle, and the Midwest. Other rides brought Agee to the home of his roommate, Robert Saudek, in Pittsburgh. Saudek was thrilled to introduce the hitchhiker-poet to the family. Attired in blue-jean overalls, a big, floppy, torn straw hat, and very much in need of a haircut, Agee fast became the talk of the Saudek clan. Robert's father, a musician at radio station KDKA, immediately took the wastrel under his wing and bought him a new blue suit, a shirt, a tie, and shoes. After bidding a protracted farewell, Agee took to the road again, a suddenly respectable hitchhiker.

On the final leg of the journey home, he narrowly escaped a fatal accident. The early hours of September 6 found him in the mountains of Pennsylvania, desperately searching for a ride to Maine. A boy stopped to pick him up. Soon after, they "drove off a mountain curve at 45 m.p.h." The car flipped over three times, "but the only injury sustained was a cut on my wrist and the startling bouleversement of a roast beef sandwich I'd just eaten." Two days later he arrived in Rockland, none the worse for wear.

In his absence, his family had worked itself into a fever pitch of anxiety over his well-being. He had unfortunately "neglected to write Mother," and the letters she had sent to him "boomeranged from various Kansas p.o.'s before I returned home." As a result, she convinced herself "I'd died several deaths." But there he was, resplendent in his new blue suit and bubbling over with all manner of tales of life on the road.

For all its rigors, the summer had proved a good one, endowing him with a welcome sense of self-reliance. The intricacies of Elizabethan poetry held no terrors for a man who had traveled across the country with ten dollars to his name. The James Agee who returned to Harvard in September 1929 was not the scared young stripling who had haunted its libraries the previous year. On moving into his new quarters in Thayer Hall, in the heart of the Yard, an unaccustomed serenity stole over him, prompting him to write to Father Flye on September 29, "I feel more and more a growth of mental balance and appreciation, and it hits me, I suppose, about as puberty did. I experience the same almost sensuous joy in knowing that I'm 'getting somewhere—growing up.' " At the same time, simply writing to the priest whom he had not seen for over four years was enough to put Agee in a wary, penitent frame of mind. He expressed the wish that the summer would effect a "reasonably permanent cure for the irrational side of my unhappiness," whose cause, as Agee had come to understand it, lay in a "gradual spiritual and ethical atrophy" in his "unconscious attitude," fostered, he need not tell Father Flye, by godless Harvard. Even as he wrote, evil stirrings threatened his fragile equilibrium. "I feel as if my mind were turning into a wart, and that I can do nothing to stop it," he feared. "I suppose this is a perfectly natural phase of intellectual development—just as a flood of unpleasantly dirty thoughts and desires are a natural part of puberty. I'll outgrow these, then, as I've outgrown (to a great extent) the dirtier of my pubescent imaginings."

A month later the New York Stock Exchange crashed, but Agee, wrapped in a cocoon of introspection, all but ignored the world outside his window. He was more interested in developing strategies to resist the temptation he felt to drink himself into oblivion. He endeavored to cultivate a taste for wine instead of the rye, Scotch, and gin he preferred. "On the whole, an occasional alcoholic bender satisfies me pretty well," he noted.

The knowledge that he was on academic probation weighed heavily on his mind and justified his self-imposed confinement. He undertook a strenuous course load: four subjects in English, two in Philosophy, and one in Latin. This year he felt more kindly disposed to all of them, especially Professor Lake's Old Testament lectures ("very amusing, very interesting, and very Unitarian") and Seventeenth Century English Literature ("a great chance for original work—if I'm capable of doing it"). To concentrate fully on his studies, he cut back on the dubious enterprise of movie going, with the sole exception of a feature starring Anna May Wong, who exerted "the most powerful and poisonous sex appeal I've ever been exposed to." There were scores of other films he yearned to see, but, as he informed Macdonald, "I'm dismally broke." In this instance, his self-discipline earned handsome dividends in the form of vastly improved marks; there was but a single D (in Philosophy) to mar his record.

Once again he shared living quarters with Saudek, and long after his roommate had gone to bed, Agee hunched over his desk to work up stories and poems for the *Advocate*. So anxious was he to perform well that he quickly lost patience with his writing utensils. Fountain pens he found infuriatingly messy and uncooperative. "Oh, God damn this pen!" he would exclaim in the midst of a particularly involved sentence. "I've never in my life owned a decent one." He switched to the more reliable pencil, at a great cost in legibility. As he matured, his handwriting contracted into a distinctive series of tiny vertical hash marks resembling insect tracks. He developed the habit of composing on unlined yellow pads, discarding one pencil after another as soon as it became even slightly blunt. He loathed being interrupted in the midst of his literary labors. "I can't write with these damned lice . . . talking to me," he complained when several students dropped in for a visit. "God, they make me sore. I wish to God I was out of this place and several thousand miles out of earshot."

Despite the care he lavished on his manuscripts, he misplaced quantities of poems, letters, stories, and ideas. When he did contrive to find the time, tools, and privacy conducive to sustained effort, he became savagely critical of the result. No teacher chastised him as severely as he chastised himself. "It needs condensation," he remarked of one story, "and has many other horrible faults—wisecracking, unnatural dialogue . . . and repetition—and some sentimentality." Occasionally he sent samples of his work to Macdonald, not for praise or comment but solely for "criticism."

This zeal for perfection led Agee to write increasingly polished if sterile poems strongly influenced by the Metaphysicals, whose technique he diligently studied. The highly formal utterances of Donne, Herbert, and Marvell seemed to the Harvard sophomore to constitute a poetic ideal as desirable yet unreachable as the religion he had formerly espoused. If the past was any guide, it would only be a matter of time until he threw off the strictures of this new, poetic religion, but for now he devoted his energies to exercises such as this:

> *Even now, a serpent swells my living skull:*
> *Its thirsty tongue, struck barbed through my brain,*
> *Sucks all the cherished beauty dry and dull*
> *As dust; and faint and failing is the pain.*
> *I murdered joy, that your love might abide:*
> *A precious skeleton lies at my side.*

The unlucky recipient of this poem was Dorothy Carr, with whom Agee continued to correspond intermittently. She could not have felt very happy about the misgivings she inspired in her ardent boyfriend's breast.

The misery and forboding Agee felt whenever he thought of Dorothy furnished the basis for his most elaborate creation to date, a work intended to rival "Ann Garner." In "Epithalamium," as the finished product was titled, he displayed a mastery of traditional versification, yet little of his personality survived the showy technique. An epithalamium is a song in honor of a bride and groom; in Agee's version, the marriage bed is transformed into a grave, the canopy into the night sky, and in the end, the lovers are but skeletons at the foot of a tombstone.

As the last word in disillusionment, "Epithalamium" failed to satisfy its creator, who judged it "redolent of mothballs." But for all its artifice, this poem, together with "Ann Garner," established Agee's credentials as a gifted writer, and in November he was elected to the editorial board of the *Advocate*. Henceforth, nearly every issue of the publication contained at least one brief poetic utterance signed "J. R. Agee." At the same time, he undertook yeoman's work by reviewing books. He now had a supply of novels to read, all gratis, but he cursed the job for taking up the little time he had to write.

The task of reviewing, however unwelcome, broke the spell of his self-imposed isolation. In the course of his reading, he came across two landmark novels of the South published in 1929, Thomas Wolfe's *Look Homeward, Angel* and William Faulkner's *The Sound and the Fury*. The ambitiousness and mastery of both works overwhelmed Agee, yet left him, as an aspiring Southern writer himself, feeling cheated of material. Wolfe, in particular, had ransacked the archetypal Southern boyhood for his novel, leaving nothing to others who wanted to portray small towns and provincial families. "I feel as though he had stolen my whole childhood," Agee lamented.

The novels taught him a valuable lesson. There was an entire world at his fingertips that Metaphysical poetry ignored, and if he wanted to cut the kind of literary figure that Wolfe or Faulkner did, he must look beyond the classroom for inspiration. Wolfe had begun as a playwright, Faulkner a poet. Considering the examples of these two, Agee recognized that the practice of poetry might not be an end in itself but merely a demanding apprenticeship.

74

He hammered out these literary theories with a number of new acquaintances, most of whom nurtured writing ambitions of their own. They were drawn together by a thirst for an audience, however small. He exchanged confidences with the gentle, secretive, and handsome Irvine Upham, who found himself all but overwhelmed by Agee's accomplished if hopelessly vague poems, which appeared with alarming regularity in the *Advocate*. It seemed that Agee could do anything with language and that language could do anything to Agee. As the friendship developed between them, Upham came to care more about Agee as a person than as a writer. To Upham, Agee's poems were but a dim, black-and-white print of their author's greatness of spirit, especially as revealed in conversation. If he could only find a way to let loose like that in print, he would be on the way to becoming a great writer. Yet even Agee's conversation had its deleterious side effects, for Upham found he could never relax in his friend's radiant presence. All that brilliance at two o'clock in the morning could be a trial for the listener, if not the talker.

Together with Upham, Agee befriended an older student, Franklin Miner, who fast became one of the very few people with whom he felt wholly at ease. Miner himself was so volatile and eccentric a character that Agee felt no need to conceal the wilder side of his nature. Jointly they roamed the streets of Cambridge in search of found objects that afforded them great delight. They rummaged through trash bins for discarded postcards, valentines, and cigarette packages. Cast-off letters held a special fascination. Who was the writer of the homely sentences he held in his hands? What sort of life had he led? He marveled at the profusion of buried voices, all living, suffering, and expressing themselves unselfconsciously. The writers of such sincere letters had no need to hide behind a cloak of outdated literary mannerisms. They spoke in forthright, direct paragraphs, revealing all, withholding nothing. In short, they told the truth. To Agee these letters were an object lesson in honest writing. It appeared that the secret of good writing lay in the natural expressiveness of speech, not a show of technique. Unless the technique furthered the writer's message, it was pointless, a positive nuisance. Agee realized that in his efforts to excel in the writing of poetry, he had embalmed the English language. These letters provided an exhilarating antidote to the dangerous tendency. If he wanted to be a great writer, he would have to be himself, not a latter-day Elizabethan. Poetry encouraged his straining after greatness, but prose allowed him to be himself, to bring his formidable gift for spontaneity to bear. It was in prose, then, that he would truly come alive as a writer.

But it would take time for Agee to find an arena suitable for the inspired prose he wanted to write. For the moment, the discovery of ordinary writing—so obvious, yet so unexpected—shattered his confidence as a poet. When the ever faithful Macdonald wrote to solicit poems for his new magazine, *Miscellany,* Agee felt so insecure about his abilities that instead of sending material he proceeded to damn the venture with faint praise. "Because I automatically and incurably expected the best magazine I'd ever seen," he replied on January 17, 1930, "I was a little disappointed in it. That was to be expected. But, coming back to it with as much common sense as I can muster—It's damned good—a great deal ahead of the average Hound & Horn, for instance, because it hasn't the snotty, pseudo-Brahministics and emasculated air about it that set that magazine apart." Macdonald continued to press his suit with the recalcitrant poet, but the launching of a new "little" magazine proved to be fatally mistimed at the outset of a fast-spreading Depression. *Miscellany* soon expired for lack of funds.

Few of Agee's friends realized how determined he was to shed his poetic skin. The problem was that he had acquired a small yet inescapable reputation as a poet, one affording too much prestige to be cast aside. Though his heart was no longer in poetry, he continued to write it, just as he continued to consider himself an Anglo-Catholic, though he no longer believed in that religion, and to correspond with Dorothy Carr, though he took little pleasure in her company. These mounting inconsistencies, of which he was keenly aware, tore at his conscience. He loathed hypocrisy beyond all measure, yet here he was, constantly acting against his principles. On all fronts, life mocked his puny convictions.

It was at this perilous juncture that he met, in February 1930, the one friend who could sympathize with these self-doubts. "On a Wednesday afternoon in the dust of a classroom, I became sharply aware for the first time of a Mr. Agee," Robert Fitzgerald has written, "in the front row on my right, looming and brooding and clutching his book, his voice very low, almost inaudible, but deliberate and distinct, as though ground fine by great interior pressure."

Superficially, the two were opposites. Agee exuded warmth and ease; Fitzgerald maintained a remote, even haughty exterior. Although they both considered themselves poets, Fitzgerald found Agee's *Advocate* verse "turgid and technically flawed"; Fitzgerald's poems were, if anything, even more rarefied—and effective—than his friendly rival's. Agee was endlessly compassionate; Fitzgerald could be ruthlessly analytical. He detected a "troubling streak of Whitman, including a fondness for the barbaric yawp" in Agee. Despite this occasional condescension, Fitzgerald, alone among Agee's early admirers, sensed that the poet's true gift lay in prose. Agee's story "Boys Will Be Brutes," describing how he had slaughtered birds as a boy in Tennessee, made Fitzgerald gasp at its author's "sympathy with innocent living nature, and love of it; understanding of congested stupidity and cruelty, and hatred of it; a stethoscopic ear for mutations of feeling; and ironic ear for idiom; a descriptive gift." To Agee, Fitzgerald became a literary conscience, a standard against which he held all subsequent efforts.

Although he tried to live up to Fitzgerald's example, Agee's aspirations were as fickle as spring in New England. Poet, critic, scholar, bum, apostle of the forgotten man—the possibilities overwhelmed him. Just when he darted toward one, another reached out to ensnare him. Now that he had given up poetry in favor of prose, his high-flown "Epithalamium" won Harvard's prestigious Garrison Prize, and on the strength of that honor he became a favorite of Theodore Spencer, the dapper young English professor who had noticed his talent the year before. In the spring, Agee asked Spencer to become his tutor—a position entailing individual instruction for credit and career counseling.

Almost at once, Spencer exerted a powerful influence over the fortunes of his prize pupil. He encouraged Agee to experiment with ever more complex and derivative forms of verse. In the world of Theodore Spencer, as in Harvard's English Department, poetry had to do with meter, rhyme scheme, historical antecedent, and translation—everything but direct contact with experience. Agee survived, if not exactly thrived, under this regime because it conferred legitimacy on his literary efforts. He did not yet dare to be himself on paper, except in letters to friends such as Father Flye.

In addition, Spencer's patronage brought more concrete re-wards. Back in Rockland, Father Wright was complaining about the expense of keeping a stepson at Harvard in a Depression, and Agee feared he would not be able to return in the fall. He carefully explained his plight to Spencer, who immediately took up the cause and lobbied hard at the Dean's Office for a scholarship. Although young Agee's academic record lacked distinction, Spencer argued, he possessed "unquestionably more poetic talent than any student now at Harvard . . . and should, in the future, be a poet of consider-able distinction." Agee received his scholarship, and as if Spencer had not already done enough on his behalf, soon had reason to be grateful for still another favor, one with far more personal conse-quences.

5

ONE GRAND TIME TO BE MAUDLIN

The Saunders family of Clinton, New York, was blessed with enough money and intelligence to live exceedingly well. Despite their remote upstate location, they ran a lively salon attracting poets, writers, scholars, teachers, musicians, and *artistes* of every stripe passing through the foothills of the Adirondack Mountains. Their large home functioned as a compulsory stopover for the famous (Helen Hayes, Alexander Woollcott), the soon-to-be-famous (B. F. Skinner), and the esteemed (Robert Frost, I. A. Richards). It was into this yeasty environment that Theodore Spencer first brought James Agee in the spring of 1930.

There they were greeted by Dr. Arthur Percy Saunders, whose craggy, bearded face might have stared from a daguerreotype by

Mathew Brady. A tall man with an Olympian presence, Dr. Saunders was an enormously popular professor at nearby Hamilton College, where he taught chemistry and until recently had served as dean. He came from a prominent Canadian family, and in his youth had aspired to become in turn a painter, a musician, and a horticulturalist. When still a young man he developed a disease-resistant strain of wheat known as Marquis that was widely planted in Canada. He subsequently turned his attention to making hybrid flowers, and at the time Agee arrived on the scene could often be found tending an enormous collection of peonies growing on a strip of land a third of a mile long, acquired especially for that purpose. In spite of his demanding duties at Hamilton, he never lost his love for music; violin in hand, he conducted an endless series of chamber concerts in the musical wing of his house. At the same time, he enjoyed the attentions of the pretty young girls who came to play their instruments, while Mrs. Saunders looked the other way.

Agee immediately fell under the spell of Dr. Saunders' attractive, comfortable way of life. Compromise, the student realized, had its attractions. "I don't know how brilliant a man he might have been, if he'd grimly fought out one of his talents," Agee observed. "At any rate, he evidently decided, when he was quite young, not to try it: rather to work calmly and hard, but with no egoism, on *all* the things he cared most about—and he's resolved his life into the most complete and genuine happiness I know." The fault he could find had to do with a decided lack of religious conviction, but so taken was Agee with this provincial paradise that he instantly decided to become a teacher.

He admired the professor; he adored Mrs. Saunders. A special bond based on complementary needs soon formed between Agee and this attractive, energetic little woman. Eight years earlier, her favorite child, Duncan, then a student at Hamilton, had died as a result of injuries sustained in a fraternity scuffle. He was fifteen at the time. Duncan had wanted to be a poet, and the day before his death wrote a few lines the family later regarded as a presentiment of tragedy.

> *O that my boat might be shipwrecked,*
> *Out in that sea of my sleep!*
> *O that I might sink forever—*
> *Sink in that starless deep!*

When Agee entered the house, he seemed to Mrs. Saunders to be the young man Duncan might have been: an attractive, tall, shy, hypersensitive poet. Yes, Agee would admirably fill the vacuum in her life caused by Duncan's death.

As Agee became her surrogate son, so she became his surrogate mother. While Laura had lapsed into a state of permanent passivity cloaked in religion, Louise Saunders emanated warmth and, most important, wholehearted encouragement of Agee's literary ambitions. In return for her maternal love, she received from Agee a vast outpouring of affection. Unable to establish a close relationship with his own mother, he was delighted to enjoy her attentions, and Louise soon supplanted both Father Flye and Dwight Macdonald as his closest confidante. Laura's manipulative piety had taught Agee to be attentive to the wants and moods of older women, and he put this training to good use with Louise, who in turn was far more attuned to his outsized emotional fluctuations than Laura had ever been.

As he came to know her, Agee discovered that Louise Brownell Saunders was a woman of formidable gifts and attainments in her "high-strung and intense, electric way." Before marrying Dr. Saunders, she had taught English literature at Cornell, where she became a *cause célèbre* over her insistence that the university list her in the catalogue as a professor rather than a lecturer. The all-male Executive Committee overwhelmingly voted that no woman could hold the title. Her struggle for professional recognition generated considerable publicity but ended in defeat; rather than stay on as a lecturer, she resigned in 1900. Her friends assumed she would go on to the presidency of a women's college, but just before leaving Cornell she fell in love with a young chemistry professor, Percy Saunders. After a whirlwind courtship, they married in 1901 and moved to Utica, New York, where she worked as an administrator at a girl's school until her four children, two boys and two girls, claimed her full time and attention.

At the time she met Agee, Louise poured her energies into cutting a social figure, counting among her closest friends Hedda Hopper and Alexander Woollcott, both of whom she visited during frequent trips to New York, where she kept *au courant*. Naturally, she was ambitious for her three surviving children. The eldest, Silvia, twenty-nine at the time, had been educated at Bryn Mawr, Radcliffe, lived in France, and subsequently established herself in

New York as an architectural photographer. Her younger sister Olivia, universally known as Via, had also attended Bryn Mawr and made the obligatory Grand Tour of Europe. At twenty-six, she was six years older than Agee, eminently marriageable, and, as fate would have it, planning to move to Cambridge. The youngest child, Percy "Frisk" Saunders, belonged to Hamilton College's class of 1933.

Agee was smitten with them all. They were "fine and lovable," he told Father Flye. "They're the most beautiful and happy [family] to know and watch I've ever seen. It's hard to write of such people without becoming mawkish." If he had only but looked beneath the tranquil surface of the Saunders' domestic life, he would have seen that the daughters, in particular, lacked their parents' gifts and ambition and resented Louise's well-intended meddling in their love life.

Once accepted by this charming if complex family, Agee scrapped the tentative plans he had formed to spend the summer bumming around France, very much the bohemian artist. No more wandering, he resolved. Instead he would make himself over into a more responsible if slightly bourgeois fellow of acceptable cultural interests. Now that he had sown his wild oats, he decided, it was time to settle down and spend as much of the summer as he could in the enlightened company of the Saunderses, Theodore Spencer, and one of their more illustrious guests, I. A. Richards.

Ivor Armstrong Richards had come to Harvard in 1930 from Cambridge University as a thirty-seven-year-old visiting professor best known for having helped to devise a simplified version of the language called Basic English. Through this invention, Richards hoped to demonstrate that an 850-word vocabulary could express the full range of concepts known to Western civilization, and to prove his point he had published a Basic English version of Plato's *Republic*.

At the same time, he was a leading figure in a revolutionary approach to the interpretation of literature known as the New Criticism, which emphasized the analysis of a poem or other text with scientific precision and in complete isolation from cultural or historical considerations. In addition, he advocated the application of Freudian psychoanalytic principles to criticism, especially in the study of character and symbol. Both Agee and his friend Robert

Fitzgerald, ambitious young poets that they were, had taken the two courses Richards taught at Harvard in the spring of 1930, one on modern literature, the other on poetry. Richards' style of teaching matched his brilliant theories. "When he spoke of the splendors of Henry James' style," Fitzgerald recalled, "or of Conrad facing the storm of the universe, we felt that he was their companion and ours in the enterprise of art."

Richards' mesmerizing personality exerted an equally compelling influence on Agee. Sitting at Richards' feet during visits to Clinton that summer, Agee felt as though he were communing with a mystic, a priest of literature, who was at the same time maddeningly elusive.

> It's perfectly impossible for me to define anything about him or about what he taught—but it was a matter of getting frequent and infinite vistas of perfection in beauty, strength, symmetry, greatness—and the reasons for them, in poetry and living. He's a sort of fusion of Hamlet and some Dostoevsky character, with their frustration of madness cleared away, and a perfect center left that understands evil and death and pain, and values them, without torment or perplexity. This sounds extravagant—well, his power over people was extravagant, and almost unlimited. Everyone who knew him was left in a clear, tingling daze.

Dazed or not, Agee acquired a new approach to writing. As he understood the great man, words possess a reality and concreteness independent of whatever they describe. They can exist in a vacuum rather than merely as a description of the world. In short, they are an end in themselves. Pushed to an extreme, this approach could lead to sterility, but seen against the background of an exhausted Romantic tradition, it spurred on Agee and other writers to uncover new ways of capturing reality on paper. In Agee's case, it encouraged him to develop his innate powers of description until he possessed a microscopic accuracy and eye for detail. It also unleashed his love of language. He had long exulted in the sensuousness of words, that magical fusion of sound and sense behind all great poetry; he now had an intellectual justification for his enthusiasm, courtesy of I. A. Richards.

When not dallying in Clinton, Agee spent his summer vacation in Exeter, where through the good graces of Dorothy Carr he had landed a temporary job with the public library. Throughout the scorching summer he commuted between Clinton and Exeter, from Dorothy's arms to the Saunders' dinner table. Alone in his cheap hotel room in Exeter, he set himself a "great program of reading from 6 to nine every evening, in the approved Eagle Scout manner." But he soon discovered he was too exhausted by work and by Dorothy "to be capable of much concentration." To complete his misery, he was forced to hobble about on one foot, the painful result of inadvertently stepping on a nail.

Under these trying conditions he fretted endlessly about money. Even with a scholarship, he did not feel he could see out another year at Harvard. If he could only teach for a while, he could save what he needed to complete his education. Drawing on her impressive array of connections, Louise Saunders soon found Agee a teaching position, if he wanted it. On June 22, he sent the following cable to her from Exeter.

> CONFIDENT THAT DESPITE YOUTH AND INEXPERIENCE I COULD HANDLE IT   NEEDING MONEY FOR FURTHER COLLEGE FOR A YEAR   AM EXTREMELY ANXIOUS TO UNDERTAKE TEACHING POSITION OF WHICH YOU SPOKE   PLEASE PARDON ABRUPTNESS OF MESSAGE   WANTED SORELY TO REACH YOU   WILL WRITE FULLY UPON REPLY   RESPECTFULLY
>
> JAMES R. AGEE

But Agee had waited too long to respond to the offer. The job went to another candidate. The disappointment stung. But within weeks Agee wrote to Louise that he felt "more and more convinced that the business of teaching turned out for the best," largely because that perspicacious woman encouraged him to pursue his dream as a writer rather than compromise out of panic or fear.

As the summer progressed, Agee spent the bulk of his time in the Exeter Public Library, amid crumbling volumes and stifled coughs, and suffered pangs of homesickness, not for his own family, but for the Saunderses. He did not know whom he missed more, old "Stink" Saunders, as he was known to his chemistry pupils, sympathetic Louise, or lovely Via. "I've been homesick ever since

I left you," he confided to them, "and the last time I was homesick, I was nine years old."

At the end of August he reluctantly exchanged the heat and humidity of Exeter for the eternal gloom of Rockland, where he was caught up in a dreary round of errand-running for his family. His sister Emma was in the hospital for a tonsillectomy, reason enough to throw the Wrights into chaos. He bewailed the fact that he had only a single short story to show for the summer, and that effort failed "to make any one of about twenty points I consider important." At the earliest possible opportunity he extricated himself from Rockland and returned to Clinton, glorious Clinton, to spend the waning days of summer with those he loved best.

He roamed the large Saunders home at will, pausing to amuse himself with the professor's powerful telescope, through which Agee gazed at shivering images of the moon and the rings of Saturn, ghostly apparitions filled with nameless promise. He played the Saunders' piano in his careless, thumping style, listened appreciatively to their impromptu musicales, and, most important, nurtured a growing affection for Via. Why had he never noticed her red hair, infectious sense of humor, and refreshing lack of pretension? In contrast to the shrill and demanding Dorothy, Via had a wholesome, carefree air. She was charming and lovely, and although no great beauty, her red hair could turn many a man's head. When she moved to Cambridge, it was understood, they would be able to see each other in an unchaperoned environment, and what bliss that would be.

"We began to sit up all night, talking without any limit of time or subject," Agee wrote of that innocent period of courtship, when they were both "very much moved and excited" by their discovery of each other. He felt more comfortable with Via than with any other woman, even if she was a few years older than he. They subsisted on promises of future fulfillment, he as a famous poet, she as a happily married woman, free of her manipulative mother. With a certainty born of years of husband-hunting, she knew James Agee was her best prospect—the most handsome, sensitive, and likely to succeed.

The combined forces of the Saunders had a tonic effect on Agee, who returned to Cambridge filled with the "glory" of starting his junior year at Harvard. He relished the bitingly clean night air, the feel of virgin textbooks, the sense of familiarity the Georgian buildings inspired. Then, too, there were good friends to greet: Upham, Miner, and Saudek, with whom Agee again shared a suite of rooms in Thayer Hall. He boasted to Father Flye that he was in good spirits, "stridently happy and energetic and writhing with schemes of regularity and moderation and with eagerness for the year to begin." And then, "It began, Bang."

As soon as he unpacked his belongings he became entangled in a web of academic and personal demands. As usual, he took on more courses than he could comfortably manage—including the perverse choice of Paleontology—in an attempt to catch up with his class. He was off probation but still a year behind his peers. He incautiously assumed the thankless role of treasurer for the Signet Society, the college's literary club. The job's petty responsibilities consumed as many as four hours of his precious time at a stretch.

Nor did he find escape from the trials of college life in the sanctity of his suite, for there he was endlessly plagued by the impossible demands of a disturbed young freeloader named Tom Raywood. Despite his fashionable attire and familiarity with Harvard gossip, Raywood was not enrolled as a student. He was a hanger-on, an impersonator. When sober, he could be a charming fellow, the best of company, but when drunk he was given to making passes at Agee, who found such behavior deeply disturbing. To him, Raywood was a "victim of manic depression, dipsomania, and a brand of nymphomania that evidently lacks the discrimination expected of a healthy two-year-old—for it seems that I am elected his official dream cutie." As he explained to the Saunders family on September 22, Raywood had been "hovering about my room for the past 3 days in various stages of drunkenness. . . . His methods of undermining my scruples against his idea of love are quaint and not very subtle. One is to tell my friends that I'm really a Greek at heart. The other is to inform me that Dorothy, common slut that she is, is ruining my life and sapping my genius, in which he has implicit faith."

Agee's bravado concealed concern about the homosexual tendencies he thought he had left behind. Perhaps Raywood responded to something that even Agee did not sense. "If I weren't so sorry for him, I'd gladly murder him," Agee commented. Rejected, Raywood shunted from one Thayer Hall suite to another in search of sympathy until Agee could stand it no longer and took pity on the poor, lost soul. He talked with Raywood until dawn on the entryway steps, muttering, "Sure, I know. . . . It's lousy. . . . Jesus knows it's lousy." As Saudek recalled, "Nothing could be more reassuring than when he went into that kind of litany." In the end, Raywood departed Thayer Hall for a mental institution, and Agee bitterly reproached himself for not doing more, no matter how infuriating Raywood's behavior had been.

His primary respite from the confusion threatening to engulf him was the small frame building that housed the *Advocate.* Surrounded by a few sticks of cigarette-scarred furniture, a broken-down sofa, a phonograph, and a cold fireplace, he holed up for long nights of writing rambling letters to friends and disciplined verse employing Richards' precepts. But much of the time he could not write at all. When inspiration failed, he resorted to theorizing about the kind of poems he wanted to create, "poems that ride halfway between informing the reader and a certain parallelism as to the psychological process that would take place in the writer—during the course of the poem *as finished.*" Only Agee knew for certain what he meant by this statement, but at any rate the new crop of verse showed a refreshing absence of the high-flown diction that had marred his earlier work. In an impressive sonnet completed in November, he contemplated jettisoning his earlier self, everything from Tennessee to Dorothy Carr, in favor of the Saunders' way of life.

> *I have been fashioned on a chain of flesh*
> *Whose ancient links are immolate in dust;*

Flesh led to desire, and desire to despair.

> *My flesh that was, long as that flesh knew life,*
> *Strove, and was valiant, still strove, and was naught.*

Only by betrayal could he escape the plight of his ancestors. For once he realized how lucky he was to be a talented young man at Harvard.

> *I have been given wings they never wore*
> *I have been given hope they never knew*
> *And they were brave who can be brave no more,*
> *And they that live are kind as they are few.*
> *'Tis mine to touch with deathlessness their clay;*
> *And I shall fail, and join those I betray.*

He immediately made a fair copy of the poem and sent it off to Louise Saunders.

As she discovered, Agee's pessimism flourished even in the best of times. Whenever he forced himself to be still, it bloomed like a poisonous black blossom. Approaching his twenty-first birthday with, it seemed, so little to show for himself, he typed out bulletins to Louise on the terrifying fluctuations of his mental state.

> I've gone through, in the last two weeks, high, low, jack and the game. Lowest depth sounded last Thursday and Friday, when I was quite sure I'd never write another good word and never had; was surer still I'd marry unhappily and murder my wife; would drink to oceanic excess; take drugs; go in for black magic and violet perversion; during which time I could not go to classes, couldn't understand a word I'd read, cared nothing for music, swore at a good sunset, felt sore and sorry for everyone on earth, and nearly killed myself.

Here was an astonishing catalogue of confessions to make to a potential mother-in-law. But Agee felt comfortable unburdening himself because Louise encouraged him to hold nothing back. When he mailed off a letter to her, he felt as cleansed as he had on leaving the confessional booth.

In an attempt to pull back from the brink of despair he made up a "monstrous series of charts" relating various aspects of his personality to the cosmos, but the effort left him feeling "horribly dead." At this low point in his young life he endured a state of mind he described as a "deliberate, painful deadening granulation of everything senseless and unimportant in everyday life, . . . a miserable twilight sleep." He tried to stop thinking all the time, but his mind persisted in chewing "each mild thought to pulp and thence to liquid, and keeps on chewing nothing." If only he could "transform" his mind. "Instead of a lazy and sick one, I work to keep and develop one that may still be sick but isn't, God knows, lazy." In this dark night of the soul, it seemed only Louise Saunders stood between him and insanity. He implored, "Please don't think of me as a promising candidate for the Psychopathic Hospital."

That Agee was miserable in the late fall of 1930 was certain; at the same time, he relished the intensity of his feelings, however unpleasant. Upham detected a "rich enjoyment in the drama of being desperate, *his* being desperate or anybody else's. His despair was an emotion as powerful as his joy." But if he fully revealed to Louise the person he actually was, he continued to tell Father Flye only of the person he wanted to be. On November 19, at the same time he was telling Louise of his suicidal impulses, he summed up his life thus far for the priest, accentuating the positive. His desire to write had all but "killed off" his two other loves, movies and music. Writing, he declared, was his "one even moderate talent." Even so, he would have to develop that talent if he were to amount to anything more than a gifted amateur.

> I'd do anything on earth to become a really great writer. That's as sincere a thing as I've ever said. Do you see, though, where it leads me? In the first place I have no faith to speak of in my native ability. . . . My intellectual pelvic girdle simply is not Miltonically wide. So I have, pretty much, to keep same on a stretcher, or more properly a rack, day and night. I've got to make my mind as broad and deep and rich as possible, as quick and fluent as possible; abnormally sympathetic yet perfectly balanced.

Once Agee got going on the theme of making himself into a great writer, he could barely contain his excitement. For once he saw beyond personal darkness to the light of inspiration; he had faith. He was a Caliban contemplating the riches of heaven.

> You see, I should like to parallel, foolish as it sounds, what Shakespeare did . . .—to write primarily about people, giving their emotions and dramas the expression that, because of its beauty and power, will be most likely to last. But—worse than that: I'd like . . . to combine what Chekhov did with what Shakespeare did—that is, to move from the dim, rather eventless beauty of C. to huge geometric plots such as Lear. And to

make this transition without seeming ridiculous. And to do the whole so that it flows naturally, and yet, so that the whole—words, emotion, characters, situation, etc.—has a discernable symmetry and a very definite musical *quality*—inaccurately speaking—I want to *write symphonies.*

Chekhov, Shakespeare, symphonies, poetry—such was the stuff his dreams were made of. The vision, so grand, impractical, and ludicrous, vanished as quickly as it had come. Unable to concentrate on a specific project, he concocted one beautiful scheme after another. The search mattered more than the discovery. Imagination held him hostage.

When he tired of agonizing over his career, he worried about how to break free of Dorothy. For tedious months he had been more or less faithful to her out of a misplaced sense of loyalty. Now he needed a woman closer at hand, and he convinced himself she needed a man willing to devote himself to her. He began dating Radcliffe students, slyly stealing away for an intimate weekend with one, then encouraging Dorothy to start seeing other men for her own good. Still, he felt responsible for her welfare. If only he could find someone who would take his place with her.

The opportunity arose late in the fall when he met a feisty senior named Bernard Schoenfeld at a student party. Fired by a love of the theater, Schoenfeld planned to attend Yale Drama School and write plays. He was immediately taken with the young poet whose face combined "teen-age innocence and intuitive knowledge, with deepset questioning eyes, bold nose, sensual mouth, unruly hair." They sauntered over to Agee's room, where they talked through the night. Schoenfeld felt bathed in a "quiet intensity which I suspected came from feelings born in the deepest levels of his guts. I discovered he was not a private, secretive person. . . . He didn't mind . . . pouring out his thoughts and feelings about the cadence of a stanza, the challenge of prose form, the enviable genius of Joyce, the rough delights of sex, the danger of loving and being loved."

To kindle Schoenfeld's imagination, Agee described in lurid detail a weekend he had recently spent with a willing Radcliffe student and, before Schoenfeld left, pressed a piece of lined paper into the older student's palm, explaining, "It's my translation of a love poem by Catullus." Over the next several weeks, Agee began playing matchmaker for Schoenfeld and Dorothy, who, luckily, responded and started seeing each other regularly. Once the liaison finally took hold, Agee moved swiftly to sever his relationship with Dorothy just in time to give his undivided attention to Via Saunders, who was soon to move to Cambridge.

The breakup with Dorothy cast a shadow over his Christmas vacation. From the safety of Rockland he sent Dorothy an impatient rehearsal of all the reasons why he could not meet her in New York, as she demanded.

> There are a lot of reasons why I can't very well come down now, as I'd be pleased to do. In fact, there are so many reasons it seems almost too plausible. But here they are.
>
> For one thing I'm *very* low on money, and feel that I'd better save whatever I possibly can, by staying home as long as possible and getting free meals. . . .
>
> My vacation lasts till Monday, Jan 5th. At 12 noon on Jan 5th, a music report is due. I did a few hours work on it before vacation, but must go down by Thursday and really get busy on it. If I came to New York, I'd (a) have to leave by Thursday —giving me only 2 or 3 days,—or (b) would have the report very strongly on my conscience. In this latter case, we'd be working under a bad handicap.
>
> Then, too, I know that you're extremely busy this vacation with your two reports. That would make trouble for you and indirectly for me—much more so, I think, than if you were busy at a scheduled job.
>
> And I don't yet know about staying with you. Dear, I wish you'd *tell* me just how it is there—I don't want to give you danger or difficulty, if I should stay.

Under this pretense of tender solicitude, James supplied every reason for their not being able to meet except the real one: He did not wish to see her anymore.

Their relationship, in his judgment, had deteriorated beyond hope. He was tired of her plaintive letters. "It's pretty impossible to answer a sad, short letter, except sadly and shortly," he complained. And he was tired of the debilitating effects of their prolonged separations. "The only way we could avoid or ever combat this, is to write each other very fully of all we're doing and thinking and feeling. . . . Lord knows we've both failed, most of the time. It *seems* as if two people who loved each other would do this perfectly naturally, but *we* certainly don't, and can't." If anyone was at fault, it was he, with his irremediable habit of taking on more than he could manage. "I'm *always* trying to do and think *too much at once*. . . . It's like having my arms too full of packages; when I stoop to pick up one, another falls."

As Agee delved deeper into his reasons for needing his freedom, he could not have failed to make poor Dorothy burn with anger, especially as she studied his explanation of how she would inhibit his writing career. He had recently finished Joyce's *Dubliners* and had been thoroughly frightened by the author's masterly description of a second-rate writer, Gabriel Conroy. He instinctively lumped Dorothy and this second-rateness together. "I don't know of anything more ghastly than the prospect of being a *definitely minor* writer, sitting around with some patience waiting for mild little ideas to turn up—then writing them in a mild little way." To Agee, moderation was the antithesis of worthwhile art; he equated extremism with value. Should he continue with Dorothy, he would become a "damned inept ass," like some Harvard professors he knew, subsiding into a life of "hearing concerts, reading other people's books, getting tight with friends, and (a) screwing my wife or (b) (if unmarried) smelling out various women or (c) both." He served notice that Dorothy would be wise to steer clear of such a troublemaker as he, nor should she entertain thoughts of reforming him to suit her taste. "I wish to God I could be a nice fat Family Man who lives for the wife and kids and does his work at the office simply that they may all live comfortably in a house with a white tile can and a Studebaker. But you know as well as I do that I'll never be that—I'm not able to be." To ward off her further attentions, he portrayed himself as a monster, "screwed up and bitched right from the start," "the most miserable feckless sonofabitch that ever lived." Should they marry, they would be like Gabriel Conroy and his faithless wife. Not only that, he advised, he had a bad cold and would probably come down with pneumonia or tuberculosis at any time. It would be a "swell idea" if he did, though, because then he would die young, and that would show the world how little he cared for himself or the trappings of the bourgeoisie, how little he cared for anything but his ambition. "If I can't, someday, be a great or nearly great writer, I don't want to write at all—and there's nothing else in the world I want to do. I'd rather not live than to live in the failure of what I might have done."

These rash statements showed Agee at his most anxious, defensive, and unappealing. It was so easy to fall in love, he had discovered, yet so difficult to extricate oneself. Despite its awkwardness, the letter had its intended effect. He ended 1930 a free man, alone with his ambition to write.

On New Year's Eve he returned to a dark, cold, deserted Harvard to celebrate his newfound liberty in splendid isolation. Ignoring the persistent cold, he released tension by walking across Boston "rather insanely and for the most part happily," getting drunk in the process. Returning to his suite in Thayer Hall, he saw in the New Year by playing Brahms recordings on a borrowed portable phonograph at peak volume throughout the night. "Being alone in a large building is a grand feeling; and I'm afraid rather conducive to megalomania." This sudden surge of confidence and well-being was so strange and wonderful that it did feel like megalomania; it had been years since he felt so responsible and unperturbed, a mood that boded well for writing. The ideal writer, he surmised, should be free to concentrate solely on the "paper in front of him and a loud roar of the driving idea in his head." He envisioned the ideal writer's mind as both a gyroscope "powerful enough . . . forever to maintain equilibrium" and a mirror "tough enough and pure enough never to be flawed or clouded."

In this radiant frame of mind he set down a ghoulish tale of unhappy lovers who end it all by taking gas. All in all, as he told Louise Saunders, "it was one grand time to be maudlin."

Following his rejection of Dorothy, Agee had more free time on his hands than he had anticipated. All those concerns he had enumerated for her turned out not to be so time-consuming after all. To make matters worse, Via did not move to Cambridge in the spring, as she had planned. In the security of the large Saunders home she entertained serious doubts about the wisdom of testing the treacherous waters of Cambridge. The bohemian life was not her style; she required a modicum of stability. Furthermore, nothing in her young poet friend's letters to the family indicated his intentions toward her. He could be leading her on, seeing other women on the sly. If she were not careful, she might very well find herself stranded in unfamiliar circumstances, without family resources.

Deprived of Dorothy's and Via's companionship, Agee sought consolation in his lonely literary mission—not that he derived much satisfaction from it. As the end of the academic year loomed, he felt an urgent need to write something—he knew not what—that the world beyond Cambridge would notice. He threw himself into an "apoplexy of work"—to no avail. Instead, he was overcome with nostalgia for the illumination he had experienced during the New Year's Eve holiday. Walking the streets of "mellow, tired Cambridge" in late spring, he wished he were crossing the snowy fields of January, the "corrupted year once more a child." The more he wished time would stop, the more quickly it seemed to progress.

Winning election as president of the *Advocate* that spring only served to increase his anxiety, for the position, while an honor, demanded an endless amount of time and energy. He had to devise and hold to a budget, read countless manuscripts, solicit advertising, count linage, settle intramural squabbles, consult with printers, proofread copy, and uphold the entire *Advocate* tradition. He felt wholly responsible for every last detail. Should he work for a magazine after graduation, these skills would come in handy, but for now they weighed heavily on his conscience.

At first he held to a conservative editorial course. Under the Agee regime, it seemed, the *Advocate* would remain the sedate literary affair it had always been: a place where aspiring authors, critics, and editors could practice their skills before a specialized audience. But after several lackluster issues Agee grew restless. Surely there must be some way to put life in the magazine. If he could only devise an issue to appeal to the general public, that would cause a sensation. But vacation interrupted these musings; his schemes would have to wait until the fall.

That summer he decided to put up with the doldrums of Rockland in exchange for the leisure necessary to the creation of one or more masterpieces. As before, he reviled the little town. Everything about the place undermined his ambition and intensity, made his goals seem worthless. Life was so predictable and tepid in Rockland that excitement was regarded as an unwelcome intruder. In the Wrights' new quarters at 41 Masonic Street he felt like a freeloader.

Out of a sense of obligation to his long-suffering family, he agreed to ferry Emma to and from her job and to care for an aged relative. Instead of the creative tranquillity and freedom from romantic entanglements he had counted on, he lapsed into a "creative flabbiness" curable only by a regimen of reading and work.

In the midst of this confusion, Bernard Schoenfeld, who had graduated from Harvard, wrote to complain about his affair with Dorothy Carr. The letter touched a nerve in Agee, who shot back:

> Your remarks *re* Dorothy Carr, while I think of it, show either rotten judgment or cruelty for its own sake or both. I don't think it's eternally necessary to be flippant every time a girl is unlucky enough to get sick of sex. . . . Some of Dorothy's breaks are pathetic enough to be misconstrued as low comedy, I suppose. And I know that ten out of nine of her resolutions . . . come to worse than nothing. I know, too, that half the fun one gets out of life comes through more or less and usually semi-conscious self-dramatization.
>
> The fact remains that she seems to have been born for a peculiarly lousy life; and her fights to get toward something better (when she has no idea what) add up to about as brave an exhibition as I know of. This isn't bullshit, and I'm not saying it out of any ex-lover's cheap obligation to defend her. But I'd like to see her given credit, one time in a hundred. God knows I gave it to her seldom enough.

His foul mood persisted. He drank himself into a stupor on several occasions "with no pleasure" and confided to Schoenfeld that he had "fucked twice," only to find that at the moment of ejaculation he wanted to vomit. His life, he moaned, had "pretty well narrowed down to a verb." To Agee there was no such thing as licit pleasure. All fruit was forbidden. Hangovers obliterated the glow of alcohol; guilt tarnished sex.

In this unpromising state of mind he made desultory experiments with one literary form after another. In an August tally of his summer's work he listed several poems; six experiments in "mixed methods"; a short story; a beginning for a long story; outlines for more poems, stories, and novels; and a play. The whole, he noted, came to a grand total of 634 lines of verse and 18,000 words of prose, nearly all of it fruitless and eventually lost, discarded, or ignored. The gyroscope had lost its bearings; the mirror, its luster.

Throughout this frustrating struggle to find himself on paper he lived in dread of graduation, fearing the loss of Harvard's protection. When he paused to count the months to graduation, the rapidly dwindling number sent a chill up his spine. His sole respite from gloomy forbodings was Dostoevsky's *The Possessed*. The lonely, self-centered Harvard undergraduate profoundly identified with the Russian novelist's God-cursed vision. Here was intensity to match Agee's need of it, and he claimed that reading the novel "set fire" to all he had learned from I. A. Richards. He might not have found himself yet, but in Dostoevsky he had found another artist-hero worthy to join Blake and Beethoven.

Shortly after the first of September, Agee put down his book, packed his bags, and left Rockland for a three-week stay in Clinton as a guest of the Saunderses, who had by now all but adopted him. He arrived to find the great Richards regaling the salon with his newest insights and apothegms; old Percy leading spirited renditions of quintets, shouting criticism as he sawed away on his violin; and gentle Via awaiting his attentions. He was gratified to learn that she had not forgotten him after all and still planned to move to Cambridge in the fall, a prospect that made him "spectacularly happy." In these congenial surroundings he recovered the good spirits he feared he had irrevocably lost. So light-headed did he become that when he left Clinton for Harvard he forgot a bundle of *Advocate* material—manuscripts, dummies, and page proofs.

Buoyed by the Saunders' love and attention, he returned to college in robust spirits. He felt more at home in Harvard's bustling precincts than anywhere else. Now that he was a senior, there was a certain sureness in his step; he had only to gaze across the vast reading room of Widener Library to find at least two or three familiar faces. Furthermore, he enjoyed impressive new lodgings in Eliot House, one of the recently completed dormitories designed to level the social inequities of student life, as President Lowell had promised three years earlier. Located at the foot of gently sloping Dunster Street, Eliot's ungainly triangular shape hugged the intersection of Memorial Drive and Boylston Street. Many rooms, though not Agee's suite on the fifth floor of Entryway G, commanded views of the Charles River. The red brick building, trimmed with white and topped by an ornate clock tower, featured a grassy courtyard and a formal wood-paneled dining room. Here, over tables draped with fine linen, students took all their meals and socialized with younger faculty members, whose presence helped raise the level of conversation. At the time Agee took up residence, the senior tutor, responsible for the academic welfare of Eliot House students, was F. O. Matthiessen, the brilliant author of *American Renaissance,* who quickly came to appreciate his tormented young charge.

Again rooming with Robert Saudek, Agee spent every free moment with Via, who had finally made her move to Cambridge. With her friend and Bryn Mawr classmate Mary Louise White she rented an apartment in a comfortable frame house at 52 Brattle Street, a few minutes' stroll from Eliot House. Very much her mother's daughter, she inaugurated a literary salon through which passed the likes of Wyndham Lewis, T. S. Eliot, I. A. Richards, and, of course, Dr. Saunders. At other times, Agee, Via, and Mary Lou spent long hours listening to records, drinking, and talking away the night. Within weeks he found himself dependent on Via "for every breath I draw." At the same time, he harbored the suspicion that he might be making a nuisance of himself at all hours. Despite these misgivings, they began a serious courtship that could well lead to the terrifying prospect of matrimony. Their relationship progressed so quickly and smoothly that Agee feared he had become very much "the smug bridegroom."

There were other Harvard students in search of significant contacts who found their way to the Saunders salon, junior edition, notably Robert Fitzgerald, recently back from a year abroad; Irvine Upham; and an acerbic young fellow named Burrhus Frederick Skinner, who had once served as tutor to Frisk Saunders. Skinner's passion for literature vied with his newfound interest in behavioral science as practiced by his hero Ivan Petrovich Pavlov. At the time, Skinner was a graduate student in psychology at Harvard.

With scientific detachment, Skinner observed the rapidly flourishing romance between Agee and Via. Having dated Via six years before, he realized that much of the Saunders' sophisticated conversation flew over her head; she would laugh at a shaft of wit without understanding the point. Skinner wondered whether she realized how complex and troubled her disheveled young poet actually was.

Nevertheless, Via's constant companionship caused Agee to live in a state of continual excitement. He slept no more than three and a half hours a night, many of them at Via's cozy apartment. He grimly fought his way through a "fairly successful death-dance" of studying for makeup examinations. Should he pass, he would be able to rejoin the class of 1932. The anxiety generated by the exams proved sufficient to undo his equilibrium. He described his state of mind as "everything going *continuously* at top speed—mind, body, nerves; and with an intensity I've never known before: with powers, pain and joy all humming at once. . . . Even dull and microscopic things seemed magnificently alive and exciting." On October 20 the Dean's Office declared that James Agee had done well enough on the examination to rejoin his class, and a cloud that had hung over his head for two years finally disappeared. His academic load lightened to three courses—two English surveys and a music history class—none of which seriously taxed his abilities.

But the ceaseless activity and moments of exhilaration alternated with black periods of utter self-absorption as he tried to imagine life after Harvard. "It's still on me," he wrote to Louise Saunders late one night, concerning his worries, "like a homicidal gorilla on a blind and feeble man: I'm doing everything I can to fight it off—but I haven't really succeeded, and I begin to think I never will." He told himself he had *"every reason"* to be happy, but saying so did not make it so.

> I'm now a long way from happiness, and it seems quite useless to try to be otherwise: as if I were hanging (by the fingernails) to the end of a gigantic clock hand, trying to hold it at high noon for a while, then as frantically trying to wrench it up toward high noon. In spite of everything I try, it makes—and will make—its circuit within a split second of untampered correct time. The thing rather to do is—especially when the hand is at six,—is to hang on calmly and pray to God my fingernails don't tear out by the roots,—or that the clock doesn't run down. I'm afraid that . . . it's most likely to stop at six. Then God help me! Only God won't. Such praying as I do is a thoroughly empty matter—so I feel—and I think I'll try to stop it altogether, as pretty cowardly.

In all likelihood this drastic image derived from one of silent film comedian Harold Lloyd's comic predicaments. But Agee's predicament was anything but funny.

When he tired of the drama of desperation, James settled back to take stock of the things worth living for.

> I'm in Harvard, with the year to finish, with no need to worry, yet, about money. I have at my disposal . . . splendid courses, two grand libraries, symphony concerts, movies, the theater, walks all over the place, two available pianos, my Advocate work. A fine large province.
>
> I have Via and Mary Lou, and Franklin Miner, and [Ted] Spencer . . . and quite a number of friends I'm fond of but see less frequently.
>
> I have writing to do.
>
> I'm sure of the love of you all, and love you all. . . .
>
> I have more to make me happy than almost anyone I know, and I absolutely don't deserve it.
>
> The other side:
>
> I'm in Harvard, with 8 ghastly months ahead. I have no job, and no prospect of one. . . . The two libraries might as well be in Idaho. My parents are spending money to make me expensively wretched when I might as well be wretched at no expense to anyone. There's no tuition in hell. The Advocate is a bore and a terrific disappointment. We have no money: it is therefore impossible to do anything I'd hoped to do. The board consists chiefly of brats who criticize my lack of effort and remedially suggest schemes I had 10 months ago.

Despite this adolescent breast-beating, Agee's bouts of introspection did yield the occasional moment of truth. In the midst of one tirade it occurred to him that such grumbling might be part of the problem. "I have a terrific Run-to-Mama complex to overcome," he immediately noted, "and I haven't overcome it yet." Perhaps, he thought, his calling on Louise Saunders as a surrogate mother could lead to damaging consequences. Perhaps his efforts to excoriate himself hampered his ability to arrive at sound decisions concerning the crucial choices he would have to make after college. If he could only force himself to short-circuit this self-involvement and look to those around him, he would feel more at ease with himself. Case in point: He had known for weeks that Louise was ill, yet he had not even written her a get-well note.

Sick with remorse, he forsook decadent Harvard for staid Rockland in late October expressly to care for Emma and a distant relative who were both hospitalized. Tending the needs of others brought him solace and well-being. Whenever he threw himself into a situation requiring compassion, the best part of his nature came to the fore. He left off bewailing his artistic and sexual frustrations and his narcissistic daydreams of literary fame in favor of relieving the sufferings of others and, by extension, his own. In the past he had detested the small-mindedness of Rockland, but now, in his own way, he followed the example of Jesus' washing the feet of the poor. For Agee, such caring was filled with spiritual implications; it was his way of praising God. Actions spoke louder than prayers. Whether consoling the hopelessly muddled Tom Raywood, a migrant worker, or children laboring at a factory, Agee reaffirmed his Christianity.

Throughout the Rockland interlude, Agee thought not of Jesus but of Dostoevsky. Only in the Russian did he find the same prodigal variety of emotions that he had experienced, the same bizarre combination of degradation and transcendence. Russian saints and sinners reeled through his mind as he trod the damp soil of Maine. "Almost everyone seems, this fall, to be . . . dying, dead, or in danger of hellfire," he observed on November 3. "I think the last month is the weirdest and most strained, and altogether one of the best—I've ever lived. It has something of the frantic and intense quality of a Dostoevsky novel."

In his final winter at Harvard, Agee set about dreaming up a literary coup that would launch his career. For all his thrashing about with poetry, novels, stories, and plays, he had failed to top his "Ann Garner" of four years before. Certainly his Harvard career had had its high points—a handful of stunning short poems and a literary prize or two—but his confidence had steadily waned. The more he knew about literature, the less easy he found it to write. Summoning all his considerable powers, he decided to write a lengthy poem that would make up for the lost years and show the world what he could do. Or so he hoped. In fact the work became a major disaster.

Drawing on his long-standing interest in demonology, he spun a fable about adoring parents who give birth to a baby whose personality is equally influenced by Don Juan and the devil. Sucking at his mother's breast, the baby draws blood and titillates his mother to the point of madness. Agee named his demonic protagonist John Carter, and as the first stanza of what was to be an interminable poem reveals, hoped to emulate a certain outlandish English nobleman's casual masterpiece.

> *Like Byron, I'll begin at the beginning.*
> *Unlike that better bard, my lad's a new one,*
> *Expert in charm, supremely so in sinning,*
> *Nevertheless he differs from Don Juan*
> *In ways enough to set your brain spinning.*

Aware of his attractiveness to women and still suffering pangs of regret over Dorothy, Agee allied himself with the archetypal promiscuous lover. So far, so good. But he drastically misconstrued his own gifts by attempting a poetic satire. For one thing, he lacked the suppleness of mind to match Byron's wit; *Don Juan*'s cheerful nihilism belonged to another age. For another, Agee's strength as a writer lay not in his talent for ridicule but in his remarkable compassion. Heedless of such concerns, he smoked cigarette after cigarette and wrote stanza after stanza of ottava rima.

He entertained such high hopes for the misguided project that he determined to submit sections for a Guggenheim Fellowship. This prestigious award, generally bestowed on artists and scholars of some reputation, consisted of a stipend on which he could live for a year, only a fraction of the time he anticipated it would require to complete the gargantuan poem. In a boldly conceived essay he described the work's major themes for the benefit of the Guggenheim judges. His protagonist would be "the typical American Young Man," and bear a certain playful resemblance to the author.

> Spiritually speaking, he is an orthodox Roman Catholic devil, God-given to the world, a New Messiah of Evil. His human personality is so completely extroverted and so childishly sensitive and intuitive that he is a perfect mirror of whatever surroundings he finds himself in. He uses his diabolic powers

never supernaturally, always humanly; in other words, moved from place to place throughout America, he destroys whom he pleases according to that person's idioms of thought and conduct.

Declaring he had embarked on no less than a "complete appraisal of contemporary civilization," Agee expected to get at the "Problem of Evil" in the course of three volumes. The first would be devoted to the "birth, baptism, infancy, behavioristic early education, grade-school education, religious and sexual education, adolescence, first love, prep-school education, Harvard maturation, and self-discovery of John Carter." The succeeding two volumes, of even greater length, would, Agee supposed, take an infinite number of years, "and since there are other things I hope to write, I have no invulnerable confidence in ever finishing it." Nor did the Guggenheim Committee, which regretfully informed him that it was unable to act favorably on his application. Despite the setback, he continued to tinker with the poem, amassing over two hundred clumsy stanzas.

Even while failing miserably with satirical verse, he guessed he might succeed with satirical journalism. Though he struggled unsuccessfully to make light of himself, he could savagely mock the world at large. Furthermore, he had the resources of the *Advocate* at his disposal. And then it came to him, the long-overdue idea for a special issue. He would revive the Harvard tradition of parodying a well-known publication.

Immediately he set about persuading the often intransigent board to accept this proposal. If done correctly, a parody would sell a great many issues, fill the coffers, and boost the editors' career prospects. To allay the fears of die-hard conservatives, he could point to ample precedent. Seven years before, Harvard's raffish humor publication, the *Lampoon,* enjoyed a succès de scandale with a takeoff on the once renowned *Literary Digest.* A disrespectful portrayal of the American flag on the cover and a risqué illustration within attracted notice in the Boston Police Department, which seized all copies and raided the *Lampoon* building. In the wake of the controversy, the humor magazine rode a wave of publicity and retaliated by publishing a doctored edition that sold more than any previous issue in the *Lampoon*'s history. At the time Agee proposed an *Advocate* parody, copies of the notorious *Lampoon* were changing hands for twenty-five dollars.

The *Advocate,* too, had tried parody. A takeoff on *The Dial,* the well-known "little" magazine, had not caused so much of a stir, but it had earned suppression at the hands of the post office and Cambridge police. Even better, the real *Dial,* regarding imitation as the sincerest form of flattery, had offered jobs to all those involved with the parody. Faced with this overwhelmingly favorable evidence, the board elected to go along with Agee, who resolved to top all previous parodies with a unique version of the newest, flashiest, and most successful magazine around—*Time.*

Certainly the weekly newsmagazine made excellent grist for the parodist's mill. *Time* relied on a distinctive formula of succinct reportage rendered in a pungent "Timestyle" consisting of cheeky neologisms such as "tycoon" and "cinemaddict" as well as startling reversals of word order. In his profile of Henry Luce, *Time*'s co-founder, *New Yorker* satirist Wolcott Gibbs summed up the quintessence of Timestyle this way: "Backward ran sentences until reeled the mind."

Board members were also acutely aware that a number of recent Harvard graduates populated Time Inc.'s executive suite. Roy Larsen, a former *Advocate* business manager, now held the same title at *Time.* The current *Advocate* editors reasonably assumed that their best hope of finding a job in the midst of the Depression lay with the Luce empire. In the early stages of planning, therefore, they inundated *Time* with letters explaining their intentions. In one, Agee threw down the gauntlet and explained the approach their parody would take.

Sirs:

Imagine your staff set down in Ancient Greece, Rome, Egypt, and Palestine, with an uncommonly long nose for news, several amphoras of rye, vivid but confused recollections of the 20th century, a somewhat cockeyed sense of TIME, and no sense whatever of chronology; and take note. *The Harvard Advocate* has already imagined you there; has used this as a device whereby to parody TIME among other things; shall issue the parody on March 18. Unless we receive objection in writing, we shall send you a copy (regularly 25¢).

James Agee
President

While Agee sought to pique interest, the *Advocate*'s business manager, David Weir, unashamedly asked Larsen to share *Time*'s adver-
tisers. While promising a full-page *Time* ad costing one hundred
dollars, Larsen requested a prepublication peek at the contents. Not
that he was worried about the parodists' barbs. By selecting mythol-
ogy as their province, the editors limited their chances of drawing
real blood. The subject matter was keyed to the educational background of *Time*'s editors, who had received a thoroughly classical
grounding in their prep schools and Ivy League colleges. Within
months, a spirit of editorial goodwill linked the offices of the *Advocate* and *Time.*

Work on the parody proceeded steadily throughout the winter. As the editors recounted various legendary events in *Time*'s
chatty, irreverent style, they realized they were on to a very good
thing indeed. The National Affairs column described a parley with
Zeus. Theater featured a review of *Lysistrata*'s opening night. Foreign News undertook to explain the significance of the birth of
Solomon to a bewildered readership. Agee threw himself into all
aspects of the issue. He contributed copy, honed that of others,
selected pictures, wrote captions, and endlessly fussed over layout,
all the while gaining a valuable education in the craft of magazine
editing.

One wintry Saturday, after putting the parody to bed, Agee
went out to celebrate. He left behind a note for Saudek to wake him
the following morning in time for their paying job as members of
a church choir. He then took a stroll along the boardwalk of Revere
beach, several miles from Boston. In the midst of his singing and
drinking bootleg gin, two policemen appeared out of nowhere to
order the reveler to keep it down. Agee reacted angrily; ignoring
his protests, the policemen lifted him by both arms and hustled him
away to their precinct station, where they booked him and placed
his valuables in a sealed envelope. When he continued to protest,
they beat him and threw him into an empty cell.

Early the next morning, Agee arranged with a bail bondsman
to post bail, retrieved the envelope, and returned to Eliot House,
where he collapsed face down on his bed. A few hours later, Saudek
came across the envelope marked "Metropolitan Police Department, Defendant's Belongings" and immediately woke Agee, who,
Saudek discovered to his horror, had been sleeping in bloody

clothes, his face lacerated from the beating. In the clear light of morning, Agee expressed more bewilderment than anger at having been beaten without reason. It was inconceivable to him that anyone should beat, much less jail, an innocent citizen. He then went to sing in the choir, bloody face and all.

Having survived his night on the town, Agee awaited the reception of the parody with baited breath. The expectations and careers of more than a dozen anxious students rode on the issue's success or failure. On March 18, the parody, sporting *Time*'s distinctive red border, hit the Boston and Cambridge newsstands—to more acclaim than even its editors dared hope for.

PARODY FEVER BREAKS OUT AT HARVARD
Usually Staid Advocate Issues Burlesque on "Time"

So ran the headline in the March 20 Boston Sunday *Globe,* which devoted fifty column inches to the parody, complete with eye-catching photographs. Agee could scarcely have written better advertising for the issue himself. "Old Mother Advocate," wrote the *Globe*'s correspondent, "has gone and perpetrated the most recent Harvard undergraduate tour de force," which he went on to describe as a "masterpiece of parody."

Not all the reviews were favorable; some were gratifyingly nasty. The stuffy Boston *Herald* sanctimoniously warned that the *"Advocate*'s cover so closely resembled the usual cover of *Time* that scores of persons bought the parody inadvertently." So that disgruntled readers would know to whom they should direct their obloquy, the *Herald* held "James R. Agee '32 of Rockland, Me., president of the Advocate" as "principally responsible for the hoax." Larsen, too, fired off a note complaining that the parody cover looked "too much like TIME's to be sold" and that the editorial content "started nowhere and ended nowhere." Even the comparatively mild fun the editors had had at *Time*'s expense was enough to ruffle a few corporate feathers.

To modern eyes, the parody, for all its skill, creaks with the coy undergraduate hijinks of a bygone era. Larsen did have a point: The copy rambles, only occasionally hitting a satirical nail squarely on the head. In one of the relatively successful gambits, ruler "J. G. Caesar" allows that he "scribbles a good deal; not for publication, just for the pure fun of the thing." And the theater reviewer finds *Electra* to be Aeschylus' "latest nerve-shatterer" and "well worth a trip to the new State Theater." The aim, if any such joke could be said to have an aim, was to demonstrate the great extent to which the medium, in this case a mass-circulation magazine, is the message. In Timestyle, gossip supplants tragedy, and purple prose smothers classical poetry. If language shapes the way we see the world, the parody implies, our sights have become comically narrow and low.

The runaway success of the special *Advocate* issue persuaded Agee to postpone his earlier plan to write in isolation after graduation. He had spent months working with all manner of poetry and prose, while this elaborate joke had come over him effortlessly and, in the process, earned him the widest recognition he had yet known. Surely there was a lesson to be learned from the experience. It seemed that the multifaceted parody proved a ready match for his talents and interests. His wide-ranging reading and movie going had made him a connoisseur of mass media. There was blissful freedom to be had in ranging across the entire spectrum of Western civilization—sampling everything, committing himself to nothing. At the same time, the parody was rife with qualities he professed to detest: It was sophisticated, lightweight, amusing, and stylish. Little of a spiritual, personal, or profound nature entered into its thirty-odd pages. It branded Agee not as the solitary, tormented poet he imagined himself to be, but as a well-educated and enterprising young man on the make. As such, he was bound to feel at home in *Time*'s fast company.

The success encouraged Agee to move swiftly to secure a job. A considerable if slightly notorious reputation preceded him to New York; he now had to demonstrate that he could fit in as well as stand out. He initiated a formal approach to *Time* by writing to Macdonald, who had keenly appreciated the send-up. However, Macdonald harbored serious doubts about the intentions of any serious writer who wanted to work for Henry Luce. In the wake of his harsh experiences in New York, Macdonald had become a fervent Trotskyite and ardent foe of capitalism. Yet here he was working for one of capitalism's biggest boosters. Macdonald found his situation so hypocritical that he could scarcely bring himself to discuss it. "In the house of the hanged man, no one talks of rope," he quipped. To further inflame his political conscience, he had recently been promoted to star writer for Luce's newest, slickest, and most blatantly capitalist publication, *Fortune.*

Of all these political considerations Agee remained, for the moment, blissfully ignorant. Preferring to act the role of the aesthete, he had eschewed Harvard's economics and government courses. He simply wanted the best-paid writing job he could find. Would Macdonald *please,* therefore, help. Putting aside his reservations, Macdonald approached Ralph Ingersoll, *Fortune*'s crusty managing editor. Of course the James Agee of *Time* parody fame could have a job, Ingersoll said. After all, *Fortune* prided itself on its "rich and beautiful prose" and incisive profiles of the business world's movers and shakers. It was anything but a technical journal, really more a showcase for state-of-the-art journalism and photography. To this end, Luce and his lieutenants made a concerted effort to hire the cream of the Ivy League literary crop. Nowhere else would an aspiring young writer make as much. If he wanted to write poems or whatnot on his own, that was fine; Luce was happy to pay the salary of any talented writer who turned in his copy on time. Luce knew that business writers were, as a breed, a dull proposition, but if he could put poets to work writing business stories, he gambled he could produce a lively product brimming with the romance of capitalism. Luce guessed that a dose of Depression desperation could cure any artistic scruple. In its third year, *Fortune* was proving him correct.

Nor did Luce care about his writers' political sympathies. They came in all varieties, from conspiracy-sniffing arch-conservatives to out-and-out Communists. Of course it galled Luce that most of his best writers happened to be left of center, but the dialectic between his principles and their passions contributed bite and sparkle to *Fortune*'s pages. Indeed, Luce was more open to his writers' ideas than they were to his. More than most publishers, Luce would know exactly how to handle a stubborn type like James Agee.

Awaiting a reply from Macdonald, Agee resorted to his "generous and evil intentioned friend Solitary Drinking." When he could stand isolation no longer, he escaped with friends to the Massachusetts countryside. He returned from one such expedition to find Macdonald's letter confirming Ingersoll's intention of hiring Agee immediately upon graduation. He would not even have to undergo the ordeal of an interview. Agee studied Macdonald's incredible letter "with eyes rolling upward & stomach downward for joy, relief, gratitude and such things." In a hastily written reply, he exclaimed, "Thank you, God, and Managing Editor Ingersoll." Then doubt set in. Perhaps he should come down to New York for an interview all the same. "If it makes absolutely no difference, I shan't; my money is low & my time rammed," he explained to Macdonald. "But if . . . there's any doubt about my qualifying, . . . *any* reason why it would be well for me to come down—will you please let me know?" Macdonald advised that Agee stay put to marvel at this stroke of luck. As the Depression strengthened its grip on the nation, fully half of Agee's classmates failed to find employment, despite their Harvard degrees. In these circumstances he knew no way to express the full measure of his gratitude. "Words fail me," he gushed. "Besides the fairly fundamental fact that I don't want to starve, there are dozens of other reasons why I want *uh* job and many more why I am delighted to get this one."

First and foremost, a position with Time Inc. was all so very exciting and respectable. His family had kept him on a short financial tether for four long years, and here at last was the prospect of financial independence. Even better, he demonstrated to himself and to his family that he could, as a writer, earn a comfortable income, even in the Depression. He would be getting about fifty dollars a week to start and in a few short years might be making as much as $10,000 a year, surely a king's ransom. In the certain knowledge that he would earn nothing as a poet and little as a teacher or a novelist, he concluded that journalism offered the magic solution to his dilemma. He had only to look to the careers of other poets to realize the obstacles faced by a serious American writer. Weeks before, Vachel Lindsay had taken his life, followed by Hart Crane, who had jumped from a ship sailing north from Vera Cruz. Both these men had been heroes to Agee's generation, and the double tragedy struck terror in all but the hardiest of aspiring poets. An ill wind blew against them, born of economic hardship and strengthened by public neglect.

From his vantage point, Macdonald was considerably less enthusiastic about the benefits of working for Luce. Life at *Fortune,* he burned to tell Agee, was no picnic. The hours were long, the Depression horrifying, and the assignments less than congenial to poets. Years later he would perceive "unbearable dramatic irony" in Agee's gratitude. "I didn't do him a favor, really," Macdonald came to believe, but he could never have persuaded his protégé of the fact.

Agee remained swept up in the excitement of *Time* for weeks. As a result, he had put off one final chore before he collected his diploma. As class poet, he was supposed to compose an ode appropriate for the graduation ceremonies. On the night before the lines were due at the printer, he wearily took up his pencil and unlined yellow sheets to await a glimmer of inspiration. He wrote and crossed out, wrote and crossed out throughout the long night, and by morning had arrived at the semblance of a suitable statement.

He was scheduled to read the ode before the assembled forces of the class of 1932, the faculty, and parents in a precommencement ceremony that took place amid the cavernous spaces of Sanders Theater. He wore a choir robe borrowed from a church and a mortarboard adorned with the long red tassel of Radcliffe College. When the moment arrived, he approached the lectern with a lump forming in his throat and prepared to recite the ode from memory.

> *Now the snows are withdrawn and the fields young in bloom,*
> *All that lives strains in strength toward the light,*
> *And the comrades who halted in doubt and in gloom*
> *Depart drunk o'er the dawn-trampled night.*

In the midst of the recitation, he glanced up; the sight of all those staring faces overwhelmed him. He lost his place, halted, fell victim to stage fright. An endless, silent interval ensued as he fished frantically for the yellow sheets on which he had drafted the ode. Finally someone shoved a printed copy of the text beneath his nose, and he bravely continued to the ode's conclusion, lines that spoke of the light and shadow of his own life.

> *And all the wisdom we wring from our pain and desire*
> *On this field between devil and God,*
> *Shall resolve to white and unquenchable fire*
> *That shall cleanse the dark way we have trod.*

He rushed back to his seat as quickly as he could. The endless round of ceremonies could not end soon enough to satisfy him. He had his whole life ahead of him, and he wanted to begin without wasting another moment on sentimentality and an all-too-ephemeral sense of fellowship.

Via had decided to remain in Cambridge, at least temporarily, but Agee was so keen to take up his duties at *Fortune* that he planned to hitchhike to New York immediately following commencement exercises in the Yard. Before leaving, he bid farewell to his loyal roommate as they stood knee-deep in "half-packed trunks, textbooks, poems, unfinished stories, letters, term papers, prayer books, sheet music, phonographs, and diplomas." They shook hands; they promised to write. Then Agee picked up the raw pine box holding his phonograph and the wicker basket he had brought with him in his freshman year, opened the door to their Eliot House suite, and clomped down the stairs. Wrote Saudek, "I remember looking down from the window as he emerged five stories below and hiked across Eliot quadrangle with the heel-lifting stride he had brought with him four years before. The heavy pine box rested lightly as a parrot on his shoulder." And he moved out of sight.

PART TWO

6

EMPIRE

James Agee arrived in a New York stunned by heat and hopelessness. In its third year, the Depression was everywhere in evidence. On street corners unemployed office workers sold apples to support their desperate families. Others formed shuffling lines in front of soup kitchens. In Central Park an ugly, festering collection of makeshift tents and lean-tos sprang up to shelter the homeless and dispossessed: a Hooverville. Nineteen thirty-two was shaping up to be the severest year yet of the Depression. Ten times as many people were unemployed as had been in 1929, and during the same period the Gross National Product had fallen by half. Families disintegrated, and the stupor of enforced idleness hung over the city.

Yet for all that, New York harbored pockets of affluence beyond the imagination of the homeless masses. Certain businesses, especially those in industry and communications, that had gotten their start in the devil-may-care 1920s, managed to ride out the economic storm, or even to reap benefits from it, especially if what they sold happened to be cheap and diverting. Among these Depression-proof businesses was Time Inc., at ten years of age one of the great success stories of the day.

The publishing empire was the brainchild of two eager, bright, and well-connected members of Yale's class of 1920, Britton Hadden and Henry Luce. They had been good friends ever since their days at the Hotchkiss School. Hadden, the more flamboyant of the two, had originally wanted a career as a professional athlete, but he put aside those dreams of glory in favor of journalism. In *Time*'s infancy, he would often steal away to Central Park to play baseball. Luce, at the same time, labored mightily to overcome a profound sense of alienation from the American scene. Born of missionary parents in Tengchow, China, he had acquired the nickname Chink at Hotchkiss, where students taunted him for his foreignness and pointed out that he could never be elected President. Everything about Luce radiated a ferocious and barely harnessed power. He stuttered at those moments when he most wanted to speak fluently, and his bushy eyebrows twitched with every thought that crossed his mind. By the time he reached Yale, his classmates caught on to how brilliant he was in a masculine, aggressive, let's-roll-up-our-sleeves-and-get-down-to-work kind of way. He possessed an uncanny knack for grasping the essence of an abstract idea or problem and a conviction that he must impose his will on any given situation. At Yale, Luce and Hadden ran the student newspaper together, and in recognition of their abilities they were voted most brilliant and most likely to succeed, respectively.

After Yale they moved down to New York to launch the journalistic enterprise they had discussed ever since their Hotchkiss days: a smartly edited summary of the week's news, gleaned from the far more detailed but much less readable columns of the daily papers. As Luce liked to say, "We reached the conclusion that people were not well-informed and that something should be done." It was highly debatable whether the format of their projected magazine would keep people well informed, but it would keep them *au courant,* able to hold up their end of a cocktail party conversation.

In search of upwardly mobile readers who wanted the edge in polite society, the Yalies sought to infuse their magazine with a faintly superior, tongue-in-cheek manner. To Hadden especially, news had entertainment as well as practical value. The world was an oyster, a circus, a spectacle. And they wanted to make up for the secondhand quality of their news by using their relatively long lead time to unearth "background" and "perspective." But the one thing they did not want to do was a journal of opinion. They calculated that an easily identifiable political slant would relegate the magazine to the fringes of society, rather than keep them in the commercial mainstream where they longed to be. For, above all, they wanted to make money. Hadden's ambition was to become a millionaire by the time he turned thirty, and he nearly achieved it. In the New York of the 1920s, where credit flowed as freely as bootleg gin, anything seemed possible.

To produce the kind of magazine they wanted they proposed a three-tiered news-gathering structure. On the lowest level, reporter-researchers would gather and verify facts culled from printed sources. When all else failed, they would resort to direct coverage of an event. On the middle level, writers (whose ranks Agee would join) winnowed through these primary sources and assembled them into an approximation of the final story. They would not be writers so much as rewriters, stylists who had more in common with advertising copywriters than with traditional journalists. On the highest level, Luce, Hadden, and other editors would polish the writers' stories to an attention-grabbing shine. In short, Luce and Hadden proposed a system of collective journalism akin to the assembly line. Everyone had a hand in the final product, but no one dominated it. They were selling the magazine's overall style, not the expertise of individual writers or reporters.

With their foolproof formula firmly in hand, Luce and Hadden approached their wealthier Yale classmates for financial support. After meeting with a predictable measure of well-meaning scorn, they tapped into the Harkness and Firestone fortunes to amass $86,000—enough to start the magazine, which they decided to name *Time.* The first issue, perilously thin and amateurish, appeared in March 1923. Advertisers proved elusive, even at the magazine's giveaway rates, and for the next five years the enterprise ran in the red. During the lean period, Hadden and Luce refined their editorial formula, persuaded promising college friends and friends of friends to join their publication, and moved from one cluttered office in Manhattan to another. They initiated, then aborted, a move to Cleveland, where they thought they would be closer to the heartland and labor would come cheaper. Not until 1928 did *Time* go decisively into the black as circulation soared over the 100,000 mark.

Now that they were past the critical period, Hadden and Luce restructured their partnership. Previously Hadden had been the supreme editor, while Luce looked after the business side with the help of Roy Larsen. They switched roles, and Luce quickly earned a reputation as an exceptionally aggressive and meddlesome editor who adopted a crisis approach to the task of assembling each week's issue. Writers (largely men) and researchers (largely women) worked late into the night taking apart and remaking the magazine under Luce's vigilant, nervous eye. A newsmagazine, he knew, could be an unwieldy beast, slow to respond to outside pressures. So he chose to experiment just when things seemed to be going well. At the same time, he had a clear sense of the limitations of journalism, his brand in particular. To the suggestion that the growing staff gather its own news, he insisted, "*Time is* a re-write sheet. *Time* does get most of its news and information from the newspapers. . . . The genius of *Time* lies in that fact."

With every jump in circulation the son of missionaries was well on the way to the life of a press baron. He bought a $100,000 plantation in South Carolina and a fifteen-room duplex in Manhattan. In the midst of success, Hadden came down with a debilitating case of influenza. Antibiotics had yet to be introduced; the infection spread quickly; and, on February 27, 1929, Hadden died. Larsen inherited his responsibilities.

Much as he mourned the loss of his partner, Luce now had the operation of a thriving business all to himself. He lost no time in impressing his fascination with big business on all facets of the magazine. *Time* itself had become a big business, Luce a prime example of the successful entrepreneur who had taken the risks and reaped the rewards. Cover after cover featured business leaders such as Walter Chrysler. To critics contending that Luce truckled to tycoons who were heedless of the public weal, Luce responded, "Business is, essentially, our civilization, for it is the essential characteristic of our times."

In accord with this philosophy, Luce decided to launch a new publication in the *Time* tradition, a magazine devoted to uncovering the secret workings of the world of big business. He brought unrestrained glee to the prospect of investigating tycoons he considered "kittenish as a Victorian subdeb or boorish as a lion . . . in captivity." Time Inc. promotion labeled the project simply "the greatest journalistic assignment in history!" Initially, the magazine was to be called *Power,* but Luce, glowing with optimism, substituted the more tantalizing *Fortune,* and, as Dwight Macdonald would later remark, "as a journalistic inspiration, *Fortune* ranks little below *Time.* " Of course Luce envisioned a magazine worthy of its subject, a monthly publication that would be the last word in luxury. The paper would be the finest available. Since Luce had become intrigued with the possibilities of photojournalism, he set aside ample space for photo essays and four-color illustrations to fill the oversize 11 by 14 pages. At a dollar a copy, *Fortune* aimed for an unashamedly wealthy audience of Luce's peers, in contrast to *Time*'s broad appeal. Circulation would be smaller, readers more influential.

Had it not been the Depression, *Fortune* would have become the gilded, bombastic tribute to big business Luce intended. But by the time Volume I, Number 1, weighing two pounds, rolled off the presses in February 1930, he was forced to rethink the magazine's reason for being. Prodded by his writers, Luce veered from his original course, and business topics yielded to thoughtful sociological studies. "At the end of 1931 the depression finally penetrated the consciousness of the editors of *Fortune,* " Macdonald found. "As though a dam had suddenly broken, a spate of articles on politics, government, and society in general inundated the magazine," as Luce discovered the action had shifted from big business to the New Deal. At the time Agee joined the staff, the majority of pieces dealt with sociology rather than with tycoons, and the magazine found a widespread public acceptance; even at its stiff cover price, *Fortune* sold over 100,000 issues a month.

To house the burgeoning staffs of his two magazines, Luce

selected the most prominent and expensive business address in town: the silvery new spire of the Chrysler Building at 135 East 42nd Street. In its size and delicacy, the Chrysler Building resembled a latter-day Chartres built in praise of a new god, the holy dollar. To Luce, capitalism *was* a religion, and material things were imbued with spirituality. From their aeries on the fiftieth, fifty-first, and fifty-second floors, the employees enjoyed eye-filling vistas of Brooklyn to the east, the rising towers of Rockefeller Center to the west, and the dark chasms of Wall Street to the south. In the lobby, the latest-model Chrysler revolved on a pedestal, as if the automobile were an object of reverence.

It was into these grandiose surroundings, so utterly unlike anything he had ever known before, that Agee walked one hot summer's day in late June. He had been warned to wear a tie and to look as neat and clean as he was able, and he did. He said "sir" to everyone, and looked on respectfully as editors, writers, and researchers went about their mysterious business. To Agee, writing had been a middle-of-the-night, intuitive endeavor, yet here everyone wrote on demand, as if they worked at a bank. Despite the opulence of the building, Luce dictated that the actual *Fortune* offices be as clean and spartan as a barracks. The walls were bare, and desks, chairs, and typewriters were in perpetually short supply. When Macdonald had gingerly requested a desk, Luce pounded on *his* and bawled, "A desk, for Godsake! What's happened to the old log-cabin spirit that founded *Time?*" The office was a place of work, not indolence. After the briefest of introductions, Agee was immediately put to work at a borrowed desk, sorting through clippings on unemployment.

As the shock of strangeness wore off, Agee became sensitive to the nuances of daily life at Time Inc. In essence, everyone danced to the tune Luce called. When the mood was upon him, the volatile publisher could become a fearfully intimidating figure, fully the equal of any of the fire-breathing tycoons he idolized. Editors dreaded meetings with him, which they called The Last Judgment or The Rack. Luce unnervingly played devil's advocate, no matter how sound the idea under discussion. He liked a good argument, and he was adept at deploying sarcasm and criticism to reduce an editor to a gibbering idiot. An editor who knuckled under such intimidation when he should have held his ground found his career in jeopardy. Even when he did not hold staff members captive in a meeting, Luce inundated them with memos, one of which explained for the likes of Agee the role of a staff writer in characteristically splenetic tones.

> Fundamentally we don't give a damn how he gets the story— whether it's written out of his head or after months of scholarship. . . . We don't care much how it's written: it could be written sixteen different ways and still be a good *Fortune* story. Furthermore, it can be about almost anything from an essay on the Gold Standard to a description of the method of making tomato juice in Alaska. All we care is that it should be a knockout *Fortune* story.

None of the above helped Agee in his struggle to acquire the knack of writing for the magazine. His best hope was to study the handful of back issues in search of clues and precedents.

All writers, not just Agee, lived in a perpetual state of anxiety around Luce, for the boss could be as obtuse as he was demanding. Macdonald, for one, described his state of mind as that of a child in church with a peashooter at the ready. Yet they tolerated his whims and psychological cruelty because they wanted to hold on to their high-paying jobs and because they found their personal relationships with one another satisfying. The research staff largely consisted of doe-eyed graduates of Seven Sister colleges, ripe for romance and marriage. With one woman assigned to one staff writer for each story, there were ample opportunities to socialize, especially as the teams worked late into the night. Such was the atmosphere of the "booming little capitalist culture peculiar to half a dozen floors of the Chrysler Building," as Macdonald defined the domain.

Although Via was still in Cambridge, Agee was at first too shy and careful to conduct an office romance, but he plunged headlong into friendships with his distinguished if eccentric colleagues. He felt most comfortable with Macdonald, with whom he had been corresponding since Exeter yet scarcely knew. Agee found him to be, in person, a cantankerous, fast-talking young journalist resplendent in brilliantly striped shirts, suspenders, and, in emulation of his hero Trotsky, small round glasses and a goatee. A long cigarette holder clenched firmly between the teeth completed his foppish appearance. He spoke with an amiably guttural twang that harked back not to Yale but to the potato fields of Long Island, where he had grown up. In moments of moral outrage he waved his hands excitedly or wagged a long, cocked finger, and he did not lack for opinions on their employer. He claimed he had taken the job at *Fortune* "strictly from hunger." Luce had hired him in an effort to recruit "the best Yale brains . . . on the current market." If Agee really wanted to be a literary artist, Macdonald implied, he should clear out, or limit his stay to a few short months at most. A real writer, Macdonald said, would let his own grandmother starve before compromising his art.

Like Macdonald, Agee was expected to grind out a five-thousand-word, unsigned article for each issue, but the veteran complained that Luce's despicable capitalist ideology made for shallow writing. It did not occur to the Trotskyite that Communist ideology, as well, could make for stultifying prose. "If the articles in Fortune are written in a sleek, inflated, cheaply melodramatic style . . . the germ of the disease is a commercial philosophy which regards money-making as the prime end of man," he would argue.

"How can you talk that way about the magazine that keeps you from starving?" Luce would reply. "Don't you have any sense of *loyalty?*"

But for all his incessant fault-finding, Macdonald had an appealing vigor, a tangy moral sense that outweighed his crankiness. Macdonald's writing reflected the better part of his nature: taut, clear, and to the point.

Through Macdonald, Agee met a true child of the 1920s, Wilder Hobson, another *Fortune* writer and Macdonald's former roommate. The tall, lean, bespectacled Hobson played a mean trombone and cultivated a fervent admiration for jazz, on which he would write one of the first serious studies. Hobson doted on talented writers—it was he who had helped Macdonald get the *Fortune* job—and instantly took to the Harvard graduate who had so ably parodied *Time.* Possessing a wild and unpredictable writing ability, Hobson seemed poised, like Macdonald, to play a major role in the New York literary scene.

Even more impressive than these two was *Fortune*'s chief writer, Archibald MacLeish, the jewel in Luce's literary crown.

After graduating at the head of his class from Harvard Law School, MacLeish abandoned a promising legal career to write poetry. With his wife, Ada, and two children, he explored Mexico, the Mediterranean, Persia, and Paris, where he fell in with Hemingway, Fitzgerald, Pound, and Gertrude Stein. He lived in poverty and wrote poems in cafés, including the notable "Hamlet of A. MacLeish." Returning to the United States in 1929 and desperate for a job to sustain his family while he completed a long narrative poem about the conquest of Mexico, he approached Henry Luce, who offered, "You can work for *Fortune* as long as you need in any one year to pay your bills and the rest of the time will be yours." MacLeish quickly established himself as the indispensable man at *Fortune* and in his spare time finished the poem, *Conquistador,* which went on to win a Pulitzer Prize.

To Agee, MacLeish furnished living proof that working for Luce did not mean an end to serious writing. Unlike Macdonald, MacLeish believed that working for *Fortune* did a poet a world of good. The magazine gave its writers the opportunity to learn about real life, not merely abstractions. Even the routine had its benefits, imparting discipline and an ability to write under pressure. To set an example, MacLeish directed his researchers to put all pertinent information concerning a given article on file cards. He flipped through the cards to write remarkably clean, error-free copy containing just the balance of fact and fancy Luce required. No one else on the staff, especially not Agee, could match MacLeish's pace. While he left the office each day promptly at five o'clock, they worked late into the night, fussing and revising. In frustration, Macdonald snapped, "The most efficient male in the place is a poet."

Managing Editor Ralph Ingersoll coordinated the efforts of these literary prima donnas. He had come to Luce with impeccable credentials: degrees from the right schools—Hotchkiss and Yale—and a position at *The New Yorker* magazine. Considered by the writers to be even more conservative than the Founder, Ingersoll hid behind a crusty facade and an exotic array of hypochondriacal ailments. He habitually sweated profusely, sneezed through his mustache, and wiped his eyes with a handkerchief. He came to be called "the weeping armpit." However repellent his personality, Ingersoll wisely gave his talented staff free reign in the creation of articles, his sole editorial dictum being "Just put all the material about the same subject in the same place."

Throughout that first summer and fall at *Fortune,* Agee did his level best to please Ingersoll and accommodate himself to the demands of collective journalism. He gravitated to his fellow poet MacLeish, with whom he worked on run-of-the-mill stories about unemployment, housing, streamlining, and machine-made rugs. In contrast to MacLeish's orderly approach to writing articles, Agee worked in fits and starts, amid a clutter of papers and files, focusing all his energies on his tiny, penciled sentences. He endlessly rewrote his copy, developing a fanatical commitment to achieving the proper cadence and precision of language. After as many as thirty drafts, his articles far exceeded their allotted space. MacLeish and the other writers proceeded to slash and simplify Agee's baroque prose until it fit neatly into place. Agee bore no grudge against those who wielded the blue pencil; it was what he expected, all part of the job.

Agee's first months at the magazine coincided with a period of rapid politicization among the other writers. "For about 3 weeks I was working on an employment story," he wrote a friend, "and half the gang turned Red overnight. The preliminary draft was disappointingly much less sore than everybody felt—but I haven't seen the final. I hope to God MacLeish can say what he means: if he does, it'll be one swell story."

The impatience Agee detected in MacLeish soon turned to full-blown disgust at Luce's adulation of wealth. It seemed to MacLeish that Luce had a greater responsibility than simply that of making money, but Luce, philistine that he was, refused to concede the point. In retaliation, MacLeish wrote an angry denunciation of his boss in a long poem called *America Was Promises.*

> *The aristocracy of wealth and talents*
> *Turned its talents into wealth and lost them.*
> *Turned enlightened selfishness to wealth.*
> *Turned self-interest into bank books: balanced them*
> *Bred out: bred to fools.*

Wishing to keep his nose clean, Agee resisted this swing to the left at *Fortune* for the time being. Nearly every point of view, he believed, had its own validity. As for his, he did not yet know what it was.

Despite his constant dread of selling out, Agee found that life at *Fortune* had compensations beyond a paycheck. After settling into the routine there, he resumed his habit of writing late at night, relishing the prospect of solitude in the gigantic, deserted skyscraper. As it swayed gently in a strong wind, the building itself seemed to come to life. He installed a phonograph in the office and proceeded to lose himself in the rapture of music played at full volume. "Something attracts me very much about playing Beethoven's Ninth Symphony with all New York about 600 feet below you, and with that *swell* ode, taking in the whole earth, and with everyone on earth supposedly singing it; all that estranged them and all except joy and the whole common world-love and brotherhood idea forgotten." Although the world was going to rack and ruin, Beethoven's throbbing music stirred Agee's hope for "a love and pity and joy that nearly floors you," and that would overcome the misery he saw below.

At other times the Chrysler Building symbolized the infuriating impersonality of the era, inflicting on Agee a "gruesome sense of not being fit for society: just one of the misfits who moped in the fiftieth story of this chromium tower being dominated by the Machine and feeling more & more like hell and a heel." In this mood he yearned to tear down the oppressive skyscraper brick by brick with his bare hands. He hated feeling that he was only an insignificant cog in Luce's great journalistic machine. His job, once so pleasing to contemplate, now seemed a form of imprisonment. He loathed bureaucratic constraints on his freedom. The mere act of waiting in line to buy a postage stamp sent him into a rage. And he would be damned if he would go through the rigmarole of opening a bank account. Uncashed paychecks littered his office and filled his coat pockets.

Agee's private misery had less to do with the vicissitudes of working for *Fortune* than with the wretched turn his personal life had taken. On arriving in New York, he lived first with his uncle, Hugh Tyler, the mild-mannered portrait painter, but Agee longed to break free of the family's tight little web and to prove he could get along on his own. He found a bleak, unfurnished room in Brooklyn, where he took up a hard bachelor's existence, sleeping on a mattress flung on the floor and cooking rudimentary meals on a tiny stove. Restaurants were out of the question; they were too expensive, and besides, he had no friends with whom to break bread. The joy of independence quickly evaporated in the unremitting summer heat. He was deprived of luxuries he had taken for granted at Harvard: stimulating conversation, a coterie of admirers, an ample supply of fetching young women, even the consolation of playing records in his room. The apartment's electric current was direct, and his machine required alternating. Nor did he have a telephone to call the people he missed most of all—the Saunderses.

In his absence, Via had been sending out the most distressing signals. Frustrated by his reluctance to commit himself irrevocably to her, she displayed symptoms of a minor nervous breakdown. Agee blamed himself for her condition and resolved to marry her —not out of love so much as a sense of obligation. Via, sensing his ambivalence, beat a tactical retreat to Santa Fe, New Mexico, with her friend Mary Louise White for the duration of the summer.

Now it was Agee's turn to play the role of the jilted lover. He avoided favorite pastimes such as movies and concerts, the better to pine away for his lost love. He assured her he took "very little advantage of what the Big City offers in the way of ruination— much less in fact than I did in Cambridge." He hoped his penance would encourage her to take pity on him and visit New York, but she refused the invitation with a curt note signed, "Sincerely, your friend." Stunned, he resorted to a humble entreaty couched in Mountain dialect. "I take this off moment . . . to ax after your health," he coyly wrote, hoping to pluck a heartstring or two, but Via remained in self-imposed exile.

Alone, Agee wrestled endlessly with the marital dilemma. All his instincts rebelled against marriage, yet his conscience persistently prompted him to take the responsible course. Should they wed, he feared he would not be able to remain faithful and consequently would bring her pain. In the midst of this turmoil, his last weapon against despair, poetry, failed him. No verse could contain the intensity of his feelings. He concluded that "poetry is the product of adolescence" and "likely to dry up" with maturity.

He hit bottom in August, as he grimly fought to resist the temptation—and, he knew, sin—of suicide. In the absence of trusted friends with whom he might talk and drink away his problems, he tried to fathom his pain in a letter to Father Flye, written on Sunday evening, August 14.

> I've been used to bad spells of despondency always, but this is something else again; it seems to be a rapid settling into despair of everything I want and everything about myself. If I am, as I seem to be, dying on my feet mentally and spiritually, and can do nothing about it, I'd prefer not to know I was dying. . . . I've felt like suicide for weeks now—and not just fooling with the idea, but feeling seriously on the edge of it. . . . I know I should be able to fight my way out of this, and I hate and fear suicide, but I don't have a thought that isn't pain and despair of one sort or another. . . . I simply am not capable of being the kind of person, doing the kinds of things, I want to be. And I haven't enough good in me to realize the filthiness of this discontent, and to reconcile myself to it. I would certainly prefer death to reconciling myself.

Under stress, Agee tended to lose sight of his immediate problems —in this case the shock of a new job and the question of whether or not to marry Via—and give way completely to feelings of panic and despair. Abroad in the city, he found external confirmation of his internal misery. The slack faces of subway riders, the heat-tormented pedestrians, the unearthly silence of the city on Sunday —everything called to mind an "*epidemic* of despair and weariness" equal to the Great Plague of the Middle Ages. The only difference was that the modern illness was spiritual rather than physical.

Alarmed by this dire report, Father Flye responded immediately with words of consolation. Agee took heart; he was not alone in the world after all. Four days later he claimed to be "pretty well out of the area of suicidal thoughts," and revitalized enough to make a joke at his own expense. "I can promise you I was never delighted with the idea," he told Father Flye. He even recovered sufficient presence of mind to analyze the causes behind his suicidal impulse: "The vicious thing which brings you nearest it . . . is self hatred, as far as I'm concerned." He vaguely realized how angry he was at Via for deserting him at this crucial time in his life, and he blamed her woefully misguided actions on "the *foul* results of feminism."

For all his empathy with women, Agee disdained feminism, a philosophy that to his way of thinking precluded romantic love. He adopted an attitude of pity toward women like Via who were "trying to live an uneasy egocentricity they can't sustain, unable to reconcile it with love, which they could, and ruined in love by the grinding of old conventions to which they've been trained, against new conventions which they honestly feel compelled to live by: wanting marriage and avoiding it." Women caught in this quandary, he observed, wound up "so hurt and dulled by the fractures and foulnesses of the love they experience that they lose all capacity for the sort they've always wanted." In essence, a woman's place was with her man.

Agee found Via's standoffishness, whether prompted by feminism or not, unusually and irrationally painful. In fact, her attitude recalled his mother's rejection of him as a young child and emerging man. Had he but paused to reflect, he would have noticed disturbing parallels between the two women. Both came from prosperous families with wide-ranging cultural interests and more than a touch of snobbery; both resented their domineering mothers. The Saunderses were, in reality, what the Tylers aspired to be—talented and well connected. And by marrying Via he would at last possess what had always eluded him. But Via stayed away, leaving him to suffer in isolation.

In the fall, Agee moved to a larger and more comfortable apartment in Brooklyn, equipped with such luxuries as alternating current, an icebox, and a telephone. There he completed a story of which nothing survives beyond its striking title, "Let Us Now Praise Famous Men"; dabbled with his failed poetic epic "John Carter"; and wondered whether he would be asked to stay on at *Fortune* after his three-month trial period came to an end. The prospect of sudden freedom set him daydreaming. "I expect I would live in France," he wrote to Robert Fitzgerald, "in some town both cheap and within reach of Paris." The magazine's offer to renew his contract cut short any such plans. If he expected Via ever to marry him, he needed to demonstrate his ability to hold a steady job.

With his career plans settled for the moment, he renewed his appeals to Via to visit, to "see a glimpse of goodness" in his "cold gray eyes." He promised he would reform his ways, curb his self-destructive habits. No more drinking, swearing, and staying up all night. He told Father Flye of "trying as never before to understand" his "hideous trait of moodiness and worse," especially as it affected Via.

> It's the sort of intangible, slippery thing that I guess is worst in the world for two faintly nervous people to cope with; and when it's out of hand, neither of us has an easy time. I'm sometimes really forced to believe I have a dirty and unconquerable vein of melancholia in me. . . . I know the most important faculty to develop is one for hard, continuous and varied work and living; but the difference between knowing this and doing anything consistent about it is often abysmal. Along with the melancholia, or a part of it, is rotten inertia and apathy and disgust with myself.

And then came word from Santa Fe that Via would move to New York in October.

The two young lovers fell contentedly into each other's arms. Armed with a formidable array of family contacts, Via found an apartment and part-time employment with a magazine called *Symposium.* She and Agee decided all at once to marry and set a date in January. In celebration of the forthcoming alliance they made a pilgrimage to Clinton, where Agee reveled in renewed relations with the Saunderses. After the visit he wrote to Louise, "When I'm with your family, peace and clarity of mind take me." His entire life, suddenly illuminated with the glow of romantic love, wore a benign and pleasing aspect. Thumbing through a lavish set of books Louise gave him for his twenty-third birthday in November, he took endless delight in the love of the happiest family he had ever known. So simple a thing as a sunset now struck him as wondrous to behold from his office in the Chrysler Building: "A very beautiful and not unusual thing is going on outside my window, that is, the very definite *edge* of darkness you see from this height. It isn't real darkness—but a heavy belt of smoke or mist that lies straight across the lower end of the island; the tallest buildings there just come above it. It has been gathering all afternoon, and within the last 15 minutes has turned from color to black—or dark blue—the streets are thoroughly dark; . . . and everything below . . . looks as if it were under water." In renewing his relationship with Via, he recovered his muse.

The imminent prospect of marriage filled Agee with a sense of seriousness and high purpose. He found himself "no more subject to high feelings, gaiety, good cheer, or sustained ecstasy than you'd be in becoming a priest or in writing a poem," he explained to Father Flye. Marriage was a "definitely Serious Estate. My own misfortune is that Seriousness means Gloom to me." Owing to these doubts about his ability to live up to his ideal of what a husband should be, Agee came to regard his engagement as a time for self-improvement, and he set Louise up as a judge of his behavior. "I don't think I'll ever be capable of living as beautifully as you do," he admitted to her, "but I can come a lot nearer to it than I am."

Once the idea of self-improvement took hold, there was nothing in the world he would not to do to please his fiancée. "More than anything on earth I want to be able to give Via a life somewhere really worthy of what she deserves," he proclaimed. "This means an unthinkable amount of care, thought, vigilance on my part." But he remained his own worst enemy, still "liable to long *depressions*" and an "almost total loss of imagination and buoyancy and vitality." It horrified him to see how this mood affected Via, the way it dragged her into the mire with him. He had no concrete method of combating depression, only a fierce resolve to "beat down such states of mind" as best he could. In an extreme moment he made a declaration that could only give Louise pause. "I'd give my death for her," he wrote of Via, "but giving my *life*—and making it the sort of life it should be—to her, is a less easy matter." It seemed he was prepared to make the ultimate sacrifice for Via's sake: "If there were any conceivable reason for it and good to be gained by it, I would get up from this desk and [jump] out the window and present her with a willing death in a few seconds."

This rage to please was simultaneously serious, pathetic, and foolish; but mothers, Agee suspected, were demanding, unforgiving creatures, accustomed to imposing impossibly high standards on unruly men. The Saunderses, he proclaimed, "are all the strongest incentives I've ever had to take myself in hand—and the best examples of what I wish to be." As a result of his insecurity about his fitness for marriage, he insisted that he and Via would have no children—at least not during the first years of the marriage. Much later Via would recall, "I never saw us as grandparents." They saw themselves as husband and wife only with considerable difficulty.

While Agee sought to improve his character, the Saunderses proceeded with arrangements for the wedding. They sent invitations, selected clothes suitable to the occasion, and debated what music would be played after the ceremony. The wedding took place on Saturday afternoon, January 28, 1933, in an Episcopal church in Utica, New York, not far from the Saunders' home. At the last minute, Via expressed the wish to convert to Anglo-Catholicism to strengthen the bond with her new husband; but Agee, perennially insecure with orthodoxies, asked her to wait until she had examined her feelings on the matter more thoroughly, "rather than simply marrying into the church." They selected a thoroughly traditional Episcopalian ceremony for the wedding. Most of Agee's college friends were in attendance, including Robert Saudek and Brick Frohock, who, shortly before the great event, discovered matching holes in the groom's shoes and socks. When Agee knelt, the holes were certain to be visible to all and sundry. Thinking quickly, Frohock inked them over with a fountain pen, and the last obstacle to marriage was removed.

Before the hushed, watchful throng, the bride and groom made their separate journeys to the altar, where they exchanged their solemn vows. In the semi-obscurity of the cold winter light filtering in through the church's windows, they made an unusual, slightly mismatched couple. Via's red hair glinted softly, and in her wedding dress she did not look six years older than the man she was marrying. For once Agee's hair was neatly cut and combed, and his dark suit fit his lean frame. As his blue eyes took in the sight of the unfamiliar clergyman presiding over the ceremony, the banks of flowers, and religious artifacts, he doubtless felt a heavier sense of responsibility than he had ever known. His wedding day was also a day of reckoning, a chance for him to redeem the hours he had squandered. "Till death do us part": The phrase that clinched their vow had just the morbid ring he found so reassuring. Via had never looked lovelier, and still he wondered if she managed to find a trace of goodness in him, as he had once implored.

Leaving the altar, he felt only a mild unsteadiness in his legs. He had acquitted himself well enough, he supposed. Now that he was married, he awaited some change to come over him, some new way of looking at the world, but to his mild surprise, even disappointment, he continued to feel very much himself. He glanced at Via; she looked herself as well. He would have to wait to see the changes marriage would bring to them over the years. In the meantime, the only thing that was certain was that the Saunderses had acquired a brilliant, unstable son-in-law and the Wrights a daughter-in-law considerably above their social station. Although Laura Wright found much to criticize about her son, she could not seriously fault his choice of a wife.

After the oddly subdued ceremony, the wedding party repaired to the Saunders' home, where they celebrated with another one of Dr. Saunders' informal concerts. As it happened, one of the guests was a talented young violist with lovely dark hair and striking green eyes. The daughter of a Utica jeweler, she was one of Dr. Saunders' newest musical protégées. As soon as she set eyes on the bridegroom, she was taken with his good looks and gentle manner, but she supposed that in the midst of his excitement he hardly knew she was alive. Her name was Alma Mailman.

7

VOYAGE

Times were hard. The newlyweds had no thought of a honeymoon. Immediately after the wedding the couple took up residence in a modest apartment Agee had found several weeks earlier at 38 Perry Street in Greenwich Village. Their new home consisted of two large, dark, basement rooms, a kitchen, and a back porch highlighted by a tall, wan ailanthus tree, one of the few varieties hardy enough to survive in the city.

Within weeks Agee was assailed by doubts about the wisdom of marrying Via. Much as he admired the Saunderses, his relations with his new wife lacked the spark of passion. They had an arrangement, not a romance. He went to work each morning and came home in the evening in a daze, wondering how he, the flaming

Romantic, had come to live in such mild, bourgeois respectability. Someone else, it seemed, was writing his life story for him; he walked through the part, reading his lines from an utterly conventional script.

This sense of uneasy compromise found its way into one of his most telling poems, written early in the spring of 1933. "Now it is competent, our common heart," he began, knowing how alien a "common" and "competent" heart was to his passionate nature. Still, he held out hope that he and Via would neutralize one another's faults.

> *And we two fragments formed to fit entire*
> *And we two whom the long night held apart*
> *Meet in the high wealth of the morning's fire:*
> *With all predictions cancelled in the fact.*
> *And our rich insufficience satisfied.*

No matter how serene the present, he could not be so dishonest with himself as to believe the mood would last. Because love was the stuff of life, and life inherently unstable, the complacency of today would inevitably lead to chaos.

> *I meditate those things our life has lacked;*
> *Some things our love must be denied.*
> *I am most envious of those careless years*
> *When full of care we knew each other not*
> *And green false love, false happiness, false tears,*
> *Ripened this whole heart, which must wholly rot;*
> *The dreamful heart that woke toward praise of day*
> *Dreams now of dawn and darkly wastes away.*

So taken was Agee by the sentiments expressed in this poem that he immediately committed it to memory, as if it were a prayer.

The poem mingled with actual prayers in his thoughts. As part of their effort to lead a stable existence, the Agees worshiped regularly at nearby St. Luke's Chapel, on Hudson Street, where they took communion and went to the confessional booth. Not since his early years at Harvard had he stood in the dark, whispering his sins. After one such episode Agee snatched a sheet of the church's stationery, on which he wrote a fair copy of the poem and mailed it to Louise Saunders, heedless of the impact its contents might have on her, but his action had no untoward consequences. She shared his enthusiasm for the poem and memorized it herself.

In addition to regular attendance at church, the Agees made a conscientious effort to reestablish relationships with friends they had neglected during the six tumultuous months before their marriage. Such friends as Robert Saudek, Robert Fitzgerald, and Irvine Upham soon found themselves wandering down to Perry Street to spend an evening with Via and Jim, talking and drinking under the skimpy leaves of the ailanthus tree. As the evening wore on, they went indoors to listen to Agee pound out sonatas by Brahms on the battered upright piano and, when the hour was late, read Shakespeare aloud. At moments like these, Fitzgerald was swept by the conviction that he shared with Agee "a vocation and would pursue it, come what might." Saudek, on the other hand, found evidence of barely concealed strife between the newlyweds. The apartment was always a mess. It was apparent that neither Via nor her husband knew how to keep a decent-looking home. They used orange crates as furniture and washed dishes only when absolutely necessary. Agee dressed even more carelessly than he had at Harvard: one pair of cracked shoes year-round; dark, baggy suits from Macy's; and a hat several sizes too small.

In the wee hours, after the guests had left and Via had gone to bed, he skirmished with his own writing. Too tired to meet the challenge of poetry, he had a go at a book of short stories because, he declared, "I'm so tied up with symbols and half-abstractions and many issues about poetry that it is very hard for me to see people as people, full of vitality and of the ardor of their own truth." At this delicate stage, MacLeish intervened with a proposition. If Agee would collect the best poems he had written over the years, MacLeish would see what he could do about getting them published. In particular, he would talk to his friend and fellow poet Stephen Vincent Benét, who headed the prestigious Yale Younger Poets series of publications. Slowly and carefully, Agee undertook the arduous task of reassessing eight years of poetic outpourings in light of their suitability for Yale. But, MacLeish warned, it would be fatal to include that infernal *John Carter*.

Heedless, Agee took one last fling at this epic of narcissism, only to recoil in stupefaction before its unmanageable dimensions. On June 21 he wrote to Louise Saunders:

> I know there is a character to be made who embodies . . . Don Quixote, Hamlet, Falstaff, Gulliver: who has also a strong dash of Myshkin and of Stavrogin: . . . he can be all these in one coherent person: can shift, without a squawking of gears, into the lanes of conduct they represent, and do so without breaking character: he will be beautiful and profound and innocent, earnest and fiendish, ridiculous: capable of tragic, comic, satirical, all kinds of handling and adventures. . . . I can feel this person to a certain extent but God knows not fully: he's of course John Carter, the hero of the poem: but with such a character, what are you to do for drink? What other characters can mean anything in the poem? . . . There's something very wrong about the straining and self-consciousness: but something very necessary, to me, anyway. The best you may ever become is what you are good enough to become, according to your own drives and characteristics: and if one of my characteristics is to entangle myself in problems too big for me and in false hopes, I may as well go right on entangling. I suspect one thing: one of the sustaining characteristics of genius must be an absolute obstinacy. . . . I don't give a damn whether I'm a genius or not: but I do want to write great poetry: I can't possibly content my mind with "good" poetry (which God knows is probably above me): and that makes the whole question of some interest to me. I wish I would stop wasting energy and time on myself and on thinking, and spend it on actual writing. I must get to work. Much love, to you and to all of you,
>
> Jim

Don Quixote, Hamlet, Falstaff, Gulliver, Myshkin—no wonder Agee suffered writer's block. Ten poets could not have accomplished the task he set for himself.

Though all the signs indicated *John Carter* was doomed, Agee could not let it go. He persisted in seeing the poem as his chance at greatness. If he could only force himself to complete the work, he would join the ranks of the immortals; like Byron he would awake to find himself famous. The success MacLeish enjoyed with his narrative poem *Conquistador* spurred Agee on. He wrote in the grip of an obsession; but was not obsessiveness an artist's privilege? While he recognized he had lost control of *John Carter,* its very excessiveness justified continued labor on it. Agee persisted in the face of certain failure because to do otherwise would be to compromise, and working at *Fortune* was compromise enough.

In the face of these difficulties, Louise Saunders valiantly stood by her son-in-law, no matter how improbable his ambitions. A former English professor, she ventured to make technical suggestions for *John Carter.* They batted around metrical patterns and rhyme schemes, but such refinements failed to solve Agee's creative problems.

To make matters worse, he fell under the spell of Joyce's *Ulysses* in the summer of 1933. Normally a writer's discovery of Joyce's verbal pyrotechnics is cause for celebration, adoration, wonder. But in Agee's case the novel's all-encompassing vision aggravated his tendency to inflate *John Carter* beyond reason. "Joyce I think sees all sides and presents them more consistently, clearly, and simultaneously than even Shakspere," he wrote on August 3, "yet even with Joyce there's a feeling of rolling chords rather than playing them vertical with all 10 fingers; and Joyce makes a brave sacrifice of pure and definitive utterance." Despite these reservations, Joyce's general excellence made Agee want to "spit on every word" of *John Carter.*

The encounter with *Ulysses* sapped Agee's confidence, and by the end of August he shelved the epic poem for good. In a mood of quiet contrition, he informed Robert Fitzgerald, who had just graduated from Harvard, that *John Carter* had become "too long, too feeble and oblique, and otherwise not at all the poem I'd like to make it." He ceased to daydream about the glorious reception it would have or even to speak of it. With a heavy heart he assembled his other, shorter poems and gave them to MacLeish to submit to Yale.

Agee's abandonment of *John Carter* led to a renewal of interest in his work at *Fortune.* In this arena, at least, he knew the boundaries and rewards. Several months earlier, Ingersoll had assigned Agee to a story the editor thought would be a natural: a thorough consideration of the Tennessee Valley Authority, one of the New Deal's more successful attempts to revive the stagnating economy. The plum assignment gave Agee a chance to demonstrate the range of journalistic skills he had painstakingly acquired in the course of churning out journeyman stories on topics as diverse as butter, cockfights, and quinine. He initially welcomed the assignment as an opportunity to revisit the state he had not seen since 1925, but once the broad scope of the piece became clear, he feared it would make him sorry he was "ever born in Tennessee at all."

In September he spent a week in Tennessee, surveying the projects and interviewing the stalwart mountain folk he had always admired. He wanted to linger, but time was short, and he was under constant pressure to get back to New York and grind out copy. But the excursion, brief as it was, revived the sights and sounds of his earliest years, sensations that had seeped into the deepest levels of his consciousness. He again listened to the soft accents of his boyhood, smelled the fragrance of forgotten fields, and looked on the changeless Appalachian Mountains. With a mild shock he recognized the inner continuity of his life. For all his fancy Northern education and acquired tastes, he remained a son of Tennessee, more at home on its red soil than on Manhattan's asphalt. Like the mythical giant Antaeus, he had roamed the face of the earth, losing strength with every step, and able to regain it only by setting foot on his native soil. Although he had changed in superficial but significant ways, the Tennessee landscape was precisely as he remembered it, a dream come to life.

On his return to New York, Agee immediately began work on the article. He gave his lyrical impulse free reign; reams of "rich, beautiful prose" flowed from his sharp little pencil. He paid lip service to the facts and sociological angles he was constrained to present and put his heart into lavish descriptions of what he had seen in Tennessee. Rivers, in particular, inspired a champion sentence.

> Near Knoxville the streams still fresh from mountains are linked and thence the master stream spreads the valley most richly southward, swims past Chattanooga and bends down into Alabama to roar like blown smoke through the floodgates of Wilson Dam, to slide becalmed along the crop-cleansed fields of Shiloh, to march due north across the high diminished plains of Tennessee and through Kentucky spreading marshes toward the valley's end where finally, at the toes of Paducah,

in one wide glassy golden swarm the water stoops forward and continuously dies into the Ohio.

A sentence this complex, while seeming to flow in one long breath, actually required an afternoon or so to construct. In terms of his reputation around *Fortune,* the effort was well spent, for the sweet rhetoric brought sighs of pleasure from his co-workers. For once, Ingersoll and MacLeish allowed his words to stand more or less as he had written them. Only Agee could devise such sentences; only *Fortune* would print them.

It was Agee's perverse luck that the success of "The Project Is Important," as the story was titled in the magazine's October issue, threatened to nudge him away from his primary goals as a writer. Agee's fondness for purple prose so alarmed Luce that he offered to send Agee to Harvard Business School at *Fortune*'s expense. There, Luce explained, Agee would acquire a solid grounding in business and learn what really mattered in life. The startled young writer declined the offer as gracefully as possible. It was one thing to write about business, another to *be* in business. He suspected Luce's offer, so generous on the surface, was calculated to break his spirit.

Taking his cue from Luce, Ingersoll resolved to assign Agee more conventional pieces. "He will feed me business stories thick and fast," Agee lamented. Still, he would "much rather succeed than fail [at] this job before I quit it." He dreaded the thought that Luce and Ingersoll might consider him inadequate, as his father had when the young Agee refused to box. Ingersoll swiftly assigned Agee to the dullest subject imaginable: steel rails. Truth and beauty, farewell. The writer had no choice but to comply, "But Lord knows with misgivings!" First he had shackled himself in a conventional marriage; now they had him writing about steel rails. "I feel the well-known prison walls distinctly thickening," he complained, yet he had to hold on to this job in order to support Via. "If I had as much confidence about writing as I have intention, everything might be much easier. But my confidence varies and is nil much of the time."

To Macdonald's way of thinking, Luce ordered Ingersoll to put Agee on the thankless steel rail story out of a puritanical notion that it was "immoral that a writer should do only what he was best at." Luce, in fact, decided to edit the story himself. Agee gave steel rails the TVA treatment, all description and obfuscation. The Founder and the red-hot young writer sat down together to discuss the article, while Macdonald listened near the door. "Now, Jim, don't you see . . . ?" he heard Luce repeat in an effort to channel Agee's wrongheaded enthusiasm. But Agee would not be dissuaded from his original approach. Eventually Luce relented and reassigned the piece to the cooler-headed Macdonald, who gave it the required workmanlike treatment. "The trouble with Agee as a journalist," Macdonald wrote of the incident, "was that he couldn't be just workmanlike, he had to give it everything he had, which was not good for him."

In the wake of the confrontation, Agee displayed a new callousness about *Fortune*. When Fitzgerald asked for a chance at a job on the magazine, Agee responded with a decidedly jaded description of what to expect at work: "It varies with me from a sort of hard, masochistic liking to direct nausea at the sight of this symbol $, and this % and this *biggest* and this some blank—billion. . . . But in the long run I suspect the fault, dear Fortune, is in me: that I hate any job on earth, as a job and hindrance and semi-suicide." Agee's recommendation on his friend's behalf did not succeed, and after much looking, Fitzgerald landed a job at the *Herald Tribune*.

They met regularly for lunch, Agee inevitably late, loping along the street in his "fast, loose, long-legged walk, springy on the balls of his feet, with his open overcoat flapping." Over roast beef sandwiches and beer, Fitzgerald would talk of his struggle to reconcile poetry with Catholicism. To his way of thinking, journalism was not a satisfactory compromise, especially the sort of "Ivy League journalistic delving into other people's lives" in which Agee participated. That activity was merely an escape from the necessity of accomplishing something either as an artist or as a man of action.

But Agee did not see matters that way. Virtually an orphan since the age of six, he depended on *Fortune* for the emotional sustenance that others found in their families. He drew no boundary between the office and his personal life; one flowed imperceptibly into the other. Time Inc. was his home, his school, his monastery. In private, Fitzgerald was appalled at how dependent Agee had become on the organization he had once so boldly parodied.

At the same time, Agee bewailed Fitzgerald's reluctance to free himself from the tentacles of the Church.

But just when it seemed that Agee had compromised himself out of writing altogether, he received encouraging news about his poetry. From Yale came word that Benét had selected Agee's poems from the forty-two collections under consideration for the 1934 award. At the time, the Yale Younger Poets series enjoyed a reputation for launching serious, gifted poets on long, productive careers. Although none of the winners had, as yet, entered the first rank of American poets, the offer to publish under the auspices of the Yale University Press was an undoubted accolade and certification of competence. Benét himself remarked that Agee's work demonstrated "extraordinary promise," and, sensing an opportunity for a splash of publicity, invited MacLeish to write an introduction for the forthcoming volume, a request with which MacLeish happily complied. Everyone but the author, it seemed, was convinced of the collection's merit.

In his introductory essay, MacLeish warned that Agee's brand of poetry would not excite either traditional or radical camps because this poet refused to assume a "Position." Rather, he displayed a "deep love of the land."

> Equally obviously he has a considerable contempt for the dying civilization in which he has spent twenty-four years. By both he comes obviously. He spent his boyhood, with his fair share of the disadvantages so generously bestowed by the not-quite-existing order, in and about the Cumberland Mountains, and some of his vacation time during his Harvard years he spent as a harvest stiff in the Kansas and Nebraska wheat fields.

MacLeish went on to extol a "poetic gift which no amount of application can purchase and which no amount of ingenuity can fake." Even if the poems were not quite finished masterpieces, they demonstrated that Agee was indeed capable of enduring work.

The introduction was quite a send-off, reminding students of American literature of Emerson's effusive greeting of Whitman's *Leaves of Grass*. It appeared that MacLeish wished to establish a similar line of succession. Even as he praised Agee's poetry, however, he propounded theories of his own. He had been coming under fire lately for refusing to declare himself an adherent of socialism. Critics considered his insistence on art for art's sake dangerously decadent and irresponsible; the true purpose of art, of course, was to advance the class struggle.

MacLeish answered his critics, who were now Agee's as well, in a poem called "Invocation to the Social Muse." In it he denounced socialism as a fad. "There is nothing worse for our trade than to be in style," he wrote. "He that goes naked goes further at last." To MacLeish, Agee was that naked man: a poet obviously sensitive to suffering but possessed of enough dedication to enduring values to resist the siren song of politics. Agee's selection of poems, made with MacLeish's advice and consent, amounted to a defense of that point of view. "Ann Garner," "Epithalamium," and numerous sonnets all bore witness to a world in which language, not socialism, reigned supreme.

At the same time, there were a number of surprises embedded in this framework of familiar poems. Agee included an ambitious suite of twenty-five new sonnets dwelling on his reservations about marriage. In them, he tried to uncover a link between his present discontent and troubled family history. In a representative sonnet, he gave full vent to his dissatisfaction with Via.

> Forbear, forbear to look at me with joy.
> I would not do you hurt who will no harm,
> But that sure smile I surely shall destroy—
> Its covert meaning and its patent charm.
> Awakened to our love's surprising hell,
> Your dream struck sleep befits it hardly well.

Obscurely, he sensed a connection between the confinement he felt in marriage and long-suppressed sorrow over his mother's unhappy lot in life.

> Not of good will my mother's flesh was wrought,
> Whose parents sowed in joy, and garnered care:
> The sullen harvest sullen winter brought
> Upon their time, outlasting their despair.

He turned his attention next to his father, quoting with bitter irony the epithet his mother chose for Jay Agee's tombstone.

> *Deep of a young girl's April strength his own*
> *My father's drank, and draughted her to age:*
> *Who in his strength met death and was outdone*
> *Of high and hopeless dreams, and grief, and rage.*

The untitled sonnet presented nothing less than a capsule history of a family's misfortunes. But reviving these painful memories brought the poet no solace. Sensitized to the enormity of the tragedy, Agee considered himself destined to form but another sad link in a desolate "chain of flesh."

Only in the collection's final poem did he attempt a muted affirmation, yet so important was this statement to him that he named the entire volume after it: "Permit Me Voyage." This time he addressed the reader directly. "My heart and mind discharted lie," he declared; "God is ruined." His sole salvation lay in love, both spiritual and erotic. Therefore, he pleaded, "Permit me voyage, Love, into your hands."

To the author's small circle of friends the overall tenor of the poems, so tame and well-mannered, bore scant resemblance to the firebrand they knew. But they were all astonished and gratified by Agee's ferocious "Dedication," a prose poem of such force that it lingered in the mind long after the poems themselves had faded. For the first time, Agee managed to encompass his extravagant personality in print. In rolling biblical cadences he dedicated the volume to "those who in all time have sought truth and who have told it in their art or in their living." His honor roll of humanity included Christ, Mozart, Dante, "Shakspere," and of course Beethoven. He proceeded to list the nameless dead by category, "those unremembered who have died in no glory," "those who died in violence suddenly," sinners, virgins, and "those who have labored in the earth."

Thoughts of the unmemorialized dead inevitably led to his own family, especially his "brave father" and his great-aunt Jessie. Via, Emma, and even old Erskine Wright found their way into the "Dedication," as did Father Flye, Dorothy Carr, Theodore Spencer, the Saunderses—all the principal figures in his life.

Agee's reach extended beyond mere mortals. He dedicated poems to the land and the "guts," and to the "flexing heart" of the English language. He went on to offer a catalogue of personal friends and contemporary heroes, as if he were on the same level of intimacy with each: Joyce, Chaplin, MacLeish, I. A. Richards, Picasso, B. F. Skinner, Yehudi Menuhin, and Irvine Upham.

There was no end to the debts he wanted to express, especially to the millions of unheard American voices.

> ... farmers and workers and wandering men and builders and clerks and legislators and priests and doctors and scientists and governors . . . : in cities amassed, and on wide water, and lonesome in the dark, and dark under the earth, and laboring in the land, and in materials, and in the flesh, and in the mind, and in the heart . . . to all those who love and must die and to those whom they breed to follow them in the earth to endure and breed and die: to the earth itself in its loveliness . . .

Having found his tongue at last, one affirmation lead inevitably to another. The "Dedication" came to resemble a prayer, part of the Anglo-Catholic liturgy, as he addressed the "Holy, Catholic, and Apostolic Church and . . . the reach of its green boughs upon the sky through Godhead into God, and to its branches withering and withered and fallen away."

> O God, hear us.
> O God, spare us.
> O God, have mercy upon us.

Here was a "Dedication" to end all dedications. Compared with its extravagance and confidence, the poems seemed merely footnotes or illustrations for this manifesto of the unity of all things under God.

Heart in mouth, Agee lobbied hard on behalf of the collection when it was published in the summer of 1934. He sent copies accompanied by uneasy notes to the prominent Southern poet Allen Tate ("Why I am . . . writing this note I don't exactly know") and to Harvard professor John Livingston Lowes ("Though I have badly failed and know it, I have tried and am trying to write real poetry."). Despite Agee's and MacLeish's best efforts, the all-important reviews were few and far-between. The collection's lack of a "Position," as MacLeish had pointed out, was not calculated to attract the critics' attention, but early the following year a thorough and favorable assessment finally appeared, thanks to his old friend and schoolmate Lincoln Kirstein. Writing in *The New Republic* of February 27, 1935, Kirstein observed that Agee's "readings in seventeenth-century prose and eighteenth-century verse had been wholly absorbed into his own unique gifts" and went on to laud the impassioned "Dedication" as a "hymn of praise, compassion, and a curse of genuine proportions."

The two-dollar volume sold only six hundred copies, but publication brought other, less tangible rewards. The anthologist Louis Untermeyer wrote to request poems for his *Modern American Poetry,* published the following year by Harcourt, Brace. In it, Agee was represented by no less than four works—an impressive number for a newcomer—and in the biographical note listed his "deepest namable interests" as music, words, the present, the future, and documentary film; poetry per se did not show up. And Agee's contributions to the anthology, hastily assembled satires of the New Deal, lacked the polish of his poems in *Permit Me Voyage.* His enthusiasm for verse was rapidly waning, and not even the prospect of publication could revive it.

Around those he knew, Agee adopted an attitude of indifference toward the publication of his first book. To Louise Saunders he complained, "I hate promise (Promise is better than none but shd be best kept to yourself) and in a lot of ways I don't like publishing anyway or the idea of it at any time." He quickly gave away all copies of the book in his possession, anything to get the slim volume of verse out of his sight. Life mattered more than poetry; he preferred living out his feelings to fixing them on paper, as if they were so many butterflies. In fact, the more he brooded on the book, the more he came to loathe himself for having become just the sort of minor poet he had promised himself he would never be. The mediocrity of *Permit Me Voyage* went hand in hand with his stultifying marriage. Like his hero Blake, he mourned the marriage hearse and suspected he would never write a major work until he achieved absolute liberty.

Feeling trapped, he lapsed into another period of acute depression. He could not bring himself to leave the "gentle, sensitive, and complicated" Via, to betray all that he held dear about the Saunderses, and yet he found himself "in most possible kinds of pain, mental and spiritual." His thoughts ran rampant, "like wild beasts of assorted sizes and ferocities, not devouring each other but in the process tearing the zoo to parts." He supposed he might find relief in self-discipline, but "without scrupulousness I am damned forever."

In this dazed state of mind he inched ever closer to suicide, he wrote Father Flye, "as you might lean out over the edge of a high building, as far as you could and keep from falling but with no special or constant desire to fall." This was no mere figure of speech. On entering Agee's office one day in October, Wilder Hobson was astonished to see his colleague's "hands clinging to the outside window sill." Hovering six hundred feet above the sidewalk, Agee contemplated with eerie calmness the tiny pedestrians scurrying beneath his feet, his mind in a state of "apathy, or a sort of leady, heavy silt that, always by nature a part of my blood, becomes thicker and thicker." All he need do was let go and he would end it forever: the unendurable guilt, the frustrations of trying to become a major writer, the mockery *Fortune* and marriage made of his ideals. A terrified Hobson cowered behind a door while Agee considered the alternatives. Monks might don the hair shirt; Agee chose to dangle from a fiftieth-floor window. As a suicide, he was well aware, he risked being damned to eternal hell. He had no choice but to climb back inside and return to his desk, where Hobson found him "strangely calm." Shortly after, Agee promised Father Flye, "I shall not suicide."

Seeking safer avenues of escape than divorce or suicide, Agee asked Father Flye about the possibility of teaching at St. Andrew's. He felt "attracted to teaching almost enough to dread it," he explained, and hoped that the relatively low-key work would lessen the chances of his suffering a nervous breakdown. But within weeks he underwent a change of heart; now the thought of teaching struck him as a "terrible idea." Only "floating on blood money"—living off his family—could be worse. He resolved to make the best of his bad situation.

Ingersoll unwittingly came to the rescue with an assignment

that promised to divert the beleaguered young man from his troubles. The managing editor wanted a study of the "Great American Roadside," a consideration of the folkways of America's highways and byways. As a former bum and bindlestiff, Agee was delighted with the project and in his imagination set off on a cross-country motor tour. With the flimsy excuse of describing a "$3,000,000,000 industry," he evoked "the welcome taste of a Bar B-Q sandwich in mid-afternoon, the oddly excellent feel of a weak-springed bed in a clapboard transient shack, and the early start in the cold bright lonesome air . . . and the day's first hitchhiker brushing the damp hay out of his shirt."

The sweet reminiscences renewed Agee's craving for open spaces and the freedom to roam at will, down among the masses and as far as possible from the Chrysler Building's vertiginous heights. By degrees he perceived larger possibilities in such experiences. "Very much like the subject and seriously think maybe I want to try to expand it into a book," he reported to Louise Saunders. With that idea in mind, he went on to write about the severe drought afflicting the Midwest and aggravating the effects of the Depression on farmers. The specter of poverty moved him even more deeply than the exhilaration of travel. In his mind's eye he imagined a "piteous meagre sweat in the air, the earth baked stiff and steaming."

The resulting article, published in October, featured, to his dismay, photographs by Margaret Bourke-White, a rapidly rising young photojournalist whom Luce had recently discovered. Agee perceived strong affinities between his own highly descriptive, impressionistic manner of writing and the art of photography; both were impersonal, immediate, and suggestive. At the same time, he harbored doubts about the propriety of popularizing the plight of the poor. It seemed downright unethical for the Margaret Bourke-Whites of the world to dip into the lives of the poor only long enough to capture a fleeting impression of their misery on film. Surely her photographs represented the height of liberal folly, as Agee repeatedly pointed out. He yearned to put aside conventional journalistic objectivity in favor of becoming at one with the poor and oppressed, to live as they did, eat their food, and sleep in their beds. Empathy was all. Now that he had a definite theme in mind —the suffering of the poor in times of economic hardship—he conscientiously awaited an opportunity to give it the full treatment it deserved.

Ingersoll, however, had other ideas in mind. He busied Agee with mind-numbing assignments on illuminated manuscripts, glass, and the renovation of Colonial Williamsburg. Grimly accomplishing each task, Agee attempted to inject subversive undertones into the articles, only to find the redeeming touches edited out of the final copy. Williamsburg, for example, he dismissed as so much "nationalist propaganda" and a symptom of the country's decline into senility, but that was not at all the angle Ingersoll wanted.

Six months of this routine, from December 1934 to mid-1935, frayed Agee's nerves to the breaking point. Each day he was confronted with the same faces, the same endless, stale, nauseating cigarettes and clattering typewriters of other writers who always seemed to be working more efficiently than he. To relieve the boredom he flirted with researchers, telling one startled young woman, "I can see the sea in your eyes and all around the brim of your hat." Via held little attraction for him now, and he stayed away from their apartment to devote the evening hours to the playing of records in his office. Having replaced the old portable with an up-to-date model with far more volume, he took to advising friends on the correct way to listen to music.

> Get a radio or phonograph capable of the most extreme loudness possible, and sit down to listen to a performance of Beethoven's Seventh Symphony or of Schubert's C-Major Symphony. But I don't mean just sit down and listen. I mean this: turn it on as loud as you can get it. Then get down on the floor and jam your ear as close into the loudspeaker as you can get it and stay there, breathing as lightly as possible, and not moving, and neither eating nor smoking nor drinking. Concentrate everything you can into your hearing and your body. You won't hear it nicely. If it hurts you, be glad of it. . . . Your body is no longer your shape and substance, it is the shape and substance of the music.

This way of listening to music afforded Agee a Bacchic release. He scarcely believed society permitted Beethoven's works to be performed, so ecstatic and obscene were they, "savage and murderous to all equilibrium in human life." If he could only get the same intensity into his writing, he might at last consider himself an artist. After a night of aural reverie he would arrive home to find Via asleep. By the time he awoke late the following morning, she had already left for work. In the clear light of day his visions of glory vanished, replaced by "trouble in the bowels, severe chills every first few hours awake, a sort of frozen feeling in the spine": the aftereffects of excessive smoking and drinking.

In the midst of this fallow period he looked about to see how his friends were faring. Perhaps he might learn from their examples. Fitzgerald, he observed with a touch of envy, had earned modest recognition as a poet; Irvine Upham had made a brief stab at a literary career in New York before leaving; and Bernard Schoenfeld had found early fame and fortune by writing a Broadway hit, *Shooting Star,* light fare to be sure, but lucrative. Nothing here set Agee's pulse racing, but Macdonald was a different matter. The lovable gadfly had dared to go on leave from *Fortune,* having become so tired of writing for the magazine that he found himself falling asleep in front of the typewriter. Such drastic measures invariably appealed to Agee, who decided that a "kick in the ass is the best idea: get going on something and carry it through to the end, no matter how outrageous it becomes." He toyed with a "picture caption-chapter head history of the United States" that would be "extremely jagged and crazy," a "mixture of lyric quotation, . . . statistic, and satire," but forgot about the idea almost as soon as he had finished describing it.

However, inspired by Macdonald's bold move, he did arrange for six months' unpaid leave to begin in November. The prospect of freedom proved as terrifying as the reality of captivity. Should he make what he laughingly referred to as "The Supreme Effort" of quitting outright, or should he hedge his bets by writing three or four stories a year for the magazine on a free-lance basis? In the midst of his indecision he heard an unlikely rumor to the effect that James Joyce was thinking of settling in Key West, Florida, and instantly turned his thoughts in that direction. "Probably shall go somewhere South," he subsequently informed Macdonald, "either into the general country I was bawn in or to the Gulf or West Florida Coast (the latter for cheap living & hot sun; former for mild winter and cheap living and pickup stuff)." Via favored tame, cozy

Connecticut, where friends had offered to lend them a house, but Agee rejected the region as overpopulated, overbred, and over-priced. He had only to hear the word *Connecticut* to see an image of farmers working the soil to the point of exhaustion. Florida it would be, and a compliant Via agreed to draw on her savings to pay for the trip. What costs Via could not cover the Saunderses promised to underwrite, including a car.

Now that everyone had rallied around him, Agee felt enor-mous pressure to come up with work worthy of their generosity. Months before leaving, he commenced a project that would occupy him on and off for the rest of his life—an autobiographical novel. There was no burst of inspiration, no sudden flash of insight. In-stead the rather vague idea went through a slow and laborious period of gestation, a gradual process of sharpening and refine-ment. Agee had a propensity for entertaining any number of whim-sical ideas that never came to anything, but the notion of an autobi-ographical novel had more staying power than most; even when he tried to put it aside, it refused to go away. He struggled through 10,000 words of reminiscence, "much the hardest" sort of work he had ever attempted. He felt as though he were walking in the dark, afraid that something was stalking him. But he was learning, acquir-ing "respect for the value of a great *thickness* of context rather than relatively disembodied & finely filled statement." At other mo-ments he threw down his pencil in despair, for the autobiographical novel, lacking an organizing principle, threatened to degenerate into an unruly mass of recollections. He claimed to be caught "in the chills & fever of a manic-depressive wrestling match" and prey to a "goosey, weak feeling that develops in your hams and concen-trates at the crest of your ass when you try climbing hard up a long rope." Afraid of what his autobiographical investigations might yield, he transposed his physical discomfort to suspicions of mental imbalance. He imagined himself dead from the effort, his tomb-stone reading,

JAMES AGEE 1909–1935.

He attempted to resurrect his courage by reading Proust, but Agee immediately became concerned that he would be over-whelmed by the densely textured outpourings of the ultimate autobiographical novelist. "He is very clearly one of the greatest people I've read any of," he wrote Macdonald about Proust. "But I think I shan't read him now. Even the little I've read convinces me that once you got going in him he wd absorb your mind & thinking for months or even a few years. Which is not at all good for when you feel somewhere near ready to write." Try as he would to resist, he succumbed frequently to the temptation of reading *À la Recherche du Temps Perdu,* finding he had much to learn from Proust, especially in terms of uncovering an organizing principle for an autobiographical novel. As Proust attributed the formation of his personality to his failing to receive a kiss from his mother, so Agee came to perceive his father's early death as the formative experience in his own life.

In August, as he was making tentative progress on the novel, Agee suffered a setback in the form of an infuriating *Fortune* assignment on the orchid, of all things. Knowing full well that Ingersoll would tamper with the first draft, Agee decided to write about the orchid as a "clear & inescapable small study of snobbism." Taking an instant dislike to the flower because it represented superlatives that he distrusted, "the Largest, the Loudest, the Most Expensive, the most supercharged with Eroticism, Glamour, Prestige," he described it in terms calculated to raise Luce's blood pressure: "The orchid gets its name from the Greek *orchis,* which means testicle; and there are those who condemn that title as understating the case, since to them the flower resembles nothing printable so much as a psychopathic nightmare in technicolor." Agee went on in this vein for several thousand words. It became a point of honor that he condemn the flower for what he supposed it was rather than celebrate it for what others thought it to be.

"Very amusing, Jim," Ingersoll commented on the manuscript, "but of course we're not going to print it." This time Agee took the criticism personally. He had not intended to be funny; the article was deadly serious. "People's reactions to it . . . are so vile that I hate its very guts along with theirs," he noted. Never before had he resented *Fortune*'s elitism so strongly. Sniffing a whiff of rebellion in the ranks, Luce fired off a memo admonishing writers to "cheerfully remember that *that*"—meaning millionaires—"happens to be the audience to which they were invited to lecture." Irritated beyond reason, Agee talked loudly and incautiously of his contempt for the Founder. When he found a sympathetic ear, and there were many, he even discussed the possibility of shooting him. Returning frequently to the fantasy, he embroidered it with ever more realistic details. He would enter Luce's office. The Founder would be seated behind his desk, unsuspecting. Agee would steady the gun barrel on the desk and fire at chest level. As Luce slumped in his chair, the shot would reverberate throughout the hallways, and the staff would emerge from their offices to cheer. If Luce ever got wind of such threats, he never bothered to acknowledge them; poets, he knew, were a necessary evil.

Reminding himself that it was only a matter of months before his six-month leave would begin, Agee eventually bit back his anger and presided over the editorial emasculation of the orchid article. The controversy, in fact, was a symptom of widespread unrest at *Fortune*. Writers, more left-wing than ever, detected a shift to the right on Luce's part. In 1935 he divorced his first wife, Lila, to marry Clare Boothe Brokaw, an attractive, ambitious, and talented editor of the stylish magazine *Vanity Fair*. Along with other *Time* and *Fortune* writers, Agee deplored Luce's new wife and feared he would turn over the editorship of one of the magazines to her or, at the very least, implement her editorial suggestions. To the absent Macdonald, Agee quipped, "You may return to find a woman's magazine in the making, so to speak."

By November Agee longed to escape the endless backbiting, petty gossip, and routine humiliation of life at *Fortune*. With great relief he and Via packed their bags into the Saunders' Ford for the trip to Anna Maria, Florida, a small island off the west coast, near Sarasota. Before heading south they made a detour to Rhode Island to attend the wedding of Agee's former roommate, Robert Saudek. As best man, he presented the newlyweds with a gift of Mexican bowls. At a reception following the ceremony, Agee, intoxicated by the throng and his newfound liberation from *Fortune*'s wheel, became so carried away that he backed into a lit candelabrum. It was left to others to point out to him that the back of his jacket was on fire. Agee quickly doused the fire before he was hurt. It seemed wholly characteristic of him to become so involved with what he was saying that he had not noticed he was on fire.

In Anna Maria, Agee and Via stayed in a twenty-dollar-a-month shack, where the slats of their creaky bed fell to the floor and the weather turned so cold that he complained there was no benefit in coming to Florida whatsoever. They warmed themselves as best they could over a finicky oil stove and devoted the first few days to unwinding and catching up on their sleep. This was Agee's first extended vacation after three and a half years of unremitting labor in the Luce sweatshop.

At first Via was delighted to have her husband all to herself for a change. They spent their days surf-casting in the warm Gulf waters and on moonlit, misty nights roamed the beach, Agee watching the waves' "edges on shallow sand with tearing, glistening sound, like a drawn zipper opening." Later they tuned in a distant "hot jazz" station on their old radio. He rapidly developed a taste for the music. It was coarse, it was fun, it was sexual, it was spontaneous; it gave him as "full and 'relevant' satisfaction as Mozart." "It may be a minor art," he noted, "but it's as great as any art of this time." Since the jazz station was located in New Orleans, Agee became infatuated with the city, to which he attributed a mystique of pleasurable, relaxed sin. "New Orleans is stirring, rattling, and sliding faintly in its fragrance and in the enormous richness of its lust. . . . The breastlike floral air is itchy with the stiletto word embroiderings above black-blood dream-throes of an eloquent cracked undiscoverable cornet, which exists . . . in the heart of Louis Armstrong." Or so Agee imagined.

The couple desperately hoped their time together in Anna Maria would ease the strains that had crept into their marriage. Via felt herself "really married for the first time." In a burst of confidence she expressed her long-hidden desire for children. No other request could have alienated Agee so quickly. The thought of becoming a father, with all the bourgeois commitment the role entailed, appalled him. And he positively loathed the American cult of motherhood. He imagined mothers as an army of pink-toenailed, big-breasted females mindlessly snapping their garters as they reared their defenseless offspring. Via was shocked, hurt. They began to fight; mistrust between them took root.

Agee's habit of analyzing each nuance of feeling, however trivial or unpleasant, aggravated tensions in the little shack on the beach. They had shouting matches; Agee threw whatever object came to hand. Both came to the painful realization that their marriage, for all its brave intentions, had been a mistake. Try as he might to conform to the Saunders' standard of living, he was forced to admit what he had known back at Harvard—that he was not cut out to be a responsible husband and father. Via deserved better.

When they were not fighting, Agee brooded over his autobiographical novel or, more specifically, his inability to produce a literary masterpiece the moment he set pencil to paper. He moaned that he would never become "a great writer" after all. He was no good, would never amount to anything. Recovering slightly, he then decided that his only problem was that his imagination warmed up slowly, like his old radio. What he needed to do, he figured, was to stimulate his imagination until it came to life. Throughout November and December he consumed quantities of current magazines, thrillers (especially those by Dashiell Hammett), and large doses of Sigmund Freud's *The Interpretation of Dreams.*

That last item made a powerful if uncomfortable impression. Agee had long heard of Freud's ideas, of course, but now that he read them for himself he ticked off one psychoanalytical theory after another to which he could not subscribe. The concept of penis envy, for instance, struck him as ludicrous. However, he admired the way Freud plumbed the unconscious for clues to man's real nature. After his reading of Proust, Agee was prepared to acknowledge the irrational as a source of inspiration, and he began to jot down his own dreams for further study. "However many heels practice his preachings, Freud is a great man," Agee declared. Yet he could not bring himself to trust Freud enough to submit to an orthodox analysis. Surely the reductive and determinist Oedipus complex could not explain the mystery of his life. In fact, he actually preferred his native Anglo-Catholicism, which offered salvation without antiseptic intellectualizing. As a scientist and a Jew, Freud belonged to an alien if brilliant species.

Despite his misgivings about Freud, he went on to devour another psychoanalytical work, *The Inner World of Childhood* by Frances Wickes, which came complete with an introduction by her mentor, Carl Gustav Jung. That the author happened to be a woman initially put him off. He dismissed Wickes as "some Jung-disciple (female)," but he kept returning to the book. As a Jungian, Wickes concentrated on the study of "archetypes" in the "collective unconscious" as the way to unravel the mystery of the psyche. Her emphasis on religion, myth, and symbol held strong appeal for Agee. Even more to the point, she applied her techniques to children, devoting much space to the way a child comes to terms with death. While turning the pages, he found himself flooded with memories of his father and Knoxville. He put aside a batch of lackluster poems with which he had been blunting his pencil and gathered his resources to write realistically about his past.

Five times he tried; five times he discarded the results. In frustration he chided himself for being "completely disorganized & undisciplined." He compared himself to a compass needle "shaking and splitting in every direction." With an objectivity that Freud might have admired, he caught one dodge after another. He abjured reading poetry for fear it would influence him. He realized he was far too self-critical. He wrote Louise Saunders, "I am a lot too serious & inhibited: have to learn to break down or postpone self-criticism & fear which currently chokes and freezes everything." With quiet determination he concluded it was more important to "break down things learned & habituated . . . & to try to begin to learn over, than to get anything written." But his lack of productivity brought on paralyzing attacks of anxiety. In the caldron of his mind, Freud, Proust, and Wickes churned with memories of the vanished world of Knoxville. Slowly he ceased worrying about writing and simply began to write.

> On the rough wet grass of the back yard my father and mother have spread quilts. We all lie there, my mother, my father, my uncle, my aunt, and I too am lying there. First we were sitting up, then one of us lay down and then we all lay down, on our stomachs, or on our sides, or on our backs, and they have kept on talking. They are not talking much, and the talk is quiet, of nothing at all.

The result was simple and straightforward. In his notebook there appeared the first tentative acknowledgment of results: "Have been working (c. 12–15,000 words) on the . . . Knoxville idea. Don't know."

Gradually the impressions of his early boyhood came back to him through the gauze of the intervening years. As he wrote, he found that his memory proved remarkably full and accurate. There was no need to fabricate or exaggerate what had happened to and around him. At times the lyrical prose broke into poetic fragments.

> Parents on porches: rock and rock: From damp
> strings morning glories: hang their ancient faces.
> The dry and exalted noises of the locusts from all the
> air at once enchants my eardrums.

Though the reverie threatened to drift off, Agee anchored it with a succession of concrete images. Never before had he described a scene with such loving attention, nor had he succeeded previously in creating a world so tangible that he could almost touch it. In the Freudian lexicon, he was abreacting, raising long-buried memories to the conscious level.

At Christmas he took time off to celebrate with Via. He attached more importance to the holiday than to any other, excepting Easter, and spending this Christmas on a lonely, isolated island caused "twinges of homesickness" as he unwrapped gifts and paid a halfhearted social call on his landlord's family. On Christmas night he treated himself to a few hours with a neglected favorite, William Blake, "and was almost sorry to have resumed because I was beginning to have lyric & language ideas . . . too nearly parallel."

He resumed work on the autobiographical manuscript shortly after the New Year. "Got quite a fair slug of stuff done," he recorded one night. "Some of it pretty good, some of it terrible, & nearly all of it half-baked as of course I must expect." Exhausted from writing, he slept fourteen hours at a stretch, and when he recuperated he compressed the unwieldy mass of recollections into about two thousand shimmering words, less than a fifth of the original length, but all the more powerful for that. After much hemming and hawing he named the result "Knoxville: Summer 1915." The story marked a new departure in his writing, a true fusion of poetry and prose, lyrical yet disciplined. At twenty-six, he had created a miniature masterpiece.

That he had begun to live up to his vaunted promise gave him little satisfaction. The battle for literary mastery had taken its toll on his marriage and his mental well-being. Spells of anxiety and equivocation diminished every gain he made on paper. As the day of departure from Anna Maria approached, his mind swarmed with uncomfortable musings about New York, and he resumed his city habits of staying up to all hours, drinking, and sleeping late. "Pleasantest event in weeks was tasting a Martini, which turns out to have as strong a recall power as the smell of a hogpen," he wrote. Bits of old conversations returned to haunt him. He had falsely expressed admiration to MacLeish about a poem he—MacLeish—had written and had later told Macdonald the truth. Would Macdonald, now back at *Fortune,* tell? "I guess it is unfailingly wrong as hell not to be frank," he told Macdonald about the matter, "but it frequently takes more courage than I have."

He dearly wanted to see Father Flye on the trip home, but he was afraid of how the priest would respond to him after a separation of eleven years. On February 17, 1936, Agee wrote to him:

> I know there are two things about me that inevitably must cause you pain and annoyance, perhaps anger, and that keep us from being able to talk easily and really fully. The first (call it cynicism for short) I think I was probably beginning to absorb about the time we were last able to see each other much, the trip to Europe; and I've steadily taken a lot of it aboard ever since. . . .

Agee also warned Father Flye about his left-wing politics, the product of "three years of exposure to foulness, through *Fortune* and the general News." Agee insisted he had yet to become a Communist, but "there are many things in that set of ideas which look to me good; and I think more of them may conceivably succeed than we have any cynical right to think." He was no longer the pious, callow youth the priest had known; Agee now considered himself a non-believer and an embryonic radical. Of his degenerating marriage he dared not breathe a word, but Father Flye, reading between the lines, could easily draw his own conclusions.

During his last week in Anna Maria, Agee reveled in the mild climate. "The weather wonderful now," he noted gratefully. "There have been days and evenings of a kind I have never seen the likes of elsewhere: like honey if the latter were breathable and weren't sticky." On April 15 Via and he reluctantly took their leave of the shack they had come to regard as a second home. Succumbing to the lure of the open road, they stretched the trip home into a month-long sentimental journey. They spent several days in New Orleans, in search of the jazz they had heard over the radio. They followed the Mississippi up to Tennessee, braving severe floods along the way, and arrived at St. Andrew's in time to celebrate Easter with Father Flye and his wife, Grace.

For three exceptionally serene weeks they were the guests of the Flyes. Agee had not seen the school since 1924, but life went on there at the same unhurried pace, unaffected by the frenzy of politics. The pine-scented mountain air smelled as sweet as it always had, and Agee temporarily became the innocent youth he had once been. He spent his days playing tennis and swimming and now and then doing a little reading and writing, but he felt no compulsion to accomplish anything of great moment. His misgivings about how he and Father Flye would get along after all the years apart proved groundless. Their rapport was stronger than ever, for now they could talk man to man, "catching up the threads, bridging the gap." Agee felt sufficiently comfortable to read "Knoxville: Summer 1915" to the priest. As a teacher, Father Flye had his own exacting standards of literature, but the story met and exceeded them. "I was tremendously impressed by it," he later recalled, certain that Agee had written a "beautiful piece of English."

It was during this charmed interval in Tennessee that Agee befriended a promising St. Andrew's student, David McDowell. The previous September Father Flye had sent examples of McDowell's work to Agee, who declared the poems "as likable and moving as the first poems of Keats are to me." On the same occasion he delivered himself of his opinion of the dubious value of formal education to a poet. "I'm not such a dope as to think I or anyone can find his own way unassisted," he wrote, "but the more of that and the less guidance & elaborate of the means, the better."

Agee enjoyed his share of admirers, but McDowell's boyish regard for him approached hero worship. They took long walks in the woods beyond St. Andrew's and at Agee's suggestion visited the swimming hole in whose murky waters he had often swum. Strolling past the cottage where his mother and sister had lived and from which he had been all but banished, he relived the waning days of his faith in God. "He made no comment," McDowell later recalled, "and . . . spoke little on these outings, except to respond to my talk about poetry or to marvel at how little things had changed." To McDowell, Agee was not so much a great talker as an "incredibly sensitive and perceptive listener." He was so taken with the area's tranquil beauty that he exclaimed it was his favorite spot in the entire world. His newly refreshed memories of the place coalesced into an impulse to write a second autobiographical novel, this one concerning the spiritual crisis he had undergone as a student at St. Andrew's, a complement to the work-in-progress about Knoxville and his father. The new idea brought the number of projects under consideration to three: two novels and a nonfiction study of the effects of the Depression on farmers.

When not communing with nature, McDowell and Agee played endless sets of tennis on the school courts. Soon Agee came to feel part of the life of St. Andrew's again. Wearing a borrowed tie, he attended commencement exercises with Via. McDowell, who was to deliver the valedictory address, nervously sought Agee's help with the manuscript. Remembering all too well his own struggle to come up with appropriate sentiments at Exeter and Harvard, Agee spent hours revising McDowell's speech.

It was now the middle of May, he had run out of money, and he could no longer postpone his return to New York. What terrors and fulfillments awaited him there, he did not know. The weeks amid the piney woods of St. Andrew's had been the most tranquil he and Via had ever known together; their lives would never be so simple again. After bidding farewell to the Flyes with the deepest regret, they followed the spring weather north. As soon as he was back in the overcrowded, unclean city, Agee wrote to Father Flye, "No time or visit ever, anywhere, has been so good and meant so much to me."

8

SPIES

A month after Agee returned to his cluttered desk at *Fortune,*
Ingersoll asked the hotheaded young writer to undertake another
sociological article, this one concerning the plight of the sharecroppers—the poorest of farmers—in the deep South. It was an assignment destined to transform Agee's literary career and personal life.

Ingersoll had good reason to consider Agee the right man for
the job. Despite his fits of intransigence, his deft work on other
New Deal pieces had earned high marks. And Agee was from the
South, that most idiosyncratic of regions. Furthermore, he was
alone among the staff writers in wanting the assignment. Others
blanched at the thought of spending long summer weeks in one of
the most desolate areas of the country, but Agee instantly greeted

it as the opportunity he had been awaiting. At last he would be able to fuse his nostalgia for the open road with his nascent radicalism.

To Agee's further delight, Ingersoll nominated one Walker Evans as the photographer for the article. Having dreaded the prospect of working with Margaret Bourke-White, Agee considered Evans the ideal choice of collaborator. The photographer's cool, unsparing style was perfectly suited to the harsh reality of the life of the rural poor; he would neither aggrandize nor condescend, as a lesser photographer might be tempted to.

Ecstatic, Agee raced to the office of Robert Fitzgerald, who had at last made the leap from the *Herald Tribune* to *Fortune*, "swallowing with excitement, . . . stunned, exalted, scared clean through," as Fitzgerald remembered, and prepared to begin "impregnating every woman on the fifty-second floor" of the Chrysler Building. Taking refuge in a dungeon of a bar on Third Avenue with Fitzgerald, Agee sang the praises of *Fortune* for having the wisdom, the foresight, the unbelievable perspicacity to pair him with Evans on this assignment. When he got home that night he dashed off a note about his stroke of good luck to Father Flye: "Best break I ever had on *Fortune.* Feel terrific responsibility towards the story; considerable doubts of my ability to bring it off; considerable more of *Fortune*'s ultimate willingness to use it." Of course, he would have to suspend work on his autobiographical novel, but after months of introspection it came as a relief to concentrate on an external issue of equal importance. To add to the excitement, Ingersoll ordered Agee and Evans to pack their bags immediately, for they were leaving at the end of the week.

At the time, Agee and Evans were acquaintances with a high regard for one another's talents, nothing more. Agee knew little about Evans beyond the fact that he was a diminutive, dapper fellow with an upturned nose, sleepy green eyes, and a brisk, reserved manner. They were a pair of complementary opposites, having little in common, least of all background. Evans came from a prosperous family in Chicago, where his father was a highly successful advertising copywriter. Evans had mastered the social graces at an early age. He played golf as a young boy and demonstrated an early flair for painting. His idyllic childhood ended with his parents' separation; he lived briefly with his mother in New York and, like many inconvenient children of the well-to-do, was sent to prep school, first to Loomis and later to Andover, where he developed an ardent desire to become a writer, an ambition he pursued during a single miserable year at Williams College. Evans dropped out in 1923 and resumed living with his mother in New York, working the night shift in the map room of the New York Public Library.

He endured three years of this shadow life. In 1926 he received an allowance from his father, enough to permit him to move to Paris, where he haunted the lecture halls of the Sorbonne and the stacks of Sylvia Beach's Shakespeare & Co., and stole glances at the famous expatriate writers he was too shy to meet. He left Paris after a year, explaining, "I wanted to write so much I couldn't write a word."

In 1928 he suddenly happened on photography, in which he gained a freedom of expression he had sought but never found in language. Disdaining the pretentiousness of the "art" photography of his day, he painstakingly developed a remarkably straightforward, self-assured style that mirrored his inner dignity, reserve, and sadness. He insisted his photographs document their subjects, not call attention to themselves or, worse, their technique. Evans hated the display of technique with a passion. Supporting himself with odd jobs, he gradually made his way through the maze of New York's gallery and art world, and in the spring of 1932, found himself collaborating with Agee's friend Lincoln Kirstein on a plan to photograph Victorian homes in Boston. Evans found Kirstein quite a catalyst. "This undergraduate," the photographer remarked, "was teaching me something about what I was doing." In the same year, Evans had his first exhibition, at the prestigious Julien Levy Gallery in New York; by now his work showed a pronounced affinity with the all-encompassing photographs of Mathew Brady and Eugène Atget.

A few years later, Evans received an appointment as "roving social historian" of the Farm Security Administration's photographic unit. Employed by the federal government to document the hard times the Depression had brought to farmers, he had become very much a part of the New Deal, though he had nothing but contempt for bureaucrats who attempted to meddle in the lives of ordinary citizens. He longed to act as an independent agent rather than as a member of a bungling bureaucracy, but a job was a job.

For the first time in his life he was able to earn a living in his chosen field. At about the time he went to work for the FSA, he successfully lobbied for assignments on *Fortune*. He held the entire Luce operation in approximately the same low esteem that he did the United States government, but the magazine had one compensation he valued highly: James Agee.

He saw in the writer, as he later recalled, a distinct flavor of "Harvard and Exeter, a hint of family gentility, and a trace of romantic idealism." On the other hand, Agee "didn't look much like a poet, an intellectual, an artist, or a Christian, each of which he was. Nor was there outward sign of his paralyzing, self-lacerating anger. His voice was pronouncedly quiet and low-pitched, though not of a 'cultivated' tone." Agee's manner of dress also caught Evans' observant eye. In this area they were a study in contrasts, for Evans was very much the dandy in his tailor-made clothes, English shoes, and fancy hats. But the threadbare Agee "would work a suit into fitting him perfectly by the simple method of not taking it off much." Evans' shoes were polished to a gleaming shine; Agee favored tennis shoes, seconds if possible; and a "sleazy cap." Where Evans was small and neat and precise, Agee was all "graceless" movement and "large, long, bony hands."

In one area, at least, Agee came off as an aristocrat, and that was in his speech. Evans could not get enough of Agee's talk, "hardly twentieth century in style; it had Elizabethan colors." Alone among Agee's friends, Evans was willing to stay up half the night listening. "Many a man or woman has fallen exhausted to sleep at four in the morning bang in the middle of a remarkable Agee performance," Evans remembered, "and later learned that the man had continued it somewhere else until six. Like many born writers who are floating in the illusory amplitude of their youth, Agee did a great deal of writing in the air. Often you had the impulse to gag him and tie a pen to his hand."

Agee, for his part, took to Evans immediately. Everything about the sly little photographer fascinated him: the fact that Evans had been exposed to the raw edge of the Depression, his contempt for the mindless adulation of power and big business that seemed to animate Luce's every waking moment. Agee seconded Evans' opinion that working for Time Inc. was "intellectually degrading and insulting." In his quietly forceful way, Evans came to exert a profound influence over Agee, who was suddenly given to exclaiming that the federal government "is certainly showing its ass off the higher it puts it in the air. . . . Needs wiping, kicking, clothing & elimination." Since Evans considered Father Flye a crashing bore and had little patience with Agee's interminable spiritual crises, the writer did his best to emerge from his habitual self-absorption. Friends soon noticed that Evans was the only person from whom Agee took advice. The photographer's astringent, no-nonsense attitude exerted a calming effect; around Evans Agee felt focused and relaxed and able to concentrate. They discovered shared passions for film, Chaplin, Mathew Brady, and the striking visual scheme of Erich von Stroheim's cinematic epic, *Greed.*

This little mutual admiration society departed New York on a warm afternoon in mid-June. As they drove south, it seemed to Evans that his disheveled companion was "in flight from Greenwich Village social-intellectual evenings, and especially from the whole world of high-minded, well-bred, money-hued culture, whether authoritarian or libertarian." And, Evans might have added, from his claustrophobic marriage.

In one way or another, Agee had been preparing for this assignment since the day he had offered his shoes and socks to the starving factory workers back in Knoxville, yet it had come so suddenly that he had had no time to prepare. He was in a panic, without the slightest idea where to begin, where to find actual sharecroppers. Perhaps they were in Oklahoma. They headed toward Oklahoma, only to discover that they would not find sharecroppers there. They would have to go to Alabama and hope for better luck. In the midst of the Depression, the kind of poverty they were looking for proved to be hard to find. They did not want any sort of poverty; they wanted a special, pure, exalted poverty, a holy poverty, if possible, because they intended to demonstrate that the poor possessed more innate dignity and strength than the bourgeoisie.

Furthermore, Agee doubted *Fortune*'s willingness to print their findings. This time he was going to write an article exactly as he saw fit, not in a way calculated to please Ingersoll and the gang, to play to their well-meant misconceptions. Those bastards could dismantle his piece on orchids, but when it came to sharecroppers, Agee felt a moral passion, a proprietary interest. They were *his* people, the wretched of the earth. Now all he had to do was find them.

Confronted by the reality of a desolate and dusty Alabama withering in the summer heat, Agee's initial enthusiasm for the project gave way to paroxysms of confusion and self-doubt. The task of depicting the lives of sharecroppers as truthfully as his conscience demanded seemed so vast and delicate that he scarcely felt equal to it. Despite the four-year-long apprenticeship he had served at *Fortune,* his approach to investigating the subject was anything but methodical. He had no official information or statistics of any kind, only his subjective impressions of the human spirit in extremis. If he could not see something with his own eyes, he was inclined to disbelieve it and would certainly omit it from the resulting article.

While they bumbled around, pausing now and then to take photographs of desolate hamlets—photographs they had no way of knowing were good, bad, or indifferent, for they could not develop them on the road—Agee fulminated against the hypocrisy and shallowness of journalism. "The very blood and semen of journalism," he came to believe, "is a broad and successful form of lying. Remove the lying, and you no longer have journalism." The pair of them were a bunch of self-righteous hypocrites; did Evans realize that? They had no right to go poking into the innocent lives of beleaguered citizens on the pretext of gathering information but in reality making money for Luce, money the Founder would probably spend on a hat for his new wife. The entire journalistic enterprise had gone from being the voice of the people to exploiting the people. Agee later wrote:

> It seems to me curious, not to say obscene and thoroughly terrifying, that it could occur to an association of human beings drawn together through need and chance and for profit into a company, an organ of journalism, to pry intimately into the lives of an undefended and appallingly damaged group of human beings, an ignorant and helpless rural family, for the purpose of parading the nakedness, disadvantage and humiliation of these lives before another group of human beings, in the name of science, of "honest journalism" (whatever that paradox may mean).

Every step of the way, it seemed, they were in danger of falling into Margaret Bourke-Whiteism. To compensate, they hashed out a new conception of their role. They were no longer journalists but spies, who, if they did their job well, might be made "witness to matters no human being may see." They did not mean spies in a political sense, but in a religious one, spies of God engaged in a covert war against evil. Throughout the Depression the tide of evil had risen at an alarming rate; unchecked, it would lead to an apocalypse. They set themselves the task of waging battle against their eventuality by acting as witnesses. In commemoration of their cause, Agee wrote Evans a poem.

Against time and the damages of the brain
Sharpen and calibrate. Not yet in full,
Yet in some arbitrated part
Order the facade of the listless summer.

Spies, moving delicately among the enemy,
The younger sons, the fools,
Set somewhat aside the dialects and the stained skins of feigned madness,
Ambiguously signal, baffle, the eluded sentinel.

Thus they frittered away their allotted month in Alabama with endless moralizing and aesthetic theorizing. Concrete findings were harder to come by. A promising encounter with the poor seemed to be in the making when they met up with a group of black singers. Yet, after reveling in their performance, Agee, "in a perversion of self-torture," gave their leader fifty cents "while trying to communicate much more." His approach, his token philanthropy, was all wrong; Margaret Bourke-White could hardly have done worse. In desperation they requested—and received—permission from headquarters to spend another month in the field.

With Agee hamstrung by guilt, Evans, the more practical of the two, took matters into his own hands. Loitering by the courthouse in Sprott, Alabama, one hot afternoon, he fell into casual conversation with a local sharecropper, Frank Tingle, eventually persuading the farmer to sit for a portrait. Soon Tingle was joined by friends, Bud Fields and Floyd and Allie Mae Burroughs, who had come to town in search of relief work. By the time Agee joined the group, Fields had decided the two strangers were helpful government representatives (a misconception Agee and Evans did little to dispel), and he offered to drive the pair to his home for a look around.

The Fields's shack—for that is what it was—came as a revelation to Agee; the primitive dwelling reeked of poverty in its purest state. While Agee feasted his eyes on every humble detail of the family's clothing and appearance, Evans, crouching behind the dark cloth of his camera, coolly snapped off photographs of the children "naked in front of the cold absorption of the camera in all your shame and pitiableness to be pried into and laughed at."

With a mixture of humility, patience, and cunning, Agee and Evans worked their way into the good graces of all three poverty-stricken families. Throughout this period of courtship, Agee devoutly wished himself to be worthy of them, rather than the other way around. Voyeuristic curiosity and a yearning for acceptance went hand in hand. They left, returned, left again, and returned again. "We could not drive along the highway past those wandlike posts between which your road levels off along the hill without . . . feeling in our chests a pulling." After several visits, Agee succeeded in earning the Fields family's trust, which he valued to such an extent that he accorded Bud Fields the ultimate accolade: Fields became "a sort of father."

During these reconnaissance missions Agee pieced together the pathetic circumstances of the family's life. They lived at the subsistence level, or even below it, working borrowed land in exchange for the most primitive shelter. The entire family picked cotton by hand, for which they received six dollars a bale. But once expenses were subtracted, they had virtually no money left over to show for their backbreaking labor. The lot of the nine Tingles was, if anything, worse than that of the Fields.

[Tingle] went $400 into debt on a fine young pair of mules. One of the mules died before it had made its first crop; the other died the year after. . . . [Tingle] went into debt for other, inferior mules; his cows went one by one into debts and desperate exchanges and by sickness; he got congestive chills; his wife got pellagra; a number of his children died; he got appendicitis and lay for days on end under the ice cap; his wife's pellagra got into her brain; for ten consecutive years now, though they have lived on so little rations money, and have turned nearly all their cottonseed money toward their debts, they have not cleared or had any hope of clearing a cent at the end of the year.

All these harrowing events had taken place on a sunbaked plateau known as Mills Hill, thirty miles below Tuscaloosa. They illustrated any number of points that Agee and Evans had hoped to make in their article: the impossible conditions under which the sharecroppers labored, the exploitation of workers by landowners, and the devastating effects of natural disasters on the vulnerable families.

After two weeks' immersion in the sharecroppers' plight, Agee and Evans required time to sort out their findings. They spent two days in a Birmingham hotel room dark enough for Evans to develop test shots he had taken of the shacks' interiors. At this juncture they could have left the sweltering region for New York, where *Fortune* editors were poised to work their raw material into a timely article, but Agee sensed he had yet to get to the heart of the sharecroppers' lives. He needed time to himself, to think and come to grips with the overwhelming suffering he had witnessed.

They agreed to part company for several hours; Evans remained in town, while Agee took to the open road in the car. Without Evans he quickly lost his bearings and plunged into a dark journey of self-discovery, having only the most tenuous connection with sharecroppers or the Depression. Caroming along sixty miles of "narrow and twisted concrete, up against the thin margin of danger," he half-consciously reenacted his father's drive into oblivion. In a trance, he drove on, "just watching the road disinvolve itself from the concealing country and run under me with its noise and the tires and the motor." Along the way, he seriously considered picking up a waiting prostitute, but found the prospect too dispiriting, "not worth the sacrifice of solitude . . . in spite of the vapor-lamp quality of her lavender and unappeasable eyes." He badly needed a drink but realized, to his horror, that it was Sunday, and all the bars and liquor stores were shut. "Of all the Christbitten places to spend a few hours alone, and of all the days to do it in," he complained. He came to a small town seeking rest, only to be plunged into depression by its grim appearance: "The sun was hitting every surface in sight, and all of them were bare and hard, and the street and walls were white." He wished he had never been born, that this entire dreary landscape would vanish in the blink of an eye.

For lack of anything better to do, he pulled over at a down-at-heels café called Gaffney's Lunch, where he partially recovered from this bout with existential dread. Again his thoughts turned to sex; he desired "nothing in the world so much as a girl," and not a prostitute and not Via, either, but "a girl nearly new to me." They would make love in a slow, relaxed fashion, Agee and this girl, who would wear a thin, white cotton dress. Afterward, "I should almost in silence cry the living blood out of myself."

Abruptly he left the café, tormented by doubts about his writing ability. Would he ever create even "one decent page"? He knew he never would, not in a million years, and if he turned to movies, he would fail to create a decent minute of film. In this despairing mood he undertook the hazardous task of reliving his father's fatal car crash, imagining himself flooring the accelerator to "twist the car off the road, if possible into a good-sized rock, and the chances are fair that I would kill myself"—just as his father had. He was both serious and jesting about death, playing with the fact of his mortality. But death was a strong adversary, not to be teased. Thoughts of Via back in New York brought him momentarily to his wits, but if his death "would do Via some bad damage," so would "continuing to live with her," or leaving her. Any way he turned, he was bound to cause her pain, and there was nothing he could do to avert that eventuality. The pain swelling in his soul erupted into the forefront of his thoughts as he silently mourned the dead: "My father, my grandfather, my poor damned tragic, not unusually tragic, bitched family."

Again he was confronted with the most crucial choice in life: whether to succumb to the misfortune that had plagued his family —misfortune not so cruel as that afflicting the Tingles and Fieldses of this world, but bad enough in its own way—or to summon the strength to resist its destiny. If the Tingles could get on with their lives, so could he. Self-destruction was a luxury sharecroppers could not afford.

It was only now, a few days after the fact, that he felt the full impact of meeting the families. They were natural artists, it seemed to him, existing unselfconsciously in a tragedy with the greatest

167

forbearance and dignity. Their lives were defined by important rituals absent in Manhattan's hollow mores. They could have been figures in a novel by an American Dostoevsky or the Bible; they dealt not with the fickle winds of politics, but with the eternals: life, death, birth, sickness, the land, and the weather. Through the alchemy of intuition, he had envisioned this primitive life in the decade-old "Ann Garner" before he had actually seen it. Obviously he was fated to come to this godforsaken plateau (or was it?) to "do the piece of work you would give all your blood to do." The years of searching for a topic to match his literary ambitions were at an end, and he had to make the most of the small amount of time in Alabama remaining to him.

Without meaning to, Agee worked his way around to the Tingles' shack, where he struck up a conversation with Frank Tingle himself, apologizing for the photographs Evans had taken and promising to keep in touch. To Agee's eternal gratitude, Tingle replied that he was always there. As the writer drove off, the weather suddenly worsened, the wind "taking up little spirals of dust among the shaken cotton," the rain bombarding the car. In the back of his mind, Agee hoped that one of the families would take pity on him and invite him into their home, and Burroughs, who lived nearby, finally did. Within, Agee's eyes fastened on a universe of poverty illuminated by an oil lamp. The journalist in him started to catalogue the homely details of the Burroughs' domestic existence—the homespun clothes, furnishings, and simple utensils—as if these possessions would explain the secret of their will to survive. There were no formal introductions, mercifully, only a "quietness, casualness, courtesy and friendliness" to indicate he was slowly earning their respect. He hoped the family would come to take his existence for granted, and then, as if he were a hidden camera or an infant, he would freely observe their unselfconscious behavior.

Burroughs repeatedly asked Agee to spend the night, but "in a paralyzing access of shyness before strong desire I thanked him and said I had better not." Agee drove off, his head pounding with the knowledge that he had passed up a golden opportunity. The heavy rainfall made the dirt road slick in spots and soft, but Agee drove on recklessly, his foot a lead weight on the accelerator, his mind swarming with memories of his father's death. One false move and a woeful family history would repeat itself. Perhaps that was not such a bad thing; he could not say. Suddenly the car veered off the road, slid into a ditch, and came to a halt. Everything occurred just as it had with his father, with this exception: Agee survived. He was not even hurt.

He tried to jostle the car loose, but the chassis remained firmly implanted in the sticky mud. Pausing to take the measure of his predicament, he lit a cigarette and "sat looking out at the country and at the sky, while the vanquished engine cooled with a tin noise of ticking" in the "very darkest kind of daylight which can be called daylight at all, . . . a cold blue-brown light of agate." He was honest enough with himself to admit the silly accident had been "half-contrived"; he had wanted to feel—not imagine, but actually *feel*—what it was like to die in a car crash. It was a dangerous stunt, but of a piece with his willingness to dangle from the fiftieth story of the Chrysler Building. His occasional need for such extreme behavior had its psychotic edge; for precious minutes at a time he lost touch with reality and fell prey to a desire to act out his fantasies regardless of the consequences. This time Death allowed him to walk away unscathed.

Afterward, when he came to himself, he gratefully experienced a spiritual rebirth. Every scrubby tree and tumbledown home in sight took on a supernatural clarity. The old James Agee, the writer from New York, had died when the car slid into the ditch; the new one was a sharecropper who had had an accident. He changed into his sneakers and rolled up the legs of his pants as the sharecroppers did. He began to walk as they did, a bit stiffly and bent, and to talk as they did, slowly and softly. Bidding farewell to his old, citified self, he "started off down the road, looking back at the car frequently from changed distances as at a picture of myself, tilted up there helpless with its headlights and bumper taking what light was left."

He now had the perfect excuse to seek shelter in one of the sharecropper homes. He chose the Burroughs and walked up on their porch—which he later described as a "great tragic poem"—to explain "shamefacedly" that he had had a little bit of trouble on the rain-drenched road. After a pause, Floyd Burroughs offered to put him up for the night and, even more gratifying to Agee, to share their evening meal. Famished, he insisted a crust of bread would suffice, but Floyd's wife, Allie Mae, spread a full meal before him: biscuits, jam, eggs, buttermilk, peas, fried pork, and four fried eggs. While Agee wolfed down the food, Mrs. Burroughs apologized for the humble fare. Through chance and cunning he had turned the tables on the family; no longer a sophisticated *Fortune* writer from New York, he had become a mendicant, more dependent on their help than they were on his.

Having partaken of their food, Agee virtually adopted the entire family. Mr. and Mrs. Burroughs "seemed not other than my own parents." Through them he hoped to reclaim a "royalty" of which he had been robbed by the "blind chance" of having become a city dweller. Overcome with nostalgia, he believed he had gained access to the "sources of my own life," undeservedly so, for he had paid "no price beyond love and sorrow." Alone in his room, he studied the family Bible, redolent of a "strong and cold stench of human excrement" and slept in a vermin-infested cot. At last he felt at one with the sharecroppers. "I don't really know why anyone should be 'happy' under these circumstances," Agee wondered, "but there's no use laboring the point: I was: outside the vermin, my senses were taking in nothing but a deep night, unmeditatable consciousness of a world which was newly touched and beautiful to me."

It can be argued that Agee's approach to the Burroughs family was as suspect as conventional journalism. He had mildly duped them to win their acceptance. The Ingersolls of the world found little value in his staying with sharecroppers; they were after the big picture, the sociological implications. Agee meanwhile sought to exorcise private demons on the pretext of writing an article. Furthermore, his sudden insistence that he had sprung from equally humble circumstances was certainly stretching a point. His father's family consisted in part of farmers, to be sure, but not dirt-poor sharecroppers. As Father Flye later observed, "His people were not illiterate country people, but they lived in the country or small towns . . . and he wouldn't have thought the life of farmers or the soil so entirely alien as some people coming from a purely urban environment would have found it." It was Agee's special gift to treat the sharecroppers without condescension, and, according to Father Flye, "they would have thought of him, 'Well, he's just like one of us' "—St. Andrew's, Exeter, Harvard, and Time Inc. notwithstanding.

Agee's impromptu stopover at the Burroughs' stretched into a three-week-long stay during which he lived, slept, ate, and worked side by side with the family. When Evans tracked him down, he found Agee "sweated and scratched with submerged glee" and had "won almost everybody in those families—perhaps too much—even though some of the individuals were hardbitten, sore, and shrewd. Probably it was his diffidence that took him into them. That nonassurance was, I think, hostage to his very Anglican childhood training. . . . To him, human beings were at least possibly immortal and literally sacred souls."

Equipped with a license to pry, courtesy of *Fortune,* Agee dared go further than he had thought possible into the Burroughs' lives. By day he observed their work, clothing, and conversation, and by night he committed his impressions to paper. He described his modus operandi this way:

> It is late in a summer night, in a room, of a house set deep and solitary in the country; all in this house save myself are sleeping; I sit at a table, facing a partition wall; and I am looking at a lighted coal-oil lamp which stands on the table close to the wall, and just beyond the sleeping of my relaxed left hand; and with my right hand I am from time to time writing, with a soft pencil, into a schoolchild's composition book; but just now, I am entirely focused on the lamp, and the light.

That light formed his center of consciousness. He worked steadily outward, noting minuscule details with the accuracy of an infant staring by the hour at the wall above his crib.

By degrees his perspective widened until the entire shack seemed a "plain shell" containing a family reduced by nature and economics to a living death, a condition he considered more revealing of human nature than comfortable circumstances. Writing of the house with surreal detail, he stretched his powers of description to the breaking point, in the process transforming into an interior landscape the inner surface of a locust shell: "In all this house not any one inch of lumber being wasted on embellishment, or on trim, or on any form of relief, or even on doubling of walls: it is, rather as if a hard thin hide of wood has been stretched to its utmost to cover exactly once, or a little less than once, in all six planes the skeletal beams." Indeed, the "power" of the hand-hewn house recalled the severity of Doric architecture or "one of the larger fugues of Bach."

Adopting a fugal approach, Agee worked variations on the "three qualities of beauty" he perceived in the lumber.

> One is the steaming killed strength of the grain, infinite, talented, and unrepeatable from inch to inch, the florid genius of nature which is incapable of error: one is the close-set transverse arcs, dozens to the foot, which are the shadows of the savage breathings and eatings of the circular saw; little of this lumber has been planed: one is the tone and quality the weather has given it, which is related one way to the bone, another to satin, another to unpolished but smooth silver: all these are visible at once though one or another may be strongly enhanced by the degree of humidity.

Even the knotholes elicited his fervor. He imagined the grain within going into "convulsions or ecstasies such as Beethoven's deafness compelled."

Working diligently to evoke the shack in terms of all five senses, Agee subjected odors to a similarly detailed analysis as the nights wore on.

> The odor of pine lumber, wide thin cards of it, heated cars of it, heated in the sun, in no way doubled or insulated, in closed and darkened air. The odor of woodsmoke, the fuel being mainly pine, but in part, also, hickory, oak, and cedar. The odors of cooking. Among these, most strongly, the odors of fried salt pork and of fried and boiled pork lard, and second, the odor of cooked corn. The odors of sweat in many stages of age and freshness, this sweat being a distillation of pork, lard, corn, woodsmoke, pine, and ammonia.

Writing as a man possessed, fully confident of his gift, he gave nary a thought to the unlikelihood of *Fortune*'s running such idiosyncratic copy. No detail was too homely to escape his inventory. When he came to cataloguing barnyard animals, for example, he evoked each with gentle irony and unforgettable images: "A clutter of obese, louse-tormented hens whose bodies end dirtily, like sheaves of barley left in rain. Several neat broilers, and a few quilly, half-grown chicks whose heads are still like lizards. A pair of guineas whose small painted heads and metal bodies thread these surroundings like the exotic glint of naturalistic dreams." Piling detail upon detail, his descriptions gained hallucinatory power; the choice of the verb *thread,* which forces the mind to visualize the movement of the fowl, was perfect. He went on to make thousands of similarly brilliant and canny word choices; there was nothing he could not do with the English language when he put his mind to it. No nuance was too small or delicate to escape his descriptive powers, no moment too alien or complex to elude his understanding.

In time the Burroughs family repaid his interest in their lives handsomely. Agee recorded the moment when Mary, Floyd's sister, made her appreciation known in a speech brimming with bashful sentimentality.

> I was on the porch, diddling around in a notebook . . . and a hen thudded among dried watermelon seeds on the oak floor, looking, as they usually do, like a nearsighted professor . . . and [Mary] appeared, all dressed to go, looking somehow as if she had come to report a decision that had been made in conference, for which I, without knowing it, seemed to have been waiting. She . . . said, I want you and Mr. Walker to know how much we all like you, because you make us feel easy with you; we don't have to act any different from what it comes natural to act, and we don't have to worry what you're thinking about us, it's just like you was our own people and had always lived here with us, you are all so kind, and nice, and quiet, and easygoing, and we wisht you wasn't never going to go away but stay on here with us, and I just want to tell you how much we all keer about you.

To Agee, Mary's sentiments justified all his hunches and tricks. It is entirely possible that no one had ever made him feel as accepted for what he was as this simple farm girl did. He, too, never wanted to leave the impoverished fairy tale he inhabited with her and responded to her declaration with a peroration of equal gratitude and, Agee being Agee, far greater length.

Though he had achieved his goal of acceptance by the sharecroppers, he despaired of writing about them as well as his conscience demanded. He called his strong suit, description, into question; it was "a word to suspect." He decided, "Most young writers and artists roll around in description like honeymooners on a bed. It comes easier to them than anything else. In the course of years they grow or discipline themselves out of it." Still in the thrall of I. A. Richards, he wanted to take words a step further than description; he wanted them to embody the things they described—or to give the illusion of embodiment. In his lust for extreme realism, he took to copying marginalia in the family Bible, remnants of torn newspapers and magazines, discarded schoolbooks—anything that would give the texture of the sharecroppers' lives. If he were to be wholly truthful, he would eliminate his descriptions altogether and make his report entirely a compilation of such material. Let the reader draw his own conclusions therefrom. But no, that plan would not work; words were inadequate to the task, he told himself. Only Evans' photographs could bring back the truth to New York, for they were unedited, undistorted by the mind. They included everything, for nothing escaped the camera lens. If Agee were to adhere to the same standard of truthfulness, he would have to resort to bringing back artifacts such as "fragments of cloth, bits of cotton, lumps of earth, records of speech, pieces of wood and iron, phials of odors, plates of food and excrement." If only such objects could speak!

Occasionally Agee's extremism got the better of his artistic judgment. His account of Floyd Burroughs' clothing may serve as one flagrant example. In stark sentences intended to suggest Burroughs' discomfort, Agee detailed a sharecropper's Sunday best.

> Freshly laundered cotton gauze underwear.
> Mercerized blue green socks, held up over his fist-like calves by scraps of pink and green gingham rag.
> Long bulb-toed black shoes: still shining with the glaze of their first newness, streaked with clay.
> Trousers of a hard and cheap cotton wool, dark-blue with narrow gray stripes; a twenty-five-cent belt strap in them always.
> A freshly laundered and brilliantly starched white shirt with narrow black stripes.

A brown, green and gold tie in broad stripes, of stiff and hard imitation watered silk.

A very cheap felt hat of a color between that of a pearl and that of the faintest gold, with a black band.

In contrast to the pathetic artificiality of formal clothes, the farmer's everyday dress radiated an authenticity no dandy could hope to imitate. Once Floyd donned his overalls ("They are pronounced overhauls," Agee reminded himself), he assumed his natural dignity and status. Agee eulogized the garment with pretentious solemnity.

And on this façade, the cloven halls for the legs, the strong-seamed, structured opening for the genitals, the broad horizontal at the waist, the slant thigh pockets, the buttons at the point of each hip and on the breast, the geometric structures of the usages of the simple trades—the complexed seams of utilitarian pockets which are so brightly picked out against darkness when the seam-threadings, double and triple stitched, are still white, so that a new suit of overalls has among its beauties those of a blueprint: and they are a map of a working man.

When the fabric aged, it turned into a "region and scale of blues, subtle, delicious, and deft" that Agee compared to the "blues of Cézanne" and "the feather mantle of a Toltec prince." He indulged in similar flights of fancy concerning poor Floyd's humble shoes and hats; nothing escaped Agee's keen eye, his incantatory prose, or his habitual exaggeration.

When not writing or watching, Agee tried his tender hands at cotton picking, but not for very long, as he found the work even more unpleasant than journalism. "It is simple and terrible work," he reflected. "Skill will help you; all the endurance you can draw up against it from the roots of your existence will be thoroughly used as fuel to it: but neither skill nor endurance can make it any easier." He found that he required several hours of picking simply to get limber, that his back ached, that the only weather worse for picking than heat was cold. With his burned hands, Floyd was a poor picker and a considerable liability, but Allie Mae was reasonably adept at picking cotton, averaging about one hundred and fifty to two hundred pounds a day. "The family exists for work," Agee concluded, as he bowed out of this crucial aspect of family life. For all his love of the soil, he vastly preferred writing about it to working it.

As his three-week-long stay drew to a close, Agee put aside his initial fondness for the surroundings in favor of a more realistic appraisal. It was one thing to visit sharecroppers for a few weeks, to savor the novelty, freedom, and elemental simplicity of such a life, but quite another to spend one's entire span of years sleeping in vermin-infested beds, wearing threadbare clothing, and doing demeaning work for virtually no wages. The hand-to-mouth existence was better observed than led. When Allie Mae burst out, "Oh, I do *hate* this house *so bad!* Seems like they ain't nothing in the whole world I can do to make it pretty," Agee's heart went out to her, for he knew the "beds, the bedding, and the vermin are such a crime against sex and the need of rest as no sadistic genius could much improve on." Still, he found much about the shack's lack of creature comforts to recommend. "I cannot unqualifiedly excite myself in favor of Rural Electrification," he wrote of that ambitious New Deal program, "for I am too fond of lamplight." Nor did he favor flush toilets, "for I despise and deplore the middle-class American worship of sterility and worship-fear of its own excrement." However, he stopped short of insisting that the Burroughses were better off without toilets and electric lights: "I will say, then, that whether or not the Bathroom Beautiful is to be preached to all nations, it is not to their advantage in a 'civilized' world to have to use themselves as the simplest savages do." Yet the middle class would do well to study and learn to appreciate the sharecroppers' mode of existence.

Of all the deprivations the Burroughses suffered, lack of privacy perturbed Agee the most. He felt twinges of prudishness when accidentally confronted with their nakedness, and he speculated that confinement in the small space of the shack seriously inhibited their sex lives. There was nowhere anyone could go to make love in private, or, for that matter, to eat, sit, read, go to the bathroom, or sleep. They were forced to carry on every function in public, much as they hated to, and Agee theorized that they had become "anaesthetized" by the situation. The most delicate of needs were tended to with a kind of vapid joylessness; the family existed in a stupor, a permanent state of shell shock.

He assumed the family was so accustomed to the lack of privacy that his presence had little effect on them, but in at least one instance their activities had an overpowering effect on him. Shortly before leaving for New York, he caught sight of Allie Mae nursing her baby "with one broken breast." Though he had earlier expressed his loathing for parenthood to Via, he underwent a change of heart and was deeply moved by this vision of maternal tenderness. "I see how against her body he is so many things in one," he wrote of the sight, "the child in the melodies of the womb, the Madonna's son, human divinity sunken from the Cross at rest against his mother, for at the heart and leverage of that young body, gently, taken in all the pulse of his being, the penis partly erected." After spending two hot and dusty months in Alabama, he was leaving with a new and startling desire for a child of his own; and, once acknowledged, the drive for paternity would not be denied. If there was any moral he might draw from the infinite series of impressions he had absorbed during his stay, it was to be fruitful and multiply.

Agee returned to New York in early September "half-crazy with the heat and diet" and utterly exhausted from nightlong bouts of writing by lamplight. When he recovered his strength he was a changed man, far more self-confident, deliberate, and endowed with a sense of gravity—the seriousness of purpose of the man who has found his mission in life.

This time around he did not dash to the typewriter to unburden himself of his impressions in a feverish rush, deeming it wiser to keep them to himself for a precious while. Otherwise he might violate the sacred spirit of the trip. In retrospect it seemed a sort of religious retreat, his version of the poet's ecstasy (meaning literally a standing-apart from the crowd). Then, too, he was concerned about preserving the anonymity of his sharecropper friends; the last thing he wanted to do was trigger a storm of publicity and subject the families to embarrassing public scrutiny. And he was concerned about what they themselves would think of the resulting article; the Fieldses, Burroughses, and Tingles were all illiterate (except for the small children), but they could see Evans' pitiless photographs for themselves.

No, he could not in good conscience pay back the three families with a cruel unmasking. Rather, he wanted to make known his gratitude in a way they could appreciate, and so he debated with Evans the propriety of donating a mule. Though Agee said he could afford the cost of the animal "by scraping the very cervix of my bank account," he worried that the gift would compromise his fragile relationship with the Burroughses in particular, who would immediately perceive Agee and Evans as "Moe and Joe Bountiful, or, as bad or worse, creditors to a friend who has too many creditors now." Agee feared, "Our position as rich guys would become even more falsified." Unable to come up with a suitable way of repaying the debt he thought he owed them, he tabled the idea until Christmas, when he sent inexpensive trinkets.

To add to his insecurities, Agee learned that his blithe friend Wilder Hobson was suffering a nervous breakdown. It seemed that after spending several weeks in Japan with MacLeish gathering information for a special issue on that country, Hobson succumbed to a writer's nightmare: he blocked. Now he sat before his typewriter by the hour, sweating, unable to tap out a coherent sentence, let alone a paragraph. The invincible MacLeish meanwhile steadily ground out his usual letter-perfect copy, further demoralizing Hobson, who soon departed *Fortune* for a less demanding post at *Time's* new competitor, *Newsweek,* where he gradually recovered his high spirits, if not his burning ambition.

Of more critical importance to the fate of the sharecropper article, the political winds at *Fortune* were shifting rather dramatically from left to right. While Agee and Evans were in Alabama, Luce decided he had had his fill of New Deal folderol and set the magazine on a more conservative course. He transferred Ingersoll, who had been instrumental in endowing the magazine with a social conscience, to a high post at *Time* and appointed the more pliable Eric Hodgins as the new managing editor. The switch marked the end of an era at *Fortune* and signaled the cadre of leftist writers that their political opinions would no longer be welcome in the oversize pages of the magazine. Heaping insult upon injury, Hodgins immediately put a strict new dress code into force. Writers were no longer permitted to wear casual clothes on the job; the last thing

Luce wanted was for some left-leaning writer such as James Agee to show up in the immaculate offices of a tycoon in rumpled khakis and a work shirt.

Dwight Macdonald was one of the first important casualties of the new regime. Assigned to a comprehensive four-part series on the United States Steel Corporation, he turned in a stinging Marxist critique of the behemoth. When Luce rejected the articles, Macdonald, long restive in this hotbed of capitalism, promptly resigned. "Dwight," his mother exclaimed on hearing the news, "you must be mad! You're making $10,000 a year and getting a raise almost every year . . . and you throw it all up on a whim."

"But mother," Macdonald patiently explained, "*Fortune* is against the New Deal and I'm for it. Also it bores me."

Whereupon Macdonald recycled his U.S. Steel article for *The Nation* magazine, an act bringing a summons from Hodgins. "Do you realize what you've done, Macdonald?" the editor shouted. "You're a traitor and a thief. You had no right to use material you collected here in another magazine." Before Macdonald could mumble an apology Hodgins showed him the door.

The corporate primal scene boded ill for the fate of Agee's sharecropper assignment. If Luce objected to Macdonald's portrayal of U.S. Steel, how would he respond to Agee's far more outlandish depiction of sharecroppers? The article's chances of appearing in the pages of *Fortune* in anything remotely resembling its original form were very poor indeed. It was in this adverse political climate that Agee began work on the piece, but, not surprisingly, he found it "impossible" to construct an article "in any form and length *Fortune* can use; and I am now so stultified trying to do that, that I'm afraid I've lost the ability to make it right in any way." He showed the misconceived result to Hodgins, who rejected it out of hand and ordered Agee to work up a more conventional assessment. This Agee refused to do, pleading that he had completed the article that had originally been assigned; it was not his fault that *Fortune* had changed the rules in his absence. To Fitzgerald, observing the controversy from close range, *Fortune*'s attitude reeked of hypocrisy: "It appeared that the magazine, committed of course to knowing what was the case, had had the offhand humanity and imagination and impertinence to send an ex-president of the Harvard *Advocate* into the helpless and hopeless lives of cotton tenant farmers, but that it did not have the courage to face in full the case he presented."

Agee reacted to the setback with surprising resilience, for he had already formulated alternate plans. If *Fortune* did not want several hundred thousand words of commentary on the lives of sharecroppers, in addition to much soul-searching on the part of their author, he would assemble the drafts into the book he had long anticipated writing. *Fortune* might have lost interest in the New Deal, but the Depression remained the principal topic in the public eye; surely a publisher for such an account would not be unduly hard to find.

To prepare himself for the task of writing the book, he set down his thoughts about experimental literature—the category to which he expected his book would belong—in an article for the left-wing *New Masses*. Appearing in the December 1936 issue, "Art for What's Sake?" was the work of a serious young man attempting to reconcile Surrealism, rejected by orthodox Marxists, with left-wing views. A truly modern art, the article explained, must contain both the truths of the unconscious and the social ideals of the Marxists. He thereby justified his book, which would, he hoped, fuse personal meditation with political outrage. He could combine the interior landscape he had explored as a poet with the external world he covered as a journalist. Before the trip to Alabama, each of the concerns had seemed mutually exclusive; now he would strive to integrate them into a well-rounded whole. The revelation liberated his literary energies. Let Luce prostrate himself at the feet of the capitalist bosses. Agee would wage a secret war against the entire filthy system.

Despite the theoretical buttress he had erected, Agee found it difficult to compress his wealth of impressions about sharecroppers into a book. From time to time he fired off brief communiqués on the struggle to Evans. One read, "I am giving myself an awful fucking still after 6 weeks work to get a leverage on how to write this Alabama trip right. O well." And to Father Flye he wrote, "I seem to be lazy, and badly organized . . . and am going to have to get violent with myself."

In frustration, he seized on the idea of making a documentary film about sharecroppers in collaboration with his new friend Jay Leyda, who had recently returned to the United States after three

LEFT: Henry Clay Agee, James Agee's paternal grandfather.
(*Photograph courtesy of Dr. Oliver Agee*)

RIGHT: Hugh James Agee, the writer's father, in Panama.
(*Photograph courtesy of St. Andrew's-Sewanee*)

OPPOSITE TOP: The three Agee brothers. *Left to right:* Frank, the undertaker; Hugh James; and John. *(Photograph courtesy of Dr. Oliver Agee)*

OPPOSITE BOTTOM: *Left to right:* James Agee; his mother, Laura; and his sister, Emma. *(Photograph courtesy of St. Andrew's-Sewanee)*

Looking west along Union Avenue in Knoxville, Tennessee, 1913. *(Photograph courtesy of the McClung Historical Collection, Knoxville-Knox County Public Library)*

ABOVE: Robert Preston and
Thomas Chalmers at the movies
in *All the Way Home*, a 1963
screen adaptation of
A Death in the Family.

LEFT: The Chapel at St. Andrew's,
scene of Agee's religious
crisis. (*Photograph courtesy
of St. Andrew's-Sewanee*)

OPPOSITE: Agee as an aspiring
writer at Harvard, a copy
of Dostoevsky's *The Possessed*
in one hand, a cigarette in
the other. (*Photograph
courtesy of Alma Neuman*)

LEFT:
Walker Evans photographed
by Helen Levitt.

BELOW LEFT:
Allie Mae Burroughs, 1936.
Farm Security Administration
photograph by Walker Evans.
*(Reproduced courtesy of
the Library of Congress)*

BELOW RIGHT:
Floyd Burroughs, 1936. Farm
Security Administration
photograph by Walker Evans.
*(Reproduced courtesy
of the Library of Congress)*

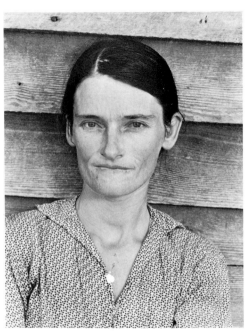

TOP:
The Tingle family
(Frank, extreme right)
singing hymns on
Sunday, 1936. Farm
Security Administration
photograph by Walker
Evans. *(Reproduced
courtesy of the
Library of Congress)*

MIDDLE:
The Fields family
at home, 1936. Farm
Security Administration
photograph by Walker
Evans. *(Reproduced
courtesy of the
Library of Congress)*

BOTTOM:
Allie Mae Burroughs
in the backyard of the
home where Agee
lived for three weeks
while gathering material
for *Let Us Now Praise
Famous Men*, 1936. Farm
Security Administration
photograph by Walker
Evans. *(Reproduced
courtesy of the
Library of Congress)*

Left to right: Alma, Agee, and Delmore Schwartz photographed by Helen Levitt in New Jersey, 1939. This photograph prompted Agee to write love letters to Alma years after they were divorced.

Agee and Delmore Schwartz photographed by Helen Levitt at Monk's Farm, New Jersey, 1939.

LEFT: Alma photographed by Agee in their West 15th Street apartment.
(*Photograph courtesy of Alma Neuman*)

RIGHT: Alma in Mexico shortly after she left Agee, 1941.
(*Photograph courtesy of Alma Neuman*)

Agee and Mia Fritsch, his third wife, photographed by Helen Levitt.

LEFT:

Father James H. Flye.
(*Photograph courtesy
of St. Andrew's-Sewanee*)

BELOW:

Humphrey Bogart and
John Huston during the
filming of *The African Queen*.
(*Photograph courtesy of
The Museum of Modern
Art/Film Stills Archive*)

Agee photographed by Helen Levitt at his home on King Street shortly before his death.

years in Moscow, studying film under Eisenstein. To Agee's way of thinking, Leyda possessed impeccable credentials. He now worked in the film division of the new Museum of Modern Art, where he often screened Russian films for Agee. "He is a smart guy all right and a likable one," Agee wrote Evans of Leyda. "I wd definitely not think a first rate director but very strong among the second-stringers and a hell of a lot more valuable than harmful to American pictures." Recasting the project as a film, Agee, working with a budget of only $350, reduced the contents to "the rhythmic howling of nearly static stuff strung together between about 4 very simple, spaced sentences in which you wd hope to give the words a sort of spaced-chord suspense value." But he soon forgot about the plan, as he did a multitude of others that he and Leyda concocted.

Agee came to realize that lack of time was his most serious problem. It was impossible to write a complex book, or even a screenplay, while toiling for Luce. He considered the possibility of signing a contract with a publisher and collecting an advance on which to live while he completed the work, though in principle he considered advances unnecessarily restrictive and, for the serious writer, immoral. However, he found it seductively easy to locate an editor willing to offer him a contract, and a very good editor it was.

Agee discovered that in New York's densely textured social life, opportunities had a way of materializing as if by magic. In this case, Via's close friend and former roommate, Mary Louise White, had just married Edward Aswell, an editor who enjoyed a reputation for sponsoring serious writers at Harper & Brothers. Having recently signed Thomas Wolfe, who had broken his long-standing arrangement with Max Perkins at Scribner's, Aswell responded positively to Via's recommendation that he consider her husband's sharecropper book. Long fascinated by Wolfe, whose Southern childhood and lyrical writing paralleled his own in so many ways, Agee ignored his reservations about contracts and advances to enter into negotiations with Aswell. If all went according to plan, he would be able to resign from *Fortune* and, contract in hand, devote his full time to the book.

Luce, however, had other ideas. Evans' photographs and Agee's text were still the property of *Fortune,* and the magazine, burned by Macdonald's escapade, was not about to let them go. To Agee's silent relief, negotiations with Aswell came to a halt. By the time Luce finally did consent to release the material, which he considered worthless, Agee was wholly absorbed in an astonishing upheaval in his personal life. For all its promise and importance, the sharecropper book received scant attention as a rough-and-tumble game of passion played itself out.

9

PASSION

The early months of 1937 found Agee preoccupied with his barely suppressed sexual longing. His four-year-old marriage to Via had become cold, abrasive, lifeless; at best they were friends. Everywhere he turned he saw women who seemed more attractive and who were ready and willing to return his interest. For the moment he confined his illicit activities to the cuddling of stray women at Greenwich Village parties, usually in the kitchen. As his restlessness became an open secret among their friends, both he and Via sensed their relationship was doomed; it was only a question of when and how it would end.

Several years after the fact, Agee re-created the events surrounding the breakup in voluminous detail, claiming that he possessed total recall and could remember everything that had ever happened to him. With his obsessive temperament and fanatical attention to detail, he recounted the story so fully and accurately that he planned to make it the basis of yet another autobiographical novel, one he never completed.

As Agee told it, he was then a young man entertaining "great delusions of worldly wisdom, of sophistication in matters of flirtation," a dangerously "passionate contempt for caution and convention," and a "passionate conviction that liberty and enjoying oneself are among the highest attemptable virtues." All these unfulfilled passions, and Via shared none of them. Sooner murder an infant in its cradle than nurse unacted desires, Agee repeated to himself, after Blake; but by this standard he had committed an untold number of crimes. To dull his senses, he resorted to a number of what he considered "secondary" pleasures: smoking, reading, listening to jazz, and, above all, drinking (highballs, at this point).

Among these minor vices, it was the drinking that Via most resented. Late one night in their Perry Street apartment, Agee later recalled, she offered him a glass of hot milk. Naked under the covers of their bed, he lifted his drink in reply. "You dope," Via said. "You don't know the meaning of enough, do you?"

"Sure I do," Agee replied. "Enough is too much."

Exasperated, Via applied camphor balm to her lips, rendering them unkissable. "I'm sorry I interrupted your little peccadillo in the kitchen," she said, referring to another of his "unseriously promiscuous" misadventures at a party they had attended earlier in the evening.

"So am I. It wasn't intentional, you know."

"That's what I mean, honey. I mean I'm sorry on your account."

Agee found his wife's lack of jealousy infuriating. If only she would make a sign, show a little passion, he might stop, but he feared she cared for him as little as he cared for her. Surely other couples felt more deeply. Not long before, he had seen one of his friends, Alice Morris, "slapping the bejesus" out of her husband, book reviewer Harvey Breit. In public, Agee denounced her possessiveness, but in private he conceded, "That's a wife, a *real* wife." When Via tentatively offered to make love, he kissed her on her cheek without desire and took another drag on his cigarette.

The next day the unhappy couple went for a walk in nearby Washington Square, where they were surrounded by "young families absolutely reeking of fecundity; and lovers who have just managed to get up after a day and night of it and are now taking in the soft air, on buttery legs, walking hip to hip." As for the Agees, they enjoyed neither sexual love nor family happiness.

Soon after, they went to tea at the apartment of Via's older sister, Silvia. Going to a tea party was not Agee's idea of fun; this pointless display of gentility sorely tried his patience, and it might even have been a ploy to restrict his drinking. But all was not lost, for among the guests was the attractive young musician who had been smitten with him at his wedding—Alma Mailman. She had just moved to New York in search of excitement and a musical career. The daughter of a Utica jeweler, she was tired of playing the role of Dr. Saunders' "lower-class protégée" and longed to make her own way in the world. At twenty-five, she was three years younger than Agee, sexually innocent, and brimming with curiosity.

Agee soon noticed the ardent, frightened girl from Utica. "She is exceedingly pretty. Her dressing and makeup are out of key with that of *any* of the people" at the party, he wrote of his first impression. Because she was "a little bit poor, provincial, garish, and movie fannish," Agee came to feel a "secret sympathy" with her; they were both outsiders. His compassion for her swelled when he saw the others looking at her as if she were a "tart," and even the Saunders sisters, who should have known better, treated her with "an ineradicable tinge of patronage." He caught her glance, she caught his, and as the party wore on they stared ever more boldly at each other.

Later, in ostensibly casual conversation with Via, Agee learned that Alma and Via's brother, Frisk, had been engaged but had broken off, in part because of pressure applied by Via's snobbish Aunt Matilda. Since Alma came from a modest Jewish background, she was something of an anomaly in the Saunders household. The more Agee learned about her, the more intrigued he became. Soon after, he talked with Evans about the girl, confiding that he was in love, infatuated, he hardly knew what. "You'd better watch out," Evans advised over drinks. "You're going to get into trouble." Hashing over his feelings with Evans usually gave Agee a measure of insight, but this time he ignored the warning and remained "at least one jump behind the truth."

Several weeks later, Agee and Alma met again at another party, where the guests were drawn largely from the ranks of Time Inc. They were given to playing a game they called Sardines. The rules were simple: When the lights were turned off, couples formed spontaneously and dashed off to a private corner for a few moments' furtive groping. After several unsatisfying encounters, Agee sidled up to Alma, and, during the next blackout, led her to the roof, where they could be alone. But once they reached their destination, they were overcome with shyness. "You know, they won't ever find us here," Agee finally said. "Sooner or later we'd have to give ourselves up."

"Why?" Alma asked. "Have you been up here before? You don't seem like the kind of man who'd hide without a girl." Agee laughed, embraced Alma, and kissed her on the cheek. She quickly slithered out of his grasp, saying, "You *know* you mustn't."

But Agee did not see matters the same way. When he liked someone, he felt impelled to demonstrate his affection; it would be dishonest of him not to. Despite Alma's show of resistance, he was utterly captivated by her "odd blend of adolescence, ripeness, flirtatiousness, and her innocence." He took her hand, murmuring, "Do you know I like you very much? . . . Why, I've been missing you badly; and I hardly know you. . . . More than anything else, I just want to be the best possible kind of friend to you. Do you see?"

"But you know so much more than I do," Alma said.

"Maybe that's one of the reasons."

By this time she had succumbed to Agee's homespun charm. In one-on-one conversations he was enormously convincing. The weaving of his hands, the extraordinary effort he made to shape each word with his lips, and the slight tremor in his face caused by the intensity of his desire to communicate—all combined in a mesmerizing display. Alma felt as if they were the only people in the world.

However, the tête-à-tête did not go unnoticed. Late that evening, Via, applying the hateful camphor balm to her lips, asked, "Do you intend to tell me about it?"

Agee played dumb. "About what?"

"You know perfectly well about what."

"Why sure I would. If there was anything much to tell.... You think I made a pass at her?"

"Of course I do," Via shot back.

"Well, I didn't. Nothing you could possibly really call a pass. Why, I put my arm around her; I kissed her once: but it was just purely in friendship and both of us knew it. Besides, she seems perfectly able to take care of herself. Half the guys in the room were after her."

As far as Via was concerned, her husband's behavior conformed to his established pattern of casual flirtation and indicated no serious threat. But their conversation continued, "in this painful blend of honesty and self-deceit and calculated dishonesty" until they went to sleep.

Again, Evans warned Agee to keep his distance from Alma. "She's a high school girl!" he said.

Agee insisted, "What excites me is seeing anyone start to *learn* a few things—start to *grow up.*" He had inadvertently made her his protégée instead of the Saunders', and the perceptive Evans was having none of it.

"She'll be a high school girl twenty years from now, no matter what happens to her." Yet even he was forced to admit there was something "God damned attractive about her." Agee heartily concurred.

He next saw Alma in, of all places, his own apartment. Suspecting nothing out of the ordinary in Agee's feelings for Alma, Via invited both her sister and the younger girl to dinner. At the last minute Silvia dropped out with a cold, and Alma came by herself in a downpour. At the end of the meal it was still raining, and, at Via's insistence, Alma agreed to stay the night. There ensued a "pitiful and ominous ritual as the two women spread sheets for the studio couch in the livingroom," while a subdued Agee quietly played the piano.

After Via fell asleep, Agee stole into the living room, where Alma, wearing one of Via's nightgowns, slept soundly on the guest bed. At first he told himself he simply wanted to watch the girl in repose. But he could not resist taking her relaxed hand and stroking her bare arm, "first the outside, then the more sensitive skin; then above the elbow, with the greatest subtlety and excitement." Sooner murder an infant in its cradle . . .

Suddenly Alma awoke "sharp as an animal" to order Agee back to his bed. He held his ground long enough to kiss her, to feel her breasts, and to sense that "despite a flicker of panic and good sense she accepts and responds." They made love, Agee experiencing a passion and fulfillment he had never known with Via. It was only when the sky lightened that he crept back into bed beside the sleeping form of his wife. Overcome with remorse, Agee considered ending this brief affair while there was still a chance to save his marriage. In the morning, Alma left in a great hurry, before either Agee or Via could speak to her. Via could not imagine what was bothering the poor girl—some personal problem, in all probability.

For the next few weeks Agee and Alma kept their distance. They were playing with fire, and they knew it. Agee could not bring himself to forget about her. Thoughts of Alma crowded his every waking moment; if he believed in the truth of sex, he had to see her again, and again. Finally, after Via fell asleep one night, Agee left their apartment "with the utmost possible stealth" and walked to the apartment Alma shared with her friend Gladys Goldstone. With Gladys asleep, Agee and Alma talked in conspiratorial whispers. As he motioned to leave, he kissed her goodnight, a kiss so fond and long that they wound up making love on a nearby couch. Afterward they felt "excited and sad" as they realized they were falling in love. To his chagrin, Agee found himself uttering the cliché that "this thing is bigger than we are." They were prisoners of their passions, hardly responsible for their actions. "After all," Agee said, "we've done about the best we could, short of not seeing each other at all. I'm not going to try to pull that crap about My Wife Doesn't Understand Me. She 'understands' me all right. And I love her very much. . . . Only it's been a long time since we felt even the least bit *in* love; and the way I feel with you, I begin to wonder if we ever did, really." And he left Alma to ponder his words in solitude.

When he returned to Perry Street, Via was awake, and he immediately knew from the look on her face that she now suspected the extent of his involvement with Alma. "*Whatever* it is, we need to tell each other the truth," Via said.

"I won't lie," Agee replied. "You know I hate to. Only I hate to make you feel bad, too."

"It's a girl, isn't it?"

Agee nodded.

"Who is it?"

He relished the act of "saying The Name." As Via expressed her shock and disbelief, Agee took her hand.

"How long has this been going on?"

"Not very long. Not with any intensity, I mean." He said the affair was "serious in the sense that . . . we're kind of in love with each other—infatuated, anyhow; it's too soon to tell which really; . . . the one thing in this world we're determined to do is not to hurt." He told Via not to worry, explaining, "This kind of thing is bound to happen from time to time in any marriage, but we'll come through it." Or so he hoped.

"I suppose the thing I ought to do is simply make life unbearable for you," Via said with that air of well-bred detachment he loathed. He gave her a look of "compassionate skepticism." She continued, "But just a few things I *do* ask you: Don't ever let it get to Mummy and Daddy that you're carrying on an affair with *her,* of all people; it would simply break their hearts. . . . And one thing more, . . . don't ever *sneak out* again; just tell me; I'll be as good as I can about it." They embraced, Via suddenly aware of the other woman's scent on her husband's body.

Agee could not help but wonder whether Via was simply giving him enough rope to hang himself. If she had only yanked the leash, how quickly he would have come to heel. Still, he feared the consequences, the "bad damage" he might do her. Via was not as strong and independent as she pretended to be; nor, for that matter, was he. Nonetheless, he continued to see Alma regularly, and the affair became an open secret among their friends.

His doubts about Via's ability to bear up under the strain soon proved justified. Coming home late one night to Perry Street, he found the apartment empty. He waited up for Via to arrive, and when she did return she was drunk and her hand was tied in a handkerchief. "Hello, honey," he said. "Where the hell have you been?"

She regarded him drunkenly "and with her hideous kind of attempt at flirtatious 'mystery.' " "Wouldn't you like to *know!*" After beating around the bush for a while, she burst into tears.

Agee discovered she had been at the Hobsons', where, in despair over the affair, she had smashed a glass and cut her hand.

"O my darling, my darling," Agee said softly as he undressed her. "Come on; come on, dear; let's clean up that hand and get you to bed. Why, you're drunk, honey. You're stinko. I never saw you so drunk in my life."

Once in bed, Via reiterated her long-frustrated desire for a child, "the one thing that might give us a chance," but Agee remained inflexible on the matter. He wanted a child very badly, but not with Via.

"We've been through this so many times before," he explained wearily. "We knew we couldn't when we married; I don't know how it all got changed around."

"Maybe because I turned into a grown woman and you turned into a grown man." Via would not drop the subject; she had to know why Agee refused to have a child with her.

"I guess I'm just—not in—not enough in love, that's all. There's nothing I can help about that."

"Tell me the truth. Have you ever wanted one with her?" Via asked, referring to Alma.

Agee nodded. "The first time I ever went to bed with her."

Via, now in a "sudden terrible fury," shrieked, "Then *go on* to her for God's sake, *go on* to your *light o' love.* Get out of here!"

Someone pounded on the ceiling to silence them. Furious, stunned, exhilarated, Agee grabbed Via, kissed her hard, and went.

What Agee did not include in his account of his disintegrating marriage was the myriad of other matters on his mind. By the time he admitted to Via he would rather have a child with Alma it was well into summer, and his career was going nowhere. Unable to sign a book contract and resign from *Fortune* altogether, he compromised by exchanging his staff position for the promise of sufficient free-lance work to keep the wolf from his various doors. Without Macdonald, Hobson, and Ingersoll, the place just was not the same anymore, and Agee sensed he would soon sever this last link to *Fortune* too.

Although he had more time to himself, he accomplished little on the sharecropper book. With Luce still refusing to release the material, work on it seemed futile. Occasionally he tossed off poems, but they were not the finely worked, reflective exercises of his youth. Now he wrote on satirical themes in verses so simple that he composed in his head. In one, he considered the reasons underlying his attraction to Alma.

> *Mumsy told me not to play with all those rougher girls and boys*
> *And perhaps that's why I sleep today with a girl in smelly corduroys:*
> *And if only Mummy had kept mum about the sunnier side of God,*
> *Perhaps I wouldn't have left Him on the seamier side of the sod.*

Once whetted, his appetite for rebellion would not be denied.

He spent his evenings with Alma or Via, and when he had had his fill of them, sought refuge at a Greenwich Village jazz bar known as Nick's, a "pinched and intensely crowded little 3 cornered joint where you have to enter past the full blast of the band." There he drank heavily, listened to the band play into the wee hours, and imagined himself adrift in a northern New Orleans. Observing Agee's dissipation from a distance, Macdonald found much to wave his bony finger at. "Even for a modern writer, he was extraordinarily self-destructive," Macdonald wrote. "He was always ready to sit up all night with anyone who happened to be around, or to go out at midnight looking for someone: talking passionately, brilliantly, but too much, and in general cultivating the worst set of work habits in Greenwich Village." If only Agee had had the knack of self-preservation, Macdonald lamented. If only he knew better than to fritter away his creative energy on pointless talk. If only he lacked the urge to punish himself, to complicate his life to such an extent that he was "rarely able to come to simple fulfillment." If only . . .

After the initial thrill of liberation wore off, Agee wondered whether his new arrangement with *Fortune* was not, after all, a mistake. He had deprived himself of a steady salary and regular raises for a partial freedom he did not use. On the one hand, he told himself, "I never intend to write at all *steadily* for another [magazine] again unless it is a hundred percent work I want to do and believe in for itself. . . . I will work for money only when I have to have it and think security and solidity . . . murderous traps and delusions"; on the other hand, he had nothing to show for his self-righteousness beyond a shattered marriage. Life had a way of holding him hostage to his beliefs.

It was in this mood of angry disillusionment that he accepted an important assignment for the "new" *Fortune* in which he was supposed to give a madcap account of a luxury cruise in the Caribbean aboard the turboelectric liner *Oriente,* pride of the New York and Cuba Mail Steamship Company. The previous summer he had devoted two months to investigating the lives of the wretched of the earth, whom he revered; now he was assigned to spend six days covering the carriage trade, whom he despised. With sure journalistic instinct, he turned from comforting the afflicted to afflicting the comfortable. In retaliation, he planned to make his account into a satirical tour de force. Even better, he would again work with Evans. And Via could come along for the ride as well.

Sailing from New York on a bright August morning, Agee, Evans, and Via decided to hide their true identities from the other passengers for the duration of the voyage. They would not reveal even that they knew one another and would meet only in secret to compare notes and impressions. While Agee walked the decks and ate the overgenerous meals, Via and Evans broke the pledge long enough to establish a rapport. They recognized they were two of a kind—reserved, thoughtful, and not given to Agee's wild behavior. When Agee realized the obvious bond of sympathy that had formed between his wife and his best friend, he was delighted for them and relieved that someone of Evans' caliber would take an interest in Via.

But the excursion aroused his disgust. So quick was he to condemn the pleasure-seeking of all those around him that he might have been a priest in a brothel. This was not a luxury liner, it was a ship of fools. The headwaiter was a "prim Arthur Treacher type," the menu "pretentious," the food "standard, sterile, turgid, summer-hotel type" fare. After a few days the average passenger, Agee guessed, was "bored with himself and with whomever he knew and sank into depression," while deluding himself into thinking that he was happy. The spectacle of enforced jollity made Agee want to vomit.

He anticipated a relief from the nonstop eating and drinking when the ship docked at Havana; he longed to steep himself in an alien culture, if only for a short while, but insensitive tour guides conducted passengers "at brutal speed through that staggering variety and counterpoint of detail whose sum makes a city as individual as a soul."

His disgust with the passengers was matched only by his surprise at their inhibitions. "Flirtation seldom attained either high temperature or seriousness" until the so-called Last Supper, when the would-be party girls drank more liquor than they could handle. To Agee the drunken women were harridans trading insults that belied their insecurity. Here and there an angry wife threw a glass of planter's punch at her sozzled husband; Via was among those tossing drinks, though Agee refrained from mentioning her by name in the article. When a waiter asked the rowdy crowd to stop breaking the glasses, they broke more out of spite. It was an ugly scene out of a novel by John O'Hara. Agee supposed the drunken rudeness stemmed from sexual frustration. An orgy might cure what ailed the drunken passengers, or a dose of poverty, but nothing else would.

When Agee sat down to write his account of the "Six Days at Sea" for the September issue of *Fortune,* his running feud with Via informed every satirical jibe. In castigating the passengers, he flaunted his contempt for her *haut bourgeois* upbringing and tastes. Much as he loved Louise Saunders, he could no longer bring himself to subscribe to her values; they belonged to the old order that a great historical wind would sweep away.

By the time he finished the article he had become so angry with the Saunders' world that he considered himself a Communist "by sympathy and conviction." His politically committed friends such as Dwight Macdonald did not take Agee's conversion all that seriously; they believed in the sincerity of his moral outrage, of course, but when it came to politics they thought him hopelessly naïve, romantic, and befuddled. In contrast, they were hard-nosed pragmatic types, interested in debating economic policy and the abuse of power, but Agee lacked the most elementary understanding of these topics; impassioned discussions of ends and means left him cold. He read no more than a smattering of Marx, nor did he formally enlist in any branch of the Party. Still, he was more Communist than capitalist. He fervently believed in the brotherhood of man, and he was prepared to endorse any political philosophy that promoted that idea.

Agee occasionally expounded his hazy social theories to a new acquaintance, Selden Rodman, during long, music-filled evenings in the Chrysler Building, that bastion of capitalism. Rodman was a darkly handsome young aesthete who had been educated at Yale; he had met Agee through MacLeish, and, small world that it was, happened to be Macdonald's brother-in-law at the time. Like Agee, Rodman cultivated a multitude of interests in the arts. He had made a name for himself as an anthologist and publisher of a leftist magazine called *Common Sense.* One day at the magazine's head-quarters at 315 Fourth Avenue, Rodman tried to entice Agee into contributing a poem to the publication, but Agee demurred, explaining, "I've got them in my head, not on paper." Rodman sat Agee before a typewriter, and without a moment's hesitation he batted out one of the poems in his head. He called it "Millions Are Learning How," and it expressed as succinctly as any manifesto his political credo.

> *From now on kill America out of your mind.*
> *America is dead these hundred years.*
> *You've better work to do, and things to find.*
> *Waste neither time nor tears.*
>
> *See, rather, all the millions and all the land*
> *Mutually shapen as a child of love.*
> *As individual as a hand.*
> *And to be thought highly of. . . .*
>
> *These poisons which were low along the air*
> *Like mists, like mists are lifting. Even now*
> *Thousands are breathing health in, here and there:*
> *Millions are learning how.*

Rodman ran the poem in the January 1938 issue of *Common Sense.*

Despite Rodman's encouragement, Agee secretly considered his career as a poet finished, a casualty of his unsettled personal life. "His skill with traditional meters declined," Fitzgerald noted. "It remained, now, mistrusted and for long periods unused, or used only casually and briefly." Reading a new poem by Robert Frost in Bickford's cafeteria on Lexington and 43rd Street with Fitzgerald, Agee recognized perfection when he saw it and conceded he would never attain it himself. So he ceased to try. And if Frost was turning rural American themes into near-great poetry, W. H. Auden, to Agee's way of thinking, was doing an even better job with international political issues. Among all the poets of his day, Agee respected Auden the most, and dearly coveted the Englishman's skill and fame. In contrast, he was an incomplete man, as he explained to Louise Saunders in a heartfelt diatribe.

> I have a fractional idea what poetry is or ought to be and do honestly try to live up to it as well as I can—but these poems and all my others, and even more myself, do nothing but make me embarrassed of myself for a fake and pretender. [I have] a feeling of having an essentially inert, cagey, and cautious mind which I will not possibly grow above since those are my only tools for growing above it. . . . I have got to use every kind of force & relaxation to quit talking, writing, or thinking about myself—and to break out of poetry-consciousness as well as my self-consciousness.

Though he despised Louise's materialistic values, he remained very much her spiritual son and protégé, even if he was, by his own standards, a failed one.

Throughout the sweltering summer of 1937 he often sought escape from personal torment by visiting the country home of one friend or another, where he obliterated his worries with bouts of tennis and drinking. He frequented the Hobsons' rented summer cottage on the North Shore of Long Island, where Wilder's brand of merriment offered a welcome antidote to the city's poisons. Hobson liked nothing so much as to march up and down of a Saturday night in the nude, playing his trombone. He took to referring to his brilliant writer friend as "the great North American Agee" and had the presence of mind to remark, when a sweet young thing appeared naked from the waist up on the tennis court, "Am I seeing double?"

During other weekends, Agee found respite at Dellbrook Farm, the New Jersey estate of Roger Baldwin, the presiding genius of the American Civil Liberties Union. Baldwin occupied the manor house, an imposing white edifice fit for a lord, and the bohemians he liked to surround himself with occupied rustic cottages dotting the grounds. Agee initially came to Dellbrook Farm through Rodman and was later joined by other members of the

Time Inc. crowd, who fished and swam in the Ramapo River and played tennis on a clay court. But the visitors were not by and large physical types; they preferred to talk and drink late into the night and sleep away lazy mornings in the stillness of the woods.

Agee became so entranced with the pastoral life that he came to consider such tranquil surroundings a necessity if he was to complete his book. The nervous instability of city life, combined with his marital dilemma, made real work in New York impossible. Though he badly needed to establish a stable domestic existence with one woman or another, he found himself unable to choose between passion and honor.

Returning to the city after these placid weekends, he was barely able to function; indecision reduced him to a state of nervous collapse. Walking through Sheridan Square with his friend Brick Frohock one evening in late summer, he began discussing his agony over Via and Alma and soon became so upset that he banged his head against the bricks of a building until blood covered his fore-head. To calm his friend, Frohock piled Agee into a car and drove out of the city. At Spuyten Duyvil Bridge a policeman, catching sight of Agee's bloodied face, stopped them and threatened to make an arrest. After showing his driver's license, Frohock quickly explained that he taught French at Columbia University and was simply taking home a friend who had suffered a slight accident; the policeman reluctantly let them go. Once they got back to New York, Agee showered and ate breakfast at Frohock's apartment before returning home late in the morning.

At some point during the evening, Agee had waxed eloquent on the incomplete sharecropper book. Fearing his friend would destroy the manuscript or inadvertently leave it in a cab, Frohock took it upon himself to visit Agee at home, find the manuscript (it was in the piano bench), and safeguard it until the fall, when Agee appeared to be in a calmer frame of mind. Agee seemed not to mind temporarily relinquishing the manuscript; he was more concerned, surprisingly, that Frohock might tell friends in Rockland of his marital problems and that word would filter back to his mother and stepfather, but Frohock promised Agee not to breathe a word.

In his account of the breakup of his marriage, Agee compared himself at this point to a mule caught between two bales of hay;

unable to choose, he had neither. While he agonized, Alma returned to Utica. Agee recalled that he planned to join her there, but she told him not to bother. He drove up anyway, and Alma, after resisting his advances as best she could, eventually yielded to his pleas and agreed to accompany him to a motel, where they renewed their affair. After she left, he sat up all night in the room they had shared writing her a letter containing his "highest idealism about living, love and sex." He tore it up, called her before breakfast, and conveyed his message over the phone. Convinced of his sincerity, Alma expressed the wish that he meet her father. Suddenly Agee was on the defensive. He had not bargained on reassuring her family of his intentions toward Alma. He looked a mess, and he was exhausted; but Alma insisted, and Agee agreed to the meeting. At her home the lovers hinted—at first obliquely, later broadly —at the secret affair. Alma's father became both excited and "scared for his daughter's virtue," a concern that touched the lovers and enhanced their feelings for one another.

Soon after, Agee had a "wild idea" that he outlined for Alma. "Let's drive to New Orleans and hear some real jazz and see the city. If we drive day and night, down and back, we ought to have about enough dough to see us through a few days there." Agee had about seventy dollars to his name and Alma fifteen. To keep their trip a secret, Alma explained to her father that she would return to New York by bus. She did take a bus, but she got off at the first stop, where Agee picked her up, and they drove down to New Orleans together. The trip marked the first acknowledgment that they were having more than an affair; it was one thing to sneak to her apartment, another to leave Via for several days to be with Alma. There would be hell to pay when they returned to New York, but Agee was not thinking of the consequences of his actions, only of his "speechless" happiness as they drove south.

As before, Agee relished the freedom of the open road, now spiced with sensual pleasure. Alma drove during the daylight hours; he drove at night, while she laid her head in his lap and drowsed. Before daybreak on the second morning they arrived at the summit of a mountain overlooking the Shenandoah Valley— broad, green, and peaceful—where they watched the sun rise. The world was so quiet they heard birds "whiffling" through the air. Descending the mountain, they paused to watch a turtle crawl across the highway. All of a sudden a car appeared out of nowhere to crush the turtle under its wheels. Alma went into hysterics. Agee eventually calmed her, but they both regarded the wanton killing as a very bad omen indeed.

Heading south again, they stopped in Knoxville. They were already low on money, but Agee remembered an old family friend, a bank teller, to whom he told a not-very-persuasive story about wanting to give money to a needy friend. The teller lent Agee thirty dollars. "Okay, honey," he said as he returned to the car. "We're in business again."

Since they were in Knoxville, Agee could not resist pointing out prominent features of his boyhood landscape. They drove to Highland Avenue, now "gone way down hill from not very high" and then to the Tyler home, which Agee discovered had been converted into an "unpainted rooming house"—much to his dismay. He wanted to get out of the car and walk around but was afraid old family friends would spot him and tell his mother he had been there with a strange woman. Truly he could not go home again, except in his imagination.

As they headed out of town, bound for the neutral territory of Chattanooga, Agee was overcome with nameless anxieties, and he feared Alma was fast "over extending her relative conventionality." To restore their spirits, they stopped to skinny-dip in a rough, rocky stream. Twice he saved Alma "with immense pleasure" from being swept away by the strong current. Over the roar of the water, a voice rang out, "Hey, have you-all gone outen your heads?" They looked around to see who was addressing them. It was only a well-meaning local who was afraid for their lives.

Refreshed, they pressed on to Chattanooga, where they went to the movies, spent the night in a "little cheap misery of a hotel," and departed in the morning for Birmingham and later New Orleans—which they reached in the "weird, pearly light of daybreak." There they collapsed in another third-rate hotel. Ever since those nights in Anna Maria, Florida, when he had listened to jazz on the radio, Agee had considered New Orleans his "Magic City," a place of hot music, plentiful liquor, and uninhibited sensual indulgence. Here Alma and he regaled themselves, eating oysters "as big as tennis shoes" and drinking potent rum. But the fun of absolute liberty did not last long; the pursuit of forbidden pleasure soon yielded to a general seediness and torpor. The sun beat down mercilessly. In the Jackson Park zoo they were horrified to see a heat-stunned lion too weak to defend its meat from a rat, and they never did hear the ecstatic jazz Agee imagined poured from every window and bar. The irony of the situation was not lost on Agee, who soon after noted, "All escapes are relative, and bestow their own peculiar forms of bondage."

On their last morning in New Orleans, Agee arose before Alma to walk the predawn streets of the Vieux Carré, where he bantered with the whores. "No thanks, honey," he said to one. "I'm married."

"Sweetie," she replied, "if it wasn't for you married men, us girls couldn't even stay in business."

"Yeah, but you don't know who I'm married *to!*"

"Oh, well, you're a lucky man, then."

"Baby! Am I lucky!" Agee exclaimed. Unable to "suppress his love for everyone," he added, "God bless you, sweetheart." And they parted with the "greatest friendliness and attraction."

When the time came to head back to New York, Agee and Alma were overcome with cold, queasy feelings of remorse. Their few moments of stolen pleasure faded fast before the dreadful permanence of the consequences. Their first night on the road north, they stopped at an "absolutely Christbitten tourist camp; little cabins like back houses; but their one recommendation is that they are set among trees so huge in the darkness that they must surely be virgin forest." Within their little cabin, they were confronted with the lamentable sight of a "bare bulb strung from center ceiling over center bed. Roaches three inches long, crawling down the cord, then dive-bombing." When he stepped on one, it crackled "like a frying steak." According to Agee's account, the situation went from bad to worse when they tried to get some rest.

> Increasing horror; hers worse than his. They turn out the light. The bed creaks dismally. She begins to be uncomfortable; ouch. He strikes a match; the sheet is alive with bedbugs. She begins to cry. They get up and get the hell out and drive all night up through the pitch black state of Mississippi, cutting east into Alabama. Nothing is open; nothing at all; except coffee for truck drivers. They get into a deep exhausted peacefulness travelling thus; a new kind of rapport; this is suddenly, terrifyingly interrupted by a breathtaking moment: out of ab-

solute darkness, travelling fast as possible, they . . . come onto a very new cement bridge; its railings glare white and make a whiffling sound; beyond, is total darkness. They get to the other side and stop a moment, not for love, but just to recover.

Later that night they arrived in Tuscaloosa, Alabama, where Agee's thoughts inevitably turned to the sharecroppers he had not seen in over a year. They planned to head directly for the forlorn plateau where the shacks were located, but the car began making "horrible noises." Running low on money again, Agee resorted to wiring Via for help. Awaiting her reply, he left the car at a garage and with Alma checked into a hotel. The following day, Via wired money; his debt to her was beyond all measure, as was his sense of guilt.

With car restored to running condition, the lovers proceeded to the Burroughses', who now seemed a "beautiful, wild, half-sane family"; Floyd and Allie Mae were "amazed and happy" to see Agee, who introduced Alma to all as his wife. He was profoundly relieved to discover that at least this one element of his past was still intact. The Burroughses seemed more precious to him than ever, the closest he had to an actual family now that he had destroyed his marriage and was in hiding from his mother and stepfather. They stayed for supper, Agee stuffing himself as he had before, while Alma went outside and vomited what she had eaten. Although Floyd implored his guests to stay the night, Agee knew Alma could not tolerate the vermin-infested bedding and reluctantly turned down the offer. After the meal, Agee, Alma, and the family sang a hymn of praise, and it was time to go. Agee knew he would never see the family again.

They swung through Nashville and lingered in Louisville, which, with its "incredible number of bars with cheap whiskey," struck Agee as a "drinker's paradise." They stormed through Steubenville, Ohio, a "cruelly forbidding small city," and Weirton, West Virginia, an "even more impressively ugly company town." On the last night of the trip, Agee slipped away from Alma long enough to send Via another telegram.

DARLING ARRIVING HOME SOMETIME TOMORROW (TUESDAY)
MUCH LOVE J.

On the last leg of the journey they were so depressed they could think of nothing to say. To cheer Alma, Agee sprang a surprise gift on her, a "small, cheap, pretty bracelet." Even this failed to lift her spirits. "I think I know how you feel, darling," Agee said.

"Do you?"

"I think so. Or maybe I don't. But I know how *I* feel."

Alma asked in a nasty tone, "How do *you* feel?"

"As if I couldn't stand to hurt anybody again."

"God, I'm so sick of hearing you say that."

"You can't be any sicker of it than I am. But I mean it, God knows. I don't want to do what *I* want anymore; I just want to do what *you* need—you and Via."

After much discussion, they agreed to be "faithful to this principle of generosity and compassion towards the others" as the George Washington Bridge appeared in the distance, "opening ahead of and above and around them like a prodigious harp."

He was back in New York, prepared to face the worst. He arrived at his "closed, dead, unused, dusty" apartment to find a present from Via—of all things, a piano score for a Mozart concerto, inscribed with love. The quixotic gesture made him feel "absolutely heartsick." There was also a note informing him that Via had spent the last few days at the Hobsons' and was now waiting for him at Nick's, the jazz bar. There he found Via, Walker, and the Hobsons: a jury of his peers ready to try him for gross misconduct in the course of discharging his duties as a husband. Via, having had a good deal to drink, slowly approached him with "enormous bravery and compassion and a strange, set smile, slowly disintegrating to the verge of tears." They embraced and sorrowfully walked home.

Late that night they sat, fully clothed, on the edge of their bed, talking. Agee revealed that the disappointments of the misbegotten journey had done nothing to temper his lust for Alma. "I still can't see why it isn't possible to conduct a love affair and a marriage at the same time without everyone being torn to bits," he wondered aloud.

After kissing him, Via flung a startling revelation in his face, one that dramatically reversed their positions relative to each other and taxed his belief in freedom to the utmost. She admitted she had taken a lover. Agee drifted on waves of alternating relief, generosity, and pain. But there was more. Now that they were being so honest and open and compassionate with one another, he had to know who her lover was; he insisted she tell him. Via simply said, "Walker."

He had set a trap, only to catch himself in nets of jealousy. What a fool he had been! There he was, weeks before, discussing with Evans the propriety of cheating on Via, loudly proclaiming his belief in sexual liberation. And now the shoe was on the other foot; it was his turn to suffer torments of jealousy. "Are you in love with him?" he asked Via. He could not keep himself from prying, especially when Via claimed the affair had saved her life.

"Do you want me to be?" she replied.

"I want you to have a little bit of *happiness* for a change."

"I don't think I'm particularly in love with him; no."

"Is he, with you?" Agee's question struck Via as painfully funny. This narrow little man with his hypersensitive tastes and absolute self-involvement—how could he be in love with anyone but himself? "Oh, he's not *that* bad," Agee said, wondering why in the world he was now defending Evans' prowess as a lover. Principles can make one do strange things.

"He's very dear to me," Via conceded. "I tell you I think he saved my life." And she wanted to know if her husband was jealous.

"Just a very little, darling. I wish to God I was more," Agee replied.

"That's just as I thought. We *really are* on the rocks, aren't we!" Tears came into her eyes; Agee took her in his arms.

"I'm not so sure about that, sweetheart," he said. "We're not if—*devotion, just even that*—means anything."

But later that night, "hideously restive," he crept from their bed and wrote Via a note: "Darling; I *am* going to see her; I've *got* to. But I promise you I will be back soon. I love you dear—J."

When he got to Alma's apartment, she sternly told him, "If you ever did the things to me that you're doing to her, I'd kill you." And she meant it. That was all Agee needed to hear; he knew Alma loved him.

If Via could not bring herself to "kill" her faithless husband, she soon demonstrated herself to be his equal in marital warfare, fully capable of extracting a terrible emotional toll, in her own quiet, well-bred way. She knew that Agee remained pathetically vulnerable to her opinion of him, that he continued to hold out the (to her, irrational) hope that she would bless his union with Alma as he condoned hers with Evans. So Via coyly suggested that Agee invite Alma to dinner, thus setting the stage for a memorable encounter.

Hearing of the invitation, Alma made a slighting reference to Via. Suddenly, Agee grabbed her by the shoulder and wrenched her around "in a cold rage."

"What do you mean by that!" he shouted. *"Don't you dare* speak about her like that! You hear me?" Eventually Agee recovered his equilibrium, but the seeds of mistrust sown by Via took root, and Alma did not come to dinner after all. Agee arrived home to find Via entertaining, even fondling, Evans in a most overt way. But he felt more embarrassment than jealousy at seeing his wife and his best friend carrying on.

He accepted Evans' continuing to see Via because the relationship allayed his own mounting sense of guilt; as long as Via was having an affair, he felt justified in continuing to pursue Alma. And when he was alone with Evans, drinking, he still confided his innermost thoughts to his friend. "I'm the guy who always thinks these things ought to be so easy, and look at the mess *I* make of it," he told a "quietly amused" Evans. "I'm the Author of Liberty; and I'm probably the most hooked man in Greater New York. I'm the guy who hates hurting anyone—and look at what I'm doing. Looks to me as if you and Via have got just about what I've always wished *I* could have: good fun, a compliant cuckold, no quarrels *. . . nuts."*

"I can think of two reasons," Evans said by way of explanation. "She isn't in love with me; and I'm not in love with her."

Agee's keen perception of the irony, not to mention the hypocrisy, of his situation was of no avail. He maintained control over his thoughts but, sadly, not over his actions. If only he could bring his better judgment to bear on his behavior. But he could no longer consider staying with Via. The real problem was not his attraction to Alma but his frustration with the Saunders' mentality. "Look here, Walker," he burst out. "Have you ever lived with a woman you felt no sexual love for, for five solid years?"

"I never intend to, either," Evans replied.

"Well, that's what I'm up against, and you know it. It wasn't any too good when I didn't have it anywhere else; and now it's just a living hell."

Evans warned, "You'd better do *something—soon*—or you'll destroy three people."

In the next few weeks, Agee, plagued by his pathological doubt, zigged toward Alma only to zag back to Via. Perhaps he and his wife, while unable to enjoy a satisfying sexual relationship, could settle for the "companionship" sustained by Louise and Percy over the years. Agee brought this section of the story to a conclusion with a scene in which he and Via, to ascertain whether their marriage has any life left in it, spend a weekend in the country. When Agee attempts to make love to her, he is impotent, but Via seems not to mind. Still pleased to be away with him, she says, "I haven't felt so happy since I don't know when."

Agee could not tolerate the thought of living in impotence with his wife. He moved out of their apartment into a small studio furnished with a few borrowed sticks of furniture. Even now they held out the hope that the separation would be temporary, a strategic retreat before they advanced into a better marriage. The separate living quarters helped buoy Agee's sagging spirits. Away from Via, he entered a state of "real euphoria."

It was now well into the fall of 1937. In this uncharacteristically positive frame of mind, Agee entered a wildly fecund period. Ideas, impulses, and fantasies that had simmered just below the surface of his consciousness now presented themselves with startling clarity. Taking advantage of the novelty of privacy, he returned to writing with a vengeance. Though a multitude of fresh projects teemed in his mind, they were distressingly fragmented and inchoate. Thrown back on himself, he drew on the subconscious for inspiration. The technique had worked in Anna Maria; perhaps it would work again. Out of dreams and daydreams he contrived a movie scenario in which he revisited a surrealistic version of Knoxville. Sinister characters and menacing nuns prowled the city streets, crucifixions occurred on every corner, and a woman clutched a phallus encircled by a wedding ring.

At first Agee's encounter with the subconscious proved oddly unsatisfying. Freed of the restrictions of journalism and the technical demands of poetry, he did not know how to arrange his visions and so took to spewing them out at random. Yet even when operating below par, his fertile imagination yielded astonishing results. The very idea of ideas inspired him, and he felt confident enough of his abilities to apply once more for a Guggenheim Fellowship. This time, he hoped, the money would come through, and he would be free at last from all obligation to the Luce empire. A cooler head might have concentrated exclusively on the highly promising sharecropper book, but not Agee. Carried away by a proliferation of ideas, he submitted no less than forty-seven projects for the Guggenheim's careful consideration. He wove the titles of the projects he had in mind into a manic, Whitmanesque poem covering the breadth of his intellectual curiosity.

"An Alabama Record" headed the list, followed by "Letters," a topic of continuing fascination to Agee. With his friend and fellow cinéaste Jay Leyda he had discussed the possibility of starting a magazine devoted exclusively to the correspondence of everyday people, and he could not pass a trash can stuffed with paper without pausing to search for discarded letters and postcards. He doted on them because they were real, and to his way of thinking, more authentic than contrived forms of writing. Fiction was a lie, and he was interested solely in truth.

After disposing of the most plausible notions, he went on to include ideas that were just taking shape in his fevered imagination. There was a story about "homosexuality and football" that would trace the "love between a twelve-year-old boy and a man of twenty-two; in the Iliadic air of football in a Tennessee mountain peasant school"—obviously, St. Andrew's. There followed:

News Items.
Hung with their own rope.
A dictionary of key words.
Notes for color photography.
A revue.
Shakespeare.
A Cabaret.
Newsreel Theatre.
A new type of stage-screen show.

Anti-communist manifesto.
Three or four love stories.

Most of these projects were self-explanatory, but others eluded definition. In "Hung with their own rope," he intended to compile examples of inadvertent self-parody by notable figures—to what end Agee could not say. And the love stories, he said, would focus "entirely on the process of love. If these are 'works of art,' that will be incidental."

He went on to propose a new type of sex book ("as complete as possible a record and analysis . . . from early childhood on"); examples of "Glamour" writing; a study in the pathology of laziness, a vice he continually accused himself of practicing; a new type of horror story; and, even more vaguely, stories "whose whole intention is the direct communication of the intensity of common experience." "Musical" uses of "sensation" or "emotion" also caught his fancy, as did collections and analyses of faces and news pictures, experiments in the fine art of caption writing and recording bits of overheard conversation, and a new form of story: "the true incident recorded as such and an analysis of it." One could argue that journalists and historians had been doing precisely what Agee proposed for centuries, but the idea was new to him and therefore new to the world as well.

As the list stretched on, it became ever more idiosyncratic, even bizarre:

A new form of movie short roughly equivalent to the lyric poem.
Conjectures of how to get "art" back on a plane of organic human necessity, parallel to religious art or the art of primitive hunters.
A show about motherhood.
Pieces of writing whose rough parallel is the prophetic writing of the Bible.
Uses of the Dorothy Dix Method; the Voice of Experience: for immediacy, intensity, complexity of opinion.
The inanimate and non-human.
A new style and use of the imagination: the exact opposite of the Alabama record.
A true account of a jazz band.
An account and analysis of a cruise: "high"-class people.
Portraiture. Notes. The Triptych.
City Streets. Hotel Rooms. Cities.

A new kind of photographic show.
The slide lecture.
A new kind of music. Noninstrumental sound. Phonograph record-
    ing. Radio.
Extension in writing; ramification in suspension; Schubert 2-cello
    Quintet.
Analyses of Hemingway, Faulkner, Wolfe, Auden, other writers.
Analyses of reviews of Kafka's *Trial;* various moving pictures.
Two forms of the history of the movies.
Reanalyses of the nature and meaning of love.
Analyses of miscommunication; the corruption of idea.
Moving picture notes and scenarios.
An "autobiographical novel."
New forms of "poetry."
A notebook.

This was not an application, it was an astonishing curriculum
vitae: in one way or another, most of the ideas set forth here would
concern Agee throughout his life, and many found their way in
abbreviated form into the sharecropper book, or, as he took to
calling it here, the Alabama record. But some of the ideas bordered
on the absurd. Agee declared that his autobiographical novel, for
example, would not rely on mere words, that outmoded form of
communication, but on recordings and photographs, the better to
represent reality with absolute fidelity. And as for the notebook,
Agee defined it as a "catchall for all conceivable forms of experience" that might, in the course of time, "reach encyclopedia size,
or more." Then again, it might not; Agee never could keep a
notebook for more than several days at a stretch.

Here and there, however, appeared a method to his creative
madness. A few of the ideas had a prophetic air about them, hinting
at multimedia and minimalist art forms that artists would embrace
decades later. But for now he was unable to articulate fully what
he meant by such ideas; he stumbled across them in the dark of his
imagination, feeling shapes without being able to recognize or
name them. Yet the sheer number of ideas, coherent or otherwise,
demonstrated how highly associative and fertile a mind he had, and
how lacking in discrimination between sense and nonsense. He was
perfectly capable of mentioning a new type of sex book, a nonexis-
tent notebook, and the sharecropper book in the same breath. They
were all of equal urgency to him, truly an embarrassment of riches.

Other, more cautious souls might have delighted in hoarding such ideas for future development, but Agee rejoiced in frittering them away. The exhilaration of the moment of discovery was all that mattered. The whole business of following up on his inspirations, of patient elaboration, made him nervous and insecure. He was inclined to mistrust the mundane and had no instinct for preservation, of himself or of his ideas. Like virtue, spontaneity was its own reward.

In the aftermath of this creative orgy, he hinted at the extent to which the effort had exhausted him. "An excess of vitality can be a great spiritual handicap," he wrote. "Most of the time I feel full enough of electricity or gas that I feel off the ground, ever-rapid and substanceless." When the creative mood was upon him, he explained to friends, he felt as though a high-voltage wire in his chest had snapped and was spewing out sparks and bolts of energy in all directions, and he was powerless to control the flow. The tragedy was that most of the sparks flickered briefly and were gone. Of the forty-seven ideas he submitted to the Guggenheim Foundation, only one came to fruition: the sharecropper book. Again the foundation rejected the upstart young writer's outlandish application, no matter how brilliant the sparks it threw off. "Hung with their own rope," indeed!

By now it was Christmas. Agee had made little progress in resolving his marital quandary during the fall, but as the year drew to a close, matters fast came to a head. In his detailed notes for the never-completed story of his marriage, he recalled spending two very different holidays, one with each of the women in his life. On Christmas Eve he gave Via a matronly bathrobe, perfume, and liquor, and she bestowed books and records on him. "Don't go to Midnight Mass without me," she asked after their "civilized" reunion, but Agee had other plans in mind.

"I'll be thinking of you at Midnight," was the best he could offer before hurrying to Alma's apartment, where he gave his mistress presents of a wholly different order: a "really bitchy kind of sheer black nightgown; black opera length sheer stockings"; and a little gold chain necklace that served as their wedding "ring." Evidently Agee considered himself married to both women by this time. As he watched Alma open the presents and model each one for him in turn, he realized that the essence of their relationship was "that of father and child." With Via, in contrast, it was mother and child, but he could no longer stand the thought of her as his substitute mother.

As the year drew to a close, the little triangle entered its "last agonies." Whenever he tried to clarify his relationship with Alma, he wound up confusing matters beyond recognition. "Surely it's natural not to want to crush Via's heart completely out of existence," he would explain to Alma ad nauseam. "Why beside her, you're just a little suburban slut and . . . I'm a goat and baboon." These were not words calculated to win Alma's heart or trust. In the grip of doubts and indecision, everyone relied on confidants for advice, support, sympathy. Via and Alma held a confabulation to try and put matters right. Alma and Evans conferred. Agee and Evans discussed what Alma and Evans had said, and Via and Evans exchanged their own set of confidences as well. The permutations of romantic misery proved endless.

Demoralized by months of Hamlet-like equivocation, Agee descended into blackness, privately arriving at a drastic thesis: "Unless you have very exceptional self-insight, or enormous strength of character, or both; or unless you are a total coward; or unless you are completely faithful or completely docile within one of the ancient conservative traditions, such as Catholicism; it would be much better for you, and for those who may ever meet you, if you were castrated at birth." Succumbing to self-pity and self-loathing, Agee now considered himself a tragic figure, but he remained blind to the forces underlying his behavior. He sensed all along that justifying his contempt for Via on political grounds—maintaining that she was too bourgeois for a radical like him—was only a smokescreen, though he never found out what lurked behind the screen. A voraciously sensual man, he required the pleasures of the body to feel alive. If he was a tragic figure, as he claimed, his flaw lay in not knowing how to enjoy sensual pleasure in the context of marriage.

Once he recognized there was no reason to continue his marriage, he collected himself sufficiently to ask Via for a divorce. It was just before the end of the year. After the months of agony he had endured getting to this point, it came as a shock when she agreed instantly. Of course he subsequently changed his mind and appealed to Via to change hers, but once set in motion, events moved forward as if of their own volition. He was free to live as he pleased.

Agee now moved with uncommon decisiveness to establish a new life for himself. With Evans' assistance he located a home several hours from the distractions of New York; he would live there with Alma and complete his sharecropper book. Via initiated formal divorce proceedings; she wanted no alimony, only her freedom. Even Luce cooperated with Agee's plans, at last relinquishing all rights to the sharecropper material Agee had collected while at *Fortune.* With this major obstacle out of the way, Agee signed the outstanding book contract with Harper & Brothers, collecting a $500 advance on which he expected to live for one year—the time he estimated it would take to complete the book.

All that remained was for Via and Agee to dismantle the life they had all too briefly shared. They packed up the contents of their Perry Street apartment, distributing unwanted items to Evans and Via's older sister, Silvia. Before leaving their "devastated home" for the last time, Agee told Via, "I don't care what happens; those five years—I'm glad we lived them. I'm grateful we lived them."

"Are you, *really?"* Via asked.

"Good God, yes." And with that he took Via in his arms.

THE RELUCTANT
RADICAL

Frenchtown, New Jersey, where Agee and Alma Mailman took up residence at the beginning of 1938, was a cozy little village on the eastern shore of the Delaware River. At that point the river ran gray and wide, with a compellingly treacherous current breaking into toothlike whitecaps. The house he had rented at 27 Second Street, just off the quiet crossroads of the town, was a narrow frame structure squeezed between a Lilliputian church, fire department, and library on one side, and a line of similar houses on the other. All had modest front porches, snug backyards, and faced a row of identical houses staring blankly from across the street. The general atmosphere—quaint, rural, provincial—was strongly reminiscent of the Knoxville suburb where he had spent the earliest and happiest years of his life. He took to the place immediately, describing it as a "small and charming, jigsawed town" where boys and dogs roamed freely and jowly proprietors sat contentedly in front of their small shops.

Although Agee believed he had at last found the right place and the right woman to allow him to do the work he needed to do, Alma had considerable doubts about the wisdom of their arrangement. The idea of living with a man to whom she was not married upset both her and her family. "My father," she recalled, "would rather see me safely, even if unhappily, married to a successful businessman or professional (preferably Jewish), than 'living in sin' with a penniless artist." To Agee there was a certain amount of irony in Alma's attitude; he thought he had exchanged the bourgeois Via for the more radical Alma, only to discover that Alma could be thoroughly conventional in her own right. He had not seen her for what she was but for what he had wanted her to be: a radical comrade-in-arms.

The spacious house afforded her at least some consolation for the precariousness of her position. They had two floors and an attic at their disposal. What little furniture there was consisted of a rocking chair and a four-poster bed so large that they were unable to carry it to an upstairs bedroom. For want of a better idea, it went into the kitchen. "What a delicious novelty, and how strangely cozy, to lie at night in that enormous bed and look over the large coal stove, barely visible in the dim light," she remembered. Sleeping in the kitchen was practical as well, for it was the warmest room in the drafty house.

During the first few weeks, the lovers devoted most of their time and attention to each other. They were on an extended honeymoon, and Alma felt as though she were merely playing house with Agee. The ever attentive Walker Evans sent them a case of Scotch and was among their first visitors. Despite the little photographer's show of good will, Alma could not help but feel "both shy and afraid" in his presence. She knew that he considered her Agee's intellectual inferior and possibly a detrimental influence on his career as well. And it was true that she had only a vague notion of the book he intended to write and scant appreciation of his literary theories.

Agee actually approved of this state of affairs. After months of emotional turmoil, he wished to enjoy the sensual life with Alma for its own sake, and she was prepared to put up with a moderate amount of intellectual condescension; she quickly learned that "the more I went along with him, the more intelligent he thought I was." She decided the best way to get along with Agee was to "leave him alone and be what he wanted me to be." At the same time, she revered him as a "saintly, illuminated man who could be moved very deeply over a slight natural occurrence." One night while they were sitting on the stairs, talking about nothing in particular, Agee paused to look at her and started to cry, about what Alma could not guess.

During this "honeymoon," they spent a fair amount of time listening to records and, once they got a piano in the house, playing instruments. Accompanying Agee on her violin, Alma discovered his approach to music "resembled his way of playing tennis. Hampered by lack of training, every once in a while he'd transcend his technical limitations with spurts of sheer physical and emotional bravura."

In this relaxed environment, a spirit of harmless mischief took hold. Alma once tied a blue ribbon in Agee's hair, as if he were a poodle. Forgetting the bow was in place, he opened the door to converse with a delegation of church ladies who had come a-calling. When the ladies left, Agee remembered the unusual ornament in his hair and groaned loudly—much to Alma's delight. Their innocent sensuality permeated the air, as penetrating and sweet as the fragrance of the night-blooming cereus in the yard next door. Agee likened this idyllic time to a convalescence, a creative exile from the rigors of the city. In his mind's eye, he and Alma seemed always to be approaching their bed with lit candles in hand, the tiny flames casting an ardent, trembling light.

With the arrival of warm weather, Agee returned to thinking seriously about how he would go about completing the sharecropper book. Since undertaking the original *Fortune* assignment he had doubted his ability to live up to the material, to capture the intensity and manifold meanings of the sharecroppers' lives. Now he hit upon the tactic of incorporating such doubts in the text itself. The book acquired a two-level structure. On one level, Agee would write as frankly as he dared about the three families in Alabama. On a higher plane, he proposed to delve into the difficulty of writing honestly about a complex reality. If the principal theme of the book was the nobility of the sharecroppers' humble lives, the secondary theme, taking up nearly as much space, was his struggle to get that phenomenon on paper, to be worthy of it as a writer and a man.

The combined approach to the project would be neither "journalistic" nor "invented," Agee noted, but rather "as exhaustive a reproduction and analysis of personal experience, including the phases and problems of writing and communication, as I am capable of." Since the result would entail "as total a suspicion of 'creative' and 'artistic' as 'reportorial' attitudes and methods . . . it is therefore likely to involve the development of . . . new forms of writing and observation."

The chief innovation Agee had in mind concerned Evans' exquisite photographs. After previewing them, their mutual friend Lincoln Kirstein exclaimed, "What poet has said as much? What painter has shown as much?" To Agee, the photographs of the Fieldses, Tingles, and Burroughses simply told the truth better than words could. Cleansed of artifice, they conveyed, with greater accuracy than the historian, greater insight than the psychoanalyst, and greater understanding than the sociologist, the meaning of the sharecroppers' lives. Accordingly, Agee insisted the finished product "should be as definitely a book of photographs as a book of words."

This multimedia, multilevel approach freed Agee to work steadily on the book. A *furor scribendi* came over him; night after night he labored over the original manuscript, expanding it to 300,000 words of description and reflection. For once he had a canvas broad enough to contain the full range of his responses to the subject matter. Did the sharecroppers' sexual inhibitions remind him of his own furtive masturbation as a boy? He would include those experiences in the book. Did their spiritual aspirations take him back to his days at St. Andrew's? He would work in memories of those days as well. He would go at reality hammer and tong, using words to pummel it into submission.

Alma knew she had to keep her distance while Agee worked, but occasionally he summoned her to hear newly minted sentences. She found the passages very effective, even if their full import went over her head. Although Agee cared for Alma's opinion, he did not encourage her to offer it or, for that matter, to overcome her intellectual inferiority complex. A woman he believed to be better suited to listening than talking.

Though he worked long hours on the manuscript now, he rarely revised—a sign of confidence in his handiwork. He felt as though he had finally achieved the long-desired, long-delayed liberation from both the constraints of polite society and literary convention; he had made the painful transition from aesthete to artist. To Father Flye he described himself as "disintegrating and 'growing up' simultaneously." He was able to give full vent to his feelings on paper with the language he required at his fingertips, and he prided himself on the writer's callus that formed on the middle right finger, "a rough yellow lump almost the size of a marble," Alma recalled.

At the beginning of May, Agee's dedication to work gave ground to an all-too-familiar restlessness. He had been out of the city for five long months. He had no phone, and visitors besides Evans were scarce. Agee grew insatiably curious about the latest developments at Time Inc. He got wind of a new magazine called *Life* that the organization planned to launch and itched to play a part in its development with Evans. Perhaps they could run a department or two in tandem. Bored with the rustic life, Alma spent days at a time in New York, and Agee was unable to cope with the solitude. He would go into the city after her and talk her into returning to Frenchtown, explaining that he was "unable even to boil a potato" without her. These brief trips failed to ease his craving for companionship. Deprived of a phone, he often wrote friends at the slightest provocation. Did Wilder Hobson need a title for a book he was writing? Agee spent half the day rummaging through his personal library in search of a dozen. Did he take offense at a recently published history of the movies by Iris Barry, film custodian at the Museum of Modern Art? He had no choice but to suspend work and bang out a "libellous" review that he termed a "beautiful chance to rape Iris Barry, who . . . badly needs it." It exasperated him to no end to lack a forum from which he might expound his carefully tended ideas about film.

The arrival of *Life*'s first glossy issues occasioned another attack of spleen. There was no way Evans and he could participate in such obvious fan magazine foolishness. In his fury he spewed out

paragraphs of anti-Luce invective intended for the book, but they
were subsequently modified or deleted to avoid a libel suit. Even
more, Agee hated the thought of being left out of the intellectual
life of New York, however frivolous its activities. Whenever he
raised his head from the sharecropper manuscript, the inconsequen-
tial nature of his free but impoverished existence overwhelmed
him, and his hunger for fresh experiences and new contacts started
to mount. He yearned to return to his old desk at *Fortune,* where
new experiences had been his stock-in-trade. His life had narrowed
down to a book he could not bring himself to finish.

His sense of displacement reached a climax when he came
across an account of a desperate young man who had spent eleven
hours on a ledge "desiring to be alone from a room of female
relatives." Recalling his perilous experiment of dangling from the
Chrysler Building, Agee decided the young man symbolized the
predicament of the artist "who will not capitulate: he capitulates all
the same in madness or death; or just very occasionally through
craft, talent, or cruelty, bursts the trap: but if so, its marks are on
him, forever." Agee recognized that he would, in a sense, dangle
from one precipice or another as long as he continued to pursue his
own literary bent. As he fretted over the book, he wondered about
the wisdom of the career he had chosen. He had betrayed the
religious and social traditions and betrayed the people—his
mother, Via, Father Flye, Louise Saunders—he loved in the name
of art, only to find that he remained at heart deeply traditional and
appalled by his actions. He was a reluctant radical.

Chastened, he set aside the iconoclastic sharecropper book in
favor of the gently evocative, warm, and conservative "Knoxville:
Summer 1915," the autobiographical reverie he had written in
Florida three years earlier. Now would be the time to bring it
before the public, to remind the literary community in New York
that he was still alive, and the key to his plan was his crony Macdonald. On leaving *Fortune,* Macdonald had joined with a group of
independent-minded writers, including Mary McCarthy, Philip
Rahv, and Delmore Schwartz, on the staff of *Partisan Review.* Until
1938 this literary bimonthly had been a partisan of the Communist
Party, but the new crop of editors, Macdonald among them, transformed it into a left-leaning, free-thinking platform for some of the
most brilliant minds in New York. Though Agee abhorred cliques,

Partisan Review's willingness to champion experimentation within the context of social responsibility won his admiration. "A magazine unqualifiedly to be respected straight through," he wrote Macdonald, "the only one in existence so far as I know."

Having greased the wheels with flattery, Agee submitted "Knoxville: Summer 1915," and, much to his pleasure, it was accepted for the August–September issue. After reading sections of the soon-to-be-published story to Alma, Agee became so excited that he proposed a midnight ride in their Ford touring car, with the top down. As they drove along darkened country roads, a wild impulse overcame Alma. She stepped onto the running board, holding the car door with one hand. The next thing Agee knew, she was taking off her clothes, item by item, throwing the discarded articles on the seat beside him. Before long she was naked, her skin gleaming in the faint light, her hair blowing behind her head and tickling her back. To increase her pleasure, he drove as fast as he dared, for once enjoying a taste of the sensual liberation he constantly sought.

Agee's various preoccupations—*Life, Partisan Review,* Alma's absences, and his exile from New York—brought work on the sharecropper book to a halt. Without warning, the book's editor, Edward Aswell, set an August 1 deadline for delivery of the manuscript. Knowing the project was timely, Aswell wanted to get it before the public as soon as possible, but he discovered that Agee could not be hurried, and the anxiety caused by the deadline actually slowed the writer's pace. The satisfaction in the practice of his craft that he had been feeling yielded to a horrible sense of inadequacy. The book was meant to be his attempt at a work of lasting value, one that would lift him out of the category of "minor writer," but his standards were so high, so well informed by years of reading literary masterpieces, that he felt unequal to the task of writing a publishable book, much less a memorable one.

Nearly every day he sent a communiqué to a friend, usually Father Flye, Robert Fitzgerald, or Evans, about the difficulties he was experiencing with the book. Taken together, the letters formed a litany of complaint and self-doubt, of tiny victories often undone. "I have in general an illusion the work is going very well: it's a more valuable than harmful illusion to have," he wrote Evans upon resuming work, adding, "I've done an entirely different kind of start which I like but which is not good enough and not right: very dense and heavily loaded with irony that reads too much like a series of exercises." Matters went from bad to worse thereafter as Agee hit a "long blind-streak" during which he wrote "eight or ten drafts of a thing finally not even to be used."

Adding to the difficulty was his training as a journalist. At first his *Fortune* experience had come in handy when he had to blend facts with personal impressions, but lately it had been handicapping him. He could afford to revise a short article endlessly, but a manuscript of several hundred thousand words' length required a different strategy. Occasional bursts of hard work would not suffice to bring the book to completion; he warned himself he had to write at a steady rate, each day, whether he felt inspired or not. In a July 1 letter to Evans he made a concerted effort to get to the bottom of his troubles, describing the agony of creation in terms many a writer might greet with a sigh of recognition.

> Several times a day it becomes physically impossible for me to sit and write even through another sentence: and having stood up and walked around it is hard to get back into as (for me) stepping into a cold bath is. . . . The only way I can do it seems to be simplemindedly and mindlessly . . . but it is very annoying and disturbing to me that I shouldn't manage to be fully and mentally eager to take hold of the work. Something is damned seriously wrong that I'm not: probably that I'm mistaken in thinking I should try to write Art at all, I don't know. I expect I had sooner or later better find out, though.

Evans did what he could to allay Agee's anxiety, so much so that Agee came to consider them full collaborators on the text, but in the end it was up to Agee to do the writing.

The weeks of seemingly thankless toil left him febrile and hypersensitive to every minuscule development, real or imagined, having to do with the book. He slept, thought, and talked the book around the clock. No escape but to finish it, but the projected length of the manuscript increased as the deadline approached. Sentences continually formed and broke apart in his mind; he rushed to his desk to set them down on paper, only to find that like pieces of a nightmarish jigsaw puzzle, they did not fit, or changed shape before his eyes. The book was all too real, his life but an illusion.

To ease the pressure on his long-suffering writer, Aswell extended the deadline to September 1. At the same time, he tried to inspire Agee by mentioning the enthusiasm of Harpers' salesmen for the book, but as with the tactic of setting deadlines, this bit of encouragement boomeranged. "That is a bother to hear," Agee remarked to Evans about the news, "but aside from resharpening and re-snotting me—I had more or less forgotten the book was going to be for sale." Nothing—not compliments or promise of fame or financial reward—brought solace to Agee, nothing but the completion of the book. "My trouble is," he wrote Father Flye on August 12, "such a subject cannot be seriously looked at without intensifying itself toward a centre which is beyond what I, or anyone else, is capable of writing of: the whole problem and nature of existence. Trying to write it in terms of moral problems alone is more than I can possibly do. . . . If I could make it what it ought to be made I would not be human."

At night weird dreams brought on by the strain of overwork tormented Agee. In late July he dreamed he was back at *Fortune,* enduring "hours of sexual nightmare." A few weeks later he dreamed of William Faulkner, mountains, libraries, Communism, Wilder Hobson, and a troop of Girl Scouts—all in the course of a single feverish reverie. "Late in the dream a large tract of wilderness lifted itself in a long sea wave, wet green on crest, red clay underneath, and lounged and folded over a quarter mile, suffocating me and all creation; yet as it sank I persisted." His unconscious rebelled at the extraordinary demands he made on himself, and yet he persisted.

During another dream, he talked in his sleep—to Alma's astonishment. "Poverty shall tear at your face," he announced in the middle of the night.

Alma awakened with a start. "What makes you think so?" she asked, assuming Agee was awake.

"Just as sure as that moist thing in the corner of your mouth is your tongue."

"What a hell of a thing to tell me."

"What would *you* say if you saw a whale shrinking and shrinking to nothing but a knot? What would you say if two elephants were charging down on you?" And with that enigmatic pronouncement, Agee resumed quiet slumber.

One of the elephants charging down on Agee, Aswell, again extended the deadline, this time to November 1, or, at the very latest, December 1, with the book to be published early in 1939. Agee's response was predictable enough: "My relief from stress is such that I already run the danger of disintegration."

In moments stolen from the ordeal of completing the book, Agee turned his attention to another, related pet project. Early in the summer, while Evans was visiting, the two had rummaged through the attic of Agee's rented house and come across a trunk full of letters written years before by former occupants. As a connoisseur of correspondence, Agee was seized with enthusiasm; they must be published as a book, an example of the unselfconscious art of the people. "The two main facts about any letter are: the immediacy, and the flawlessness of its revelations," he wrote. "In the sense that any dream is a faultless work of art, so is any letter." He believed them "the best available document on the power and fright of language and of mis-communication and of the crippled concepts behind these. The variety to be found in any letter is almost as unlimited as literate human experience; their monotony is equally valuable."

The letters in the attic fitted these conditions admirably; they were clumsy and monotonous, prattling on about the petty misfortunes that had befallen the correspondents. After sorting through them, Agee could not refrain from parodying their misspelled, matter-of-fact pathos: "P.S. Abbie stept on a bedbug last night and J. fell and broke her pelvis. Well, I must wash now."

Agee expected Aswell would share his enthusiasm for these documents and rush them into print on the heels of the sharecropper book. At the same time, Agee would collect another advance, by now desperately needed, since he was low on funds. Furthermore, he had specific ideas about the physical appearance of the collection; it "should be colorless and non-committal, like scientific or government publications. It should contain a great deal of facsimile, not only of handwriting—but of stationery." He assigned Alma the task of typing the letters, but despite his enthusiasm, the project slowly succumbed to the demands of the sharecropper book.

As a result of his interest in these artless letters, Agee now paid more attention to his own correspondence, endeavoring to write regularly about his daily life. He nominated Evans as the prime recipient of these effusions and suspected that they would reveal him as he really was, not as others perceived him. It is difficult to resist the conclusion that he anticipated the arrival of some unknown amanuensis on the scene who would bring samples of his correspondence before the public. His inspired, disorganized utterances cried out for the attentions of a latter-day Boswell.

Letters written to Evans in September reveal Agee threatening to rewrite everything he had thus far completed. "I am wanting and hoping I may find a way of doing the whole thing new from start to finish and am trying holding off in hope of some such crystallization," he explained, but the sheer difficulty of writing was enough to kill his enthusiasm for continuing: "It is very painful, in a deadening way, to keep on feeling no excitement or vitality about the work." Two days later: "I think it would be very nice if suddenly in high spirits and perfect self-confidence I sat here and wrote 60,000 words on you know what subject."

As if the book were not sufficient trouble in itself, a series of minor illnesses plagued him as summer slipped imperceptibly into fall and his bank account dwindled to nothing. First his eyes began a strange "twiddling"; perhaps he required glasses, but measurement involved a trip to the city and precious time, and he was ashamed, moreover, to set foot in New York without the completed manuscript under his arm. "I am sufficiently superstitious of that city at present that superstitions bear themselves out," he remarked to Fitzgerald. Next he was afflicted with "a bad boil in each ear, with bad pain, loud beating of blood, and a stench of straight death which has almost ceased to be interesting." To combat the illness he "overdosed" himself with aspirin and played as many sets of tennis on the town courts as his strength would permit. Perhaps in sympathy, Evans came down at the same time with a nasty "grippe."

When trouble avoided Agee, he went out of his way to find it. In one instance, he invited Via's older sister, Silvia, to visit Frenchtown, immediately dreading the consequences of this rash act, but the visit went smoothly enough. "None of it was so bad as I feared," he subsequently related to Evans, "some of it was even pleasant or relaxed, which was practically orgasmic relief." In another instance, he pored over photographs of Freud and Joyce, persuading himself of marked physical similarities between the two. This spurious finding prompted him to wonder whether geniuses possessed a distinctive facial type, and if they did, was he, an aspiring genius, endowed with it? He turned to the discredited science of phrenology for an answer. Examining the bumps on his forehead, he noted "a round lump at centre of forehead just above the hair line, which has developed & has receded, yielding to strong rounding growth at the temples." The findings proved inconclusive; nonetheless, he now toyed with the idea of compiling a catalogue of distinctive facial features. In the most masochistic instance of all, he initiated negotiations with *Life* for a staff position, although he reviled the slick magazine. Not surprisingly, the prospect of returning to "Luce Inc.," as he now termed his former employer, left him in a peevish mood. "A fair way of indicating to them why neither you nor I would give a fuck to work on the Magazine Proper would be to present for their looking-over your scrapbook as is, and my advertising and hate art similarly arranged," he wrote Evans.

Agee's obsessive hatred of *Life* and its new competitor, *Look,* stemmed from their contrived photographic essays, which to his way of thinking violated the free and spontaneous spirit of photography. When Evans published a book of photographs in September, Agee considered the act a sacrilege, a way of relegating the work to respectable obscurity. To publish was the equivalent of hanging a picture in a museum, where it was deprived of power and relevance. He declared, "The world has not the slightest idea what to do with these productions, can neither throw them away nor have them around, and so has invented a sort of high-honorable day nursery or concentration camp for them, so that they will not be at large, staring the world in the face and making it uneasier than it can stand. Then all criticism and art history would also be a rationalization of guilt."

In contrast, Agee preferred a primitive art that remained a part of the fabric of life from which it emerged. A streak of genius lay buried in everyone, he believed, and those who managed to root it out were worthy of the name artist. He soon happened on a specimen of what he considered to be an authentic artist in the person of Cleo Crawford, a thirty-five-year-old black bricklayer who lived in Haverstraw, New York, on the west bank of the Hudson River. Strolling through Haverstraw on a fall afternoon with friends, Agee discovered Crawford's freshly completed oils drying on a porch. "Not an inch of meekness or imitation about him," Agee instantly decided. The painting, which he later described to Evans in great detail, portrayed local houses in bold, vibrant colors. Agee imagined he had a real discovery on his hands and feared that adulation would ruin the artist's talent. "Some bitch has already tried to get him to go to Art School," Agee remarked in disgust. "He knows better, but maybe not enough better. But as he is now everything he does is wonderful and he is incapable of doing anything that isn't."

Inspired by Crawford's example, Agee filled the quiet evenings in Frenchtown by sketching Alma; soon she was sketching him. They were, she recalled, "always surprised by the discovery of new, hitherto unsuspected details in the other's face. Jim's eyes would no longer be laughing, or tender, or just looking, but suddenly opaquely blue, intense, even cold." The coolness lurking beneath the surface of his eyes haunted her, made her feel lonely. "It was a part of Jim I could never know, and which was, perhaps, unknowable even to him." For his part, Agee valued the sketches as an extension of his highly visual style of descriptive writing. "I would never have known how much even a little of it sharpens your eye and gives you more understanding and affection for even some small part of a human or architectural feature," he told Father Flye. He felt he possessed the spirit of whatever he drew, especially Alma's face; he was learning to see the world with new, more perceptive eyes.

The urge to discover and possess moved beyond Alma to various inhabitants of Frenchtown. In the course of an afternoon walk, the couple impulsively bought a black-and-white baby goat, which they kept in the backyard of their house to nibble at the uncut grass. Eventually the goat's insistent bleating prevented Agee from concentrating on his writing, and he let the animal live in the kitchen, where it was quiet. Figuring the goat was lonely, they took it with them on a weekend excursion into New York to visit Evans at his tiny studio apartment at 441 East 92nd Street. They planned to let the goat roam on a bit of roof just outside one of the windows. ("We didn't think Walker would mind," Alma remembered.) Naturally the precise and fastidious Evans reacted with a show of disgust and horror at the appearance of this beast in his home. The goat became even more bothersome when they returned with it to Frenchtown, and after unsuccessfully hunting for a mate, they guiltily gave him to a local butcher.

Soon after they got rid of the goat, an itinerant beggar showed up, looking for food. By now it was late in the fall, too cold for sleeping in the open air. Having spent time with such marginal men and profoundly identifying with them, Agee invited the hobo, who gave his name as Walter Clark, to stay with him and Alma. During the next two weeks, the stranger, a quiet, shy man, mesmerized Agee with tales of hopping freight trains and cadging meals. As an experiment, Agee took Clark to the movies, where the hobo watched the feature in uncomprehending, stony silence. However, he responded enthusiastically to a Mickey Mouse cartoon—a reaction Agee carefully noted. From now on he resolved to pay closer attention to cartoons; perhaps they were a more valid form of expression, more truthful because they were more naïve. Later that evening, Agee took Clark to a relatively lavish restaurant, an indulgence Agee could ill afford, but again, he wanted to see how the hobo would react. After studying the menu carefully, Clark selected but a single dish: pork and beans.

Before long, the question of what to do with their guest became a major issue. It was December, the book was still incomplete, and after paying the rent they had only $12.52. Furthermore, the lease on the house was due to expire at the end of February 1939. To raise cash, Agee decided he would return to New York with Alma to write several articles for *Fortune* on a free-lance basis. Through a fortunate coincidence, Hobson came to the rescue with the generous offer of a rent-free home in Brooklyn in which they could live as long as they pleased. Agee and Alma agreed to spend the winter in Brooklyn and return to New Jersey in the spring, this time to a ramshackle farm they had located near Frenchtown. But where would poor Clark go? Alma wanted to adopt him as a surrogate child, but Agee could not bring himself to follow this course of action. Caught between necessity and guilt, they had no choice but to leave the hobo alone in the dark, empty house once they vacated it.

While on the subject of plans for the future, Agee and Alma decided, very much on a whim, to get married. His divorce from Via had become final in November, and on December 6 they drove to Flemington, New Jersey, where they were married in a five-minute ceremony in a dusty courthouse. After tying the knot for a second time, Agee experienced an overwhelming surge of elation and ran down the courthouse steps three at a time, later telling Alma how astonished he was to feel such "clarity" and "happiness." These emotions stood in contrast to the bewilderment and forboding he had felt at the time of his marriage to Via. Now he was all confidence and optimism.

Word of the marriage got back to Louise Saunders, who valiantly conveyed her felicitations to the newlyweds. But Agee's reply to her was decidedly glum and self-involved. "I wish my book was done," he complained, "and that it was as good as it ought to be." At the tail end of the note, he added, as an afterthought, "God bless you all this Christmas, and I hope you'll forgive and not despise my saying it." Certainly Via seemed to have forgiven him, since she went to Frenchtown in late December to convey her best wishes to the couple. Despite the potential for mischief and hurt feelings, the reunion of the three turned out to be "thoroughly to the good," according to Agee, who wrote Evans, "It looks as if a corner was now pretty well turned, though there of course remain reverberations." Via, for her part, had long since broken off relations with Evans.

With his personal troubles seemingly resolved, Agee radiated happiness throughout the Christmas season. After long neglecting his sister Emma, he insisted she come to New Jersey to celebrate the holiday with him. Now twenty-seven, she had lived much of her life in the shadow of her accomplished older brother, of whom she was in awe. Several years before, she had followed him to New York, and, desperate for work, had landed a clerical job at *Time,* where she was to spend her entire career as a copy-room assistant. Many of Agee's friends admired her vivaciousness and sense of humor. Like her brother, she had a fondness for jazz, alcohol, and poetry. She wrote reams of verse but never showed her work to anyone. Only Agee realized how lonely she was beneath her carefree façade. She had weathered a brief, unhappy marriage to a pilot and was constantly in search of companionship. (She later married Donald Ling, an engineer for Bell Telephone.)

As Christmas approached, Agee turned his mind to presents. At Emma's suggestion he bought clothes for Alma. For Evans he had a more precious gift in mind: the manuscript of the sharecropper book, at such time as it was finally complete. On Christmas Eve Agee found the sight of Alma decorating their tree a "pleasure people claim . . . to be had out of children." It was Alma's first Christmas tree; at her father's insistence she had never had one before.

Now that intimations of Christian charity and sexual happiness played about his head, Agee wished the entire world to share his overflowing love and good will. As a concrete step in that direction, he patiently and skillfully lobbied to unite the two people closest to him, Evans and Alma. It gratified him enormously to behold a friendship developing between these two former adversaries. "All these shifts enlargements mutualities and witnessing of . . . desire or affection or love do wonders . . . for me, and for Alma, and between us," Agee revealed to Evans. The blossoming friendship served to "substantiate & enlarge much I have already believed in or needed as important both in myself & in all relationships." So grand and glorious were feelings among the merry little band that Agee was moved to reflect on the teachings of great artists and religious figures, particularly Blake, Beethoven, Dostoevsky, and "certain aspects of Christ." With his inclination to take matters to the illogical extreme, Agee insisted that "much more needs to be learned, investigated, synchronized & tried." To be more specific, he hoped that Alma and Evans would make love, and if they did, Agee would be glad for them, as well as himself. It seemed possible that he had eradicated sexual jealousy from his heart, but only the acid test would offer proof.

Agee's attempts to encourage a liaison between Alma and Evans at this time were strongly reminiscent of his feelings during the ill-fated "romantic friendship" back at Exeter. He exhibited the same idealism laced with lust, the same urge to ensnare those he loved in a web of desire. Yet he himself did not perceive any similarities between the two cases, separated as they were by fourteen years. Nor did he imagine the dire personal consequences of his actions. A little optimism went a long way toward covering a multitude of sins.

Agee's unshakable optimism extended to the book as well. By January 1939 he believed he was "getting into the home stretch" on it. He spent two exhausting weeks writing until five o'clock in the morning each day, but despite his best efforts, the work resisted completion. He was forced to acknowledge the painful fact that he would have to return to New York with weeks, if not months, of work remaining. To add to the delay, he would have to hold off further labor on it pending completion of the free-lance article for *Fortune.*

He had given his all, and it had not been enough. He would have stayed in New Jersey throughout the winter if he could, but it was the end of February and time to relinquish the house where Alma and he had lived for over a year. The night they returned to New York, Agee and Alma left Walter Clark, their resident hobo, a thoughtful going-away present: two quart bottles of whiskey, cheap eating utensils, half a dozen cans of pork and beans, and matches. Their last sight of the hobo sent shivers up their spines. Through the window, they saw Clark sitting on the living-room floor, legs outstretched before two candles, staring dully at his presents and scarcely noticing his guilt-stricken caretakers saying goodbye forever.

At the beginning of March the Agees moved into the Brooklyn home Hobson had promised them. Belonging to their patron's in-laws, it was located on St. James Place, a thoroughly ordinary city street. Alma took an instant dislike to the place, rent free or not; it was cold, drafty, cheerless. Agee meanwhile quickly decided that Brooklyn was an unsatisfactory compromise for a writer, neither close enough to the center of literary action in Manhattan nor remote enough from it to confer blessed isolation. And the idea of living on charity, even the charity of Hobson, who was a great admirer and glad to help, tore at Agee's conscience.

On the other hand, he was again able to avail himself of the pleasures of city life. He had the luxury of a telephone, whose presence meant a sudden decline in the number of letters he would write from Brooklyn. And he could catch up on all the movies he had missed during the previous year. Though he had been no farther than New Jersey, he felt so out of touch with the cultural crosscurrents of the moment that he might as well have been abroad. True to his movie-going experience with Clark, he found more to admire in the animated exploits of Daffy Duck and Porky Pig than in the slick, vacuous feature films whose sumptuous sets only served to aggravate his sense of poverty.

Despite the reservations Agee had about Brooklyn, it did serve as a convenient base of operations for his first *Fortune* assignment. The magazine planned to devote its June issue solely to New York, and Agee was to contribute a comprehensive survey of the borough. He undertook the project with a reluctance that showed in every line of the manuscript. Where *Fortune* required a straightforward, factual account, Agee, under the influence of his deeply subjective, eccentric sharecropper book, drafted a halfheartedly impressionistic survey mingling rhetorical flights of fancy with grotesque detail. Brooklyn he described as "the collaborated creature of the insanely fungoid growth of fifteen or twenty villages, now sewn and quilted edge to edge." Villages, quilts, fungus—never before had he mixed metaphors with such abandon. He called attention to a woman in Prospect Park who "sits alone on a bench with her fecund knees spread and her hands folded on her belly." His portrayal of Jewish neighborhoods and families was so acerbic as to give offense, and he went on to include verbatim transcripts of inane conversations he had overheard and obscene graffiti he had seen. Clearly he was daring the magazine's editors to reject the four-thousand-word phantasmagoria, which they were glad to do, not once, but twice.

Agee considered the rejection, which he had all but brought on himself, as the formal conclusion to his career at *Fortune.* He had outgrown the limitations of the magazine. If he was no longer the red-hot writer straight out of Harvard he had once been, *Fortune* was simply not the socially aware magazine it had been in the heyday of the New Deal. Many of the old faces were gone, and with them the old esprit de corps. Among those who had left, Agee missed most keenly his friend and mentor Archibald MacLeish, who had taken a teaching position at Harvard, but not before delivering a scalding attack on Luce for betraying *Fortune*'s promise. "I will admit (with resentment) that *Fortune* is not the association of mutually assisting journalists it was for five or six very exciting years," he wrote at the time of his departure. "I will admit (without enthusiasm) that it is now part of a publishing enterprise in which not more than a dozen or so people know each other's names." MacLeish concluded, "I wish you hadn't been so successful." But Luce had, and there was no more room at *Fortune* for journalist-poets, only business writers. The truth was that the upstart *Life* had usurped *Fortune*'s pride of place in the Luce empire.

Despite these profound changes, "Luce Inc." continued to hope that Agee would return to the fold. As an olive branch to this talented writer, *Fortune* excerpted a single line from his rejected Brooklyn article to serve as the epigraph for its tepid replacement. It read:

> *"It is one of those terrifying mileages of the world."*
> —JAMES AGEE

Agee regarded the quotation as a badge of honor, an acknowledgment that he was now an independent author in his own right.

Freed of the burden of writing for the magazine, Agee frittered away much of the spring contemplating twenty or so projects that came to nought; meanwhile, Alma dutifully typed sections of the sharecropper manuscript. In May, Macdonald forwarded a questionnaire that yanked Agee's head out of the clouds. It was a *Partisan Review* survey of writers' attitudes toward their work and society. The tenor of the questions—faintly stuffy and academic— aroused Agee's righteous indignation. "It sounds like a meeting of the Junior League of Nations at Wellesley; or the Blairstown Conference; or a debate between an episcopal and a unitarian minister on the meaning of god in human experience." Relishing the prospect of tweaking Macdonald on the nose, Agee went on to say, "I think nearly everything I have read in the Partisan Review is quite as seriously corrupting, and able further to corrupt the corruptible."

One question in particular caused Agee's adrenaline to flow; it concerned the possibility of a serious writer's earning a living.

No; no living. Nor do I think there is any place . . . for "literature" as a "profession," unless you mean for professional litterateurs, who are a sort of high-class spiritual journalist and the antichrist of all good work. Nor do I think your implied desire that under a "good system" there would be such a place for real "writers" is to be respected or other than deplored. A good artist is a deadly enemy of society; and the most dangerous thing that can happen to an enemy, no matter how cynical, is to become a beneficiary. No society, no matter how good, could be mature enough to support a real artist without mortal danger to that artist. Only no one need worry: for this same good artist is about the one sort of human being alive who can be trusted to take care of himself.

In striving to become an artist, Agee realized, he had made himself into an outcast.

Having exercised his formidable talent for invective, Agee calmed down and after due consideration decided his replies were "intemperate, inarticulate, and at times definitely foolish." He had not meant to take a hard line after all, and to his relief the magazine, assuming his remarks were a personal attack on Macdonald, chose not to print them. In the wake of this decision, Agee reversed himself yet again and included the questionnaire, answers, disclaimers, and an apology to Macdonald in the text of the sharecropper book. He titled the section devoted to the material "Conversation in the Lobby" to point up its irrelevance, but the issues did have a bearing on the book's secondary theme of his struggle to write. To what Aswell would make of such an outlandish digression he gave nary a thought.

It was now the end of June, and he had grown heartily sick of living in Brooklyn. "It has been a very bad three months," he wrote Father Flye, "full of a good many kinds of anxieties. . . . I'm pulled apart between them so that I'm seldom good for much." Even the book left him cold: "I feel nothing about it, pro or con, except a wish to be done with it, a sense of serious gaps in it, and a knowledge that it is 'sincere' and that I made no attempt to take an easy way on it."

The underlying reason for his paralyzing anxiety had to do with Alma, who was now pregnant. He had longed to have a child with Alma almost since the day they met, but now that the reality was upon him he had serious misgivings about becoming a father. He was all but broke, out of work, and saddled with a seemingly unfinishable book. "Whenever we made love," Alma remembered, "he'd say, 'I want to have a child with you,' but I wasn't convinced." To preserve her husband's peace of mind, she reluctantly took an injection designed to induce an abortion, but when Agee learned what she had done, he had a change of heart. He wanted a child, no matter what. Fortunately, the injection failed to work, and the pregnancy proceeded normally.

Happy in the knowledge that they were going to be parents after all, Alma and Agee left Brooklyn and all its dreary associations for the twenty-five-dollar-a-month farm they had rented the previous winter. Located in Stockton, New Jersey, Monk's Farm consisted of an old stone house and plenty of open country, but precious little else. To friends from New York in search of a bathroom Agee exclaimed, "Why, all God's outdoors is a toilet!"

Here Agee expected to put the finishing touches on the book, but throughout the summer he dawdled over revisions. He padded the already bloated text with newspaper clippings that had caught his attention, especially a frivolous profile of his old nemesis, Margaret Bourke-White. Near the end of the manuscript he appended a list of several hundred words he considered capable of causing debate and misinterpretation ("lesbian, labor, laborite, write, author, musician, composer," and so forth). At once a linguistic tour de force and a deliberately provocative gesture, the list was certain to incur Aswell's displeasure.

Even more damaging to the book's prospects than these questionable interpolations was the endless delay. With every passing month the immediacy of the subject matter waned. At the time Agee had visited the sharecroppers, three years earlier, the Depression had been public issue number one, but it had since been supplanted by ominous developments abroad. While Agee worked in bucolic isolation, Hitler made threatening gestures against his neighbors. Radios on both sides of the Atlantic reverberated with shouts of "*Sieg Heil!*" As a vital issue, the Depression had dated.

As if to underscore the risk of delay, another writer, John Steinbeck, had come along and made the plight of the disenfranchised his literary turf. *The Grapes of Wrath* had appeared in May to great acclaim. By the time Agee's book on the same theme appeared, if it ever did, it would seem to be little more than an eccentric footnote to yesterday's literary sensation.

Agee fended off these pressing concerns with bouts of tennis, swimming, movie going—anything that would take his mind off his worries. Visiting friends, and there were many this summer, found him in a particularly carefree, relaxed mood: trim, tan, and fit. One weekend a photographer friend of Evans, Helen Levitt, came to Monk's Farm, where she snapped several revealing portraits of Agee. They showed the young writer in his prime, his eyes seeming to radiate an unearthly illumination. Another guest at this time was the poet Delmore Schwartz. Levitt photographed the two ambitious writers conversing placidly beneath a shade tree.

For the benefit of his guests, Agee spent hours reading aloud completed sections of the book. In fact, he devoted more time to reciting than he did to writing, but with good reason, for his audience greeted the work with great praise. "It's gospel, Jim, gospel," Hobson proclaimed during his visit. Another appreciative listener was Selden Rodman, who convinced Agee to allow an excerpt to appear in Rodman's magazine, *Common Sense.* After much debate Agee titled the excerpt "Three Tenant Families," and it ran in October, attracting little attention.

The only ripple in the ocean of serenity formed during Father Flye's stay. Throughout the 1930s, Agee and the priest had been drifting apart politically. To get Father Flye to take his politics seriously, Agee eventually resorted to scare tactics, telling the priest, "I am essentially an anarchist, with the belief that the operations of human need and acquisitiveness, in concentration on purely material necessities . . . is tragic, mistaken, and eccentric from the root up, and cannot come to good." Society was now so corrupt, foul, and accursed that the only truth left in life was not love but sex.

While Flye was able to tolerate such radical notions in his favorite "son," he could not bring himself to subscribe to them. Arriving in New Jersey, he felt compelled, as friend and priest, to put matters right. They discussed their differences, but they did not come to terms. The best they could manage was to agree to disagree. Agee's impatience with Father Flye reached its zenith when the time came to read aloud sections of the book. The priest took strenuous exception to the obscenities studding the text. To be sure, his standards of propriety differed sharply from those of the author. Even the word *guts* bothered Father Flye. Agee defended the obscenities on the grounds that "it is possible to be quite as foul mouthed using a euphemism or an aseptic or so-called scientific word. . . . I feel no word can be quite as dirty as the word sexual intercourse where it is used wrongly." To Agee the real obscenity lay not in the words, which were merely symbols, but in repression of them.

Father Flye's virtuous attitude also incurred Alma's dislike. She detected a "falseness in his goodness" and suspected he harbored right-wing sentiments. Much to her embarrassment, she found herself vying with the priest for Agee's attention. In this charged atmosphere Father Flye suddenly indicated a desire to bless her. For Agee's sake she went before the priest on bended knee to receive his benediction, but afterward she burned with indignation at the humiliation she had brought on herself. To decorate a Christmas tree was one thing, but to kneel before a priest—that was going too far.

To clear the air, Agee impulsively decided that the time had come to deliver the manuscript to Aswell in New York. For weeks the chorus of praise—at least for selected excerpts from the book —had been filling his ears, fortifying his courage until he felt comfortable showing the work to his editor. Accompanied by Father Flye and several friends, he drove off. The day was hot and beautiful; it was a festive occasion: Agee was taking his book to market. After the initial elation wore off, he began mentally to rehearse sections of the complex book. Before long he decided he had left undone those things he ought to have done and announced to the astonished passengers that he had just thought of an entirely new way to write the book. Of course they would have to turn around and go home; Aswell would have to wait until he had finished the book once and for all.

Several weeks later, at the end of August, Agee, having completed the latest set of revisions, again drove to New York to deliver the manuscript. This time he accomplished his mission. With the greatest possible trepidation he returned to Stockton to await word from Aswell. If the editor deemed the manuscript acceptable, Agee could collect the rest of the advance Harper & Brothers owed him, a badly needed $500. But days crept by without a sign from New York, and Agee was forced to borrow money, which he hated to do. "More delay from Harpers leaves me again without a cent," he wrote Evans on September 8, "and because I can't stand asking the same people I've been asking again, I'm now asking you: could you loan me anything until (supposedly within a few days now) the money comes through from Harpers." When —and if—it finally did, Agee proposed they tour the South to celebrate the occasion.

Evans' immediate offer of financial relief induced paroxysms of gratitude in Agee. He repeatedly tried to express how much the loan meant, but he tripped over his words in a profound embarrassment that masked another, related matter—his continuing campaign to unite Alma and Evans. He took to referring to the potential liaison in childish double entendres. "I have organized . . . an advanced sexual program," he wrote on the back of a penny postcard, "and we would appreciate it if you will give us some advice on apertures." Later, Agee regretted the undignified tone of such suggestions and promised them both that he would cease and desist. "Though I am still adolescent-capable of making myself & others trouble, I am getting over it," he said, preferring to let matters take their course. Any sexual encounters should remain in the realm of "purely chance pleasure if pure & independent chance so happens to shape them."

While Agee pondered the mysteries of sexual attraction, Aswell developed grave doubts about the wisdom of publishing *Three Tenant Families,* as the sharecropper book was now called. He gave the obscenity-studded manuscript to another editor, who wrote a memorandum to the effect that he could take the language but was afraid readers would not. In addition, Aswell had reservations about Agee's baroque manner of expression. The book seemed to him a disorganized jumble of impressions; it lacked a clear-cut beginning, middle, and end; and some sentences were so long and complex as to be meaningless. He carefully relayed these objections to Agee, who, desperate for his $500, agreed to tone down the offending passages if Harpers would print the memo in the front of the book. But that Aswell refused to do.

Humiliated, Agee drafted a disclaimer of his own.

I wish to call attention to some last minute modifications in this text, and to state why they have been made.

As the manuscript stood completed, it contained certain

things which in the opinion of the publishers would be fatal to the interest of the general reader and to certain areas of sale. . . . I was told that unless these obstacles were removed, they could not publish the book.

It has been possible to concede to these wishes, on one condition: that I make as clear as need be what these changes are, and why they have been made.

Agee's willingness to compromise induced Harpers to proceed with the book. At considerable expense, the publisher made up photographic plates from Evans' pictures, but even here, the engraver "censored" one shot by omitting unsightly flyspecks. Now Agee and Evans realized they were in serious trouble; they could think of no justification on earth for sanitizing the photographs, and so they resolved to have it out with Aswell. In the hours before their meeting with him, Agee was a knot of tension. With the ever helpful Hobson he debated endlessly the question of what clothes he should wear—the dark suit of the corporate lackey or the work shirt of the proud laborer. At the last moment Agee opted for casual dress as a gesture of defiance. But the result of the meeting would have been the same no matter what he wore. Aswell told Agee and Evans that Harper & Brothers had officially rejected the manuscript; they were free to take it elsewhere if they wished, but the editor doubted that any publisher would risk bringing it out.

The decree stunned Agee, who expected such shenanigans from the likes of Henry Luce, not from a serious publisher of books. To Agee publishers were the trustees of a sacred responsibility toward society and posterity; it never occurred to him that legal or financial considerations would sway their behavior. And if the renowned Edward Aswell, editor of Thomas Wolfe, felt this way about the book, how would other, less reputable editors react? He thirsted for revenge against Harpers, but there was none to be had. He wrote to Father Flye of feeling "weak, sick, vindictive, powerless and guilty" in the wake of the rejection. No longer did he consider himself the footloose young writer ready to take on the world. He was nearly thirty, and he had "missed irretrievably all the trains I should have caught."

As the fate of the book hung in the balance, Agee entertained any number of whims about it. If he ever did succeed in finding another publisher, he wanted them to price it at $1.50, cheap enough for a sharecropper to buy. Not only that, but the cover should be a facsimile of a hymnal or made of the flimsy cardboard used to bind government publications. In essence, the book should be as cheap and ephemeral as the sharecroppers' meager possessions were.

At the same time, he chose a new title, *Let Us Now Praise Famous Men,* to emphasize with savage irony the obscurity of the three families about which he had written. The title, which he had used once before, in a short story, came from Ecclesiasticus, an Apocryphal book of wisdom dear to the hearts of many Anglo- and Roman Catholics. (And not to be confused with the better-known Ecclesiastes.) Agee made room for a lengthy excerpt from the ancient book near the end of *Let Us Now Praise Famous Men,* where it took on the force of a eulogy, especially the passage's closing lines: "Their bodies were buried in peace; but their name liveth for evermore." Thus Agee mourned the death of his book and the apparent waste of three years of unremitting labor.

II

THE CAPTIVE POET

The fall of 1939 found James Agee in desperate straits. He had a seemingly unpublishable book on his hands, a child on the way, and no money whatsoever. In the name of integrity he had recklessly ignored warnings about the obscenities in his book, only to witness Harper & Brothers reject the manuscript. In the name of sexual freedom he had adopted a course sure to drive Alma away from him. His twin crusades had the sad and ironic effect of bringing him full circle, once again in New York and in search of a job with his former employer. The cost of rebellion had been too great to sustain, and he had no choice but to capitulate to circumstances. He returned to the city a broken man.

Avoiding the purgatory of Brooklyn, Agee and Alma borrowed enough money to rent an apartment at 322 West 15th Street, an unfashionable, windswept district dominated by warehouses and factories. They lived on the second floor, directly above a bar where the jukebox played nothing but "Roll Out the Barrel" until all hours. They reached the apartment by climbing a flight of dark and dingy steps. Their thrift-shop furniture was old and frayed, dirty clothes cascaded from a closet, and sections of *Let Us Now Praise Famous Men* were scattered everywhere. The living room and bedroom were separated by an alcove containing Agee's beloved piano and record player. A tottering bookshelf held volumes of poetry, a complete edition of Shakespeare's works, and a copy of Krafft-Ebing's *Psychopathia Sexualis.*

It was here, in these grim surroundings, that Agee finally goaded to consummation the long-delayed liaison between Alma and Evans. As always, Alma was willing to go along with her husband's desires, no matter how extreme. If Agee wanted her to sleep with his best friend, she was willing, even though she was pregnant and did not find Evans particularly appealing. Consumed by love for the two of them and by curiosity, Agee remained blind to her reservations. Nor was it enough that Alma and Evans make love—he proposed to watch them in the act. In doing so, he expected to learn more about the truth of sex and in particular the revelation of the male orgasm. He persuaded himself he knew what he was getting into, but he did not figure the intensity of his response into the equation.

When the time arrived, he sat at the foot of the bed, watching Alma and Evans make love. Instead of scientific detachment, he was overcome by spasms of pain, love, and jealousy. The conflicting emotions the sight aroused within his breast were so strong that he had no recourse but to cry. Never before had he felt the full panoply of his emotions simultaneously, everything from extreme love to extreme hate, from extreme tenderness to extreme cruelty. The spectacle of the bodies writhing on the bed was more than he could comfortably handle, and his emotional devastation was complete.

Afterward he was overwhelmed by guilt. He realized he had, for once, gone too far, and, even worse, he had brought pain to those he loved most. He apologized to both Evans and Alma for the debacle, all the while attempting to deceive himself that the episode had little or no meaning. "I have caused each of you a certain amount of bother & am of course sorry and contemptuous of myself," he wrote Evans. "However much . . . you happen to like each other, good: I am enough of an infant homosexual or postdostoevskian to be glad. However much you don't, that's all right too: I am enough of a 'man' not to care to think particularly whether I care or not."

The dismissive shrug masked profound disillusionment. If sex had no meaning, his marriage to Alma, based on sex, was seriously diminished. If sex had no truth, he was deprived of yet another force in which he had fervently believed. The orgy had proved heartbreaking enough to satisfy the masochist in him but devoid of revelations about truth, beauty, or spirit. The bright vision of communal love he had imagined in New Jersey collapsed into so much heavy breathing and embarrassment. He had preached a transforming love, not this bewildering, cold lust.

By now his career was also in disarray. Propelled by financial necessity, he turned to his network of friends to help him find a full-time job. As it happened, Robert Fitzgerald had recently inherited the position of "Books" editor at *Time* magazine, and he invited Agee to join that department at a starting salary of forty-five dollars a week. In accepting the offer, Agee told himself the job would be no more than a temporary, makeshift solution to his problems, to be discarded when the crisis had passed.

Any major decision at *Time* meant consultation among a number of editors, who now carefully considered the case of James Agee. Here was a writer who was as difficult as he was talented. His 30,000-word-long drafts for *Fortune* articles had become legendary around Time Inc., as well as his drinking and volatility. Still, they were not likely to find another book reviewer who was as sensitive and capable and who had been to the right schools. His prospective boss, T. S. Matthews, was a tall, lean-jawed Luce loyalist who, in his own words, valued "the steady man, the slogger, the writer who got his copy in on time and did what he said he would." Agee, Matthews suspected, was none of these; he was "in journalism but not of it," the kind of writer who was contemptuous of authority and responded only to vague inner promptings and the bottle. The kind who would throw tantrums and give way to despair, who would sulk and mock the efforts of other, less talented journalists. The kind who was worth a dozen of the other sort. In all, Agee was just the kind of writer Matthews wanted to hire—and to bring to heel. The editor welcomed the opportunity to tame the man he took to calling his "captive poet."

On meeting Matthews, Agee saw in him a stern conscience and father figure whose lash (or blue pencil) was to be revered rather than scorned. The Time Inc. juggernaut had a reputation for crushing writers as diverse as Hobson and Hart Crane, but Agee looked forward to the imposition of discipline as the price of respectability and solvency. Nor was he immune to the organization's intoxicating perquisites: the high offices commanding eye-popping views, the bevy of beautiful researchers, the fraternal feeling among the writers. Although admission to the elite fraternity demanded a sacrifice of literary ambition, he found it reassuring to merge with a large corporate entity. All he had to do was follow orders. A chain of command replaced individual initiative; deadlines took over where inspiration left off.

Agee's life at *Time* bore scant resemblance to his job at *Fortune*. In the spring of 1938 the company had moved from the Chrysler Building to the top seven floors of a new tower, this one at 9 Rockefeller Center. From his twenty-eighth-floor office Agee enjoyed sweeping views of the Hudson River and the Rockefeller Center skating rink.

His work proved to be as new and different as his quarters. As a weekly magazine designed to be read quickly, *Time* thrived on a high-pressure atmosphere, where deadlines reigned supreme and style yielded to necessity. He was no longer a reporter, responsible for facts and figures, but a critic. He read six books a week, usually of his own choosing, and wrote several thousand words about each, far more than required. As editor of the cultural or "back of the book" departments, it was Matthews' task to whittle Agee's reviews down to a few terse paragraphs of standard Timestyle. Like many magazine editors short of time and space, Matthews believed he was doing the writer a favor by slashing the reviews to ribbons, and even Agee came to think that Matthews and he together struck a balance between inspiration and clarity. Nonetheless, reams of fascinating, if long-winded, observations were discarded each week, and none of Agee's published book reviews matched the caliber of

his other writing. Still, Agee was inclined to take the editing in
stride, as if he were doing penance for his personal and literary sins
of excess. And *Time* was only too happy to put his masochistic streak
to productive use. He fast yielded to what Evans termed the "satanic naïveté" of editors who expected "gifted, intelligent employees . . . to work hard and long hours under crushing pressure
at many tasks no man with a mind could put his heart into."

Although the job turned out to be more demanding than Agee
had bargained for, he had no choice but to stick with it until he
discovered a way to support his family through his own writing.
Consequently, he displayed symptoms of profound melancholy. He
settled into a routine of arriving at the office late in the afternoon,
disheveled, unshaven, and, in solidarity with the sharecroppers,
wearing a blue or black work shirt stained with sweat at the armpits.
Occasionally he adopted a studied bohemian air, alternating a wrinkled, shiny, double-breasted blue jacket worn over a checked shirt
with a velvet suit fastened at the waist with a bandanna or length
of rope. He tried, but soon discarded, a pair of steel-rimmed eye-
glasses to combat farsightedness. And his drinking, until now only
an occasional problem, became more serious. He became so dependent on alcohol to relieve the pain within that he kept a bottle at
the ready beside his typewriter. His tolerance of the substance was
so high that he did not feel drunk when he imbibed, merely more
or less normal. Though he was not aware that he had a problem,
he was becoming an alcoholic. But the disease had a way of insinuat-
ing itself with deceptive slowness. He assumed he would cut back
on drinking, too, as soon as his problems had eased to the point
where he felt in control of his life again.

For sheer eccentricity, Agee could not match his office-mate
and fellow book reviewer, Whittaker Chambers. Before joining
Time, Chambers had been a professional, card-carrying member of
the Communist Party. He had not been merely a sympathizer, as
many of Agee's friends had, but a dedicated subversive. Working
out of his home in Baltimore, Chambers had for six years acted as
a buffer between Soviet spies in Washington and his superior officer
in New York, a Russian military intelligence official named Boris
"Peter" Bykov. In 1938 Chambers underwent a conversion, disavowed Communism, and deserted the Party. The following year,
at thirty-eight, he found a job with *Time,* at twice Agee's salary. It

was the first conventional job Chambers had ever held, and it marked the end of a dark period during which he and his family, fearing for their lives, had gone into hiding. Now he preached the gospel of capitalism with the zeal of a reformed sinner; no one at *Time* was more aware of the Red Menace than Chambers, who perceived the conflict between East and West as the decisive historical battle between the forces of good and evil.

Few at *Time* besides Agee knew the full extent of Chambers' involvement with Communism. But the short, stocky former spy did stand out; others regarded him as laughably strange but enjoying unusual access to Luce. Chambers, on the other hand, considered his colleagues naïve college lads pitifully ignorant of the desperate realities of global politics. Everyone, whether they knew it or not, was a soldier in an apocalyptic conflict; he was not on the job at *Time* but at war against Communism. Considering left-leaning reporters dupes of the Soviets, he made it his job to flush them out of hiding.

As a soldier, he believed himself in constant danger of being assassinated. To avoid this ignominious end, he appeared only in public places, slept with a gun, and carried a knife wherever he went, even to *Time.* If he was to meet a friend at, say, Keen's English Chop House on 36th Street, he would take the subway to 14th Street, change trains, and go back uptown to shake off a supposed tail. When Fitzgerald tried to voice moderate criticism of his Communist paranoia, Chambers shot back, "Hush, the walls have ears."

Chambers' political obsession appealed strongly to Luce. Several years earlier, the Founder had installed at the Foreign News desk a notorious reactionary, Laird Goldsborough, one of the very few *Time* writers to escape editing. Goldsborough's anti-Semitism and open admiration of fascism incurred the wrath of others, especially MacLeish, who had urged Luce to dump "Goldie." This Luce reluctantly did, only to turn the department over to Chambers, who had long campaigned for the post.

For all their differences, Chambers and Agee, who were both fond of night work, discovered they had quite a lot in common and after a trial period became fast friends. Both nurtured religious convictions that went deeper than their politics. To them the key issue in life was belief, whether in religion, a political system, or art.

They were both misfits who had paid an enormous personal price for their misguided beliefs and were grateful to *Time* for offering them a chance at rehabilitation. Although they were at opposite ends of the political spectrum, Agee felt that Chambers' suffering validated his Communist phobia. If he was sincere, he was right, and that was all there was to the matter. Gradually Chambers' brand of patriotism influenced Agee, who, under his friend's patient tutelage, modified his political intransigence. No more was he the fire-breathing radical and enemy of the establishment. Despite the ample justification he had seen for such attitudes, they had gotten him nowhere. Communism, he belatedly realized, was only another church, with its own forms of sin and penance. As a passionate devotee of liberty, he could not bring himself to believe in anything as absolute as economic determinism. He demanded mystery out of life, a quality Communism failed to provide. Within months he ceased to claim he was a Communist and discovered he was, much to his surprise, a pro-Roosevelt Democrat. Given time, he might even summon the faith to step into the voting booth.

This mellowing of his beliefs extended in every direction. The old Agee—confrontational, impulsive, extreme—was dying; the new—tolerant, forbearing, able to see many sides of a question—was about to be born.

Agee's newfound willingness to see at least some value in contemporary society paved the way for a promising new development concerning *Let Us Now Praise Famous Men,* thanks in large part to an acquaintance named Eunice Clark. Young, Vassar-educated, and well connected, having herself worked at *Fortune,* she had gotten to know Agee several years earlier, during those lazy summer weekends at the Baldwin estate in New Jersey. She harbored doubts about his wholesomeness as a person, but when she heard him read sections of the book, she recognized he was onto something important. Not long after, she became a talent scout for Houghton Mifflin, the Boston-based publisher, who looked to her as its link to promising young writers in New York. With the encouragement of the ever attentive Hobson, she brought the rejected manuscript of *Let Us Now Praise Famous Men* to the attention of Houghton Mifflin's editor in chief, Paul Brooks.

Although he had graduated from Harvard just a year earlier

than Agee, the two were virtual strangers. To the extent that Agee was a "typical" writer—brilliant, moody, and improvident—Brooks was a "typical" editor—tall, forbearing, and scholarly. He would not have been out of place in Harvard's English Department, for he combined fastidiousness with an open mind. Both he and another Houghton Mifflin editor, Robert Linscott, were enormously impressed with Agee's book, recognizing it as a classic work of dissent to rank with the writings of Henry David Thoreau and Harriet Beecher Stowe. Thus they became the first editors to recognize the inherent value of *Let Us Now Praise Famous Men.*

Not that all was sweetness and light. Brooks saw problems ahead with the obscenities, but he proposed a commonsense solution. He told Agee and Evans that Houghton Mifflin would include any language in the manuscript that was legal to print in Massachusetts. A few of the coarsest expressions would have to fall by the wayside, but the text would retain its original pungency. Realizing that Brooks offered the last, best hope for publishing the troublesome book, Agee readily agreed to the condition.

However, when the two men subsequently conferred in New York, Agee, twisting and turning his hands in the air, attempted to lay down a condition of his own. "Paul," he said, "I want this printed on newsprint."

Brooks was aghast. "But Jim, in five or ten years it'll powder up."

"That might be a good idea," Agee replied.

In time the newly mellow Agee dropped his demands, and Houghton Mifflin used conventional paper and a dignified dust jacket with a marble pattern. The engraver carefully nicked the photographic plates to simulate the flyspecks the Harpers engraver had omitted.

Although he was willing to compromise on the book's physical appearance, Agee did what he could to thwart its chances for popularity. He warned Brooks that Houghton Mifflin should not attempt to "ingratiate it with the public." At the same time, he proposed that the publishing company put him on salary. The unflappable Brooks suggested Agee wait until the next book before committing himself to such an arrangement, but he did offer a small advance for this one, which Agee gratefully accepted. Having come to terms, Houghton Mifflin proceeded to schedule publication of *Let Us Now Praise Famous Men* for early 1941.

Friends had helped shore up Agee's sagging careers, but they were powerless to repair his disintegrating home life. His relationship with Alma entered a vicious cycle. As she focused ever more intently on the impending birth of their child, he felt unjustly ignored and consequently kept his distance. His remoteness made Alma insecure, contentious, and demanding. Yet Agee felt the need of some feminine companionship, and if Alma would not suffice, he was prepared to look elsewhere. It was at this time that he met the woman who was to become his third wife, Mia Fritsch.

She could not have been more different from Alma. Mia was tall and intellectual, an Austrian Catholic émigrée who had lately landed a job at *Fortune* as a researcher. As it happened, she was working on an article with one of Agee's friends, Christopher "Goofy" Gerould. The two men were having lunch at a local restaurant, when Mia appeared on the scene. Agee struck up a conversation with the woman with the swept-back hair, pronounced German accent, and sparkling blue eyes. Further meetings, both spontaneous and arranged, ensued. Agee learned that she had been born in Vienna, the cradle of psychoanalysis, a science of considerable interest to her. Rebelling against a proper bourgeois upbringing, she felt drawn to the bohemian life, especially as it was practiced in that capital of Western decadence. Her parents had divorced years before, and eventually the whole family emigrated to the United States, where she set her sights on a medical career. In Chicago she found a job assisting two psychiatrists and lived in an apartment near the university. But the job lasted eighteen hours a day, taxing her formidable energies, and she was unable to save enough money to put herself through medical school.

Finding the Midwest not at all to her liking, she moved to New York, which had far more in common with Vienna. Here she found her first job through the luckiest of accidents. Arriving at the Benton & Bowles advertising agency for an interview, she caught an error in a report and was hired on the spot. But, last hired, first fired. On her own once more, she found a safe haven at *Fortune* in 1939. Her starting salary was $25 a week, later raised to $30—

enough to pay for her $35-a-month Greenwich Village apartment.

Unlike Alma, the bookish Mia comprehended the complexity of Agee's literary aspirations, as well as his enormous difficulty in attaining even a fraction of what he wanted to do. Furthermore, Mia was cool and subdued, and she was as cultivated as Via, though far more uninhibited. Of greatest significance, she was enough of a realist not to be swept off her feet by the charming James Agee. While acknowledging his sensitivity and powers of empathy, she was equally aware of his proclivity for dissipation. Mia had few delusions of reforming him; if he wanted to drink to excess, that was his business. She was willing to accept him as he was.

As Alma's delivery date approached, Agee was increasingly attracted to the nonjudgmental, undemanding Mia. His insecurity about becoming a parent was more than he could comfortably bear; looking at Alma's swelling form, he was filled not with expectation but with numbing confusion. He lost his precious "clarity of mind" and became prone to a "dangerous" and "terrifying lack of . . . discipline of thought and conduct" aggravated by a marked "tendency to melancholia" and the deadly sin of sloth, *"acedia."* With his feelings for Mia growing by leaps and bounds, he was aware that his romantic history was about to repeat itself, but, as before, he felt powerless to stem the tide of passion. There seemed to be no end to the miseries he was able to inflict upon himself.

The curious thing about his alienation from Alma was that it did not concern the central issue of sex. To his mind, they enjoyed an "intensely satisfactory sexual relationship" along with "tenderness and poetry and illumination and a sense of fun." The problem, he decided, was their lack of intellectual common ground. Alma did not appreciate him enough; he assumed she was "bored, bewildered, and disappointed by him." After nearly two years of marriage, they knew too much of one another's weaknesses. Ultimately, their relationship revealed itself to be "very deep, but very narrow." He had considered sex his salvation and had abandoned Via in pursuit of it, only to find that sex alone could not sustain a marriage. He decided that what he needed now was a friend, not a sex object. Mia could be that friend, the first woman he had ever known whom he considered his intellectual equal. As before, he kidded himself into thinking their relationship was "casual" and "transient," as his early flirtation with Alma had been.

It was in this highly sensitive and insecure atmosphere that

Alma gave birth to their child on Wednesday, March 20, 1940, at 12:59 P.M. at Lying-In Hospital on East 70th Street in Manhattan. The rosy, healthy baby boy weighed six pounds, eleven ounces. "I know these statistics are ludicrous but for some reason are interesting and necessary," noted Agee, ever the journalist. The statistics assumed such great importance because they were, at the outset, all he knew about his firstborn. To his fury the hospital had not called him until after the child was born, and he felt cheated of experiencing the birth with Alma.

The giddy, exhausted new parents named their boy Joel, after Agee's maternal grandfather, who by now had assumed mythological dimensions in the proud father's mind. Alma recovered rapidly, and on Saturday Agee brought his wife and child home from the hospital. They had previously purchased clothes for the infant, but these he forgot to bring with him to the hospital, remembering only Alma's three-inch heels. Already parenthood was taxing his limited powers of organization to the utmost.

Three weeks later Agee confessed to Alma that he had been sleeping with Mia Fritsch. He explained that he was making this confession because it was necessary to purge their marriage of doubt and mistrust. As a defense, he pleaded that the enforced celibacy of the late stages of pregnancy had been too much to manage. He had to have a woman, and Mia was available. Alma was tolerant enough to understand her husband's having an occasional fling. But why, she wanted to know, did he bring that woman into their apartment and make love with her on their bed? The idea so angered her that she turned into a "wild animal," as she later recalled, jumped up, and slapped Agee. He protested that Alma need not worry, that she was the center of his life; from now on he would devote his full attention to her.

But Alma was having none of it. She instantly recognized the seriousness of the threat Mia posed. Alma had once been the "other woman" in Agee's life herself, and she knew that he would be incapable of giving up Mia, no matter what he said. As a result, Alma became "furiously, even hysterically jealous." In response, Agee took offense at what he considered to be her overreaction to a casual fling, a mere lapse of marital fidelity, not a full-blown love affair. Despite his disclaimers, Agee could not bring himself to break off with Mia in the subsequent weeks and months.

Alma found this state of affairs intolerable. Repeatedly she tried to run away, but Agee prevented her. Once she went flying out of their apartment and down the stairs. Agee caught up with her and dragged her back by the hair on her head. In their apartment he banged his head against the wall and struck himself with his fists. In punishing himself for his misconduct, he hoped to win Alma's forgiveness; instead he aroused her anxiety about his fitness as a husband and the father of their child. On another occasion she dropped by his office at *Time* to declare her intention of going to Mexico with Joel and the photographer Helen Levitt. To thwart her plan, Agee threatened to jump out the window and went so far as to dangle one long leg over the sill while looking back in defiance at her. Equally adept at confrontational tactics, she calmly strode out of the office and headed for the elevator. No, she would not allow herself to be blackmailed by childish threats. But while waiting for the elevator, she lost her nerve. What if he had jumped? In a state of panic she ran back to Agee's office. The room was empty, the window wide open. She was on the verge of realizing that the worst had happened when she discovered him crouching behind the door. Fury quickly followed relief.

These confrontations alternated with attempts at reconciliation, protestations of love, more deceptions, and a resumption of their intense sexual relationship. In the process they neglected Joel. They thought nothing of going out for dinner while the baby slept at home unattended. And at the Baldwin estate, they made themselves noticeable by their absence. There it often fell to Eunice Clark, handmaiden of *Let Us Now Praise Famous Men,* to care for Joel while Agee and Alma cavorted in the bushes. Through it all, Agee cultivated an ever deepening relationship with Mia.

Occasionally events brought him up short, and he was stricken with guilt over his inability to provide an adequate domestic setting for his child. He had revered his own father above all other men, yet he found himself unable to emulate his father's steadfastness as a parent. When Louise Saunders sent Christmas gifts to Joel, Agee replied with an exploration of his uneasy state of mind. "I feel mainly two things—terrific responsibility, almost paralyzing, and a near certainty . . . that that degree of intensity in the effort to do right is perhaps the most damaging single atmosphere one could surround a child with." If only he could be like the Negroes, he explained, "who lack science, conjecture, and tension, but have ease, resilience, animal depth and response." He dared not reveal to Louise Saunders that his marriage to Alma was all but finished; instead, he commended his wife for possessing the characteristics of an ideal mammy, "because she is more sound and simple than I am." Once committed to this line of reasoning, he found it plausible to claim an "easy and happy certainty about Alma—much more solid confidence in her qualifications than in mine." And he went on to weave a fantastic vision of languid summers in the country with "simple" Alma and their child, full-time work on his own writing, and an end to book reviewing. All that was missing was the antebellum plantation.

The contrast between the grim reality of Agee's domestic life and the fantasy he presented for Louise Saunders' benefit was poignant enough, but even more distressing was his inability to comprehend why he felt compelled to betray Alma at her time of greatest need. That he was extremely possessive of her was plain to all their friends; she had only to look at another man (Evans excepted) for Agee to become agitated. He wanted Alma all to himself, and he regarded anyone else she loved, even a helpless infant, as a rival not to be tolerated.

By the time Agee wrote to Louise Saunders, Alma could take no more of his neglect and deceit. She packed a few belongings, the baby (now a year old), and fled with Helen Levitt to Mexico, leaving Agee to contemplate the consequences of his actions in wretched isolation on West 15th Street.

He mourned the loss of his wife and child as if it were another death in the family. Throughout the early months of 1941, he endured bereavement, sorrow, depression. That they were self-inflicted only made matters worse. He knew that if he wanted Alma back he would have to break off with Mia, but he found it impossible to sacrifice that rare woman for the sake of a tranquil domestic life. He had always known he was not the stuff of which good husbands are made. His sense of absolute failure sat "constantly in the bottom of my gut," he wrote Robert Fitzgerald. He felt a "bottomless sadness, impotence, and misery in which one can neither move a hand nor keep it still" compounded by a "punch-drunk numbness and blandness." He went on to fill in the details of a bleak self-portrait.

I'm in a bad period: incertitude and disintegration on almost every count. Somehow fed up and paralytic with the job; horribly bad sleeping rhythms; desperate need to live regularly & still more to do new work of my own; desperate knowledge that with all the time on earth I would as I spiritually feel now be capable of neither. Bad enough, though, that I'm calm as ever, bland rather than tortuous; and the beginnings, at least, of a "grip" on it, by bullying myself awake.

At his lowest ebb, Agee drew up a comprehensive survey of his situation, beginning with the impending publication of *Let Us Now Praise Famous Men,* as a way of strengthening his "grip" on reality.

The book is supposed to be published January or February— no proofs yet, though. I thoroughly regret using the subtitle (Let Us Now Praise Famous Men) as I should never have forgotten I would. I am rather anxious to look at it, finished and in print—possibly also, to read it in that form—but I have an idea I'll be unable to stand to. If so, it might be a healthy self-scorching to force myself to: but that's probably New England Chapel-crank blood. Mainly, though, I want to be through with it, as I used to feel about absolution, and to get to work again as soon as I can. I am thirty-one now, and I can conceivably forgive myself my last ten years only by a devotion to work in the next ten which I suspect I'll be incapable of. I am much too vulnerable to human relationships, particularly sexual or in any case heterosexual, and much too deeply wrought upon by them, and in turn much too dependent in my work on feeling, as against "intellect." In short I'm easily upset and, when upset, incapable of decent work; incapable of it also when I'm not upset enough. I must learn my way in an exceedingly quiet marriage (which can be wonderful I've found but is basically not at all my style or apparent "nature") or break from marriage and all close liaisons altogether and learn how to live alone & keep love at a bearable distance. Those are oddly juvenile things to be beginning to learn at my age: what really baffles me is that, knowing them quite well since I was 15, I've done such thorough jobs in the opposite direction. Well, nothing would be solved or even begun tonight by anything I wrote or thought, or at any time soon: my business now and evidently for quite a while to come is merely to sit as tight as I can and careful as I can, taking care above all to do no further harm to others or myself or my now vertically destroyed needs or hopes, and doing a timorous or dramatic piece of mending or wherever there seems any moments' chance to. I haven't been very intelligent—to say nothing of "good"—and now it's scarcely a chance for intelligence or goodness—only for the most dumb and scrupulous tenacity. On the whole, though, it's time I had a good hard dose of bad going, and if I find I'm capable of it the winter will be less wasted than it otherwise might be. Meanwhile, though, I find I'm so dull I bore myself sick. A broken spirit and a contrite heart have their drawbacks: worst of all if at the same time a spirit is unbroken and ferocious and the heart contrite only in the sense of deep grief over pain and loss, not all in true contrition.

In sum, he was not fit for marriage, only for work. A major writer, he conceded, required major torment. Of torment he had suffered enough for a lifetime. His only salvation lay in work, now that he could not be saved by love. He had no choice but to press on, continue to review books for *Time* to pay the rent, monitor the final prepublication stages of *Let Us Now Praise Famous Men,* and begin a new domestic arrangement with Mia, keeping his expectations on all counts low.

He commemorated the decision in a sonnet. The long-neglected form felt awkward and confining now. He had lost the hard-won facility with verse. Still, it was good to remind himself of its discipline and elegance, qualities he sadly lacked. He began by addressing Alma.

> *Two years have passed, and made a perfect wheel*
> *Of all that love can know of joy or pain.*
> *All that lovers hope or dread to feel*
> *We've felt, and arrived at naught again.*

Disillusioned by romance, he cautioned himself to

> *. . . set no stars*
> *On other loves; all love's a ceaseless bend*
> *From naught to naught: farewell: make fast your door.*

Having shut the door on his old life with Alma, Agee resumed work on *Let Us Now Praise Famous Men.* Brooks informed him that publication had again been postponed, this time to the summer of 1941, but the deadline was close enough to instill a sense of finality in Agee's mind. There was no time left for equivocation, doubt, or sudden inspiration; all that remained was the task of correcting the manuscript, but this predictable exercise imparted a sense of control lacking in other areas of his life.

His friend Alice Morris, whose slapping of her husband Harvey Breit had made such a memorable impression on Agee, assumed responsibility for typing the manuscript where Alma had left off. An acquaintance of Morris, Charles Fuller, an architect, offered to pay her a modest stipend for the work, thus becoming, indirectly, Agee's patron. As she labored over the manuscript, Agee's tiny handwriting reminded her of angels dancing on the head of a pin. She worked at Evans' tiny apartment, where the photographer constantly hovered over her, terrified that she would inadvertently alter a word or punctuation mark. Everything had to be letter perfect, precisely as Agee had written it.

Elated by her progress and believing that he had at last put his troubles behind him, Agee dashed off a note to Fitzgerald describing his relief at being able to function as a writer, if not as a person.

> I am, thank God, beginning (by way of mechanical and rewriting efforts) to get back to work, and accordingly am happy again. The lack of it is very literally like anemia. Getting back the feeling of it I know (more completely than with just [my] head) a bromide better than I ever have: that it is, finally, barring a negligible amount of food, the only thing completely necessary to life.

As he surveyed the neatly piled, finished pages, a rare sense of accomplishment and pride stole over him. "I regret parts of it and have doubts of some other parts," he related to Fitzgerald, "but on the whole have a feeling I've never before much enjoyed, of knowing why I have done this . . . and of believing in the why I have done it." When he reflected that nearly five years had elapsed since the inception of the project, his confidence momentarily faltered, yet he still considered the book "worth the try, so far."

Feeling pleased with himself, he turned over the last sections of the 150,000-word manuscript to Brooks and Linscott in March. When the proofs came back, Agee made further corrections in his minuscule hand. The editors at Houghton Mifflin were accustomed to deciphering unusual handwriting, but Agee's scrawl baffled them to the point of exasperation. In a carefully typed letter, he hastened to apologize to Linscott for the trouble he had caused: "Please give my most abject regrets to yourself and all who have suffered; illegibility is the worst possible manners, and I am ashamed of myself."

While Agee immersed himself in correcting the manuscript of *Let Us Now Praise Famous Men,* his principal confidant at the moment, Robert Fitzgerald, took a leave of absence from *Time* to do exactly what Agee had long wished to: write poetry in splendid isolation. When Agee learned that Fitzgerald planned to return to *Time* in the fall, he offered to subsidize an extended sabbatical for his friend. "Why don't I continue at this work and you continue at yours, for 6 months or 8 months a year (we can arrange that) during which I could send you and Eleanor [Fitzgerald's wife] $100 a month," Agee proposed in June. The amount came to about a quarter of Agee's *Time* salary. At the same time he suggested the Fitzgeralds move to Mexico, where a small amount of money could go a long way. "This would involve living where perhaps you might rather not; but a living, and free time, would be assured."

To ease Fitzgerald's sense of indebtedness, Agee proposed they switch roles as poet and patron at a later date. Early in the summer, Agee sent Fitzgerald the first installment under this plan, explaining, "Nothing on earth could make me feel worse than that you should for any reason whatever have to come back now that you are ripe for so much." He went on to offer a series of replies to what he imagined would be Fitzgerald's protests.

> As for the money, I feel as you do, that it belongs to him who needs it at a given time—your need for it for the next year or so is so far out of proportion to any I would have short of a year or so of freedom. . . . I think neither of us should think twice about your later paying me back—that is the wrong conception of the whole thing. I'll be able to take care of myself, one way or another, when my time comes for it— meanwhile I'll be best taking care for things I care for most,

if I can make freedom and work possible for you when you can make best use of it.

I'm talking badly out of turn in all this walking-in and urging—I hope you can forgive it. It seems terribly crucial to me that you stay free at this particular time, and criminal if you don't.

Fitzgerald was sincerely grateful for this display of generosity, particularly in light of Agee's perilous financial situation. Agee also sent small amounts of money to Alma in Mexico, where she and their son, Joel, were now living with a German Communist writer, Bodo Uhse, whom she had met shortly after her arrival.

Without meaning to, Fitzgerald drew Agee still further into this tangled web of marital guilt. Through mutual friends, Agee learned that Fitzgerald was in the throes of a divorce from his wife, Eleanor. Until now he had looked on Fitzgerald as a paragon of integrity; unlike Agee, Fitzgerald had held fast to the ideals of Catholicism, poetry, and marriage. Shocked and saddened by the impending divorce, Agee relived the pain of his own two marital failures. "I feel the deepest kind of sympathy with both of you," he wrote to Fitzgerald. "I don't think that people who appear to—who are in the habit, or think they are, of taking marriage rather lightly—go through this nearly as painlessly as one thinks. It is certainly the hardest thing I have known, and I can't think of anyone it could be harder for than you and Eleanor."

On that grim note, Agee expressed the wish that Fitzgerald would come to rely on him as a cross between a psychiatrist and a father confessor. Perhaps he might teach Fitzgerald lessons he had learned from his own mistakes. As a start, he advised that the "paralysis" following separation was "only a stage, and God help the person unlucky enough to exalt it into a permanent deadlock." He hinted broadly that Fitzgerald's troubles gave rise to religious sentiments, and while he stopped short of offering to pray for his hard-pressed friend, his response had distinct echoes of the warm, patient, and often fuzzy advice he had received over the years from Father Flye. "I hope you can trust me," Agee wrote, "for if you can, I hope and feel I might be of some use to you . . . based on three main things working together—my deep concern and sympathy; whatever ways I am like you or at least on communicating roads with you, morally or religiously; and the ways in which we most differ." Once his empathy was engaged, Agee felt little distinction between private misery and the suffering of others. The universality of basic emotions—especially pain, loss, and separation—carried him, as if on a wave, to sublime heights. In these moments he earned a respect from his friends that redeemed his darker side. Even the cantankerous Macdonald insisted, "It was impossible to dislike James Agee."

While he found it natural and therapeutic to offer advice and sympathy, he found it harder to accept the concern of others when he was in need. Worried about Agee's mental state after Alma's departure, Father Flye gently lectured his young friend on the importance of exercise, sleep, and a regular schedule. But Agee could not bring himself to heed the priest's words. Discipline reminded him of his mother, and his mother reminded him of the loss of love and freedom. "Nothing makes me more frantic than . . . always being sure to wear my rubbers. That of course is at the root of my almost total lack of sense and discipline," he replied to Father Flye.

Undaunted, the priest recommended that Agee look to a good psychiatrist to help him cope with his emotional upheavals—a suggestion Agee was inclined to take more seriously. He had flirted with the idea but still could not bring himself to subscribe to Freudian dogma. Then, too, he looked on analysis as a humiliating admission of defeat. It seemed that only the certifiably insane underwent analysis, and he doubted that a functioning adult could benefit from the process. He prided himself on his willingness and ability to contend with problems on his own, no matter what the cost. But the more he explained his reservations to Father Flye, the more obvious it became that he could benefit from treatment.

> Psychiatry, and for that matter psychoanalysis still more, interest me intensely; but I feel reluctant to use either except in really desperate need, and suspect in fact that I'll probably pull out of this under my own power. Yet I realize that I have an enormously strong drive, on a universally broad front, toward self-destruction; and that I know little if anything about its sources or control. There is much I might learn and be freed from that causes me and others great pain, frustration and

255

> defeat, and I expect that sooner or later I will seek their help. But I would somewhere near as soon die (or enter a narcotic world) as undergo full psychoanalysis. I don't trust anyone on earth that much; and I see in every psychoanalyzed face a look of deep spiritual humiliation or defeat; to which I prefer at least a painful degree of spiritual pain and sickness.

He loathed the thought of relying on a clinically detached observer, nodding politely and noting his shortcomings on a pad. Then, too, he would not be able to confuse and manipulate a trained psychiatrist as he did his friends and family. He would be trapped.

Nonetheless, he would have made an eager, perceptive patient, for he was always attempting to analyze himself with more ruthlessness than any psychiatrist would have brought to bear. His latest technique for attaining self-knowledge consisted of studying photographs others had taken of him. To candid shots Father Flye had snapped during a short visit to New York, Agee recorded these reactions: "When I saw the picture . . . I (a) thought I was someone else, and disliked him rather, and (b) recognized myself and was shocked, seeing in the face complacency, coarseness, a kind of intelligence which over-estimated itself, and a kind of duplicity." So ugly was he that he felt shame at having tricked Father Flye into liking him; the priest should have had the sense to see him for the beast he was. To Agee's way of thinking, this experiment in self-examination was as valuable as orthodox psychiatry. The unsparing camera lens provided instant analysis, and at a fraction of the cost of the conventional kind.

Agee's proud and self-reliant attitude drew strength from his deepening bond with Mia. In mid-1941 they quietly began looking for an inexpensive apartment to share. Marriage was not an issue. Agee believed that to marry Mia would put an end to their love affair, and she took a similarly casual attitude toward formalizing their relationship. It was enough that they were together without entering into a covenant they might not be able to sustain. Early in the fall they located a fifth-floor walk-up apartment at 172 Bleecker Street, in the heart of Greenwich Village.

He drew additional satisfaction—and relief—from the imminent publication of *Let Us Now Praise Famous Men*. Compared with the amount of effort he had expended in writing the book, his expectations for it were very modest. He knew it would not be an easy book to love, for he had created an aggressively antipopular, avant-garde work whose value, if any, would in all likelihood not be recognized in his time. He supposed it would baffle and offend the casual reader in search of entertainment and diversion. In emulation of Joyce, the patron saint of modern letters, he had written a book most likely to be appreciated not by the general public but by other writers.

At long last Houghton Mifflin published *Let Us Now Praise Famous Men* in August 1941. The 471-page volume, with its sedate brown-and-black dust jacket, cost $3.50 and contained sixty-two of Evans' photographs "reproduced through the courtesy of Farm Security Administration, United States Department of Agriculture." The coauthors insisted in a brief introduction that the "photographs are not illustrative. They, and the text, are coequal, mutually independent, and fully collaborative." And they advised that the text was written "with reading aloud in mind." To preserve the anonymity of the book's subjects, Agee changed their names; the Burroughses became the Gudgers, the Tingles the Ricketts, and the Fieldses the Woods. At the last minute Agee decided to dedicate the book to them all, "To those of whom the record is made. In gratefulness and love."

The world at large, poised on the brink of war, was ill prepared for such a demanding and provocative work. The first major review, in the *New York Times* of August 19, was a disaster. Plainly irked by Agee's slighting references to journalism, the reviewer, Ralph Thompson, dismissed *Let Us Now Praise Famous Men* as "the choicest recent example of how to write self-inspired, self-conscious and self-indulgent prose." After sparing a few kind words for Evans' photographs, Thompson proceeded to ridicule Agee for being "arrogant, mannered, precious, gross," and incapable of writing a clear sentence. In this instance, Thompson was only taking his lead from the author, who, in his ill-advised introduction, had written, "If I bore you, that is that. If I am clumsy, that may indicate partly the difficulty of my subject, and the seriousness with which I am trying to take what hold I can of it; more certainly it will indicate my youth, my lack of mastery of my so-called art or craft, my lack perhaps of talent." Thompson was willing to take Agee at his word. In general, the reviewer felt that Evans' austere photographs said more about the plight of the sharecroppers and said it better than all of Agee's literary contrivances. While it may be true that there can be no such thing as bad publicity, a review as harsh as Thompson's, appearing in the pages of the *New York Times,* was not likely to bolster sales.

On the heels of the *Times* debacle, Agee's literary acquaintances rallied in support of the book. Forming a benign conspiracy on its behalf, they submitted their own reviews to various influential publications on a free-lance basis. In doing so, they hoped to counter what they thought was the *Times*'s scandalous mistreatment of their friend's difficult masterpiece. Selden Rodman, who had excerpted *Let Us Now Praise Famous Men* in his own magazine, turned up in the *Saturday Review* with a lengthy consideration of the book's merits. He warned that it might cause the unsuspecting reader to "throw down the volume in rage, and curse the author for a confused adolescent, an Ezra Pound in Wolfe's clothing, a shocking snob, or a belligerent mystic posing with a purple pencil on the Left Bank of *Fortune,*" but, he insisted, the book's "greatness and unique quality" lay in its "over-all failure" to satisfy conventional expectations. He predicted that the book "will be spat upon —and years hence . . . read," a prophecy that proved to be accurate. And he went on to laud the work for combining the unmistakably personal feelings of the 1920s with the broad social concerns of the 1930s. "Our generation," he declared, "not only sees the connection but . . . insists on it stridently."

Next, Harvey Breit, whose wife had helped type the manuscript of *Let Us Now Praise Famous Men,* came to its defense in the *New Republic.* Like Rodman, he conceded that "Mr. Agee does a good deal to antagonize the reader" but insisted that he "writes brilliantly" and "is extraordinarily sensitive." He was especially impressed by Agee's barrage of literary techniques for getting at the truth of the sharecroppers' lives: the poetry, self-analysis, interior monologues, footnotes—an entire arsenal of devices. Much as he admired Agee's obvious skill and determination, Breit could not bring himself to accord the book more than grudging admiration. "It is a book about Mr. Agee," he concluded. "It is a book that refuses to call itself a book."

At *Time,* the problem of how to treat a controversial work by one of its own writers set the stage for intrigue. Matthews assigned

Fitzgerald to the book. As soon as Agee heard, he dispatched an airmail special delivery letter to his friend, promising, "I'll gladly make the agreement we once made on it, a long time ago: that I (a) will never read your review at all or (b) will let a long time—say a year—lapse before reading it." Feeling constrained nonetheless, Fitzgerald submitted what he thought to be a "stiff and reverent" review to Matthews, who refused to run it. He preferred to write his own, more objective appraisal. To Agee the change was an ominous one, for Matthews was notoriously blunt and caustic in his opinions.

When Matthews' review appeared in the October 13 issue of *Time,* it was not nearly so bad as Agee had feared. In fact, the lean-jawed editor proclaimed the book "the most distinguished failure of the season," and not because Agee might have done a better job but because he had "willed it so." Matthews did accuse the author of "bad manners, exhibitionism and verbosity," not to mention a certain "foredoomed failure to convey all he feels." And now that Matthews thought of it, Agee did "clumsily intrude between his subject and his audience, even when the subject is himself," but once the editor got these reservations off his chest, he had to admit that "Agee has a delicacy and power that make the total effect of the book overwhelming." Lapsing into Timestyle, Matthews sensed that a spiritual quest had inspired "Preacher-Poet Agee" to write "some of the most exciting U.S. prose since Melville." Considering Matthews' penchant for tearing apart the work of talented writers, such praise was highly unusual.

Other publications reviewing *Let Us Now Praise Famous Men* echoed these conflicting attitudes. In *Partisan Review,* Paul Goodman took exception to the book's perverse organization. *Commonweal*'s reviewer decided Agee was "in a much more tragic condition than any exploited sharecropper." And, closer to home, Agee's mother added her voice to the chorus of disapproval. She told her son that she objected to the book's obscenities. Having a son who possessed such a filthy, impertinent mind only added to her worldly cares.

Not until the following year did a review finally appear that went beyond the book's stylistic novelties. Writing in the scholarly *Kenyon Review,* Lionel Trilling, one of the rising stars of Columbia University's English Department, singled out *Let Us Now Praise*

Famous Men as a "great book" and "the most realistic and important moral effort of our generation." Trilling's laudatory review signaled the New York literary establishment's acceptance of Agee as a worthy, if unpredictable, writer. As a veteran of Luce's journalistic sweatshop, Agee had considered himself incapable of attaining this distinction, but now that he had this densely woven, challenging book to his credit, his reputation finally exceeded the boundaries of journalism. No longer an aesthete, a minor writer, he became a cult figure to the cognoscenti, respectably disreputable and roguish.

The lack of favorable reviews in the popular press dampened the book's chance for commercial success. True to form, Agee did nothing to enhance the reputation of *Let Us Now Praise Famous Men.* He made none of the expected polite gestures toward reviewers on its behalf, and with the bombing of Pearl Harbor on December 7, public interest in the plight of some sharecroppers in the summer of 1936 plummeted, no matter how rich and beautiful Agee's prose.

By the year's end the book had sold only six hundred copies. It quickly vanished from bookstores and the public eye. Following the practice of most trade publishers, Houghton Mifflin remaindered the book, selling leftover copies to stores at a large discount. These could be had for as little as nineteen cents. Although Houghton Mifflin continued to list *Let Us Now Praise Famous Men* in its catalogue until 1948, the book was, for all intents and purposes, dead within weeks of publication.

Agee refused to blame either Brooks or Houghton Mifflin for the book's spectacular commercial failure, nor did he consider the tiny sale a surprise. He remained grateful that Houghton Mifflin had published the work in the first place; considering the legal risks involved, it had discharged its responsibilities about as well as could be expected.

Nor did the scathing reviews rile him. Quite the opposite. He came to agree that the book was, in fact, a failure. To Father Flye he insisted, "It is a sinful book at least in all degrees of 'falling short of the mark' and I think in more corrupt ways as well." Not even the priest, for all his reservations about the book's obscenity, seconded this opinion. He wrote back that the book was, when all is said and done, "deeply religious." But Agee seemed to think he deserved punishment and censure for having put pen to paper. At the same time, he told himself the censure meant nothing; criticism was irrelevant. As he explained in the book itself, he had not written a work of art, but rather a "human effort which must require human co-operation." And he insisted on sharing what little credit he thought the book deserved with Evans. But when Evans signed a friend's copy, he wrote, "This is of course Jim's book, which I have no right to inscribe."

Despite Evans' high regard for the text, he lost the precious manuscript Agee had given him as a Christmas present. The photographer inadvertently left it behind when he moved out of his tiny studio, and the building was shortly thereafter demolished. He regarded the loss as one of the great tragicomic episodes of his life —tragic because of the waste, comic because Agee's wish for the book had been fulfilled; the manuscript, at least, vanished into thin air.

But the strange history of *Let Us Now Praise Famous Men* did not end there. In 1960, when Houghton Mifflin reissued the book, it was hailed by critics as a great "lost" work and made a significant impact on the public as well. In the sensual and heady days of the 1960s, readers were at last prepared for the verbal pyrotechnics of *Let Us Now Praise Famous Men*. Campus activists looked to it as a harbinger of the decade's social upheavals and reforms, and journalists seized on it as a precursor of a new approach to reporting, the New Journalism. Like Agee, the New Journalists discarded evasive objectivity in favor of a personal, visceral re-creation of their subject matter. Like Agee, they often made themselves the heroes of their accounts; what mattered most was not the facts but their reactions to the facts. And, like Agee, they were prone to making autobiographical digressions and outlandish statements— anything to push journalism to the stylistic extremes Agee first explored over twenty years before.

IN THE DARK

Following the publication of *Let Us Now Praise Famous Men*, the tornado that was James Agee, after a decade of twisting wildly across the literary landscape, began to slow and decrease in violence. At great personal cost he had made the arduous transition from poet to journalist, and from journalist to independent author. But now he tumbled from that lonely summit to the intermediate level of journalism, though he came to practice it in a more sophisticated guise.

His versatility was at once cause for admiration and for concern. It was, of course, testimony to the great variety of his interests and abilities. At the same time, there was something disturbing about his habit of abandoning a form once he had gained a certain amount of recognition for it. Who knows what wonders might have flowed from his pen had he continued to write poetry or to pursue his personal brand of social commentary? There are writers who spend their lives at their desks, who live primarily in their heads; and there are writers hungry to experience all of life, who are determined to live out lives as dramatic as anything they write about. Agee belonged to the latter group. Unfulfilled possibilities beckoned him, tormented him, and, in the fall of 1941, led him to choose, if so driven a man can choose, to revolutionize film criticism.

To Agee movies were not primarily a form of entertainment, although they were, fitfully, entertaining. Nor were they the modern equivalent of bread and circuses designed to lull the masses into a state of passivity. Rather, they were, as he had known since his Exeter days, *the* indigenous art form. Good or bad, vulgar or exquisite, they were, more than any literary form, the mirror of American life. They were cheap, rude, hypocritical, democratic, occasionally inspired, usually humdrum—in short, they were American. For this reason he longed to find his way, however roundabout, into them. Once again he was slowly but inexorably setting out on the journey west.

The return of Robert Fitzgerald from his poetry-writing sabbatical in October set in motion events that would lead to Agee's securing a permanent post as film reviewer for *Time,* the first leg of that journey. He had long been restive as a book reviewer for the magazine. He was as careful a reader as he was a writer, and he found it impossible to express snap decisions about complicated matters in a few terse paragraphs of Timestyle. With the "Books" department now up to strength, he agitated for and received a transfer to "Cinema."

In this as in no other department at *Time* he felt thoroughly at home and confident. He now had the ideal pretext to indulge his movie-going habit to the utmost. He saw at least four or five movies a week, some of them several times. He whiled away pleasurable months stretching into years in the dark, escaping the pressures of his personal life and later the war. To Agee, watching a film was nearly as satisfying as making one, and he instinctively remade in his mind's eye whatever he saw on the screen. If a film was absolutely terrible, he could find some reason, however insignificant, to embrace it. Publicity and box office grosses made no impression on him. It scarcely mattered whether a given film was good, bad, or indifferent; he demanded only that it be interesting, and often the very worst films were the most interesting, though not in ways their makers intended. As Fitzgerald said, "To see and hear him describe a movie that he liked—shot by shot, almost frame by frame—was unquestionably better in many ways than to see the movie itself."

Agee's first review for *Time,* a brief appraisal of W. C. Fields's *Never Give a Sucker an Even Break,* appeared on November 24, 1941, days before the bombing of Pearl Harbor. "Fields is a beautifully timed exhibit of mock pomposity, puzzled ineffectualness, subtle understatement and true-blue nonchalance," Agee commented. It was his first distinctive observation to appear in *Time*'s glossy pages. From the outset his movie reviews exuded a self-confidence and stylishness that his book reviews lacked. Henceforth, his film reviews appeared in virtually every issue of *Time.* They were usually no more than several hundred words long, rarely over a thousand, and covered the subject in four or five tightly packed paragraphs.

Although Agee threw himself into his new assignment with vigor and enthusiasm, he was, as always, beholden to Matthews' savage blue pencil. To complicate matters further, some anonymous hand sprinkled Agee's copy with Timestyle's annoying neologisms, staccato sentences, and bizarre word order. Despite this bowdlerization, Agee's voice usually survived the editing process intact, and he enjoyed the challenge of writing to space. After all, he had written a lengthy book exactly as he had pleased, only to see it sink from view almost before it was published. At least *Time* provided him with a faithful audience of several million readers, even if he could not be completely himself in front of them.

In a playful rather than subversive spirit, Agee did whatever he could to stretch the limitations of his format. He wrote (and counseled his colleagues to write) reviews that were longer and more repetitive than necessary in the hope that a decent amount of the writer's opinion would survive the editing process. He refused to type his copy, instead scribbling it in a hand so crabbed and tiny that researchers resorted to using a magnifying glass to read it, but when they did, they found little to query. He deliberately mispronounced Matthews' name as "Mathoos" and continued to wear tennis sneakers and ragged pants, even after the advertising department, fearing that he might accidentally meet a potential advertiser in the elevator, took exception to his uncouth appearance.

On a more serious level, he persisted in drinking on the job. Music critic Winthrop Sargeant, who occupied a nearby office, discovered to his dismay that Agee would "tank up on whiskey while he was writing until . . . he could no longer concentrate. Then he would take benzedrine to sober up, reach the point of concentration again, and remain there until he felt he needed more whiskey." Agee was aware of his propensity for addiction to alcohol and tobacco, but he felt powerless to stem his growing dependency on them. The least amount of stress—a deadline or inconvenient assignment—brought on a craving for narcotic relief. Movies were as potent a drug as any other, offering brief, blissful escape.

At *Time,* the progress of the war was uppermost in everyone's mind, but the conflict failed to inspire a deep personal response in Agee. Often he wished it would simply blow away. The Depression was the only political issue that held his interest. He had, in his own small way, participated in it and written about it, but he wanted nothing to do with war, unless it was another Civil War, for which he felt great nostalgia. But this one was an overseas war, it was immoral, and he held the United States morally culpable for entering it, even in self-defense.

By October of 1942 the war threatened to become more than an abstraction to Agee. From the upper echelons of *Time* came word that he could expect to be drafted at any moment. Numerous other employees, including his friend Fitzgerald, were in one branch of the armed services or another. For the moment his draft status was 3-A, exempt, but when he underwent and passed a physical examination his anxiety reached fever pitch. Pleading with the *Time* brass to come to his rescue with a continued deferment or an overseas assignment, he outlined his objections to being reclassified 1-A, immediately draftable.

> Not satisfied with this classification, but doubt it can be successfully appealed. 1) My wife and child, though we are not "maintaining a bona fide home," are entirely dependent on me; the Army pay would not adequately support them; and I cannot rightly assume that TIME can continue indefinitely, if I am

drafted, to send my dependents a percentage of my salary. 2) I suspect I am a better writer than soldier. . . .

My chief contingent desires are two. 1) To assure adequate support of my dependents. 2) To maintain, if possible, an intact relationship with the person most important to me.

This person is an employee of this company. My preference for where I work is influenced by the question of whether, in the course of time, we might work in the same place. Of the ability and usefulness of this person in such work I have no question, and doubt her employers would have. If, in the idea I might do useful work abroad, or away from New York, TIME thinks of asking for my deferment, I would like to talk to you . . . personally.

Plainly the prospect of being drafted threw Agee into a panic. He would not be able to write, of course, but that was the least of his worries. He dreaded separation from Mia, "the person most important to me," and while he asked *Time* to consider pairing them on an assignment, it was unlikely that the magazine would look favorably upon that request. Finally, he falsely claimed he was supporting his dependents, Alma and Joel. More likely he wished he were supporting them; in fact, they were still living in Mexico with Bodo Uhse, and the small amount of money Agee contributed was not enough to sustain them.

Although Agee's memorandum smelled of desperation, *Time* acceded to his wishes and obtained a deferment for him. He would not have to don a uniform after all, at least not for now. But the war did affect his life in other, more subtle ways. For one thing, travel restrictions were in effect, and he was rarely able to leave New York; when he did, he journeyed no farther than the surrounding countryside for brief respites from the pressures of work. For another, his avoidance of military duty damaged his self-esteem. As the war continued and the sacrifice of lives mounted, his sense of shame increased to a nearly intolerable level. He felt himself a coward, a misguided pacifist in a world ruled by hate. His new involvement with Hollywood offered little escape from these concerns, for, it seemed, every star appeared in uniform to sell war bonds, every feature was preceded by a newsreel highlighting the latest exploits of our boys overseas, and, worst of all, the studios started to grind out one war movie after another.

At the time Agee began his film reviewing career, Hollywood was suffering its first major slump in years. Box office receipts failed to keep pace with the rest of the economy, and for a time it seemed that the ailing industry might go into hibernation for the duration of the war. Then came *Mrs. Miniver,* Metro-Goldwyn-Mayer's patriotic story of the effects of war on a stately Englishwoman. Starring Greer Garson, the movie was a hit at the box office, taking in over $6 million, and a hit as well with President Roosevelt, who, sensing it would boost the war effort, lent it his personal support. It went on to win a clutch of Oscars and to unleash a spate of war movies attracting ever larger audiences to the theaters.

With few exceptions, Agee deplored them all as examples of typical Hollywood shallowness, and he wrote about them with a pen dipped in acid. But to express dislike for war movies when patriotic feelings in the land were at an all-time high was tantamount to treason, and before long he had run afoul of *Time's* senior editors, who urged him to overlook the movies' intrinsic quality—or lack of it—in favor of their propaganda value. But Agee was having none of it.

The controversy reached a flash point with his caustic review of the popular *Wake Island.* A flood of mail from irate readers took Agee to task for condemning this noble depiction of the American war effort. To one of his critics, Edwin Westrate, a veteran, Agee explained what he looked for in a war movie.

> I have not seen combat service, nor do I think I need to have, to know a half-good film depiction of combat from a really good one. I have seen men who were badly hurt, and they looked it. I have also seen films about combat or violence which convinced me—newsreels of the Memorial Day fracas in 1937, some of the shots in *The Battle of Midway,* and such pictures as *The Birth of a Nation, Potemkin,* and *Ten Days That Shook The World.* About fictional ones among these films I cannot, it is quite true, qualify as a first-hand observer. But a work of fiction is "convincing" through doing well or ill by laws of its own, only one of which is physical or medical authenticity. If I am not convinced that 10 men are dead just because that many actors fall to the ground and lie perfectly still, it is the business of those who make the film to convince me.

And to Westrate's insistence that *Wake Island* must be a good picture because it was popular, Agee declared:

> The box office record of any picture is a fair measure of the picture's popularity and of nothing else. I could regard it as a yardstick for cinematic victory or defeat, as you appear to recommend that I do, only if my judgment of pictures and my respect for good ones were far less responsible, even, than you think. And I cannot share your opinion that my judgment, insofar as it differs from your own, is "infantile."

To the beleaguered Agee it came as a great relief to learn that Luce had a new, top-secret magazine in the works. Given the military-sounding name of "Project X," it promised to attain an even higher level of sophistication than *Fortune*. Under the supervision of Willi Schlamm, former editor of a Communist newspaper in Vienna and now one of Luce's in-house radicals, Project X was supposed to be a noncommercial but widely circulated version of the late, lamented "little" magazines of the 1920s. The prospect of Time Inc.'s undertaking such an intellectually ambitious venture sent tremors of anticipation through the corps of *Time* writers, whose good salaries and stock options never quite compensated for the suspicion that they were working well below their tastes and gifts.

Once Agee got wind of the new magazine, he worked overtime to come up with new ideas, standards, and approaches for it. In the process he refined considerably his notion of responsible journalism. He had earlier walked away from *Fortune* in disgust, declaring all journalism a "broad and successful form of lying." In a memorandum he now expressed a new vision of what journalism could be.

> It is the business of journalism to report; of comment and analysis it does very little and that, as a rule, is inevitably brief and usually superficial. Nominally editors, columnists, radio commentators, and the "class" magazines make comment and analysis their business; but the results again are almost without exception that the mere surface has been scraped. . . . I suggest that this magazine could work a pincer-movement on experience or "reality," with journalism functioning very impor-

tantly as a part of the opposite arm of the pincers. We could use the findings of journalists, in other words, as they in turn use the findings of researchers. . . . Our technique of review would be quite untraditional; we would, in fact, have to invent it. A best-seller, for instance, should be reviewed not only on its "entertainment value"; we should investigate the causes of that particular "value"; and we should treat it, chiefly, as the valuably suggestive anthropological exhibit which it essentially is.

In writing the memo, it dawned on Agee that perhaps he was, after all, ideally suited to the role of reviewer. He had so many reactions to all sorts of artistic expression that perhaps the review was the best way to present them. Among all the standard literary forms, it came closest to his gift for brilliant, spontaneous conversation; only letters were better suited, but by definition they were not for public consumption.

Warming to his theme, he proposed that Schlamm and Luce subject the entire range of mass communication to careful scrutiny. "Advertising and art copy," he said, were "frequently poisonous; their poisons need naming and analyzing." When it came to movies, he suggested that a "study of merely clothes worn, of sets, of the ways people walk, of the ways people kiss, of the ways children are represented, would yield extremely rich results." He returned to his old weakness for letters; they would provide raw material for studies of the "psychology and ethics of private . . . conduct." Along the same line, he suggested experiments in "sound-photography": recording casual conversation for subsequent analysis. And the art department, he emphasized, must not concern itself with empty appreciation of beautiful objects but with the "scandalous economics involved in art" as well as reproducing the work of "every good little-known or unknown artist whom we can find." Agee would turn over the photography department, of course, to Walker Evans, "one of the three or four best photographers alive," and he warned that "serious photography, today, is far more nearly unpublishable than serious writing; and the economic situation of the serious photographer is even more hopeless."

Having exhausted conventional departments, he threw in wild cards. What about reprinting a magazine Dostoevsky had once edited? Include an Inquiring Photographer with one hundred faces per issue. Devote space to a study of sexual ethics. Look at the "wave of the future," whatever it might be. Shed light on "malpractice" and "corruption" in the world of music.

Finally, Agee insisted that the magazine should not be self-supporting. Luce must consider himself its indulgent patron rather than its publisher. Advertising must be banished from its pages, because it would be "immoral" in a truly serious publication. Furthermore, the editors should earn "no more than a modest living wage." In exchange for enough editorial influence, Agee would be glad to make the necessary financial sacrifice.

So caught up in his enthusiasm was he that it never occurred to him that Project X would be anything less than splendid in all respects. But the heyday of the little magazine, so much a product of the anarchic 1920s, was long gone, as Luce well knew. Agee's elaborate proposals met with sublime corporate indifference, and Project X vanished without a trace.

Fortunately, Agee managed to salvage a heightened awareness of the role of a reviewer, one he soon put to good use, but not for Time Inc.

The Nation, founded in 1865, bore little resemblance to *Time. Time* was glossy and brassy; *The Nation* was printed on newsprint. The ink rubbed off on the fingers. It exuded an aura of cigar smoke and argument, long-winded columns and constant reassertion of liberal principles. It was a venerable old sheet, not a slick advertising medium. Over the years, its politics had run the gamut from liberal to Communist, but it escaped the straitjacket of doctrinaire rigidity; contributors agreed to disagree. The current editor, Freda Kirchway, happened to be a Stalinist who left her political imprint on the front of the book, but she permitted the back of the book—the cultural departments—to pursue an anti-Stalinist course. At the same time, the magazine relented in its zealous campaign against social injustice, and, as a partial consequence, the back of the book became its claim to fame in the early 1940s.

The little-known steward of that domain was the elusive and legendary Margaret Marshall. Born a Mormon, she had come to New York as a young woman, married an English professor at New York University, had one child, a daughter, with him, gotten divorced, and set out to earn her own living. Blond, short, and pleasant-looking, she was cursed with manic-depression so severe that she might spend the entire evening at the home of a friend without uttering a syllable. At one time she had entertained literary ambitions, but she found herself chronically blocked.

Despite her afflictions, she knew a good writer when she saw one, and she knew enough to let her staff work with a minimum of editorial interference or bullying. Indeed, she was glad not to have to enter into her reviewers' problems. When, in late 1942, the position of movie reviewer at *The Nation* fell vacant, several regular contributors urged Marshall to invite *Time*'s cinematic savant, James Agee, to write the column. She took the advice, and Agee, with *Time*'s blessing, immediately accepted the offer. He would write about movies for the magazine on the average of twice a month, receiving only twenty-five dollars per column, barely enough to keep him in popcorn. At the same time, he continued his reviewing duties at *Time.* At first it seemed that his *Nation* contributions would be akin to moonlighting, but in time they came to assume far greater significance than his "real" job.

The new assignment made for an unusual double life, for there was a certain amount of bad blood between the two publications. The *Nation* crowd roundly condemned *Time* as a dangerous, war-mongering publication and considered Luce an exploiter of talents such as Agee. Few, if any, other writers were able to bridge the gap between *Time*'s philistinism and *The Nation*'s elitism, but Agee easily won acceptance by the other reviewers on the latter magazine. Together, they were known as the Four Horsemen of *The Nation:* Clement Greenberg, Bernard Haggin, Diana Trilling, and James Agee—as diverse a group as could be found on the staff of any publication. The fussy, stringent Haggin wrote about music with the fervor of the true believer, though he was blind to the merits of contemporary works. Nevertheless, Agee held him in the highest regard. Diana Trilling, wife of Lionel Trilling, who had admired *Let Us Now Praise Famous Men,* covered books with sympathetic acerbity. Then there was Greenberg—shrewd, hawklike, and icy, who would in the 1950s emerge as the most influential art critic of his generation. Even while admiring Agee, Greenberg considered *The Nation*'s new critic an "unrealized great writer." He suspected Agee's facility with words got him into trouble. Agee wrote so well that he cut corners and avoided the cloistered existence necessary to the creation of art. Greenberg was hard-pressed to imagine how anything worthwhile could come of Agee's penchant for talking, sharing, collaborating. One had to work in isolation; the writing was all that mattered. Yet there was Agee nattering on endlessly at cocktail parties about fleeting trends. Greenberg later declared, "He had the ability to be sincere without being honest."

When it came to writing about movies for *The Nation,* Agee put the discipline he had acquired at *Time* to good use. For once, he was able to write at the level of his abilities in a journalistic format. He wrote quickly, "like shit through a goose" in the words of one admiring colleague, and had little trouble turning in his copy on time to *The Nation's* offices on Vesey Street in lower Manhattan. Furthermore, his columns required little or no editing, and even if certain sentences required repeated reading to be understood, they never sounded less than intelligent.

In his inaugural column, on December 26, 1942, Agee explained that he approached the movies as an amateur, a status he defended as an advantage "in so far as a professional's preoccupation with technique, with the box office, with bad traditions, or simply with work, can blur, or alter the angle of, his own judgment." For Agee, analysis of a film called into play the entire motion-picture industry, the American system of government, and "the temper of a civilization." He believed movies revealed the national experience in a way that higher forms of art did not. They were a sort of found art, naïve but revealing. As a result, he went out of his way to shortchange movies that had scored a significant popular or commercial success. He sniggered unashamedly at *Casablanca* ("obviously an improvement on one of the world's worst plays") and dismissed *Citizen Kane's* innovative techniques ("most of them are simply retakes of tricks used—and discarded—in the 20's"). Having no interest in becoming an Eastern adjunct of Hollywood, he was constantly on the lookout for the odd, unappreciated movie deserving more consideration, though such gems were maddeningly scarce. In frustration he often turned his attention to cartoons and short subjects, the stranger the better. If Hollywood offered the American public a "collective dream," with all the pitfalls and subjectivity of any dream, he proposed to play analyst to the national psyche.

Agee's *Nation* column quickly attracted a cult following. For the first time in his career he found an appreciative audience that greeted his ruminations with respect and glee. *The Nation*'s 60,000 readers consisted largely of intellectuals, it was true, and he was reviewing movies rather than writing poetry, it was also true, but he made these limitations into strengths and emerged as a writer's reviewer. His reaction to films, and by extension to the larger world of art and ideas, was so finely tuned, so eloquently expressed, that it took a fellow practitioner to recognize the full extent of Agee's accomplishment.

He responded to his newfound popularity by writing reviews of constantly developing richness and vitality. He was on a hot streak, and he knew it. Everywhere he went, people had read what he had written, and nothing is more intoxicating to a writer than having an appreciative readership near at hand. Here was the writer of the extraordinary *Let Us Now Praise Famous Men* turning out film reviews that seemed destined to enter the select category of criticism that outlasted its subject matter. A few literary critics—Johnson, Coleridge, Hazlitt—had brought off this feat, but Agee bid fair to become the first film critic to achieve a similar status.

As his circle of admirers grew, an Agee legend sprang up. Younger journalists at *Time,* in particular, looked up to him as a shining example of what they wished to be. They spotted him lunching at the Maison de Winter restaurant, discoursing on the latest movie he had seen. To illustrate the editing rhythms, he pounded on his table so hard it turned over. The Depression, the war, sex, poetry, and popular entertainers spun through his conversation like so many spangles.

Even *Time* added to the Agee legend. T. S. Matthews pointed to Agee as the "house ideal," a writer who could take on any subject, no matter how abstruse or trivial, and find some personal connection with it and thereby make it his own—and the reader's as well. To sit in Agee's presence, surrounded by smoke, inhaling the alcohol on his breath, hearing his intoxicating conversation, was to be lifted onto a dizzying plane. The rapturous conversation flowed more freely than ever and gave life to his *Nation* column.

One of his youthful admirers, Alfred Kazin, then at *Time,* remembered the thrill of being in Agee's presence.

> Like so many Southern writers I knew, his rhetoric, his open suffering and mountainous declamation in taxis and barrooms were hurled at you along with great literary shrewdness. His authentic insight was dizzying in its cruel gift. What I loved most about him was his gift for intoxication. At any given moment he swelled up to the necessary pitch, he made everything in sight seem equally exciting. Never bored, afraid only of missing some exaltation on the air, he seemed at any time to be all there and primed to go off.

Kazin was only one of Agee's supporters in wartime New York. Such was the esteem in which Agee was generally held that no less a luminary than W. H. Auden was moved to write to *The Nation* to express his regard for the magazine's new film critic.

> Dear Sirs:
>
> ... I do not care for movies much and I rarely see them; further, I am suspicious of criticism as the literary genre which, more than any other, rerecruits epigones, pedants without insight, intellectuals without love. I am all the more surprised, therefore, to find myself not only reading Mr. Agee before I read anyone else in *The Nation* but also consciously looking forward all week to reading him again.
>
> In my opinion, his column is the most remarkable regular event in American journalism today. . . .
>
> One foresees the sad day, indeed, when Agee on Films will be the subject of a Ph.D. thesis.

Believing Auden to be the most significant and accomplished poet of the day, Agee took greater satisfaction from this unsolicited testimony than any other form of adulation he received.

To Auden as well as many other artists and intellectuals, Agee played a pioneering role in the history of movie criticism. Although not the only critic to take American film seriously, he was widely recognized as the first to see more in the movies than fleeting entertainment value. Emphasizing craft over stars, he discussed film more from the point of view of an informed insider than a consumer. Making brilliant use of his passion for detail, he took the reader behind the scenes to notice fine points of camera work, lighting, set decoration, and editing.

At the same time, his reactions were bracingly subjective rather than drily pedantic. He made a point of interjecting himself between the reader and the movie. His distinctive voice—now sweetly seductive, now bitter and ironic—gave the reviews immediacy and urgency. As a result, they were—and remain—compulsively readable. This innovative approach exerted a strong influence on succeeding generations of film critics, who looked to Agee as the first real practitioner, if not the founder, of their profession.

Agee's sudden notoriety as a film critic brought with it an unfamiliar set of responsibilities. People were just as likely to take a crack at him as applaud him. On May 22 he touched off a donnybrook with an agonized review of a film titled *Mission to Moscow,* a glorified account of Soviet-American relations. In his discussion, Agee was forced to address a political question of prime importance to many intellectuals: whether or not to support Stalin. As a starting point, Agee took exception to the movie's simplistic equation of "Stalinism with New Dealism with Hollywoodism with journalism with opportunism with shaky experimentalism with mesmerism with onanism." It seemed to him that the film's makers wanted the American public to "think the Soviet Union is . . . a great glad two-million dollar bowl of canned Borscht." So far, so good. Then, almost as an afterthought, he made a remark that enraged both pro- and anti-Stalinists.

He admitted that the propaganda aspects of the film so depressed him that he refused to take sides on the Stalin question. "It may be that this painful impotence is an impotence merely of my own spirit," he wrote. "In any case I can attempt to learn the truth, and can defend, or attack, only in areas where I can rely in some small degree on the hope of emergent truthfulness in the material and those who are handling it." Implicitly he accused those who had taken sides of willfully obscuring the truth, and he refused to be taken in by this political confidence game.

Agee's intransigence sent shock waves through the New York intelligentsia. Diana Trilling thought his attitude one of "uninformed superiority to the film's political content." Dwight Macdonald fanned the fires with a long, strident letter to *The Nation* beginning, "What kind of doubletalk is my friend James Agee handing us in his review of *Mission to Moscow?*" To Macdonald's way of thinking, it was impossible to arrive at a fair assessment of the film without taking its politics into consideration. At the very least, Agee would do well to "harmonize" his political and artistic opinions.

Agee's refusal to reveal a distinct political leaning isolated him from his peers. Almost alone among them, he failed to perceive any heroism in the war. Since war was an unconscionable evil, anyone who practiced it, even in self-defense, deserved condemnation, not a vote of confidence. "I expect the worst of us and of the English," he wrote to Father Flye on October 30, "something so little better in most respects . . . than Hitler would bring, that the death of a single man is a disgrace between the two. I would expect very little good of Russia (of Chiang Kai-shek even less), but hope at best there will be a balance between these two powers, forced by the final chance outcome of the war."

Sensitized to the issue of war films, Agee went to considerable lengths to seek out those presenting what he thought to be a truthful vision of the conflict—films that were the antithesis of the slick, hollow *Mission to Moscow*—and came to this conclusion:

> Our only really good films have been our straight record films. Of these, the best have been of war, whose special intensity requires a minimum of intelligence to do fairly well with. . . . Of the material we have seen it is clear that nearly always, when there has been chance to prepare for the shot through the mind's eye rather than the eye purely of courage and of the camera, the mind has been painfully inferior to the possibilities offered. The presentation has invariably been worse. The prevailing quality has been that of American commercial romanticism, as taught, for example, by the *Life* school.

This and other swipes at Time Inc. in the pages of *The Nation* raised eyebrows at the Time & Life Building. Must he insist on biting the hand that fed him?

Agee, too, felt the strain of trying to serve two masters: *Time* and *The Nation*. "The pressures of work are such . . . that I am in a daily nerve-rending frustration," he complained to Father Flye, but his burgeoning reputation encouraged him to persist. On his own recognizance he wrote an article for *Partisan Review* denouncing an assessment of folk art by Louise Bogan, *The New Yorker's* poetry editor. In "Pseudo-Folk," as the piece was called, Agee lambasted the attempts of several recent Broadway shows, especially *Carmen Jones, Oklahoma,* and *Othello,* to portray the common man or what was then called the Negro. Fair enough, but Agee asked for trouble when he admitted in the article that he had not bothered to see the productions he took to task. Hearing about them from friends was enough, he explained, "because I felt sure they would be bad. People who spoke well of these shows have reinforced in me the feeling. . . . People who spoke ill of them, I regarded as even more trustworthy."

By the time his article was published in the *Partisan Review,* Agee had cause to regret his words, because his casual approach to criticism confirmed the view of his detractors who thought him too interested in his own prejudices to watch what was going on in front of him. A "Talk of the Town" item in *The New Yorker* twitted Agee for the lapse, and he gained an unfortunate reputation as a critic who dared to criticize without first seeing. If any good came out of the ignominious affair, it was that Agee never again made the mistake of attempting to write about works he had not seen.

As if he were not sufficiently busy with his two reviewing posts and all their attendant celebrity and controversy, Agee accepted a third position, this one of a unique and clandestine nature. The offer came through his old friend and mentor Archibald MacLeish, who, after leaving *Fortune* for Harvard, had become Librarian of Congress, where he now oversaw the administration of the archive begun by Thomas Jefferson in 1800. MacLeish wished to bring the library's catalogue of motion pictures up to date, and Agee, he hoped, was just the man for the job. He wrote the critic a letter marked *"Confidential and Urgent"* to request a list of films worth preserving, together with a brief explanation for each suggestion.

As Agee later discovered, the request was more complicated than it seemed. While soliciting recommendations from Agee, MacLeish worked closely with the Museum of Modern Art's film specialist Iris Barry, whom Agee loathed beyond all reason. Aware of Agee's habitual procrastination, MacLeish suspected that an informal competition between the two would spur Agee on. He gingerly advised Agee that he had asked Barry for a similar list. Stunned, Agee threw himself into the task with the intensity he brought to his other work. He did not mind that his work was secret and unpaid; he would do anything to prevent Barry from having her way.

Tightening the screws a notch, MacLeish sent Agee Barry's list of films to preserve. Agee's reaction can be imagined. He was apoplectic and worked day and night to correct what he considered to be her grievous errors. MacLeish's ploy worked, and Agee got his list in on time, but the strain involved robbed him of sleep and drove him to rely ever more heavily on alcohol. Still, he had the thrill of being a consultant to the Library of Congress, even if he was not permitted to tell anyone—except Iris Barry.

In the spring of 1943, Mia and he took their first extended vacation since the outbreak of the war. They journeyed south to Jacksonville, Florida, where they had rented a small house near the beach.

The highlight of the vacation was to be a grand tour of Knoxville on the way home. Agee longed to drive, but with gas in short supply they were forced to take the train. Leaving Florida, he fell ill with a severe throat abscess. As a result, the sentimental journey through scenes of his youth that he had intended shrank to an hour's anguished walk through the shabby center of Knoxville while they waited for the next train to New York.

On his recovery, Agee's fragile equilibrium received a further blow when he learned from his draft board that his draft status, once considered a secure 3-A, was about to change, and he could expect to be inducted in July or August. "I would be glad enough . . . to have a nervous breakdown if I could arrange it," he wrote to Father Flye on June 14, "but my constitution . . . is of the particular, amphibious sort which will pass tests without much reducing the quota of misery to me." But then, another reprieve. The draft board passed him over, and he remained a civilian, content to experience the war at a safe distance.

On the basis of this always revocable assurance, Mia and he decided to have a child, and by early 1944 she was pregnant. This time Agee was determined to prove he could be a reliable and trustworthy father and head of a family. But fatherhood was, in its own way, as challenging as his multiple jobs. Waves of doubt and anxiety washed over him. In April he had a dreadful nightmare that left him "seized by fits of crying" the following day.

He considered the dream important enough to record in detail. In it, he found himself "revisiting a once familiar college" reminiscent of Harvard. In a "garden part of the college grounds," he "met a 3-year-old girl, very lively, leading a great lizard by a chain. The lizard is from Brazil." It reminded him of a "fairy-tale dragon—about 4-feet tall, walks on hind feet a good deal." The girl led the creature about on a chain. Suddenly another, even more lovely girl appeared, wearing a "loose cotton dress which exposes her very pretty breasts. By them, her hair, her eyes, her mouth, and her manner and her walk, I am fascinated. . . . I also notice that the lizard is now, though still docile, much more clearly dangerous."

A sense of danger pervaded the rest of the dream, which came to a violent conclusion.

We are joined by a decent, slightly officious young professional type, who urges us to hurry & fit the lizard into the lecture room. . . . He takes the children in hand and takes them along to the room, asking me before I bring along the lizard to take the knife out of his collar (main implication, suicide). I am left in a shadowed narrow rear garden and for the first time see the knife—a very sharp one—in the collar; also that the creature is carrying a . . . battle-axe—his equivalent in the world of weapons. And now that we are alone, the docility is gone. It is replaced by a cold, quiet fierceness and hatred . . . and all his hatred and venom are focused on me, through his eye. Around his eye, his scaly eyebrow muscle intensifies and locks and I have perhaps never been more frozen than by this eye. I make no effort to remove the knife. . . . Instead, along with fear, I am impressed and sympathetic. I turn aside and pretend not to look, to see what he will do. Immediately he takes the axe, quietly but openly, and brings it down on the chain (which I have fastened to a wall or arbor). I realize he has only done the wild animal's equivalent of burying the trap-chain, and watch for what next. He turns . . . and with the same tremendous dignity of his axe-blow, walks toward . . . his escape. I wait, with pity, deeply moved by his dignity; the chain pulls tight and pulls him backward in a brutal fall. . . . The look of woe in his eye is incredibly deep woe to me. It is suddenly intensified greatly; for now . . . a whole wood-frame wall falls on him, whether intentionally thrown or dropped on him, or pulled down by the chain I don't know; breaks on and breaks open his body. I wake gnawing and crying.

Inevitably, the impending emotional crisis colored his perceptions of the movies he reviewed. He had previously conceived of them as a safely impersonal "collective dream." Now certain of them mingled with his own, idiosyncratic dreams and longings. He had taken refuge in darkened theaters to escape, but the images flickering across the screen illuminated the darker recesses of his heart. Inspired, he gave thought to taking up poetry again. Once a poet, he knew, always a poet. For a poet not to write was like a priest not to pray. But poetry did not come easily this time, and he wrote inferior verse.

While contending with the turbulence swirling within, Agee fell behind in his reviewing duties. In June, MacLeish began hounding him for overdue contributions to the Library of Congress film archive. To prod Agee into action, MacLeish offered an admittedly modest stipend of $100. When that failed to produce results, he offered to make Agee's contribution official and public. Agee could even name his price, if he wished, but would he please send the material he owed. The overburdened reviewer wanted to oblige, but at the moment he was busier than he could remember having been in ages. He was working late at *Time,* filling in for vacationing colleagues. His mother was in town to meet Mia, now that she was carrying her son's child. And of course he was continuing his *Nation* responsibilities. On July 26, Agee dashed off a noncommittal reply to MacLeish: "I'm grateful for your offer of a check (I'm very glad to do it for nothing though) and for the longer term offer."

Now MacLeish's letters metamorphosed into urgent telegrams bristling with impatience. He took the liberty of setting a deadline: August 1. The date came and went without a reply. On August 4, MacLeish learned why, when he received the following telegram.

TERRIBLY SORRY TO DEFAULT WILL DO BEST TO SEND TO-
MORROW BUT CANT PROMISE   MY WIFE SERIOUSLY ILL
REGARDS—

JIM

As the telegram suggested, a calamity had been visited upon the Agees. On July 30, Mia had given birth to a boy who was nearly two and a half months premature. Agee subsequently explained to MacLeish the pathetic circumstances surrounding the birth.

> He had some pitiful small statistical chance of living in an adequate incubator and managed to live, in the inadequate one obtainable, for a little over forty hours. Those days and the next few, virtually nothing was possible, of course, except to be what use and good I could to my wife. She is better and home from the hospital now, and since she is both strong and apparently incapable of self-pity, whatever hits her, I have no fear for her, either psychological or physical. But I can imagine very little that would be harder for a woman to come through well.

Following the death of their child, Agee gained a heightened appreciation of Mia. He came to regard her as a truly noble figure, a strong, independent, accomplished woman. Earlier, he had known women who, it seemed, were but shadows of what they might have been. His mother had yielded to religion, Via to gentility, and Alma to passion; but Mia emanated a natural grace and dependability that was entirely of her own devising. Where the promise of a newborn had once threatened to divide Agee and Mia, the reality of death united them. For this reason Agee was not exaggerating when he referred to her as his "wife" in the letter to MacLeish, for she was now to all intents and purposes just that.

Barely a week after the death of his premature infant, Agee put aside fatigue and misery long enough to type and mail his material to MacLeish. Agee's observations about movies so impressed the Librarian of Congress that he showed them to his friend Robert Penn Warren, who felt sufficiently moved by them to express the wish that this fellow Agee apply his formidable command of film technique and history to the making—not merely the reviewing— of movies. MacLeish relayed the compliment to Agee, who took it very much to heart. The same idea had occurred to him, but it was a question of connections and getting to know the right people in Hollywood. Not long after, he began a campaign for *Time* to send him to the West Coast for purposes of "research." He argued that by staying in New York he was too remote from the film industry to write about it as perceptively as he should. But with the war on, *Time* was reluctant to concede that a trip to Hollywood was really necessary.

Restless and frazzled by Mia's ordeal, Agee felt an urgent need to go somewhere, even if it was not California. In late August, when Mia had recovered, they spent ten blissful and carefree days on Monhegan Island, off the coast of Maine. The island featured spare, unspoiled vistas and tangy North Atlantic breezes. There Agee contemplated scenery as striking as an engraving by Rockwell Kent, a former inhabitant. Nothing mattered now but the rhythms of nature—not the war, not literature, and certainly not the movies.

It seemed to Agee that in this soothing environment he was at last free from all temptation and interference. He was astonished by how quickly the cares and pressures of city life fell away, "very encouraging and almost unbelievable," he noted. He felt cleansed, renewed, healthy. The most important reason behind this change in mental attitude was his sharply reduced intake of alcohol. His sleep returned to normal rhythms, and he relished every minute of the morning hours he had previously been too drugged to appreciate. On taking his leave of Monhegan Island, he lamented, "To live in a state of positive, conscious well-being, as tangible as a sack of flour, makes you know how sick you are whenever it isn't tangible."

On the trip home, Agee's sense of well-being was such that he decided to make Mia his wife in the only way she was not—in the eyes of the law. Somewhere along the way—to this day Mia professes not to remember where—they were married with a haste befitting their bohemian status. And then it was time to return to New York and their fifth-floor walk-up on Bleecker Street.

After the open spaces and tranquillity of Monhegan, the city seemed unendurably hot and crowded to Agee. He wondered why he had ever chosen to live here, where distractions by the score waited to ensnare him. He tried "with conspicuous lack of valor . . . to revise my life and get some work done," but a mild depression settled in, accompanied by the all-too-familiar insomnia. "I suppose if I manage even by midwinter to wake up when I want to it will be more than I have reason to expect of myself," Agee recorded on September 12.

He was soon stirred from his lethargy, however, by word from

Time that the magazine was willing to send him to Hollywood on a reconnaissance mission. In October he left New York for his first glimpse of California since he was a hitchhiking college student. During the war, air travel was a virtual impossibility for all but VIPs; he was forced to make a tiring journey by rail. Soldiers crowded into cars stripped of their seats, and civilians like Agee were expected to stand too. He slept fitfully, for the train stopped at hamlets throughout the night, loading and unloading men and supplies, but after four days he was rewarded for his troubles by gleaming California sunshine. In Los Angeles he checked in with the local *Time* bureau and became acquainted with a young reporter named Dwight Whitney, who was to act as his emissary to the studios.

Agee was inclined to amble around the empty studio lots and sound stages at will, stopping, thinking, daydreaming, but he quickly discovered that in Hollywood life was every bit as ritualized as it was in the East. He needed a pass to go here, permission to go there, and realized that much of what he would have liked to see was out of bounds. His first real taste of Tinseltown came when Whitney introduced him to Darryl F. Zanuck, the reigning presence at Twentieth Century-Fox. More impressive than Zanuck was the office he occupied. It looked as though it belonged to the emperor of an imaginary kingdom. It contained a grand piano; the desk sat on a raised platform; and the walls were covered with photographs of Zanuck shaking hands with movie notables. Downstairs there was a steam room with a masseur at the ready, should Zanuck feel the need of relaxation in the midst of his busy day. Agee was so awed by the setting that he initially overlooked Zanuck but after a moment realized the man swinging the foreshortened polo mallet and smoking a two-dollar cigar was not a statue, he was a real live mogul who made movies Agee deplored.

From the start, the Hollywood establishment considered Agee an oddball from the East. In an era when neatness was the rule, Agee's ill-kempt hair trailed every which way. He wore his usual work shirt and, in deference to the region, a black string tie. Furthermore, his slow manner of speaking and mysterious intensity put off moguls who valued short questions and crisp replies. If Agee had not had the power and influence of *Time* behind him, Zanuck would not have wasted a minute on him. Even Whitney had his doubts—until Agee returned to the bureau's offices and wrote eloquent articles as fast as he could type them.

When he was not haunting the studios, Agee roamed the nearby beaches, where he was mesmerized by the sight of muscular young men sunning themselves and splashing in the surf. He found himself so attracted to their open, narcissistic sensuality that he suspected himself of homosexual tendencies. Not since his loneliest days at Exeter had he experienced these feelings, and they both intrigued and repelled him. It seemed to him that homosexuality opened up new areas of sensual exploration, new approaches to all his relationships. On his return to New York he discussed his attraction to muscular young men with his *Nation* colleague Clement Greenberg, who was quick to dismiss Agee's feelings as transient and baseless. In a Freud-ridden era, he later explained, "It was the fashion to suspect one's self of homosexuality."

Aside from raising the possibility that he had homosexual tendencies, the trip caused Agee to look on commercial films with a new affection. Suddenly he declared himself a fan of Elizabeth Taylor: "Ever since I first saw the child, two or three years ago, in I forget what minor role in what movie, I have been choked with the peculiar sort of adoration I might have felt if we were both in the same grade in primary school. . . . I hardly know or care whether she can act or not," he wrote in *The Nation*. He held Mickey Rooney in the same high esteem: "He is an extremely wise and moving actor, and if I am ever again tempted to speak disrespectfully of him, that will be in anger over the unforgivable waste of a forceful yet subtle talent."

It seemed scarcely possible that this was the same James Agee who had roundly condemned Hollywood only months before for having reached an all-time low, "so far." His *Nation* column of January 20, 1945, began with this broadside:

> If you compare the moving pictures released during a given period with the books published during the same period—or with the plays produced or the pictures painted or the music composed—you may or may not be surprised to find they stand up rather well. I can think of very few contemporary books that are worth the jackets they are wrapped in; I can think of very few movies, contemporary or otherwise, which fail to show

that somebody who has worked on them . . . has real life or energy or intensity or intelligence or talent.

His reverence for film led him to see ominous signs in the development of television. He dreaded its "ghastly gelatinous nirvana," its emphasis on style over content. "I would about as soon see all that kind of skill and devotion used in embroidering the complete text of the Solemnization of Matrimony on a pair of nylon drawers," he remarked. Indeed, the threat that television posed to movies was so serious that "only men of murderous creative passion can hope to save it." From now on, Agee declared to his *Nation* audience, he would be on the lookout for such men, especially the "dangerous sort . . . who does great work."

His search for a cinematic savior was interrupted by a sudden complication in his personal life. Without warning, Alma returned to New York with Joel, now five, in tow. Agee had seen neither since she had fled to Mexico at the end of 1940. Her subsequent marriage to Budo Uhse had proved to be troubled, and when Alma came back to New York she thought she would never see Uhse again.

Shortly after her arrival she got in touch with Agee, who felt at least partly responsible for her predicament. To help smooth her way, he installed her in his writing studio at 33 Cornelia Street, around the corner from the Bleecker Street apartment. The studio occupied the top floor of a narrow, three-story house. Equipped with a fireplace, a double bed, and a gas stove top, it was, predictably, a rather messy place. The sheets were dirty, and the passageway smelled of urine. It was also something of a retreat; Agee did most of his writing here, and Mia almost never set foot in the place. No matter how grimy and remote it was, Alma was grateful—both for her sake and for Joel's—to find shelter in the city.

When word got around that Alma was back in town, Agee's friends assumed she would try to steal him away from Mia, but Alma had no such designs. When Agee introduced the two women, Alma overcame her jealousy and discovered she actually liked Mia. The threat that she might steal her former husband from his current wife ended when Alma found her own apartment on Gay Street and left the studio.

For Agee, the most rewarding aspect of Alma's return was the opportunity it gave him to become acquainted with his son. The relationship was especially important to him since he had lost his subsequent child. Truly Joel was the prodigal son; he had been lost, and now he was found. By mutual agreement, Agee and Alma did not tell Joel that the big, friendly man known as Jim was his father, because, as Joel later wrote in his autobiography, *Twelve Years*, "I already had a father in Bodo."

Nonetheless, Agee regularly dropped by Alma's apartment to take Joel on walks in Washington Square Park, where the child liked to feed peanuts to the squirrels scampering up and down the leafless trees. In his autobiography, Joel vividly recalled Agee's reaction when one of the squirrels bit the youthful hand that fed him.

> Jim squatted down next to me and kissed the hurt finger and explained that the squirrel hadn't *meant* to hurt me, that it had thought my finger was a peanut. That didn't make any sense to me at first, but then Jim held up the tip of my finger and said, "Doesn't it look like a peanut?" And it did. We laughed, and he dried my tears with his hand, and then we walked on.

Later, having come down with a sore throat and fever, Joel recognized the bond between them, a bond exceeding simple friendship.

> Jim came into my room and softly closed the door. He sat down on the edge of my bed and took my hand in his. Then he touched my forehead with his cool palm. That felt good and we both smiled. Then he held my hand between his two hands and gazed into my eyes, smiling gently for a long time. I didn't feel at all uneasy, as I might have with someone else. The room became very, very still. A strange thing happened. It was as if he were telling me everything with his eyes. If the words "love" or "father" had been spoken, I might not have been able to understand. But this way . . . there was no confusion. I felt wonderfully content.

As Agee and Joel established a growing rapport, Bodo Uhse began pleading with Alma by mail to return to him. In February she gave in and decided to go back to Mexico with the child at the end of the month. The two of them spent their last night in New

York at Agee's Bleecker Street apartment. In the middle of the night, he left Mia's bed and came to Alma. They were both naked, and they fell into one another's arms. They cried for all the sadness of what might have been between them and for the pain of separation. Inevitably, they were reminded of that night long before when Agee had crept away from Via's bed to make love with Alma. But this time they refrained. Agee returned to Mia.

In the morning he drove Alma and Joel to the airport, where they caught an early flight to Mexico.

13

A DANGEROUS MAN

In the wake of Alma's visit, Agee experienced a surge of good will and a sincere desire to make peace with old adversaries. He was prepared to forgive his mother her severe limitations and started to communicate with her on a regular basis. He wrote a friend to say how "thankful" he felt now that he had "gotten fully around to liking her and enjoying her a great deal—not too hard, because my war with her had not had to be a very bloody one—and felt very sorry about my neglect, and moved by how much she enjoyed hearing from and writing me."

The renewal of family ties led him to reconsider the role of religion in his life. The approach of Easter 1945 hinted at a personal resurrection as well, one of recovery of long-buried warmth and charity. On March 29 he wrote to Father Flye:

> It seems unlikely that I will ever become fully religious or a communicant again. But I hope I need not tell you, and feel sure you will not scorn, how grateful I am for such religious feelings as I do have. . . . I have to doubt so much that at the same time I trust: thoughts and realizations mixed with personal and historic memories and projections so fill me with tears, and with faith and certainty, that it seems incredible to me not to be a Christian and a Catholic in the simplest and strictest senses of the words.

His newfound traditionalism proved to be positively contagious, spreading outward from family to religion and finally to politics. The sudden death of President Roosevelt on April 12 moved Agee very deeply, calling forth memories of his own father. In an instantaneous, sustained inspiration, he wrote his most eloquent *Nation* column to date on the event. The Rooseveltian mannerisms that had always struck him as slightly effete and ridiculous now seemed signs of a "vivid, sensitive intelligence" and an "extraordinary gallantry." He no longer dismissed Roosevelt as an opportunistic politician but venerated him as a man endowed with a "singular, triumphant, essential gaiety," whose passing would cause ordinary men to fall back on "metaphysical yet very literal faith in unanimity and massiveness of spirit. I believe that this exists, and that if it is known to exist it can have very great power."

Agee perceived the same massiveness of spirit among Southern blacks. He lectured Father Flye on the importance of antidiscrimination legislation, insisting that a great change in the country's social structure was at hand, and "nothing on earth is going to stop the change." Reading Richard Wright's autobiographical novel *Black Boy,* Agee identified so intensely with the protagonist that he considered himself more of a black than a white Southerner, and he had the neglected middle name of Rufus to prove his claim. His zeal for social transformation encouraged him to toy with the idea of inaugurating a new column, this one devoted exclusively to social commentary and the revival of old-fashioned liberalism.

"Such a thing as a true 'liberal' hardly exists anymore," Agee lamented. "One no longer knows one's friends from one's enemies."

In an attempt to play the role of polemicist, Agee wrote an impassioned defense of legislated integration, intended for the *Sewanee Review*. Curiously, as his argument rambled on, it betrayed a nostalgia for the "Old South" rather than a zeal for the New.

> I know . . . by personal experience as well as inclination, that some of the finest personal relationships conceivable can develop between whites and Negroes of the South—thanks to their inequality, not in spite of it—and that virtues are developed in some Negroes, in that predicament, which will vanish along with those excellent friendships, when the Negro has won his equality.

To his Northern liberal friends, Agee's supposed defense of integration sounded more like a justification for separatism, but to Southerners this statement rang with the truth of experience. In any event, Agee abandoned the article before it could be published and turned his attention once again to the movies.

Auden had declared that "poetry makes nothing happen," but Agee had come to believe in the power of works of art, especially film, to bring about constructive social change. In *Let Us Now Praise Famous Men* he had attacked the social structure; now he was more reform-minded. He was looking for a movie—and a director—that would not necessarily make the audience take to the streets but would bring about a heightened state of awareness and sensitivity.

In this frame of mind, Agee happened on the "dangerous man" in movies whom he had been hunting for months on end, and his name was John Huston. In May, Agee saw Huston's war documentary *The Battle of San Pietro* and instantly decided it was the best movie of its kind that he had ever seen. "It is clear that Huston understood what he was recording, and how to record it, with a wonderfully vigorous and whole maturity, at once as a soldier and an artist and a man," he wrote in the May 26 issue of *The Nation*, keeping his flow of compliments throughout the review on this entirely personal level. He loved the movie, but he loved the man who made it even more.

Like all film aficionados, Agee had been aware of Huston ever since the latter's breakthrough film, *The Maltese Falcon,* of 1941. But Agee paid scant attention to it and to Huston's other early efforts. Then the war altered the course of Huston's career, sending the writer-director overseas as a member of the Signal Corps to make documentaries of military action. Working with Signal Corps cameramen and equipment, Huston's *Battle of San Pietro* recorded the attempts of American infantrymen to capture a strategically valuable Italian village.

The result was unlike anything Huston had done before and very controversial. Not everyone shared Agee's opinion of the documentary. The War Department thought it unpatriotic and antiwar because it was too realistic in its portrayal of military operations. There was none of the standard heroic veneer to soothe the national conscience or offer justification for the brutality of war. To such objections Huston replied, "If I ever make a picture that is pro-war, I hope someone will take me out and shoot me." Before long the film was classified as secret so that impressionable enlisted men would not be able to see it.

Rushing to Huston's defense, Agee condemned the Hollywood establishment. "I am forced more and more to the narrow, dismal hope that if good movies are to be made any more at all, in this country anyhow, they will have to be made on shoestrings, far outside the industry, and very likely by amateurs or at best semiprofessionals," he proclaimed in his column. It was not clear exactly who Agee had in mind for the role of independent filmmaker-artist, himself or Huston, but he was certain he would not be satisfied with anything less than "perfect liberty, discipline, and achievement."

As the summer approached, Agee decided to take these matters into his own hands. He proposed to make a movie himself or, failing that, collaborate with those more familiar with film technique. To find the privacy he required to plan a film, he fled the city in June for a farmhouse in the foothills of the Pocono Mountains, not far from Stroudsburg, Pennsylvania, where he discovered he much preferred spending time out of doors to struggling with ideas at a desk. He and Mia came to like the region so well that they debated buying a house that was for sale, but at the last minute Agee balked at the expense and the idea of owning anything beyond the necessities of clothing, writing supplies, and a car. By the time Mia persuaded him to see matters her way, the house had gone off the market. Agee bitterly regretted losing what he belatedly realized would have made an ideal writing haven. "The mere thought of it still makes me very sad and homesick," he wrote to a friend, "not to mention my sadness at causing Mia to be done out of something she wants so much." The struggle over the house occupied so much of Agee's attention that he made little progress on the movie. It was going to be about a soldier on leave. He comes to New York, where he has many interesting experiences . . . but then it was time for Agee to return to the city.

There he renewed his interest in photography with Helen Levitt, the photographer and close friend of Walker Evans. Her work fascinated Agee to no end. He would sit by the hour discussing her oddly humorous shots of New York street life. She was especially drawn to black children in Harlem, whom she captured in arresting poses reminiscent of the work of Henri Cartier-Bresson. When the possibility of publishing her photographs arose, Agee wrote an introduction that maintained:

> Some of the best photographs we are ever likely to see are innocent domestic snapshots, city postcards, and news and scientific photographs. If we know how, moreover, we can enjoy and learn a great deal from essentially untrue photographs, such as studio portraits, movie romances, or the national and class types apotheosized in ads for life insurance and feminine hygiene.

Levitt's freewheeling, spontaneous photographs stood in the greatest possible contrast to these examples. To Agee they revealed the living world as it really was, with no distortion beyond the flare in the lens of Levitt's secondhand Leica.

Agee's excitement over the book, which promised to become an urban counterpart of *Let Us Now Praise Famous Men*, grew daily, but in the midst of preparations their publisher went out of business. The material intended for the book—Agee's lengthy analysis and Levitt's photographs—would not come before the public for another twenty years.

Despite this disappointment, Levitt and Agee surmised that their subject matter—the children of Harlem—would lend itself to an experimental movie, for the children were nothing if not kinetic. Levitt was not sure how to proceed at first, but to Agee the answer was obvious: borrow a 16-millimeter camera and take to the streets. This he and Levitt did on three occasions. They called the result, naturally enough, *In the Street.*

Agee's contribution to the film went beyond that of cameraman. His evocative commentary included as succinct a statement as he ever made on the nature of the artist: "There, unaware and unnoticed, every human being is a poet, a masher, a warrior, a dancer," he wrote of life in the street. "And in his innocent artistry he projects . . . against the turmoil of the streets an image of human experience." Thus everyone qualified as an artist, but only a precious few had the wit and self-awareness to recognize that fact about themselves. Yet the knowledge carried a penalty, for it meant a loss of innocence, an acceptance of a burdensome and potentially dangerous responsibility that could only be compared to a religious calling.

To Agee, blacks epitomized the phenomenon of natural artistry. Ever since the day he had discovered Cleo Crawford, unemployed bricklayer turned painter, he had looked to blacks as the incarnation of all that was unspoiled and true in art, and he feared that once they achieved equality with whites or even began to strive for it, they would compromise these God-given attributes out of existence. They would become no better than the white man.

After Agee began shooting material for *In the Street,* he became enmeshed in another independent film of considerably greater sophistication. His involvement came at the request of Levitt's friend Janice Loeb, a painter with a private income. It was Loeb who had put up the money for *In the Street,* and she now wanted a film made about a school for delinquent children. The school, Wiltwyck, was then located in Esopus, New York, about two hours' drive from the city. Loeb invited Agee, Levitt, and a director, Sidney Meyers, to visit Wiltwyck and come up with ideas for a movie. But there was a catch: The film had to show the school in a positive light if the staff was to cooperate with them. This particular limitation did not bother Agee in the slightest; he applauded anyone willing to help troubled youths. Working with his collaborators, he was able to create a remarkably complex and subtle portrait of a typical student, who was, of course, black.

In striving for an unsparing treatment of social conditions, Agee hoped to emulate the realism of *The Battle of San Pietro,* but beyond this sliver of inspiration there was little precedent for this kind of movie. Studios retained their iron grip on the industry; independents were relegated to an insignificant role. There was no chance of an independently made film such as *In the Street* winning widespread commercial distribution. A showing in a local art theater might be arranged, but that was all. Despite these obstacles, Agee worked on and off with his collaborators for months that stretched into years.

Characteristically, he pursued such projects with great enthusiasm but never for very long. Again and again events pulled him away, and he was only too willing to drop whatever he was in the midst of in favor of a new passion. He much preferred to be tantalized than to be fulfilled. Inspiration was everything; execution bored him. And his association with *Time,* that universe of information and stimulation, repeatedly furnished him with ideal excuses to abandon private projects.

The latest distraction came in the form of an event of worldwide importance. On August 6 the United States dropped the first atomic bomb on Hiroshima, killing 130,000 people at a stroke. The bomb—death incarnate—instantly obsessed his every waking moment. The following day he sent the first fruits of his meditations on the tragedy to *Time* colleague James Stern.

> I would suppose it is the worst thing that ever happened—so far: anyhow, that it pretty thoroughly guarantees universal annihilation, within not many years. . . . I would expect, among other things, tremendous abortive religious convulsions—not to mention the political—and, at best, a great many people maturing much beyond possibility under any other circumstances. . . . Since the destructiveness is still by no means infinite (though it will logically become so), we will somehow absorb the enormity as we have absorbed every other.

Only when a madman "pushes the plunger," Agee added, will "our will and understanding . . . be adequate to have prevented it." Writing to Father Flye, Agee took his gloomy predictions a step further: "At the end of the next war we either survive or don't survive almost total annihilation. . . . As for averting the next war, I see no use even to try. Everything should be rather preparations for the aftermath."

What made the tragedy all the more lamentable to Agee was that the United States had dropped the bomb. He believed the deed placed the country on the same low moral level as its adversaries, writing:

> O my poor country I have so much hated
> How can I ever hate you now your doom is near?

Convinced that the United States should never have entered the war in the first place, he now envisioned a "petulant and flattered" American populace deaf to the groans of the dying, a populace "incurable through pity, love, guilt, fear." Indeed, the bomb made him feel personally implicated in the slaughter of thousands of innocent victims. Rather than celebrate victory, the United States ought to writhe in shame at its vicious death-dealing.

Agee soon had a chance to put the powerful emotions the event stirred to work in a constructive fashion. For the issue of August 20, *Time* planned special coverage of the bomb and subsequent surrender of the Japanese. Casting about for an eloquent, profound story, managing editor Matthews turned to the man he considered the best writer in the Time & Life Building, James Agee. The film critic said he would see what he could do.

When the issue hit the newsstands, it was distinguished by a strikingly simple design: Japan's red sun obliterated by a crude black X. Within, Agee's account of the most significant occurrence of the decade ran as the lead article.

The greatest and most terrible of wars ended, this week, in the echoes of an enormous event—an event so much more enormous that, relative to it, the war itself shrank to minor significance. . . . When the bomb split open the universe and revealed the prospect of the infinitely extraordinary, it also revealed the oldest, simplest, commonest, most neglected and most important of facts: that each man is eternally and above all else responsible for his own soul. . . . Man's fate has forever been shaped between the hands of reason and spirit, now in collabo-

ration, again in conflict. . . . If either or anything is to survive,
they must find a way to create an indissoluble partnership.

To his *Time* colleagues, Agee offered a pithier assessment. Hiroshima, he said, was but the *"second* worst thing that has happened to the human race. The worst was Creation."

Agee's account of the bomb and the surrender worked wonders for his reputation at *Time.* He had passed with flying colors the supreme test of a journalist: to write clearly and movingly about a complex issue under pressure of a deadline. "When people tell me . . . that *Time* was always written in some form of pidgin English," Matthews later boasted, "I remember Agee—and this piece in particular."

Luce also took note of the accomplishment. He had come to regard Agee as the best film reviewer in the land but at the same time a self-indulgent aesthete. Now here he was, eloquently discussing Luce's favorite topic, global politics. Obviously the writer had unused talents. The better to cultivate them, he was invited to join *Time*'s elite Special Projects department. There he would write more large-scale political stories. But movie reviewing would have to fall by the wayside. Agee naturally hesitated in the face of the challenge. Perhaps the bomb story had been only a fluke. On September 19 he wrote to Father Flye, "My two great doubts about the job are 1) causing resentment and insecurity among writers whose articles I take away and 2) that I'll be working harder than on movies, thus reducing seriously my spare time for my own work." After expressing his worries, Agee plunged into the task. Before he knew it, he was writing a lengthy assessment of postwar Europe and finding that it "interests me as much as any piece of personal writing I could possibly be doing."

Although constantly distracted by his *Time* and *Nation* commitments, Agee sought throughout the fall of 1945 to write a substantial work on his own recognizance. Drawing inspiration from world events, he began two works about the bomb: the first a short story, the second a nonfiction book, but he soon gave up on both.

The approach of his thirty-sixth birthday in late November set his imagination on a different course. Now that he had reached the age, very nearly, at which his father had perished, Agee assumed he had run out of time. He was too old to be considered promising

anymore; he had wasted his life. He had nothing to show beyond
a neglected book, a neglected child, too many neglected women.
He had nothing to live for. As if to force him to dwell on the fact
of his mortality, his stepfather, the Reverend Erskine Wright, fell
ill with cancer. There was little love lost between Agee and Father
Wright, but to the writer the affliction demonstrated once again the
cruelty of the universe. In the eyes of the Lord, the clergyman had
lived a blameless life and had done nothing to deserve this punishment. Flying to Maine with Emma to visit the dying man, Agee
confided to his sister that his own death seemed imminent, but, if
he managed to avoid it somehow, he might live for a considerable
time to come. And he later expressed his feelings on the matter in
a poem.

> *I, who by chance walked safely past a war,*
> *Shall not by any chance the world has known*
> *Be here, and breathing, many autumns more.*

Despite Agee's forebodings, Father Wright clung to life. But
the writer's dread of death continued to mount, reaching its peak
on his birthday, November 27. He stayed up late, drinking himself into oblivion. Yet once the depressive effects of the alcohol
wore off, its sugar content acted as a stimulant. His overactive
mind was assaulted with dire imaginings. At two o'clock in the
morning, while Mia slept and wind whipped the deserted city
streets outside his window, Agee poured out his heart to Father
Flye.

> This is . . . half drunk, and probably not too legible (I'm
> writing each word like walking on ice in tennis shoes) so
> regard each unreadable bit as the Smile of the Mona Lisa
> whose main significance is easily explained: more whiskey,
> please. So I am now 36. For days I have had premonitions:
> more solemn than any in years. Now I am tight, very regret-
> fully, slightly ashamed, as if I had turned up in that condition
> to watch by my own deathbed. A very strong sense of death.
> . . . There are premonitions I superstitiously fear to write, but
> will: 1) I will die during this year, unexpectedly (parallel to my
> father's death at just that age): 2) I will be killed after long
> torture . . . probably by Stalinists.

How long Agee would have continued in this dark vein can only be guessed. But Mia, in a stroke of inspiration, came to his rescue with a Rorschach test, which she gave him as a birthday present. The ten famous inkblots designed to elicit memories and associations seized Agee's imagination. His mind had always been highly associative, so much so that he was barely able to control it. Now he was overwhelmed by the associations the vague black shapes called forth. He spent hours working with the test, far longer than normal, reliving long-forgotten memories, sights, sounds, textures. Surely he was uncovering material he could use in a work of fiction, but he realized he required help in assembling the fragments. He needed someone who understood the pain he had suffered as a child, who would help him overcome his self-destructive urges. He required a psychiatrist, but not just any psychiatrist, for he continued to resent the determinist Freudians. He wanted one familiar with the creative capacity of the unconscious. His thoughts turned to *The Inner World of Childhood,* the book he had read in Anna Maria a decade earlier. If only he could find the book's author, Frances Wickes. Perhaps she was still practicing.

After some investigation, Agee discovered that Dr. Wickes was alive and well and practicing Jungian therapy in New York. When they met, he discovered she was an easygoing older woman with few intellectual pretensions. It was doubtful that she could comprehend the depths of his despair, but she was easy enough to get along with. That she was a woman simplified matters greatly, for Agee did not look on her as a secular father confessor or surrogate priest. Rather, she was the forgiving mother he had never had. Like Mia, she was inclined to accept the vagaries of his life rather than condemn him for them. Quickly grasping his profound, unresolved grief over his father's death, Dr. Wickes offered a choice: "You can either work this out in analysis or write it out." True to his indecisive nature, Agee elected both options. He entered an on-again, off-again analysis that would last for three years. And he began a work of fiction.

"I've started a short novel about adolescence in the 1920's, a fairly good start," he reported to Father Flye in late November. "But in ten days I haven't come back to it. And by now it looks too flimsy. With so little time from work and so very little time left for anything faintly recognizable as civilization, it seems rather too obligatory to work only on the best things possible. But those are even harder to hold to—for anyone of my weak will." Despite his ambivalence, he fought for time to work on the story. If he could set aside just three days a week for it, if the world escaped "atomic liquefaction," he might see his way clear to a decent work of fiction.

The task he set himself was difficult: to re-create the spiritual crisis he had undergone at St. Andrew's when he was twelve. The idea had been in the back of his mind ever since he had spent a charmed interval there with the Flyes a decade before. Only now did he realize that he had, at long last, put enough distance between himself and the unhappy schoolchild he once was to write of those days with sufficient objectivity and understanding.

Remembering everything, he proposed to invent nothing. Yet he was careful to protect the anonymity of friends and faculty members he portrayed. To keep the real and invented names clear in his own mind, he drew up a cast of characters. The originals appeared on the left, their "fictional" counterparts on the right.

> Dave Mooney – *Hobe Gillum*
> Raymond Kersey – *Jimmy Toole*
> Bob Stewart – *George Fitzgerald*
> Paul Green – *Claude Grey*
> Deaconess Barbour – *Deaconess Spencer*
> Fr. Whitall – *Fr. Whitman*
> Fr. Flye – *Fr. Fish*
> Fr. Lorey – *Fr. Weiler*
> Fr. Orum – *Fr. Ogle*
> Fr. Campbell – *Fr. McPhitridge*

He exchanged the name by which he had been known at St. Andrew's, Rufus, for the more dignified Richard. In general he made all the names he chose as close to their actual counterparts as he dared, devoting special attention to Father Flye. By renaming him Father Fish, Agee invoked the ancient symbol of Jesus to suggest that the priest was indeed Christlike.

As Agee wrote, the story revealed itself as a mood piece. There was little action, less dialogue. Memories were all that mattered. It was a microcosm of his entire childhood. With surprisingly little hesitation he decided to call it *The Morning Watch,* after the

Maundy Thursday vigil it commemorated. But it was not enough simply to remember, he warned himself; he had to shape the story. The work required constant redefinition.

While Agee shuttled between *Time* and his novel-in-progress, Mia again became pregnant. On November 7, 1946, she gave birth to a healthy baby girl. Agee was characteristically indecisive about a name until he saw the little wrinkled face of his first daughter. At that instant, he knew what to call her: Julia Teresa Agee.

The process of writing *The Morning Watch* was for Agee literally a matter of life and death. Either he mastered his fears of death by writing thoughtfully about them or he succumbed to them, as he constantly threatened. But the energy he devoted to the short novel did not hurt his film reviewing in the slightest; on the contrary, his success in realizing his own work emboldened him to take new strides in his film career. If he was fecund in one area, he was fecund in all, and he was determined to cut a larger figure as a critic than ever before.

The opportunity for Agee to make a name for himself in the film world occurred at the beginning of May 1947, when he saw Charlie Chaplin's latest effort, *Monsieur Verdoux.* To Agee, Chaplin, more than anyone else, incarnated the magic that was movies. A wonderfully skillful and compassionate comedian, he was, as well, a champion of the common man in the best sense of the term. However, by the war's end Chaplin, once the most famous actor if not the most famous man in the world, had fallen into disrepute. Despite his well-received attempts to adapt his comedic pantomime to the talkies, he remained essentially a silent-movie performer. A well-publicized paternity suit had blackened his name in hypocritical Hollywood, and even his subsequent vindication did nothing to restore his ailing reputation. And his espousal of left-wing causes flew in the face of the popular mood, which was rapidly shifting to the right. For all his former glory, Chaplin had become by 1947 distinctly persona non grata in the United States. Agee was one of the few who had never stopped believing in Chaplin's integrity and artistry, and he went to *Monsieur Verdoux* with the highest expectations—expectations that the film met and more.

Monsieur Verdoux marked a complete reversal of Chaplin's heretofore sympathetic portrayal of the common man. Instead of the saintly Little Tramp, he played a charming, calculating, capitalist version of Bluebeard, based on an actual criminal. Henri Verdoux, having lost his job as a bank teller, supports his child and invalid wife by meeting, marrying, and murdering wealthy heiresses. He goes about his business with little passion and with the utmost fastidiousness, utterly blind to the moral inconsistency of killing to maintain a travesty of domestic happiness; he sees himself as the perfect husband and father.

Needless to say, Chaplin's drastic alteration of his cinematic persona meant that *Monsieur Verdoux* was a commercial fiasco. Most reviewers castigated Chaplin for abandoning comedy in favor of the most sickening satire. The film confirmed everyone's worst fears of his leftist immorality and closed within six weeks.

Everyone except Agee, that is. A voice crying in the cultural wilderness, he rushed to the defense of the movie and of Chaplin with the fervor of a neglected prophet. Beginning with the issue of May 31, he devoted not one but three full *Nation* columns to defending the film, enjoining readers to "disregard everything you have heard." He claimed that Chaplin's performance was "the best piece of playing I have ever seen," and went on to extol *Monsieur Verdoux* as a great work of Western art, comparable in significance and quality to Michelangelo's *Pietà*. It was, in short, "one of the few indispensable works of our time."

By making such extreme claims for the film, Agee inevitably called attention to himself as an advocate of artful dissent. He defended the work as though it were his story and not Chaplin's, and to a certain extent it was. He abandoned all pretense of objectivity when it came to *Monsieur Verdoux* because he identified intensely with its protagonist. In the life and times of Henri Verdoux, Agee saw himself writ large; the repellent fable encapsulated his own sexual nature—his deep ambivalence toward women, his often calculating use of them to further his own ends. He was endowed with the same fatal charm and ruthless cunning as Verdoux, and he was prone to the same slobbering sentimentality. And like Verdoux he had discarded a number of women—Dorothy Carr, Via, and Alma—in the name of principles that had blinded him to the reality of the cruelty he had inflicted on them. In reality, of course, Agee's relationships with women were not so simple as the movie encouraged him to feel, but he relished this feast of cinematic self-loathing.

To see his innermost secrets revealed on the screen by his boyhood hero was a dazzling experience.

In no other film had he seen so much of himself; therefore he proclaimed it the best film he had ever seen. "We can hardly bear to recognize ourselves in him," Agee wrote. "He is the committed, dedicated soul, and this soul is not intact: we watch its death agonies. And this tragic process is only the more dreadful because it is depicted not gravely but briskly, with a cold savage gaiety; the self-destroying soul is rarely aware of its own predicament." At this point not even Agee could have said whom he was writing about, Verdoux or himself.

Having established himself as a champion of the unpopular film, Agee took advantage of his notoriety to bring himself to Chaplin's attention and, he hoped, one step closer to Hollywood. Shortly after the movie's New York premiere, Chaplin held a press conference to confront the expected attacks on his politics and personal life. An ugly scene ensued. Prosecutorial reporters accused him of consorting with known Communists and of dodging income taxes. Then a lone voice rose above the din. "How does it feel to be an artist who has enriched the world with so much happiness and understanding of the little people, and to be derided and held up to hate and scorn by the so-called representatives of the American press?"

The conference came to a standstill. Chaplin fumbled for a reply. His publicity representative whispered that the speaker was James Agee, of *Time* and *The Nation,* the one critic who had liked the film. Chaplin asked Agee to repeat himself. "I don't know if I can," Agee replied.

"I could think of no answer," Chaplin later recalled, "so I shook my head and said, 'No comment . . . but thank you.' I was no good after that. His kind words had left me without any more fight."

In the aftermath of the press conference, Chaplin and Agee formed a mutual admiration society. Chaplin clipped Agee's *Nation* reviews for safekeeping in a drawer in his Hollywood home. Meanwhile, Agee wondered whether the former clown prince of motion pictures would be open to a collaboration. The Chaplin who had dared to make *Monsieur Verdoux* might well be receptive to an idea Agee had in mind, inspired by his obsession with the bomb: What if the Little Tramp were let loose in a world destroyed by a nuclear holocaust? As fond as Agee was of the notion, he was forced to set it aside when his worship of Chaplin led to an unpleasant controversy at *Time.*

While continuing in that magazine's Special Projects department, Agee had resumed reviewing movies on an occasional basis at the beginning of 1947. In the debate surrounding his three-part review of *Monsieur Verdoux* in *The Nation,* his *Time* appraisal had been all but ignored. Here Agee passed over the film's castigation of male sexuality in favor of emphasizing its assault on capitalism. His cardinal sin, from his employer's point of view, was his endorsement of the movie's dubious thesis that the "logical extension of business is murder" and that war was only business on a grand scale. "At a time when many people have regained their faith in war under certain conditions and in free enterprise under any conditions whatever," Agee wrote, "[Chaplin] has ventured to insist . . . that there are elements of criminality in both."

The outlandish assertion attracted the attention of Luce, who in July sent Agee a memorandum designed to make the writer's palms sweat and temples throb. Above all, Luce could not accept Agee's blithely equating business with murder. "It would violate, I think, most of the small store of truth which men have intuitively or intellectually hit upon in their curious and painful pilgrimage," Luce carefully explained, as if to a naughty child. And he reminded Agee that Chaplin was hopelessly naïve when it came to politics. Certainly *Time*'s star writer should be capable of recognizing an egregious political blunder when he saw it.

In a long, rambling letter of reply, Agee knuckled under to Luce. He expressed regret for having implied that business equaled murder and admitted that Chaplin had been seduced by the "peculiar logic of his picture's scheme." On further reflection, Agee wrote, "It seems to me that Chaplin's greatest error is in apparently holding modern society accountable for Verdoux, and . . . in holding Verdoux guiltless as an individual." Significantly, Agee kept his recanting over *Monsieur Verdoux* utterly private; in public, he continued to champion the movie.

This attempt to humble himself before Luce was too little and too late. The Founder decided that any writer capable of endorsing *Monsieur Verdoux*'s skewed morality was not to be trusted with political assignments. Though Agee remained nominally attached to the Special Projects department, he never wrote another political article for *Time,* dwelling instead on cultural topics. Sensing Luce's impatience with Agee, Matthews was increasingly of the opinion that his star writer, talented though he was, had overstayed his welcome at the magazine.

Aware of the cooling of relations with his employer of nearly fifteen years, Agee reserved his best journalistic efforts for the *Nation* column, where he broadened his critical scope to include the whole of American society and, on occasion, Western civilization, in addition to such minor matters as movies. Finding himself at odds with the repressive Cold War climate, he sniped unrelentingly at self-appointed guardians of freedom and decency, such as the Hays Office, the Legion of Decency, and the government itself. "Civilization has come a long way since the days when, in Vienna, the High Altar of Western Music, Mozart and Schubert could die so young, largely for want of mere patronage," he declared with brutal irony. "Today we appreciate our men of genius. In Russia we make corpses of them, living or genuine; here we drown them in cream."

Wherever he looked, he beheld the persecution of outspoken filmmakers who preoccupied his imagination. The Catholic Veterans waged a "holy war" against Chaplin. Congress cited ten Hollywood screenwriters for contempt when they refused to answer questions about their politics, a precedent made all the more chilling when the studios fired the writers. Impotent rage gripped Agee. "For the nothing that it is worth, I cannot imagine how any self-respecting man could, under such circumstances, hold Congress otherwise than in contempt," he wrote in *The Nation* of December 27. And Huston's latest war film, *Let There Be Light,* a harrowing study of combat fatigue, languished in obscurity, banned by the War Department. "I don't know what is necessary to reverse this disgraceful decision," Agee commented, "but if dynamite is required, then dynamite is indicated."

The reactionary national mood forced Agee to look abroad for a sane response. Fortunately, he happened to find solace at this time in Vittorio de Sica's neorealist *Shoeshine,* an account of vagrant boys in postwar Italy. Agee was so moved by the film's insistence on human dignity in times of adversity that he proclaimed a newfound belief in the daringly secular faith of humanism. Ever since he had lost his faith as a boy, he had been subject to a nostalgia for the old certainties of Anglo-Catholicism, but as soon as he got serious about it he remembered the negative connotations traditional faith held for him and withdrew. Humanism, however, endowed him with a sense of well-being and free will. By humanism he meant the primacy of the individual over God, together with the freedom and responsibility the leading role carried. Not that he had much hope for a humanist revival in the postwar era. He supposed it was "still nominally the germinal force of Western Civilization . . . but no attitude is more generally subject to disadvantage, dishonor, and misuse today." Even so, he regarded *Shoeshine*'s humanist spirit "as restoring and jubilant a piece of news as if one had learned that a great hero whom one had thought to be murdered or exiled or corrupted still lives in all his valor."

Agee had two kinds of heroism in mind: the spirit of great works of art and, on a more personal level, his revered father. In a list of "favorite stories" he now drew up, he perceived the humanist-heroic spirit in "the Oedipus legend-myth, Plato's account of the death of Socrates, and the Gospel according to St. Matthew." On a profoundly intuitive level he began to conceive of a work of art of his own that would place him in the company of the great storytellers. Unlike *The Morning Watch,* it would be free of the iron grip of religion. And it would feature as its hero Agee's father, who, to his son, was quiet heroism incarnate.

Dreams supplied further stimulus for a major work about his father. Under the influence of his sporadic Jungian analysis, he had been paying increased attention to them. In one, he ventured into an old well house, where he saw an enormous green frog. He dreamed of the frog several times, an indication of the image's importance, and he felt compelled to discuss it with bewildered colleagues at *Time.* In all likelihood this dream encapsulated the way he saw himself, surrounded on all sides by insurmountable difficulties, as ugly and guilt-ridden as a frog.

On other occasions he dreamed of St. John the Baptist. In these, Agee would be walking uphill, pulling a sled with a rope over his shoulder. When he turned to look at the sled he saw the saint's head resting on it, staring at him. Agee had this dream so frequently that he came to feel that he was personally acquainted with St. John the Baptist. Even more than the frog dream, this one expressed his unresolved feelings about his father's death and the fear that it would follow him wherever he went.

Inspired by the St. John the Baptist dreams, Agee wrote a chaotic, surreal "Dream Sequence" in which he reencountered his father. "Thank you for coming," Agee says to him. "Goodbye, God keep you." In the story, if not in life, Agee learned to accept his father's permanent absence. "His father did not say goodbye, but he knew . . . his brief smile, much as it always had been, and then he was gone," Agee wrote. "He was alone again now, but that was no harm—for in a way in which he had been alone for so many years, he knew he would never be alone again."

All these dreams, reflections, and exploratory pieces of writing gave Agee the impetus to make his father the basis of a novel. Taking his cue from the autobiographical reverie "Knoxville: Summer 1915," Agee initially planned a long work combining the discursiveness of Proust with the stylistic virtuosity of Joyce. He wrote scenes of his childhood in servile imitation of Joyce's *Portrait of the Artist as a Young Man.* In one:

> It is Thanksgiving and I am four years old and this is my birthday, and we all dawdle in from the living room through the greenroom into the diningroom to the table and granma puts down the bell when she sees us. Grampa says sherry. Unc hugh gets another big book and puts it on the book in the chair and daddy hise me up, there you are, here I am. Happy birthday.

This highly subjective manner of writing went against the grain. As a journalist, he felt far more comfortable re-creating domestic scenes from an objective point of view, able to dip into his characters' minds at will. So enamored with the idea of writing objectively did he become that he was inclined to look on the still incomplete *Morning Watch* as a mistake, for it was both too religious and too subjective.

Undiscouraged, he made a new beginning on the novel about his father, this time treating it as if it were an assignment Matthews had given him. To collect his thoughts on the matter, he wrote a lucid declaration of intent.

This book is chiefly a remembrance of my childhood, and a memorial to my father; and I find that I value my childhood and my father as they were, as well and as exactly as I can remember and represent them, far beyond any transmutation of these matters I have made, or might ever make, into poetry or fiction. I know that I am making the choice most dangerous to an artist, in valuing life above art; I know too that by good use of fiction or poetry one can re-enter life more deeply, and represent it more vividly, immediately, and truthfully than by any such means of bald narration as I propose; but it now seems to me I have no actual choice, but am in fact compelled, against my judgment and wish as an artist.

The compulsion to document forced him to compress the sprawling autobiography he had originally projected into a tightly focused reminiscence of the circumstances surrounding his father's death; all other material would have to fall by the wayside. He had described three hours of his life in *The Morning Watch;* now he would widen the lens of his memory to encompass three days.

Throughout the early months of 1948, Agee battled his *Time* and *Nation* commitments to make room for the new novel. On March 2 he complained of his difficulties to Father Flye.

Week after week has gone by in frustration compounded of my job, unexpected pieces of hard work for the job, the NATION, or in personal relationships, and besides, my own inertia, inefficiency and capacity for waste of time. This has gradually brought on an unusually deep and lasting depression, mental and physical, from which for several weeks I've had only a few hours escape per week.

He desperately wanted to describe the novel in detail to the priest, but a mixture of "hopefulness . . . lack of confidence, apathy, panic and despair" prevented him. That Agee could not bring himself to talk about the novel was, in fact, an encouraging sign. Previously he had talked away too many promising schemes over too many drinks. This time he had the presence of mind to confine his inspirations to paper.

When he did find the time to work on the novel, he wrote with extreme care in his crabbed hand, and he revised often. The scenes he described came to him in brilliant fragments. Now he recalled the sight of his father's corpse laid out in the living room; now shopping downtown with Aunt Jessie; now his father singing him to sleep. Some of the scenes did not fit into the strict three-day time-span he had chosen, but many of them were too good to discard. In spite of this troubling inconsistency, Agee pressed on, making a further commitment to objectivity by abandoning the first person he had used in early drafts in favor of the third. In the same spirit, he chose to employ actual names for all characters and places: Rufus, Jay, Laura, La Follette, Knoxville. There was no pretense of artifice or evasion.

Even when the going was good, he constantly challenged himself to refine his vision of the novel, as his working notes indicate.

> Theme: I worship him: I fail him: I need his approval: he is killed: everything is changed.
> [2nd theme: he is at an uneasy time of life. My failure hurts him.]
> Set up just enough to make worship understandable. . . .
> Either the episodes should be linked and dramatized, further than I have, or they should be hazy + anti-dramatic.
> I must decide between a completely detached and a deeply subjective treatment.
> I doubt if in complete detachment there is a story there.
> Rather, do the subjective, as detachedly as possible.
> Cut out the crap about the child of darkness.
> I had better figure out a good deal more about a short version, but I suspect in the long run I had better stop worrying about length or even form.

With effort, Agee developed an achingly clear vision of precisely what he wanted to accomplish in the novel and why. Always the lover of spontaneity and free association, he now left nothing to chance. The great temptation, he realized, was to fall into the trap of succumbing to his personal feelings about the events he described. As he wrote of them, he relived them, and it was all he could do to step back and gain perspective.

With his passion for fidelity to actual events, Agee realized he was prone to go into these matters in excessive detail. He warned himself that the style must remain "maximum simple: just the story of my relation with my father and, through that, as thorough as possible an image of him: winding into other things on the way but never dwelling on them."

Following these self-imposed guidelines, he wrote with a new lucidity and warmth. Though he was recalling the most painful moments of his life, he suffered little in the process. Only when he could not write did he feel fretful. Nowhere did he complain of the difficulty of shaping the work, as he had ad infinitum with *Let Us Now Praise Famous Men*. Most of his friends were unaware that he was even engaged in such a major undertaking; there were no collaborators, no confidants this time. Nor did Agee work with the expectation of creating a masterpiece, as he had with his earlier book. To his way of thinking, the novel was only one of a number of projects, including journalism, screenplays, and experimental movies, that held his attention.

The isolation and secrecy carried penalties, however. Lacking critics and listeners, he had little sense of proportion concerning his story. He tended to ramble on interminably about some minor matter until he lost his train of thought. The strengths of his writing —its precision and richness and language—served to point up its weaknesses. In a number of instances judicious invention would have smoothed over the rough spots, but Agee was too caught up with feeling and respect for his subject matter to pay heed to such problems. Only by maintaining his commitment to absolute authenticity could he keep his principal goals in sight. That sense of detachment and serenity informed every line of the novel and even his choice of title: *A Death in the Family*.

Once he had tasted the freedom and psychic rewards of doing his own work, Agee saw little reason to continue at *Time*. It seemed to him that he was living on two levels. On one, he attended a round of screenings and pointless cocktail parties, wrote his reviews, and attempted to understand the absurdities of postwar politics. On another, more profound level, he delved into the haunting mysteries of his past and strove to come to terms with his demons. Finding far more value in the latter course, he began early in 1948 to extricate himself from his journalistic commitments and devote himself fully to his two novels-in-progress. If his luck held, he would begin the year as a *Time* veteran and end it a fledgling novelist.

The difficult transition did cause strains in his work. His latest *Nation* reviews betrayed increasing irritation with both Hollywood's recent piffle and the craft of reviewing itself. He resorted to writing portmanteau notices, giving movies he would have considered with great care the year before the shortest of shrifts. Often a single review discussed as many as twenty-five films, usually in dismissive tones. He wrote off an adaptation of Arthur Miller's *All My Sons* as "a feast for the self-righteous; Ibsen for beginners." A curiosity called *Bill and Coo* prompted this flash of wit: "Over two hundred trained birds, complete with neckties, hats, etc., waddle around an anthropornithomorphic community called Chirpendale. By conservative estimate, the God-damnedest thing ever seen." Even the documentaries that had formerly commanded his respect now seemed "a synonym for dullness . . . special pleading, dishonest thinking, and perception, and again, dullness."

The sole exception to this dismal state of affairs was John Huston's latest, *The Treasure of the Sierra Madre.* "I have no doubt at all that Huston, next only to Chaplin, is the most talented man working in American pictures," Agee wrote in the January 31 issue of *The Nation,* "and that this is one of the movie talents in the world which is most excitingly capable of still further growth." Ever since his glowing review of *The Battle of San Pietro,* Agee's journalistic mash notes had come to the personal attention of Huston, who abandoned his usual practice of ignoring critics to send Agee a letter of appreciation.

On receiving word from the director, Agee began to seethe with schemes for self-advancement. He would meet Huston. He would write a profile of the director for one of the Luce publications, even *Life,* if necessary. He would cultivate a relationship with Huston, who would ask him to write a screenplay. With the proceeds, Agee would be able to quit *Time* for good and, supported by the easy money from the screenplay, complete his two novels before the year was out. Any number of reputable novelists had adopted the same course of action, preeminently Faulkner, but Agee failed to factor into the equation his chronic inability to do any work, however slight, with less than his customary intensity.

In preparation for his departure from *Time,* Agee put phase one of his plan into action by arranging to sell a profile of Huston and an assessment of silent film comedians to *Life* magazine. He airily assumed that the two pieces would require perhaps six weeks to complete, an estimate that turned out to be pathetically inaccurate. In the multifaceted career of James Agee, there was no such thing as easy money.

At the same time, he decided to bring his illustrious reviewing career at *The Nation* to a close. He had gotten all he could from the job—respectability in a field he no longer respected—and he was in danger of repeating himself. His tastes had changed since 1941, the year he began reviewing movies, but the industry itself had not —at least not enough to hold his interest. He proposed to go out in a burst of glory with a lengthy assessment of the founder of American film, D. W. Griffith.

Problems developed soon enough. Huston regarded the prospect of Agee's writing a flattering profile with alarm. Assuming that Agee would continue reviewing indefinitely, the director argued that a personal relationship would hamper the critic's ability to arrive at independent decisions. Concealing his contemplated career switch, Agee wrote to Huston that "any critic is a fool who thinks he can be completely detached and fair." He went on to explain that the only people he dreaded knowing were those incapable of carrying out their good intentions, a category to which Huston obviously did not belong. Mixing flattery with artistic scruples, Agee entreated Huston to meet him for a drink, even dinner. "My wife also likes your work a great deal," he added, to clinch the argument.

Huston enjoyed Agee's attentions, but he did not require them. Agee, in contrast, convinced himself that he needed Huston as badly as he had needed earlier mentors such as Macdonald and MacLeish. He endowed these men with the mysterious ability to do for him what he believed he could not do for himself. At the same time, friends of Agee, notably Leyda and Matthews, longed to tug at his sleeve and warn him about Huston. Despite the director's formidable reputation, they regarded him as a director of B movies that he managed to pass off as A movies. They wanted to tell Agee that Huston was not the next D. W. Griffith, that he was shallow, cynical, and manipulative. He was a dangerous man, as Agee had guessed, but even more dangerous than Agee knew. They feared for a vulnerable, malleable creature like Agee around Huston; they suspected he would do anything to prove to the director that he was not some sissified Eastern intellectual.

Agee had no interest in their words of caution. He was consumed with his mission of extricating himself from the shoals of journalism. Paradoxically, the task left him busier than ever. The pace of work on his novels slackened. At the beginning of April he came down with appendicitis, an affliction he imbued with a fatal mystique. Just when he had begun to live, death was coming to claim him. As pain lanced his abdomen and Mia urged him to hurry to a hospital, he frantically tried to tie up the loose ends of his life. He barricaded himself in his apartment, where he wrote farewell messages to Mia and Father Flye. When he finally did get to a hospital, he refused to see any visitors, preferring to read and meditate alone.

In his isolation, he came to desire at least a taste of death, but the operation came and went without a mishap. Since he was unconscious throughout, it might as well not have happened. Soon after, he sent an account of the ordeal to Father Flye.

> It is a drastic thing to be put to sleep and to have your body opened, for the first time (before, my total anaesthesia has been for little things like circumcision, adenoids, tonsils, or infected hand); and late the night before, I felt grave about it. . . . Then I looked out over Lexington Avenue, without any particular feeling, until I fell asleep. It did not occur to me to pray, before I slept. In the morning I felt so much better I was sure this immediate attack and infection were over. . . . A nurse came in and gave me an injection. I thought it was the routine "quieting" injection, which I'd heard is nearly always given you before wheeling you in; so I made no objection. My only chance to talk with my doctor was bang in the operating room. I was blandly told that I was full of morphine, and so couldn't of course be taken seriously. . . . So I submitted—and throughout my unconsciousness apparently delivered myself of my entire complex on the subject of the pseudo-sacredness and power-mania of doctors and scientists.

Even while undergoing these trials, Agee was, almost involuntarily, absorbing impressions that he planned to use in his writing. He wondered what the world would be like if these power-mad scientists reigned supreme. Agee loathed their knowing ruthlessness, their absolute power of life and death. The only thing worse than a mother's advice was a doctor's orders. After some groping about, he decided to work these concerns into the nuclear holocaust script for Chaplin—if he ever found the time to sit down and write it. For the moment, he was glad simply to have escaped death. Elated, he claimed he had recovered his "gaiety of 20 years ago."

In fact, the operation had come at the worst possible time for Agee. He had been looking forward to meeting Arthur Koestler, the writer then reaping a whirlwind of controversy over his dissatisfaction with Stalin, but now the engagement was out of the question. Still more disappointing, he was forced to miss the world premiere of a musical composition based on "Knoxville: Summer 1915." The eminent American composer Samuel Barber, a contemporary of Agee's, had set a section of the prose-poem to music. With his gift for melodic lyricism, Barber was well suited to the task, and the resulting composition for soprano and orchestra became one of the highlights of the composer's oeuvre. The performance took place in Boston on April 9, with Serge Koussevitsky conducting the Boston Symphony Orchestra. Considering his love of music and frequent attendance at BSO concerts when he was at Harvard, Agee would have taken the greatest satisfaction in the event, but he remained confined to his hospital bed.

On returning to *Time* later in the month, Agee again faced the problem of how and when to give notice. He toyed with the idea of asking for a leave of absence, but he suspected that if he left the door open behind him, he would be back within a year. No, this was the time to make the long-deferred leap into fiction and screenplays, before old age or another war left him stranded.

Unaware of Agee's determination to leave, Matthews gave Agee what was to be the writer's final major assignment, a cover story on Laurence Olivier's filmed version of *Hamlet.* But when the time came to write the piece, Agee was overcome with paralysis born of guilt and conflict over leaving the *Time* fold. He spent grueling hours on the story, but the words refused to come. Quite unlike the Agee of recent years, he turned in his draft a day after the magazine's normal Saturday deadline.

A vaguely disappointed Matthews offered a mild critique of

the piece, but it was too late for changes. Ignoring the deadline, Agee worked around the clock throughout the weekend, vastly improving his earlier draft. Even though he was leaving *Time,* he wanted to give the magazine his very best effort as a going-away present. The rewritten article made a highly favorable impression on Matthews, but the editor, knowing he could not now substitute it for the earlier version, wondered why Agee had gone to such needless trouble. He failed to realize that Agee was trying to teach him a lesson, namely, that no writer could work to the best of his ability under pressure of a deadline.

In June, Agee summoned the courage to write his letter of resignation. His rationale for leaving revealed both remorse and hope, gratitude and impatience.

Dear Tom:

. . . I've saved up enough money to do my own work exclusively for perhaps as much as 18 months to 2 years or—if I can't undermine my wife's noble prejudice in favor of supporting herself—for longer than that. . . . I can't be such a fool as to hope that I'll ever sufficiently be able to make a living by the writing I most want to do; I know that, sooner or later, I must take a job again; and there's no place I would like to work on a job as well as here. On the other hand, I assume that no leave can be granted for longer than a year at the outside; and I do have the wherewithal to work longer than that for myself; and after years of non-productiveness and semi-productiveness, I desperately feel the need to use all the time I can get. Also, more perhaps than I sensibly should, I always work myself into a hell of a self-obstructive mess if I commit myself to something I can't feel whole-hearted about.

Now Agee alluded to the *Hamlet* cover ordeal, which he assumed demonstrated his unfitness for journalism.

I'm not and never was a natural journalist, and essentially would always work at anything other than my own, chiefly non-journalistic writing because I, or others depending on me, had to eat. . . .

Tom, I'm grateful to you for many things.

Affectionately,
Jim

With mingled reluctance and relief, Matthews accepted Agee's resignation, effective August 30.

By this time Agee had spent the better part of sixteen years with Time Inc. The company had become more than his professional base; it had become his home, his crutch, his excuse. As he approached his thirty-ninth birthday, he was astonished that he had finally summoned the strength to walk away from it. No longer would he while away nights in the splendid isolation of the Time & Life Building. Nor would he have the pleasure of seeing his words in print, week after week, secure in the knowledge that millions were reading them; he was abandoning an audience as well as a job.

"Perhaps he was torn apart by all the different things he was or might have been," Matthews later wrote in as tidy a eulogy as Agee ever received, "an intellectual, a poet, a cinéaste, a revolutionary, God's fool. A wild yearning violence beat in his blood, certainly, and just as certainly the steadier pulse of a saint. He wanted to destroy with his own hands everything in the world, including himself, that was shoddy, false, and despicable; and to worship God, who made all things."

PART THREE

Photograph by Florence Homolka.

14

THE OPPORTUNIST

As soon as Agee had thrown off the golden shackles of *Time* magazine, he beat a hasty retreat to a rural hideaway in Hillsdale, New York, that he had acquired several months earlier in a haphazard manner. His friend Christopher Gerould, who had acted as an informal matchmaker for Agee and Mia, had found the perfect farm for them several hours from the city and insisted they take a look at it.

Driving to Hillsdale for the first time, they discovered an isolated farming community nestled in the foothills of the Berkshire Hills, just west of the Massachusetts border. The terrain was strewn with rocks, the climate often rainy owing to the presence of the mountains, but here and there the landscape reared back to afford splendid forested vistas. Hillsdale bore a strong resemblance to the deep mountain country of La Follette, Tennessee, country Agee had always loved. The farm itself occupied 130 acres of mostly wooded land. The farmhouse sat halfway up a steep hill and was thoroughly decrepit, having neither an adequate roof nor running water nor electricity. The mailbox was a mile away; the nearest town, three miles. Agee fell in love with the place at first sight and, with the help of Mia's *Fortune* salary, bought it at a nominal price.

When he came to his farm in the late summer of 1948, he came alone. Mia remained in New York to continue her job and look after their daughter Teresa. Away from family, friends, and deadlines, Agee cut back on his drinking. He fell in with the rhythms of nature, rising and going to bed with the sun, and sleeping soundly. Amid these idyllic surroundings he had no excuse not to write. After all, he was nearly forty, and he heard time's wingèd chariot hurrying near.

Sitting down to work, he counted an imposing number of projects competing for his attention: the profile of Griffith for *The Nation,* two articles for *Life,* two novels—*The Morning Watch* and *A Death in the Family*—awaiting completion, and a screenplay about nuclear war for Chaplin. The first order of business was the Griffith piece, which proved easy enough to write. Agee recalled the master's films in such minute detail that they might have been poems he had memorized. The charm of his assessment of Griffith was its utter lack of the pedantry such an exercise usually involves. "To watch his work is like being witness to the beginning of a melody," Agee wrote in a sweetly seductive voice, "or the first conscious use of the lever or the wheel; the emergence, coordination, and first eloquence of language; the birth of an art: and to realize that this is all the work of one man."

Since they were both transplanted Southerners, Agee discovered any number of traits he thought they shared. "He was a great, primitive poet, capable . . . of intuitively perceiving and perfecting the tremendous magical images that underlie the memory and imagination of entire peoples." Agee considered himself a natural heir to this bardic legacy, and the more he probed Griffith's work, the more the director came to resemble Agee the budding novelist.

He was remarkably good, as a rule, in the whole middle range of feeling, but he was at his best just short of his excesses, and he tended in general to work out toward the dangerous edge. He was capable of realism that has never been beaten, and he might, if he had been able to appreciate his powers as a realist, have found therein his growth and salvation. But he seems to have been a realist only by accident, hit and run; essentially, he was a poet.

This splendid assessment, one of the finest of its kind, was Agee's farewell appearance in *The Nation,* September 4, 1948.

From film criticism Agee turned immediately to film scripts. He had intended to write his script for Chaplin, but at the last minute he was able to land a more secure screenwriting job. On the advice of Huston, neophyte film producer Huntington Hartford signed Agee to write a screen adaptation of Stephen Crane's evocative short story "The Blue Hotel." Hartford was an eccentric heir to the A&P supermarket fortune; he was prone to undertaking any number of dubious enterprises with sudden enthusiasm and, just as suddenly, dropping them. Since graduating from Harvard two years after Agee, he had tried his hand at inventing, writing, art patronage, and now producing—never with the greatest success. His main claim to fame was as an expert in graphology, the "science" of handwriting analysis. Before he would hire Agee, he required the writer to submit a sample of his handwriting as a condition of employment. As Agee was eager to get to work on a screenplay and eager to be paid, he readily complied. Even though his handwriting was enough to alarm the most casual reader, Hartford approved and Agee went to work.

He knew that Crane had published "The Blue Hotel" at the age of twenty-eight in a collection of stories called *The Monster,* which appeared shortly before his death in 1900. The story dwelled remorselessly on the spiritual afflictions of small-town life, the plot revolving around a dim-witted Swede who taunts an innocent man into killing him. The dark fable revealed the failure of conventional morality to contend with the subtle shadings of evil in the human heart.

Agee adapted the story with startling alacrity. In three days and nights of ceaseless writing he released a torrent of pent-up creative energy. By the end of this brief period he had accumulated over a hundred pages of manuscript, an amount far exceeding the length of the original story. It was an astonishing outburst; never before had Agee written so rapidly. The result, however, posed insurmountable technical problems, for Agee had, in his passion for visual detail, all but smothered the story's simple plot. When he should have been developing character, he piled on exquisite descriptions of the town, the landscape, and the stars. The director did not exist who was capable of translating Agee's highly literary images to the screen. Drawing on the vocabulary of film technique he had acquired during his seven years of reviewing, he experimented with all manner of visual and sound effects. His depiction of the Nebraska town in which the story was set is a joy to read but a nightmare to film.

> It is not snowing and the night sky is overcast, but the snow on the ground gives off enough light—using infra-red if need be—to establish the station *(extreme l.s.)*, the hotel *(dead center)* the edge of town *(extreme r.s.)*. Even in darkness the hotel gives off something odd and curdled. Beyond and between these buildings, as our eyes become accustomed to the darkness, we see an immense perspective of snowed land, and a very distant low horizon against a black sky which holds two thirds of the screen.

In his mania for observation, he paid scant attention to the practical necessities of screenwriting; the finished script bore more resemblance to a novel than a drama, but Agee was intoxicated with the freedom of writing as he wanted. In the back of his mind, he had been hoping against hope that Huston would direct the script, but such an introverted and eccentric project was not likely to attract financial backing.

Caring little whether or not his adaptation of "The Blue Hotel" actually reached the screen, Agee proceeded to his long-postponed nuclear script. As the mornings grew chilly and the days short, he assembled a sixty-three-page treatment for Chaplin with the working title *Scientists and Tramp*. The unpublished manuscript began with what would become a staple of Agee's screenplays, a shot from on high, in this case outer space, in which an all but dead earth revolves. The ensuing story described a world ruled by a handful of calculating scientists modeled on the doctors Agee had come to hate during his stay in the hospital.

Into this forbidding environment Agee inserted the Little Tramp, who has managed somehow to survive the holocaust. After wandering through a devastated New York, he comes upon a group of survivors who have formed a primitive commune in which kindness and civility flourish. "It is a barter community," Agee explained. "The basic necessities are taken care of with considerable seriousness. . . . The great drives in the community are not for security, far less for Getting Ahead in the World, or for power over others or over materials; the basic drives are those of enjoyment, spontaneity and affection." To administer justice, the community has its "people's court," which spends most of its time solving romantic dilemmas. "Possessiveness and jealousy are recognized as eventually unavoidable emotions, but emotions to be resisted, not indulged."

The great virtue of Agee's utopia was that it played to his personal prejudices and forgave him the lapses in his own life. Children, for example, did not have to be reared by their natural parents. And any kind of group or clique within the community was actively discouraged; the individual enjoyed absolute primacy. *"It can be demonstrated that five convened in a room are five times as stupid as each one, and that 50 are 50 times as stupid,"* the writer insisted. Thus, whenever the community's population reached one thousand it split into smaller groups.

Agee became so entranced with creating his utopia that he soon forgot all about the Little Tramp. Suddenly, he realized, *"In this relatively good community the Tramp can hardly . . . function as the Tramp. We see for the first time how thoroughly he has depended on being an outcast in a bad society."* The writer overcame the problem by making the Tramp a *"study in what the good man does with power: i.e. tries constantly not to have it—to awaken . . . awareness instead, in others."*

Once established in the community, the Tramp comes up against the ruthless scientists, whose "genius for gadgetry" poses a great threat to the charming simplicity of life after a nuclear war. These scientists can raise vegetables from seed to basketball size within thirty seconds. They are hopelessly addicted to computers. The Tramp pleads with them to abandon their gadgetry in favor of the good life and humanistic values, but they decide instead to wage war on the community. In the end, they defeat the helpless Tramp, who is utterly alone in the world.

The complex, suggestive fable resisted Agee's best efforts at elaboration. He made numerous false starts, wrote vivid science-fiction descriptions of a world in chaos, and outlined any number of promising scenes bereft of context. The problem was that his rigid social theories kept his imagination at bay. As an experiment in social satire, *Scientists and Tramp* was both mad and brilliant, in the manner of a half-remembered dream. After repeated attempts to make the story more coherent, Agee finally realized the script had gotten completely out of hand, and he set it aside.

When the weather became too cold for Agee to remain in the unheated farmhouse, he fled the serenity of Hillsdale for the distraction and confinement of his Bleecker Street apartment, where he learned of a growing controversy surrounding his friend and former office-mate Whittaker Chambers. Under subpoena, Chambers had appeared before the House Committee on Un-American Activities in August to denounce a prominent lawyer, Alger Hiss, as a Communist, an allegation Hiss hotly denied under oath. To most journalists covering the controversy it seemed highly unlikely that Hiss, a former secretary to Supreme Court Justice Oliver Wendell Holmes and one of the prime movers behind the United Nations, had in fact been an enemy agent.

The matter might have rested there, had not HUAC committee member Richard Nixon insisted that the investigation continue, while President Truman looked the other way. Hiss and Chambers subsequently confronted each other at the Hotel Commodore in New York, where Hiss admitted having once known his accuser. Emboldened, Chambers went on national television to repeat his accusation, and the controversy attracted national attention. Two camps formed: the enlightened liberal supporters of Hiss, which included virtually all of Agee's friends, and conservative, patriotic supporters of Chambers. Soon *Time* was dragged into the controversy, when it emerged that the magazine was paying Chambers, a confessed former Soviet agent, upward of $30,000 a year.

Agee's interest in the matter increased in December, when Chambers surrendered microfilm copies of incriminating documents, many of them in Hiss's handwriting. Then came a bizarre twist. Chambers said he had hidden the microfilm in a dumbwaiter shaft of his Brooklyn home. Rising to the bait, Nixon subpoenaed Chambers for more information, whereupon Chambers led investigators to a pumpkin on his Maryland farm, took off the top, and recovered another batch of microfilm that quickly became known as the Pumpkin Papers. These were microfilmed State Department documents that Chambers claimed Hiss had given him years before. Needless to say, Chambers' unusual precautions drew howls of derision from Hiss supporters. His integrity, if not his sanity, in question, Chambers resigned from *Time,* which was only too glad to dissociate itself from him.

Agee arrived at the conclusion that no matter how ridiculous Chambers seemed, the man was incapable of lying. Virtually alone among his friends, he sided unequivocally with Chambers. Even if Chambers were lying, he would still have sided with him, for Agee held personal loyalty above politics. Ultimately, Hiss was tried, convicted, and jailed, and Chambers retired to his farm to write a sensational, fire-breathing apologia, *Witness.* Published in 1952, the book was strewn with accolades for his steadfast friend James Agee.

Throughout this political furor Agee remained on the lookout for new screenwriting opportunities, even at the cost of postponing work on the two novels. One such opportunity presented itself in December, when he attended a party at the West Fourth Street town house of Frank Taylor, then the thirty-two-year-old editor-in-chief of Reynal & Hitchcock, publishers. Taylor was about to leave New York with his wife and children for Hollywood, where he had agreed to become a producer at Metro-Goldwyn-Mayer. As befitted a sophisticated New York editor, his first project was to be an adaptation of F. Scott Fitzgerald's *Tender Is the Night.*

Agee took to Taylor at once. He was tall, slim, poised, well-dressed, and bore a strong resemblance to the actor Montgomery Clift. If anything, Agee liked his attractive wife, Nan, even more, for she was endowed with the endearing brashness of another Barbara Stanwyck. "You are the only woman I know whom domesticity has not dulled in any way," he later told her. The Taylors, in return, were highly impressed by the charming writer. Rarely had they witnessed such an infectious combination of drinking and talking. After ten minutes in Agee's presence, Frank Taylor felt as though the writer and he were lifelong friends. Nan prized Agee as a man who, she said, "could be a real friend to a woman" because he possessed extraordinary powers of empathy. They promised to keep in touch.

In Hollywood, Taylor soon ran into difficulties with the Fitzgerald movie. It seemed that David Selznick wanted the property as a vehicle for his wife, Jennifer Jones, and Taylor was forced to yield control. He turned his attention to a low-budget thriller called *Mystery Street,* a grisly tale of murder and revenge set in Boston. Ricardo Montalban and Elsa Lanchester were to star. From Hollywood, Taylor sent word to Agee in December that the job of writing the script was his for the asking, provided that he commence work by January 10, 1949.

The offer sent Agee into a panic. He desperately wanted to work for Taylor; at the same time, he was beholden to *Life* for two lengthy articles. If the deadline were a bit later, Agee explained to Taylor, he would jump at the chance. "The way things are going, I have no right to be sure I can finish my two pieces for Life by then," Agee wrote on December 29, "—even to the point of handing in drafts. And once the drafts are in, I can only guess how much mishmash & delay there may be with editing, tinkering, picture-choice, caption writing, etc." He complained bitterly of the difficulty of writing the comedy piece in particular; the "organization, binding 'theme,' if any, & overall form" proved infuriatingly elusive. The best he could offer under these circumstances was to be of "fragmentary, informal use" on the script. Taylor, meanwhile, assigned established screenwriters, Richard Brooks and Ben Maddow, to work on the movie.

The chief reason for Agee's difficulty with these rather straightforward articles was his increased drinking. After virtually abstaining during his weeks in Hillsdale, he was now drinking harder than ever—with more serious side effects. He hinted broadly to Taylor that he had suffered memory blackouts under the influence: a sure sign of dependency and impending nerve damage. He promised himself time and again that he would cut down on his consumption, but he never could remain on the wagon for more than brief periods. Yet none of Agee's friends considered him an alcoholic because he never acted drunk or out of control. He held his liquor so well that he drank them all under the table, often consuming an entire bottle of bourbon in the course of an evening. Indeed, the more he drank, the more relaxed and sociable he became. He experienced a glow and sense of well-being that was painfully absent when he was stone cold sober.

But when his mind was muddled by alcohol, he was unable to focus his thoughts and write as well as he normally did. He blamed himself for not completing the articles without knowing why they were so difficult, and he blamed the articles for cheating him of the opportunity to write *Mystery Street* for Frank Taylor. Nonetheless, he still refused to admit he had a serious problem with alcohol. In his confusion, he consoled himself with his large collection of records, the envy of his friends. After listening to 78-rpm recordings of Bessie Smith and Louis Armstrong, he often tried his own jazz improvisations on the piano, though never with happy results. Hymns were his forte now, and these he banged out with appropriately martial enthusiasm, much to Mia's dismay. "It was one of the things I could not share with him since, aside from the fact that I knew very little about them, I didn't like what I knew," she later recalled.

As the winter wore on, he moped around the apartment in a constant state of weariness, unshaven and bleary-eyed. He put on weight, and his once trim midriff thickened. Showing the effects of the alcohol he consumed, his features were often puffy, imparting an unattractive coarseness to his face. Snapshots taken of him at this time reveal a somber, unsmiling Agee, in distinct contrast to the photogenic radiance he had emanated a decade earlier. His two front teeth badly needed fixing, but he could not make himself submit to the attentions of a dentist. Instead, he resorted to concealing his mouth behind his hand whenever he laughed or smiled.

Looking back over the grim period, Agee wrote Father Flye, "This has certainly been as bad an eight months for me as I can remember. I feel phases of something different from my ordinary depression and apathy, more like galloping melancholia. . . . Yet in general I feel I just have to wait out, very likely, an even worse period when I am fully free to do the work I quit my job for—and that if I manage to wait those bad stretches out, I will come through all right."

The final blow occurred in February as Father Wright hovered near death. Agee went to his stepfather's side. The two men, long estranged, had a deathbed reconciliation. Then Father Wright suddenly took a turn for the worse. Agee summoned the night nurse just as his stepfather breathed his last. When all was still, Agee fell to his knees and prayed.

When Agee returned to New York, the recent death in the family prompted theological debates with Mia, later recalled for Father Flye's edification.

> I don't see God's providence or inscrutable mercy in such a thing. My intuition is that God is not a vulgarian. I don't think He so directs traffic that one truck miraculously stops short on a precipice and another demolishes a child. . . . I could suppose that God leaves the universe to its own devices (largely, anyhow), and he leaves human beings to theirs. . . . He knows, sees, and cares what is happening; and the tests, the relationships of all of it to God, remain vivid and unfathomable; but He does not interfere with the law of Nature (which as their creator he gave autonomy), or with the human lives of creation or self-destruction.

In contrast, Mia took an absolute position: either God was responsible for everything or He did not exist. Agee concluded that her attitude demonstrated that she was, at bottom, a Catholic, while he remained "the essential Protestant," seeking belief without miracles.

The tide of Agee's fortunes turned late in the winter. After three years of travail, the makers of *The Quiet One,* the drama about the Wiltwyck School, found a distributor willing to handle their hour-long film. On February 13 it opened at the Little Carnegie theater in New York to rapturous reviews. Writing in the *New York Times,* Bosley Crowther hailed the study of a troubled black youth as "a genuine masterpiece . . . comparable to those stark film dramas we have had from Italy since the war." Crowther accorded the film the ultimate accolade—from Agee's point of view—by calling it the *"Shoeshine* of American urban life," and he singled out Agee's commentary for special praise. The movie later won an award for Best Film at the Venice Film Festival. On the heels of this triumph, Agee unexpectedly received a $1,000 grant from the National

Institute of Arts and Letters; the award was designed to encourage "younger persons" in their artistic pursuits.

Heartened by this windfall, Agee returned to Hillsdale, this time with Mia and Teresa in tow, vowing to cut back on his drinking and complete both his *Life* articles and the novels before the summer was over. Of course he did not accomplish all that he intended, but at Hillsdale he did manage to put the finishing touches on the first piece he owed *Life,* which appeared on September 3 under the title "Comedy's Greatest Era." Many associated with the magazine considered it the single best piece of writing to have appeared within its glossy pages. Scores of readers sent letters of praise to *Life,* an outpouring that helped take the sting out of Agee's protracted battle to finish the article. And, in fact, the piece was a tour de force, even by its author's exacting standards.

"In the language of screen comedies, four of the main grades of laugh are the titter, the yowl, the belly laugh and the boffo," Agee wrote in one superbly evocative passage. "The titter is just a titter. The yowl is a runaway titter. Anyone who has ever had the pleasure knows all about a belly laugh. The boffo is the laugh that kills." In achingly precise terms, Agee described the way laughter brings a "victim" up a "ladder of laughs by cruelly controlled degrees," and "then, after the shortest possible time out for recuperation, he would feel the first wicked tickling of the comedian's whip once more and starts up a new ladder."

As Agee discussed the techniques of the silent film comedians, he developed an analogy to his own carefully contrived approach to writing.

> When a silent comedian got hit on the head he seldom let it go flatly. He realized a broad license, and a ruthless discipline within that license. It was his business to be as funny as possible physically, without the help or hindrance of words. So he gave us a figure of speech, or rather a vision, for loss of consciousness. In other words he gave us a poem, a kind of poem, moreover, that everybody understands.

It seemed to Agee that the essence of silent film comedy was a mysterious, unearthly dance of which Chaplin, of course, was the master. "The Tramp is as centrally representative of humanity

. . . as Hamlet," Agee maintained. "It seems unlikely that any dancer or actor can ever have excelled him in eloquence, variety or poignancy of motion."

When Agee returned to the city after a tranquil and productive summer, he suffered the realization that he had discharged but a fraction of his literary obligations. To add to his sense of urgency was the knowledge that Mia was again pregnant. They would need more money, more help, and more space for another child. In November a milestone birthday threw the rapid passage of time into sharp relief. "It was a deeply melancholy day for me," Agee wrote of the occasion to Father Flye, "forty of all things. I imagine by fifty one is a little better able to accept—by then it would be utterly impossible to retain any confusing delusions of youthfulness, or of living forever. Now that the day is over, I feel neither here nor there, except that Time's a-wastin'." When not brooding over his lost youth, Agee exploded into a rage brought on by the pressure he felt to fulfill the promises he had made himself. He struck a table so hard that his right hand, the one with which he wrote, remained sore and bruised for several days; he was lucky not to have fractured it.

While entrenched in this dark mood, he reluctantly agreed to participate in a *Partisan Review* symposium on "Religion and the Intellectuals." This was just the sort of dreary exercise he would have disdained in his past, but since he was trying to discover a less absolute form of belief than he had known, he decided to contribute. At least he would be in the best of company: Hannah Arendt, W. H. Auden, John Dewey, and I. A. Richards were among the other participants.

Clearly the idea of discussing such a private matter as religion in a public forum embarrassed him to no end. The resulting essay was as awkward a piece of writing as Agee ever published. In it he described himself as "pro-religion," though he doubted he would return to the faith of his fathers. Instead he preferred to remain an "amateur" capable of rescuing gems of insight from the ruin of theology to adorn his writing.

He sent a copy of the article to Father Flye together with an apology for having been so bold as to make these rash statements. "Any expression of religion is probably best indirect, if at all," he explained. At the same time he felt moved to offer this footnote:

"I feel virtually sure that nothing short of coming back into a formal religion . . . will be nearly enough for me. . . . But at all times I feel sure that my own shapeless personal religious sense is deepening and increasing."

With the greatest possible relief he returned to *The Morning Watch*. Although the book was virtually complete, the compulsive reviser in him dictated that he work over each sentence as carefully as if he were a goldsmith fashioning a tiny, intricate bracelet. Every word had to shine and lend strength, or it was discarded. On February 6, 1950, he wrote to Huston to announce, "The book will be finished in two months, or 6, or else six years; I count most on six months. I'll certainly send you as early a copy of it as I get, wishing only I might enter this proviso: that for God's sake you'll feel no concern on my account. . . . I'll be reasonably surprised if more than a few others think well of it, and much surprised if you do."

In a misguided attempt to persuade Huston of the book's insignificance compared to movies, Agee proceeded to disparage his handiwork with masochistic gusto. Richard, his autobiographical hero, was but a "backward, scrub-team version of Stephen Dedalus," the protagonist of *A Portrait of the Artist as a Young Man*, and "in so many respects a complete little shit." He advised Huston that the story was "strictly domestic stuff, trying for a kind of tragicomedy, but largely deadpan and in general very low-keyed; trying to do as well as I can what as a rule now is generally best handled in a . . . comic strip. Some Russian critic cracked about Anna Karenina that it reeked of the odor of diapers. He ought to be alive to smell this one."

There was much that was pathetic in Agee's striving to humble himself before Huston, and much that was calculating. Privately, Agee held *The Morning Watch* in much higher esteem than he admitted to Huston, but he did not want to give the director the impression that he was committed to writing novels. He continued to hope that Huston would at some point hire him to write a screenplay; this self-deprecation was his way of making himself seem available.

Huston was much on Agee's mind at the moment because the writer was making a last-ditch effort to finish the *Life* profile. The main obstacle to its swift conclusion was not alcohol, as had been the case with the comedy article, but Agee's need to present a balanced assessment of his subject while attempting to persuade that same subject to hire him as a screenwriter. By delaying, he might get away with landing the job before the article hit the newsstands, but so far Huston had resisted all his heavy hints. By May, Agee had no choice but to deliver the profile to *Life* (nearly two years after he expected he would complete it), grit his teeth, and pray that it would satisfy both his journalistic scruples and cinematic ambitions.

Days later, domestic matters demanded his attention. On May 15, Mia gave birth to a healthy girl. Agee had named his earlier children without difficulty and with much pride, but this time he was stymied. After a week of equivocation, he settled on Andrea Maria. The infant had the red hair of the mountain-dwelling Agees and a fiery temperament to go along with it.

As soon as Mia and the baby came home from the hospital, Agee resumed work on *The Morning Watch*. At this late date he appealed to Father Flye for confirmation of various details relating to St. Andrew's. "What time, about, is just daylight, *Standard* time, at St. Andrew's in early April (say April 1) and around April 12?" he queried. "And what time is *sunrise* at St. Andrew's, April 1 and 12?" Agee emphasized his need of information in Eastern Standard Time because the school was located near the border of that time zone, and locals tended to keep two clocks operating simultaneously in their heads.

Shortly after mailing the letter to Father Flye, Agee repaired to Hillsdale to make a final push on *The Morning Watch*. It was June, the weather was beautiful, and distractions abounded: children, pets, household repairs, and, of course, anxiety over Huston's reaction to the profile. Learning that the director was thinking of shooting an adaptation of Stephen Crane's novel *The Red Badge of Courage* on location in Virginia, Agee saw an opportunity to escape the domestic merry-go-round for a brief time. On July 6 he wrote to the director, begging for permission to visit. "I'd give anything if I could come down for a while and watch some of the shooting. Is that possible from your end? Or am I doing wrong in asking? Regardless of that I repeat, I hope to God you can do it in the East." Agee was sincerely interested in observing Huston at work; at the same time, he was angling for the right time and place to ask for the all-important screenwriting job.

As it happened, Huston and crew remained in California for the duration of *The Red Badge of Courage,* and Agee's escape from his family and novel vanished. By remaining at Hillsdale, however, he did manage to complete what he considered to be an acceptable draft of *The Morning Watch.* The next problem was to find a publisher willing to handle it. The obvious choice was Houghton Mifflin, publisher of *Let Us Now Praise Famous Men.* Months before, Agee had inquired as to its interest in bringing out a collection of his film reviews for *The Nation,* and the company had refused to take on the project. Stung, Agee decided to look elsewhere for his novel. On a trip to New York, he talked at length with an editor at another publishing company about the book, but, according to Mia, the editor concluded that anyone who was capable of talking as brilliantly as Agee could not write well, and he rejected the novel without bothering to read it.

Frustrated, Agee decided he had no choice but to try Houghton Mifflin. He noted sending Paul Brooks the manuscript "with a one-to-hundred expectation they'd even consider," but to his amazement, the novel met with a favorable reaction. "They are publishing it . . . without a murmur outside the 4-letter words, with apparent real liking, and, I gather, with again the illusion (not I think as wrong as before but still wrong) that it may sell." Publication was set for the following spring. Now that Agee was wiser to the ways of publishing, he made an effort to serialize the novel in magazines before its appearance in hardcover. Two literary journals, *Botteghe Oscure* and *Partisan Review,* agreed to print the entire text: a notable coup for any book, especially for a first novel.

Agee's rising star in the fictional firmament attracted the attention of a longtime admirer, David McDowell, the former St. Andrew's student whose valedictorian speech Agee had helped polish. Now McDowell was an editor at Random House. In a late-summer visit to Hillsdale he listened carefully to Agee's discourse on his second novel, *A Death in the Family.* McDowell was so impressed by the amplitude and eloquence of the writer's feelings on the subject of death that he later wrote to beseech Agee to give that novel to Random House rather than Houghton Mifflin. While McDowell was aware of Agee's loyalty to Brooks, the young editor emphasized that Random House would do better by the book than the competition would.

Unknown to McDowell, however, Agee harbored a long-standing dislike for Bennett Cerf, one of Random House's founders. To the writer, Cerf represented a certain kind of sleek, frivolous, upper-crust New Yorker who had been corrupted by success. When Agee heard of Cerf's having laughed off the Spanish Civil War, he howled in righteous indignation. How could he now allow Cerf's company to publish his precious novel? In his letter of reply to McDowell, Agee wrestled openly with his conscience over the issue of changing publishers.

> In every objective way I can see I'm convinced you're entirely right, that I owe no obligation of gratefulness, or loyalty or what not. That I feel I do is doubly curious when I realize how "neurotic" I am on the whole question of publishers—my whole general feeling . . . that even under the best of circumstances writer and publisher are, and perhaps should be, at least slightly at odds. Considering that, it's darn funny that I feel any concern except for my own best interests, which seem, pretty clearly, get out of Boston, and also to get with Random House (thanks all but entirely to your interest and concern).

He then took stock of his feelings about Houghton Mifflin's treatment of *Let Us Now Praise Famous Men* nine years earlier.

> They took it on with, so far as I could see, honest liking, and even enthusiasm; and the only edit-changes they asked for were those fucking legal ones required in their state. It's true they began to think they might be able to sell it, but I don't hold that against them and didn't at the time: I just felt rather sorry for them, and bet them, very accurately that within the first year they would sell about 400 copies.

Agee supposed that Random House offered larger advances than his current publisher did, but, he insisted, "I don't ever want to take one except on finished and accepted work," and *A Death in the Family* was nowhere near completion. Even if it were, Agee still preferred to stay with Houghton Mifflin, despite McDowell's flattering offer.

With publication of *The Morning Watch* shaping up as a significant literary event, Agee sent Huston a synopsis of the novel in the hope that the director would want to adapt it to the screen. Agee himself realized that it was a "long, very slow, winding, deeply introvert story, or cud chewing, developing in its last pages into a short piece of violent action with heavy symbolic and ambiguous charges," but it was just possible that the director of *The Red Badge of Courage* might see dramatic elements in the story that the author himself had overlooked. The more Agee discussed his novel, the more it sounded like another *Red Badge of Courage,* but, after thinking the matter over, Agee admitted to Huston that *The Morning Watch* was far too literary to survive on the screen.

While Agee succeeded in eliciting no more than mild, avuncular interest in his novel from Huston, he knew for a fact that the director was keenly interested in every word of the *Life* profile, scheduled for September 18. Considering Agee's mixed motives for writing it, he turned out a remarkably objective, candid appraisal. Eschewing the verbal pyrotechnics of his earlier evocation of the golden age of silent comedy, Agee sketched a portrait of a talented, amiably wicked man of the movies. For a change, Agee did not seek an idealized reflection of himself in his subject; the profile was all Huston and peppered with any number of interesting facts.

Readers learned that Huston was considered the outstanding "young" director in Hollywood, the man most likely to earn a place beside such silent film masters as Griffith and von Stroheim. They learned that he was born in 1906 in a town supposedly won by his grandfather in a poker game; that his father, the well-known character actor Walter Huston, had turned to film late in life, after an earlier career as an engineer; and that the director's mother was a newspaperwoman. Because his health was fragile, Huston was confined as a child in a sanitarium, where "every bite he ate and breath he drew could be professionally policed." Years later Huston told Agee, "I haven't the slightest doubt that if things had gone on like that I'd have died in a few more months." Grasping at freedom, the child stole from his bed at night to ride a nearby waterfall, and in time his physical symptoms disappeared.

Agee was obviously awed by the variety of careers his subject later tried: boxing, soldiering, painting, and writing. And there were several marriages along the way. His first wife drank herself to death; the second, Leslie Black, invested him with the discipline to make himself into a crackerjack screenwriter and later director. Of this odyssey Agee laconically noted, "John was well into his twenties before anyone could imagine he would ever amount to more than an awfully nice guy to get drunk with."

Indeed, for every compliment Agee included a subtle but telling criticism of Huston. For example, the director had earned the nickname "The Monster" for goading his stars beyond reason. He was on his fourth marriage and had acquired a "reputation for being attractive to women and rough on them." He was a prolific drinker, gambler, smoker, and a "natural-born antiauthoritarian individualistic libertarian anarchist, without portfolio." Master or monster, Huston did possess an undeniable mystique. Tall and gravel-voiced, he had a way of training his triangular-shaped eyes on a listener with hypnotic results. Curiously, he was not especially articulate, but he exuded an aura of concentration and determination enhanced by his classic punched-in boxer's nose.

When it came to assessing Huston's films, Agee was even more ambivalent than he was about the man. As a former reviewer, he knew how slender Huston's contribution was compared with that of the outstanding directors of previous generations. "His range is surprisingly narrow, both in subject matter and technique," Agee remarked. "In general he is leery of emotion—of the 'feminine' aspects of art—and if he explored it with more assurance, with his taste and equipment, he might show himself to be a much more sensitive artist." Nor did Agee approve of Huston's tendency to abandon films in the editing stage, leaving crucial work to others. To a compulsive perfectionist like Agee, that sort of cavalier attitude toward one's craft was unconscionable. Then there was the thorny problem of Huston's cinematic style, or rather the lack of it. His technique was invisible, even to Agee's practiced eye. Either the director possessed the art that concealed art, or he wore the emperor's new clothes. Ultimately, Agee came to the conclusion that Huston could be considered no more—or less—than a "brilliant adapter" who lacked the imagination and capacity for reflection of a first-rate artist.

Late in September, Agee emerged from the dungeon of his artistic conscience to face the cruel light of Huston's reaction. He sent letters to the director, shamelessly apologizing for the article and blaming *Life*'s editors for the nastier comments. "What irks and sickens me . . . is that . . . I'd never had nearly enough room to write about your work as I'd wanted to, and have never seen anyone else do it half well enough either, and that to a great extent I flubbed the chance," Agee wrote. But Huston had nothing but kind words for the profile; the criticisms, couched as they were in diplomatic language, made little impression. Agee wrote again to express his evident relief: "I'm above all glad it was clear to you in reading that whatever was done was done in affection; it sure as hell was."

To demonstrate that there was no offense taken, Huston invited Agee on a shooting trip in October in the Bitterroot Range of the Rocky Mountains. Though Agee deplored the senseless slaughter of animals, he accepted the offer with alacrity. Here was the break he was hoping for. He would be able to hobnob with Huston; the director's wife, Evelyn Keyes; and the actor Gilbert Roland. No more would he be a struggling writer, toiling away in isolation. He would ascend to another order of being—a member of the movie colony.

Prior to his departure for Idaho, Agee worked hard literally to put his house in order. With winter coming on, he hurried to paint the doors, screens, and windows. He nervously shuttled back and forth between Hillsdale and New York on minor errands, all the while missing the "great good and pleasure of being mostly alone up here during these most beautiful months of the year." Now that he was entering a new phase in his life, he was overcome with a nostalgic sense of leavetaking. His youth was dying with the summer.

His sense of aging increased when he realized that his older daughter Teresa was old enough to begin school. On the morning Mia took her to class for the first time, Agee felt prompted to write to Father Flye of his deep concern over the effects of his absence on the child.

> She's been a lovely and happy child so far; and I've felt, how-
> ever foolishly, always within my sight and reach. I know that
> from now on will be just as before, the usual mixture of good
> and terrible things and of utterly undiscernible things: but all
> I can feel is, God help her now. I begin to get a faint sense of

what heartbreak there must be in it even at the best, to see a child keep growing up.

Agee's sense of expectation was matched by an unshakable foreboding. He planned to return to New York late in the fall to work on *A Death in the Family* and assist with the publication of *The Morning Watch,* but he feared that once he left the security of home anything might go wrong. In fact, events did not turn out as he had hoped. Unwittingly, he had arrived at a crossroads in his life.

15

THE GIRL WITH THE GOLDEN EYES

The location Huston chose for the hunting expedition was so isolated that no airplane had ever ventured there before they touched down. The Bitterroot Range loomed large and forbidding before the tiny band of artists on safari. For two weeks they spent their days trekking through virgin wilderness, their nights playing poker or listening to their pilot's tall tales.

Throughout, Agee refused to lay a hand on a gun, much less fire one at a living creature, but he faithfully accompanied Huston on every outing. During their peaceful hours together, Huston warmed greatly to Agee, finding the writer to be a man of raw intelligence and fine sensitivity, all in the service of truth. "He loved to talk," Huston later reminisced of that time, "and I felt he often gave people credit for being more interesting than they really were because of his way of reading deep meanings into commonplace remarks." As the talk continued late into the night over the dying embers of a campfire, Agee drank endlessly, but to Huston's astonishment he never appeared drunk. "I wouldn't call it self-destructiveness, but carelessness," Huston said of Agee's drinking. "Jim didn't give his corporeal self any thought." Repeatedly Huston urged him to fix his unsightly front teeth, but from the way Agee reacted, the director realized he was wasting words.

Agee might not have lifted a gun, but in his own way he too was stalking big game: John Huston. During one late-night drinking session, Huston recalled, Agee "shyly confessed" his desire to write a screenplay for the director. The remark seemed casual, but it was heartfelt and the product of a long-standing desire. Huston said he was receptive to the idea of a collaboration, but he was still embroiled with *The Red Badge of Courage.* It was too late for Agee to work on that movie, but he had another project in mind that he thought would interest the fledgling screenwriter, an adaptation of C. S. Forester's 1935 adventure novel, *The African Queen.*

Huston explained that the novel, set during World War I, was a skillful blend of action and romance. Two mismatched characters, Rose, a pious sister of a missionary, and Charlie Allnut, a rebellious ship's captain, are forced to make a downriver journey together through the heart of Africa to escape certain death at the hands of the Germans. To their surprise, the spinster and the confirmed bachelor wind up falling in love. The only problem with this tale was the ending; Forester had written two, one for the English edition of the novel and one for the American. Huston thought neither satisfactory but supposed Agee and he could concoct a new one when necessary.

What excited Huston about the movie was the chance to make it under the auspices of his own production company, Horizon Pictures, rather than a studio. He had begun the company in 1948 with the producer Sam Spiegel. As Huston exemplified the cowboy-director, Spiegel epitomized the enterprising immigrant producer. Of Austrian birth, he had knocked around the German film industry before migrating to Hollywood, where he worked under the name S. P. Eagle. Huston and he had recently completed a disastrous film, *We Were Strangers,* and Horizon Pictures was now deeply in debt. Huston hoped that *The African Queen* would come to his financial rescue. At the time of the hunting trip, he had scraped together $50,000 to purchase the property from Warner Brothers and had arranged for distribution through United Artists. And Spiegel had scored a coup by persuading Humphrey Bogart and Katharine Hepburn to star. In the way of Hollywood, the flimsy book would make a sturdy vehicle for outstanding performances. The two leads dominated 90 percent of the scenes and ran the gamut of emotions.

Agee unhesitatingly accepted Huston's offer. At last he would be working within the mainstream of the motion-picture industry, secure in the knowledge that his script would go before the cameras, not into a desk drawer. At the same time, he realized, he would have to abide by the limitations of the job; but these Agee was willing to accept, as he had the constraints of writing for *Fortune* and *Time*. Chief among them was the need for an agent to represent him in business negotiations. Though he had been a professional writer for nearly twenty years, Agee had always scoffed at the idea of having an agent. His books earned little money, he resented the intrusion on his work, and, as he well knew, many "serious" writers avoided them. But when he weighed these liabilities against the $500 per week he could expect to earn for writing *The African Queen*, he accepted Huston's suggestion that the director's agent, Paul Kohner, represent him as well, at least for screenplays.

The new job turned Agee's relatively tranquil existence topsy-turvy. Since *The African Queen* was to begin shooting in the winter, he returned to New York after the hunting trip for only a few days, then flew to Los Angeles, where he installed himself in the Garden of Allah, a well-known screenwriters' retreat. Here cottages hid demurely behind lush foliage, and the weather remained eternally, disconcertingly warm. After his years in the Northeast the mild climate troubled Agee, who associated cool weather with work. He soon immersed himself in the strange business of being a Hollywood screenwriter. He took pains to catch up on the latest studio gossip and to absorb the lingo of the industry: options and contracts, rushes and properties. He seemed to exist in a dream world sustained by an army of public relations experts and shady entrepreneurs. No one troubled himself over the Cold War or the bomb;

everyone talked money. It was all so different from the down-at-heels existence of a serious Eastern writer.

In hours stolen from the script of *The African Queen,* he visited the set of *The Red Badge of Courage,* offering suggestions to Huston as shooting proceeded. In one instance he advised the director that for the sake of authenticity there should be a delay between the sight and sound of cannon fire. Impressed, Huston added the detail. Watching the rushes at the end of the day, Agee, like other members of Huston's retinue, judged the film to be a masterpiece.

In mid-December the reporter Lillian Ross, who was writing an account of the making of *The Red Badge of Courage* for *The New Yorker,* caught up with Agee and Huston as the men discussed their plans for *The African Queen.* While Ross listened, Agee attempted to persuade Huston to envision the trip Bogart and Hepburn make down the river as a symbol of "the act of love."

Overwrought from the pressure of making one film while thinking about another, Huston exploded. "Oh, Christ, Jim, tell me something I can understand," Ross heard him say. "This isn't a novel. This is a screenplay. You've got to demonstrate everything, Jim. People on the screen are gods and goddesses. We know all about them. Their habits. Their caprices. But we can't touch them. They're not real. They stand for something, rather than being something. You can't have symbolism within symbolism, Jim."

The exchange revealed much about the problems Agee faced when trying to adapt his working methods to the demands of a commercial screenplay—and much about Huston's rather conventional notion of film. But such arguments were normal in an intense collaboration. It was Huston's method to react intuitively, Agee's to be conscious of the tiniest nuance. Although Huston appeared to dominate, the two were well matched, and Agee's symbolic interpretation of the river journey eventually informed every scene of the script.

As the screenplay took shape, Agee's expectations for it steadily rose. At about the time he was wrangling with Huston over symbolism, he wrote to Father Flye, "If everything works out right, it could be a wonderful movie. If much works out wrong, it could be lousier than most. I think most likely it will wind up as good, maybe even very good, but not wonderful, or lousy. The work is a great deal of fun: treating it fundamentally as high comedy with deeply ribald overtones, and trying to blend extraordinary things —poetry, mysticism, realism, romance, tragedy, with the comedy." He went on to describe his disturbingly pleasant new life as a highly paid Hollywood screenwriter. "I haven't read a book, heard any music to speak of, or seen a movie or but one play since I have been out here. For the present I don't miss them either. I see a lot of people and like most of them. Compared with most of the intellectual literary acquaintances I avoid in New York (who are—wrongly —my image of New York) they are mostly warmhearted, outgoing, kind, happy, and unpretentious—the nicest kind of company I can imagine."

By "people," Agee meant first and foremost Charlie Chaplin. In Los Angeles the two cemented the friendship they had begun in New York two years before. Coming to know the god of his boyhood had a potent effect on Agee. Whenever he encountered Chaplin, he seemed to be shaking hands with a dream, a wraith, a sprite. Here were the same gestures and expressions that had held him fascinated in movie theaters now tangible before him, answering his questions, responding to his presence. "Very interesting (to put it mildly) to see what a man of real genius—which I am convinced he has—is really like," Agee told Father Flye. "A very active, self-taught, interesting, likeable man: a blend of conflict in him of sensitiveness with icy coldness, which sometimes disturbs me and would I think put you off. . . . The 'genius' is a mixture of these things with tremendous self-discipline and technical mastery and hard work, with incandescent feeling and intuitiveness." However, Agee's tendency to fawn on his hero had its awkward moments. One evening he found himself at a Hollywood party where Chaplin held court in one corner, Huston in another. Agee nervously alternated between the two while trying to interest Chaplin in the farfetched *Scientists and Tramp* script. Although the comedian responded enthusiastically to the idea, he was not willing to make any firm commitment.

In addition to Chaplin and Huston, Agee sought the attentions of Frank and Nan Taylor, now ensconced with their three children in a spacious house in Brentwood. It was there that he met Nan's beautiful younger sister, Patricia Scallon, who had come to Los Angeles to get a divorce. To his astonishment he found her irresistibly attractive. At twenty-two, the diminutive Pat was as attractive and vulnerable as a movie starlet. She had auburn hair; pale, creamy skin; and golden eyes encircled by a dark rim. Her physical charm and obvious sensuality seduced him; her intelligence and sensitivity, whether real or imagined, overwhelmed him. She was in every way the opposite of Mia: small, soft, irresponsible, and young. To Agee she incarnated the California mystique of rootless hedonism. After a short while in her glowing presence, he knew he had to possess this young woman no matter what the consequences.

And Pat, for her part, was enthralled by this brilliant writer from the East. He seemed terribly mature and understanding, and while she had serious reservations about entering into an affair with a married man, Agee persuaded her that impulse and feeling mattered more than caution and conscience. As the affair got under way, he discovered they had much in common. Like him, she was fond of late-night drinking. Like him, she could find delight in the simplest incidents. As she later recalled, they could be "happy as a hoot just sitting on the steps of a building, watching the world go by."

After several weeks with Agee, Pat's conscience got the better of her. She returned to her family home in St. Paul, Minnesota, determined to end the relationship before it developed into more than a casual fling. Agee phoned her every night to try to persuade her to return to Hollywood. When she resisted, he discussed the matter with her parents, assuring them of his good will and honorable intentions toward their daughter. Soon the entire Scallon family was utterly charmed by him; the only stumbling block to marriage was Agee's wife and children in the East. Agee still loved and respected Mia, but he so prized his sexual relationship with Pat that he seriously contemplated divorce. He raved to friends about his spirited lovemaking with Pat, calling her the most "far out" woman he had ever met. Though he talked often of her, he rarely introduced her to his friends in California, for fear that word would get back to Mia. To them, Pat was a phantom, a femme fatale. He consulted the much-divorced Huston about whether to seek a divorce from Mia and marry Pat, but even the freedom-loving director advised Agee against the move.

Nan, meanwhile, saw another, darker side to the affair. It seemed to her that both Pat and Agee drank too much when they were together and, despite their protestations of love, were never truly happy in one another's presence. When she asked her younger sister if she was in love with Agee, Pat replied, "I don't know. All I know is that he is my mother, my father, my sister, and my brother." That obsessive quality gave Nan further cause for worry; she saw nothing but misery ahead for both parties.

In certain ways the affair recalled Agee's tempestuous relationship with Alma. Like her, Pat was young and sensual, and once again Agee was in flight from the responsibilities of marriage. But in other significant ways it was utterly different. When he was courting Alma, he had come to loathe Via and her family. In contrast, he continued to hold Mia in the highest esteem. Despite these differences, there was one outstanding similarity between the two situations—Agee was again behaving like a mule caught between two bales of hay and unable to choose.

On January 2, 1951, Agee and Huston moved to San Ysidro, a resort ranch near Santa Barbara, to complete work on the script of *The African Queen.* Agee looked forward to two weeks of intensive work with the director before returning to New York. Pat remained in Minnesota, but she was very much on his mind.

At the ranch, the filmmakers lived a productive, strenuous existence. "I was all for having a health regimen: up early, tennis, work, lunch, relaxation, work, tennis, drinks, dinner, and bed," Huston remembers. "But Jim was a night person. With him it was drinks, dinner, and writing. I said, 'Jim, you can't do this. You're not getting enough sleep.' " Agee insisted that he could get along with only a few hours' rest at night.

Under the double strain of finishing the script and contemplating divorce from Mia, he often drank alone in his bungalow, a habit he carefully concealed from Huston. Under the influence of the alcohol he became intoxicated with the great changes he thought were in store for him. To his *Time* colleague James Stern he wrote of a "sense of hope and of turning a corner and really beginning, at last to get some work done, with all my sense of years wasted and of life shortening with a rush." He took particular pride in the forthcoming publication of *The Morning Watch,* "the first piece of work I feel really good about," and remained "astonished" and "grateful" to Houghton Mifflin for its continued support. "They already published one commercial lemon of mine," Agee wrote, unconsciously slipping into the jargon of Hollywood, "and I can't see any money in this one for them."

The excitement of working with Huston matched his enthusiasm for the novel. "Movie writing, at least on the level Huston works, I love," he told Stern. "It's as demanding and accurate and hard as poetry and as any prose except the very best to write. . . . Working double is exciting and fascinating, and so is watching that particular intelligence and instinct work. And so is learning from him—any number of basic things a day, which had only vaguely occurred to me before, about good craftsmanship and taste and imagination."

On January 9 a large photograph of Huston and Agee discussing *The African Queen* appeared on the front page of the Santa Barbara *News-Press.* Both men looked exhausted; a jowly Agee held a cigarette, his constant companion. He told the paper, "I'm the guy that's doing the work here right now, and in less than a month I'll be on my way back to New York. Lucky me, eh?"

Despite his jocularity, Agee took exceeding care with the script for *The African Queen.* This was no rush job, as his experiments in screenwriting at Hillsdale had been, but rather a well-thought-out commercial effort designed to deliver maximum audience impact. He worked hard to please the demanding Huston. "Jim was a willing collaborator," the director noted. "We quickly worked out a routine. We'd discuss a sequence, then block it out and write alternate scenes. Then we would exchange scenes and rework each other's material. This method was all right, except Jim got too far ahead. I marveled at the volume of material he was turning out."

Wherever he could, Agee embellished the bare bones of the original novel. One of his chief inspirations concerned an embarrassing rumbling in Allnut's stomach. Agee feared that audiences would suspect that he had filched the routine from Chaplin's *Modern Times,* but Huston encouraged the writer to work it in. The result, one of the film's comedic highlights, demonstrated Agee's typically microscopic approach to screenwriting.

All of a sudden, out of the silence, there is a SOUND like a mandolin string being plucked. At first the sound is identifiable, though instantly all three [Allnut, Rose, and her brother] glance up, each at the other two, then away; in the next instant they recognize what it is and each glances sharply, incredulously, at the other two—and then again, quickly away; then Brother and Rose glance with full recognition at Allnut, at the instant he knows the bellygrowl is his. At the moment of recognition, he glances down at his middle with a look of embarrassed reproach. He glances up quickly and slyly—hopeful they've missed—to find the eyes of both still fixed on him. The instant their eyes meet they bounce apart like billiard balls, and fix on the first neutral object they happen to hit. Then Allnut looks at them again. Neither will look at him.

For sheer vividness, not even the actual filmed scene could outdo Agee's description. His novelistic image of eyes bouncing apart like billiard balls eluded all but the camera of the mind.

He lavished similar care on the choice of hymns sung by worshiping Africans in the film's opening sequence, and he conveyed the quality of their voices in exact, if impossible to record, detail.

The singing of most of them is weirdly shy and inchoate—a little like that of a neighborhood audience when a group "sing" is imposed on them. But on certain high phrases a glad, rich, wet-soprano lifts out large and happy, very child-like; and a big male voice bleats forth joyous, jazz-like improvements on the time, a little off-key.

A profusion of similarly inspired details fleshed out the remainder of the script, but thanks to Huston they never obscured the flow of dramatic action or development of character.

Agee's contribution to the screenplay went beyond mere effects and details. He poured a considerable amount of his own personality into the character of Allnut and a considerable amount of his mother's into Rose. Like Agee, Allnut was a hard-drinking loner who sought freedom but usually found oblivion, and like Agee's mother, Rose was a repressed, self-righteous, Bible-thumping woman. That they would meet and come to fall in love was purely wish fulfillment on Agee's part. Like Agee and his mother, Allnut and Rose were sinner and saint, heroic scalawag and pious biddy. In the movie, if not in life, they made a splendid couple.

Huston and Agee played as hard as they worked at San Ysidro. Sweating profusely, they spent hours smashing the ball around the tennis court under a hot sun. Huston was fit enough to withstand the exertion, but Agee was seriously out of shape. Alcohol had dulled his reflexes, cigarettes had diminished his wind, and he was overweight. Nevertheless, he felt an urgent need to keep up with Huston in tennis as well as in screenwriting.

While playing on the morning of the fifteenth, Agee felt slight discomfort in his left arm, but since he held the racquet with his right, he paid it no heed. Later in the day, Huston departed for San Francisco to inspect a collection of pre-Columbian art he was thinking of buying. That night Agee returned to his bungalow, where, as usual, he began working his way through a bottle of bourbon. To pass the idle hours he telephoned Pat. During the conversation he experienced what he later described as "a series of attacks of pain (keen aching) in my chest, teeth, and forearms."

Ashen, Agee emerged from the bungalow to complain of the pain to the actor Joseph Cotten, who happened to be visiting San Ysidro. Cotten insisted that Agee go immediately to the Cottage Hospital in Santa Barbara. On admission to the hospital, Agee was diagnosed as having suffered a coronary thrombosis. For the next several days his life hung in the balance. He was on the critical list and under heavy sedation. Two friends of Huston, David Selznick and his wife, Jennifer Jones, heard of Agee's condition and called the director in San Francisco to urge him to return immediately.

While Agee underwent tests to determine the extent of the damage to his heart, Huston, Selznick, and Jones maintained a vigil at San Ysidro, playing Scrabble through the night. Four days after the attack, Agee's doctors were able to offer some tentative conclusions. They believed he had escaped death, at least for the moment, and with three or four weeks' bed rest could leave the hospital and resume light work. In fact, the doctors thought he would be almost as good as new if he cut back on drinking and smoking and worked on a curtailed schedule—not for a brief period, but for the rest of his life. If the patient refused to cooperate, they predicted more heart attacks, of increasing severity.

One of Agee's first visitors in the hospital was Huston. The director was taken aback to hear his conscience-stricken screenwriter apologizing for the trouble and delay he had caused. Although the script was nearly complete, the all-important ending remained to be written. Raising a finger to his lips for silence, Huston promised to send a rough draft to Agee for approval and comments. Relieved, Agee asked for a cigarette. "My God, no, Jim," Huston replied, aghast at Agee's reckless disregard for doctors' orders.

"John," Agee said, "I really must have a cigarette. I beg you to give me a cigarette."

"If I give you a cigarette, the doctor would lose his patient."

"Well," Agee said with a note of resignation, "I'm not going to change."

Huston did not give Agee a cigarette on that occasion, but on a number of others he bribed nurses to allow him to enter the writer's room after midnight, where they continued to discuss the script's nettlesome ending. Still, they were unable to arrive at a satisfactory conclusion to the story.

Throughout the long days, Agee was alone, a circumstance he detested. To ease the burden of solitude he summoned imaginary company by writing letters to his friends in the East, who by now would have heard of the heart attack and were doubtless concerned for him. To Father Flye he downplayed the seriousness of the illness, insisting, "This whole thing is brought on by too much alcohol and tobacco, too little sleep, too much emotional or nervous or other strain or anxiety, or even just too much excitement. The alcohol, tobacco, and sleep I can and will see to. On the rest, I'll have to take my chances."

Writing to Walker Evans the following day, January 21, Agee sounded far more vulnerable and overwrought. "I'm in a hospital with the effects of a heart attack—a modest edition of a coronary thrombosis, which is one of the most majestic things to be afflicted by that I can think of—the least one can do is drop dead, and apparently that is often done. However, I got off light. . . . Quite a show at 41, but so far, outside occasional depressed moments, I don't much mind. I guess I'm still feeling too lucky at being alive and at not being turned into a permanent invalid."

Mia's impending arrival added to Agee's worries, for he now felt remorseful about his affair with Pat. He confided to Evans:

Christ how I wish I could pray, and mean, "From all adulterous liaisons and deceptions of the truthful, and divisions of the heart, good Lord, deliver us." I couldn't. But how lousy it is.

It's bad enough when, as seems the usual, only one woman is involved. But this I *really* hate, and of course as the ultimate mark . . . of my regard for her, or of her goodness—is a feeling I've had ever since I first knew her; I don't like hurting anyone, but I'd rather hurt anyone else than her. By "her" I mean Mia, and I think the bottom of it is that the one thing you can rightly *never* forgive yourself is to hurt or otherwise misuse genuine nobility. Much more mixed things in Pat, as in me; only abortive streaks of nobility, in either. That makes it sound, may be, as if nobility bored me or I preferred ignobility. That is why I said *genuine*. There's nothing about the *genuine* that bores me, or that I less than love and revere. But I do also like the messier mixtures, being one myself.

Awaiting Mia's arrival, Agee debated the wisdom of telling her about his affair with Pat. He loathed the idea of deceiving his wife, especially when those around her knew the truth. Surely such nobility could accept this admission of weakness.

In bedside conversations with Huston, he tried to justify the affair on the grounds that it was a masculine prerogative. "We arrived at [the] same ringing affirmation of the minimal, irreducible right of a man: that he has the right, even the obligation, to write (or other vocational work) and to fuck as much as he can and in the ways he prefers to, even if doing so shortens his life or kills him on the spot. And that he hasn't got any other fucking right in the world that can't be taken away or proved invalid in two seconds," Agee wrote Evans in a particularly extreme moment.

Clearly, he was chafing at the bit illness had forced him to accept. He hated being told what to do, especially by doctors. As far as he was concerned, the heart attack had come at the worst possible time, when he was in the midst of finishing a screenplay, publishing his first novel, and conducting a passionate love affair. How it galled him to realize that he could not handle all these matters. To add to his aggravation, Huston suddenly picked up and left for Africa to scout locations for the movie. Agee would dearly have loved to tag along; instead he was confined to his hospital bed, listening to the newly introduced long-playing records—a gift from Jennifer Jones. But the music brought no solace; he brooded on lost opportunities, lost salary, lost love.

To fill the empty hours he did sums, calculating how much his illness was costing him and how long he would have to work to extricate himself from debt. His hospital bill was already over $1,000, the phone bill over $400. After fretting about money, he turned over his scratch sheet to calculate the bargain he would strike with liquor and tobacco in order to survive, pondering questions that had once seemed petty but now loomed as life-and-death issues.

Tobacco—with or without the tar?
Any filter take out nicotine?
maximum c. 6? i.e. smoke only so much   120/mo?

Alcohol—
  what is the maximum?
  tight? drunk? ever? favor mixed drinks
gradual erosion? through alc. + tobacco?

Minimum sleep I shd have? 8 hrs? 9?
  nap in middle of day? Sh'd not stay up
  far beyond **my** normal bedtime? i.e. a good
  night's sleep gives me a surplus of energy—
  I can go 20 rather than 16—in fact it's hard to
  go 16 instead.
Exercise + exertion: tennis doubles? (about ⅓ to ¼
the exertion of singles.)
The warnings are *so* clear and, if heeded constantly,
safe?
  short of breath; I think the trouble was, my
  wind got too good—lifting; climbing—palpitation;
  congestion, pain—
  What type of pain in legs means embolism?

That he would have to limit his drinking and smoking was plain enough, but the amount of effort he expended in writing eluded such easy quantification. "My work as a rule involves a lot of tension," he noted. "Not as a rule when it's going best—but—disturbingly so, on the way there, + sometimes there. It can be very important sometimes to ride a spell out, and I've always done so: have good stamina for that. Dangerous? One safety valve: If I feel too sick or too exhausted, it usually lowers the quality of the work so that I quit anyhow." Nonetheless, he realized, "It is extremely

351

unnatural to me to *avoid* stress, strong feeling, what's known as trouble." And he wondered, "Should I try to?" He suspected he would fail in his effort to reform himself, for he was always "much more interested in complexity + contradictions than in conclusions."

On January 24, nearly ten days after the heart attack, he elaborated on his doubts to Stern. "I am supposed . . . to avoid emotional strain, conflict, complexity, even excitement," Agee wrote. "Well most of this, of course, is just a laugh. . . . Imagine anyone who would even *try* to govern feelings of love, or the whole plexus of things which go into writing, according to any kind of expediency!" By this logic, even the prospect of sudden death was but another "expediency." Five days later he again wrote to Stern to explain that he now felt "no worry" over the necessary "adjustment in physical indulgence and habit." Only his mental state gave cause for concern.

> It's hard to know where, or how, you're being faithful or unfaithful to yourself, whatever yourself may be, or mean. To really try to militate against my habit of anger, I'm for—but I'm afraid I'm for, because I've been wanting & even trying to for quite a while; I'm not doing it for the sake of my heart. To try to modify, for my health's sake, the ways it comes natural to me to write, I'm much less sure about.

This endless muttering about convictions and being true to oneself belied Agee's profound bewilderment over his predicament. Though he dared not admit it, he was frightened and had little notion of how best to conduct his life after he left the hospital.

Mia's arrival added to the confusion. She had come west with their two daughters, and they were staying at the Garden of Allah. Agee was alarmed to find her "completely dislocated and in mild panic" over his condition. Despite her state of mind, he broached the topic of his affair with Pat, and as soon as the words were out of his mouth, he realized he had made a terrible mistake. Though Mia tried to be understanding, she was deeply hurt by the revelation. For the children's sake she would not seek a divorce, but the affair marked a turning point in their marriage. Agee recognized that he would never be able to find complete happiness with one woman, and Mia, true to her bohemian life-style, tacitly permitted him to continue the liaison, if he felt he must. Under this arrangement, she became more of a companion or caretaker than a full partner in marriage. In a way, she felt sorrier for Pat than for her husband, because Pat had no one else to turn to, while Agee could always rely on his family. But Mia's sympathy for Pat did not make the affair any less of a blow.

As the weeks in the hospital slid past and Agee gradually recovered his strength, he synthesized his worries over his uncertain health and sullied marriage into a striking, symbolic fable called "A Mother's Tale." The 10,000-word story opens with an ominous image of cattle herding into boxcars waiting to transport the animals to an unknown destination. A calf observing the sight prods its mother into telling the tale of The One Who Came Back, a harrowing description of a trip to the slaughterhouse from the animal's point of view. "He was upside down and very slowly swinging and turning," the mother explains, "for he was hanging by the tendons of his heels from the great frightful hooks, and he has told us the feeling was as if his hide were being torn from him inch by inch, in one piece." Speaking in a disconcertingly sweet voice, the mother goes on to relate how "knives would sliver and slice along both flanks, between the hide and the living flesh; then there was a moment of most precious relief; then red hands seized the hide and there was a jerking of the hide and a tearing of tissues which it was almost as terrible to hear as to feel."

Miraculously, the skinned beast escapes the slaughterhouse and, though severely wounded, returns to the herd, where it preaches a baffling doctrine: *"Each one is himself. Not of the herd. Himself alone."* When asked by the calves if this statement is true, the mother replies, "Of course not, silly. It's just an old, old legend designed to frighten children."

Published in the July 1952 issue of *Harper's Bazaar*, "A Mother's Tale" was replete with dark meanings and reflected Agee's pessimism following the heart attack. Like the calf who had escaped the slaughterhouse, Agee had narrowly missed what seemed certain death, and like the calf, he had a woeful message for mankind: Nothing matters but the survival of the individual; to follow the norms of society is to die.

By the time Agee had finished work on the bleak story, he had been in the Cottage Hospital for five long weeks. At last his personal physician, Dr. Arthur Koefed, authorized his release. However, there was no one on hand to drive Agee to the Garden of Allah, where he planned to continue his convalescence. Mia had returned to New York with the children; Huston was in Africa, Pat in Minnesota. At the last minute, Nan Taylor volunteered to accompany him to the hotel.

Looking pale, weak, and thin, Agee was wheeled from the dimness of the hospital into the cruel brilliance of the California sunshine. As they drove away, he startled Nan by saying, "We're going to the Santa Barbara Museum." He insisted on the detour because he had learned that the actor Charles Laughton had lent his collection of Monet's paintings of water lilies and he was extremely anxious to see them. When they reached the museum, Nan nervously helped him out of the car and watched him shuffle past the evocative, indistinct daubs of green, pink, and blue that suggested the innocence of the irretrievable past. After gazing his fill, Agee permitted Nan to drive him to the hotel, where he would try to begin his life over again.

In April, Houghton Mifflin published *The Morning Watch.* It was a small volume, only 120 pages long, but so dense was the writing that it contained as much substance as novels of far greater length. As Agee predicted, sales were small, reviews glowing. In general, critics showered the author with praise for having produced a sensitive, finely wrought novel of early adolescence.

In the *New York Times,* Richard Sullivan called the book a "dark poem" and commended Agee for having found a "style that adjusts nicely to his intention." In *The Nation,* F. W. Dupee commented perceptively on the novel's place in Agee's varied literary career. "He has fraternized not so much with the North itself as with a certain domain of popular art and feeling," Dupee wrote, alluding to Agee's years of film reviewing. "Spared the patrician pathos of many Southerners, he found at the same time congenial objects for his passion"—these objects being movies. But Dupee detected a "failure of correspondence between their worthiness and his words. Genius he surely had; the trouble perhaps lay in his trying to read that genius into things not of his making." Fortunately, *The Morning Watch* rectified the situation, at least for

Dupee, who concluded that it contained "the *kind* of writing that seems to answer best to his genius for piety and style."

Still other reviewers lauded the author for his "tour de force," his "liturgical and poetically spiritual rhapsody" and "classic finality." Yet the odd voice of dissent did arise. Robert Fitzgerald's heart sank when he read the novel; he considered the writing too "showy" and wondered whether Agee had lost his "irony and edge." Perhaps his friend had gone to stylistic extremes to "make the break with journalism decisive." Fitzgerald had a point; the writing was intimidating. Although Agee did not antagonize the reader as he had in *Let Us Now Praise Famous Men,* he continued to write primarily to please himself.

Despite the critical plaudits, the novel dropped quickly from sight. The Kohner Agency circulated it among the film studios in the hope of stimulating a movie deal, but there were no takers. Still, one admirer fought to keep it in print. When Frank Taylor eventually resumed his publishing career in New York, he included *The Morning Watch* in a collection of short novels published in paperback by Dell.

Agee took little joy in the book's warm critical reception. He was so depressed about his chaotic life that as far as he was concerned, the novel might just as well not have been published. He was far more interested in landing another film assignment, but without Huston's patronage he was cut off from the mainstream. Huston pitied Agee, but he felt powerless to help. The director was now stranded in England, trying to stave off creditors. At the time of Agee's heart attack the script had been about three-quarters complete. Huston and Agee had left off at the miraculous moment when Rose and Allnut, seemingly marooned in a swampy jungle, awake to find themselves at the edge of the lake they have been struggling to reach. " 'African Queen,' 1st draft, was 160 pages," Agee noted. "The first hundred were mine and brought it through almost exactly half the story. The last 60, except a few scenes and interpolations, were Huston's." In collaboration with another screenwriter, Peter Viertel, Huston roughed out a sensational conclusion in which the wreck of the *African Queen,* loaded with homemade torpedoes, destroys the German vessel on which Allnut and Rose are about to be executed. Even though the abrupt and incredible ending violated the carefully thought out manner of all that had gone before, Huston went ahead and filmed it. When Agee later saw the result, he disapproved of the jarring conclusion.

With the film beyond his grasp, Agee concentrated on recovering his health and Pat's attentions. By the summer he looked his old self again and felt well enough to fly to New Orleans, his "Magic City," to rendezvous with his mistress. After spending several days in the city, the lovers drove lazily west, often stopping for the night in seedy motels that sprouted at random across the stark Southwestern landscape. They made an odd couple, this fugitive, middle-aged writer and the young woman who promised to restore his vanished youth, and their unbridled pursuit of pleasure brought Agee little satisfaction. Worse, he resumed drinking and smoking at his former pace, though he knew he risked dire consequences.

Reaching San Antonio, Texas, Agee paid a surprise call on his old college friend Irvine Upham. Once the thrill of the reunion died down, Upham was disturbed by the changes time had wrought on Agee. He did not look fit, and he boasted incessantly of his sexual escapades with Pat, who remained mysteriously sequestered in a motor court, claiming that she was suffering from constipation. Upham was also puzzled by the restaurants Agee chose to frequent —among the worst in town—and by his chain-smoking. For the sake of his heart, Agee had switched from unfiltered Camels to filtered Marlboros, but he felt the need to apologize to Upham for smoking this effete type of cigarette. Most disturbing of all was Agee's reliance on alcohol. Over a cup of coffee one afternoon he asked sheepishly, "Is there any place we can. . . . Is there a liquor store anywhere near here?" They went to a liquor store, Agee bought a pint of whiskey, and they returned to the coffee shop, where he poured himself a stiff drink. Only then was he able to resume the conversation.

The dismal trip ended in July, when Agee returned to Hollywood and began to scout the prospects for work. Now it was Frank Taylor's turn to come to the writer's rescue. The producer had switched from MGM to Twentieth Century-Fox, where he persuaded Darryl F. Zanuck to hire Agee at $500 a week. While Taylor could not vouch for Agee's reliability, he remained convinced of his genius.

For the next three months Agee led a harrowing existence as an alcoholic screenwriter, his life drawn equally from two of his favorite recent films, *The Lost Weekend* and *Sunset Boulevard.* He inhabited a Spanish-style bungalow on the studio grounds, equipped with a writing room, kitchenette, and bedroom. Never had he worked in such posh surroundings; never had he so little to show for his efforts. He worked haphazardly on any number of stillborn projects. One, *The Gun and the Cross,* was to be an original Western about a priest and a gunman. The studio considered Agee's draft well written but too hokey to film. Another, *Bloodline,* was a Civil War tale set in "the gentle countryside of Middle Tennessee" and was strongly influenced by Stephen Crane. *Bloodline* contained far more atmosphere than story. He submitted a detailed, sixty-page treatment on September 11, but the studio quickly abandoned the project.

When not fumbling with scripts in the lavish bungalow, Agee pursued Pat with terrifying ferocity. Living with the Taylors in Brentwood, she often refused to speak to him, thereby setting the stage for a series of highly unpleasant scenes. Agee often haunted the grounds of the house, hoping to speak to Pat. When angry, he attempted to break down the doors and windows to gain access to her. Nan, Frank, and Pat were perfectly miserable under the onslaught.

To permit her sister and brother-in-law to recover their peace of mind, Pat moved into the nearby home of Nan's friend Dorothy Parker, the legendary wit of the Algonquin Hotel Round Table. As it happened, Parker's husband, Alan Campbell, had just walked out on her, "pressing," she explained to Nan, "a twenty-dollar bill in my hand." Campbell told her not to worry, that the mortgage on the house was paid for a year, but he neglected to mention that the furniture was about to be repossessed. As a result, Pat took up residence in a house stripped bare of all movables except for two beds: one used by Parker, the other by Pat and, inevitably, Agee.

"Dottie" Parker and Agee quickly became friends. They were both transplanted New York intellectuals and hard drinkers. Like Agee, she had flirted with Communism and had come to prominence as a reviewer. And she was a poet, one of the few certifiably famous ones of her generation. To those who idolized her, she combined lightning wit with sudden heartbreak. But her reputation was in eclipse. She wrote little poetry these days and was now a highly paid screenwriter, her gift for verse all but extinguished by alcohol. Nevertheless, she remained an attractive, vivacious woman.

Parker took the unusual position that Agee's affair with Pat had actually improved him. "You know," she told Nan, "Jim's taking baths. I think your sister's bought him a little blue duck." Furthermore, she was glad to have a man around the house. On one occasion she was tripped by a large dog she kept and fell unconscious in the garden, where she remained until Agee rescued her. For the most part, however, Agee and Pat kept to themselves. In a town accustomed to unusual ménages, the Agee-Scallon-Parker trio, drinking away in an unfurnished house in Brentwood, attracted little notice.

Though relatively docile now, Agee steadily deteriorated. Each day he wore the same ugly black shoes, sweat-stained black shirt, and dirty pants. He neglected to fix his teeth, have his hair cut, or even to bathe. His smell alienated those around him. The studio warned Frank Taylor that if Agee did not improve his manner of dress, he would no longer be permitted to eat with the other writers in the commissary—a demand the producer considered disgraceful. Without telling Agee why, he encouraged the writer to take better care of himself, but he knew he was wasting his breath. Banished from the commissary, Agee now took his meals alone.

At the end of October a second heart attack brought this ignominious period of his life to an end. He spent ten days in a Los Angeles hospital, "hellishly bored" but unrepentant. The doctors had warned him that if he did not modify his habits he would ruin his health, but Agee was too dependent on alcohol, in particular, to listen. To a large extent, drinking had become his reason for being; he arranged his life around the getting and consuming of liquor, and he could not imagine how he would survive without it.

As before, Mia and the children came to visit him in the hospital, but this time she was determined to stay in California to keep an eye on her husband. She knew he was a very sick man and incapable of taking care of himself, though he would never have admitted the fact. The appearance of Teresa at his bedside on her fifth birthday, November 7, gave him some reason to hope that he might reform himself. He called the day "St. Teresa's Day" in her honor, and wrote to Father Flye, "She really isn't a saint but she is much nicer company than I can suppose most saints would be." Later in the letter, Agee sought to hide the seriousness of his condition from both the priest and himself.

> This hasn't been at all a severe attack; I'll presumably be out of the hospital by this Saturday or Sunday. But to have to return to the hospital within so few months and after so slight an occlusion as last winter's, does begin to bear in on me. Just the things you say of it—the possible difference between 40 more years to live, and 5, and that this in every visible controllable way, anyhow, is up to me. I wish I could take it a good deal more seriously, though. Several things seem to prevent this. One is my continuing sense that if I smoke, for instance, really very moderately, I'll get away with it. Another is the whole habit of physical self-indulgence. . . . Another is in some way caring much too little whether I live or die.

Let the doctors prescribe their low-fat, 1,200-calorie-a-day diet; he would continue "fiercely to enjoy what I eat." Fruits, he complained, "bore me sick." Salads "leave me cold." He much preferred to eat high-cholesterol cheese. "I abominate health foods," he declared. And as for fish, "Between Fridays and the Coast of Maine, I've had enough sea-food to carry me well past the grave." His favored food was steak, prepared in a special way he had learned in California: covered with rock salt and charred over an open flame.

As the days in the hospital passed and Agee returned to his senses, he grew "depressed at being broke and unemployed with no job in sight—unless—which will be my last resort—I go back into *Time,*" he confided to Father Flye. He noted that three years had passed since he quit the magazine, and yet it seemed to him that he had accomplished so very little, merely a novel and some screenplays. Sensing that his agent, Paul Kohner, was losing confidence in him, he switched to another representative in the Kohner organization, Ilse Lahn. Like Mia, she was an Austrian émigrée with a strong protective instinct. She considered herself a good agent because she was a good talker, and she promised to find Agee work, but the prospects were dim. The arrival of television sent the motion-picture industry into a tailspin, and there was little need for free-lancers like Agee.

At this grim impasse, he wallowed in self-pity, a habit Mia had come to loathe. "In another 3 weeks I will advance one more official notch into the forties," ran one characteristic diatribe, "with so little done and much wasted of irretrievable life, rather distinctly behind where I was . . . when I turned 30, when, God knows, I felt things were going bad enough." His entire life struck him as "quietly sad and mildly sickening—like a tinny taste"—the taste of death. "Nearly everything I see or can conceive of is terribly pitiable: I can't suppose I'm an exception," he wailed. "I'd rather pity myself than be pitied by others."

As the stay in the hospital neared its end, Agee's bouts of self-pity lessened. He was almost willing to admit he had become an alcoholic, a realization that is often the first step on the road to recovery. Freed from the dulling effects of drink, his mind once again teemed with projects. Reading Boswell's *London Journal,* he flirted with the idea of keeping his own diary, but he doubted he possessed the discipline to make daily entries. He thought of writing an account of his love affair with Pat. The result, he imagined, would be "a long, anguished love-letter in which the writer analyzes . . . the entire course of a hopelessly unhappy relationship." Against all expectations, Lahn managed to find him work, not in stagnant Hollywood, but abroad. Agee agreed to write the narration and dialogue for a Filipino movie about Genghis Khan, to be directed by one Emmanuel Conde. Though the job was nothing on the order of *The African Queen,* it was enough to raise his morale.

By the time Agee was well enough to leave the hospital, Mia had found a house with the help of another of her husband's college friends, Bernard Schoenfeld. After his rapid rise as a playwright, Schoenfeld had switched to film, with less spectacular results. However, he remained as professional in his work and as feisty in person as ever. Hearing of Agee's need of a home, he recommended Mia look at a property near his. Located at 18716 Topanga Beach Road in Malibu, it was a large, two-bedroom clapboard structure with a fenced-in sandlot in the back. Despite its glamorous-sounding address, the house resembled a simple shack on the beach. Finding it to her liking, Mia rented it, and Agee joined her and the children there in late November.

Although they now inhabited a new and very different kind of home from the apartment they shared in New York, they retained their bohemian domestic habits. Neither Agee nor Mia had the slightest interest in housekeeping. Dust and magazines accumulated on the floors; dirty diapers and dishes filled the sink. With all the chairs hidden beneath piles of clothing, guests sat on the floor. Unsold copies of Agee's book of poems, *Permit Me Voyage,* sent by Yale University, rotted away in the heat and humidity—a poignant emblem of the decay of his youthful aspirations.

With Mia in attendance, Agee's erratic life regained a semblance of normality—except for his continued pursuit of Pat. Learning that he was now living with his family, the hapless young woman determined to make a clean break. After bidding him farewell, she drove with her twin brother, a medical student, to San Francisco, where she kept an apartment. With each passing mile she grew increasingly grim. It was in this downcast state that she opened the door to her apartment to find Agee waiting for her. While she had been driving north, he had impulsively caught the first plane to San Francisco in order to be with her. "Let's go out on the town and have a wonderful time," he announced. And so they did, spending the night hopping from one jazz spot to the next, mad with gaiety. It was obvious to all concerned that Agee would no more give up Pat than he would cigarettes and alcohol.

In his flamboyant pursuit of pleasure, no matter how destructive its effects, Agee seemed to be determined to reverse Flaubert's classic dictum on the way an artist should conduct his life: "Be regular and orderly . . . like a bourgeois, so that you may be violent and original in your work." To Agee, his life was his art, and on this basis he felt justified in going to extremes in it. But where his life threatened to veer out of control at any moment, his work—what little there was of it at this time—became ever more conservative and traditional in form and content. For example, several weeks after the San Francisco escapade, Ilse Lahn landed her client his first domestic screenwriting assignment since *The African Queen:* an adaptation of another Stephen Crane story, "The Bride Comes to Yellow Sky." The plot concerned a newlywed couple. The man, Jed Potter, is the marshal of Yellow Sky, Texas; his bride hails from San Antonio. The day they arrive in town, the local villain, Scratchy Wilson, goes on a rampage, getting drunk and shooting up the town. When he confronts the marshal, who is both unarmed and accompanied by his wife, Scratchy realizes he has been defeated by decorum and leaves town of his own volition. It was a nice story, but even Agee realized how slight it was.

As with Agee's earlier Crane adaptation, Huntington Hartford was the producer. He arranged to release *The Bride Comes to Yellow Sky* as a short feature making up part of a double bill. Despite the movie's modest status, Agee gladly accepted the assignment, but Mia had her doubts. At the time, Hartford sponsored a screenwriters' retreat notorious for its hazardous driveway, which posed a particular danger to hard-drinking writers trying to demonstrate that they could negotiate its twists and turns while under the influence. Mia feared her husband would crash if he availed himself of its facilities, and Agee worked on the script primarily in their Malibu home.

He turned out the adaptation with a minimum of fuss and bother, applying screenwriting lessons he had learned at Huston's knee. Gone were the pretentious visual minutiae of old. He kept his scenes moving at a fast, not to say frantic, pace, in the process creating a first-class piece of screenwriting. He did take one noteworthy liberty, however, by adding a character of his own invention. He called the fellow Frank Gudger, and it was the third time he had employed the name. The first had been in a short story dating back to Exeter, the second in *Let Us Now Praise Famous Men;* the latest Gudger was the town drunk, a likable man who let himself in and out of jail at will. He was entirely harmless to anyone but himself and an acute observer of events taking place around him. So closely did the writer identify with the drunk that he prevailed on Hartford to permit him to play the small role when the script was filmed.

This personal touch, at once charming and deadly earnest, was new evidence of the commitment and originality he endeavored to bring to all his writing, even when the project at hand was beneath his gifts. He threw himself into movies with a seriousness and ferocity that astonished his screenwriter colleagues, who wrote primarily for the money, not personal satisfaction. He was incapable of tossing off a hack screenplay, even to extricate himself from debt, or of feeling cynical about the routine artistic humiliations of the life of a Hollywood scriptwriter. During his prolonged stay in California, his view of the movies had changed. No longer did he regard them as a lucrative subsidy for the novels he wished to write;

they were an end in themselves, and a very worthy end at that. Screenwriting, he believed, was *the* literary art of the future. In comparison, novels were a quaint anachronism.

Among those who heard Agee expound such theories, Schoenfeld, for one, was irritated that "my dear friend who had once seriously hoped to emulate Joyce should now wish to write for a medium that, from my broad experience, depended not on inner voyage, or discipline or loneliness, but rather on social alliances, collaboration and budgets." To which Agee would have replied that he was not interested in being consistent, only in making the most of the opportunities that came his way. For example, once he had mastered the art of the screenplay, he would move on to directing, exactly as his hero Huston had. How he would find the time to complete *A Death in the Family* while directing he did not know. In his attempt to excel at a variety of forms—poetry, journalism, fiction, film—Agee was truly a maverick among writers of his generation. Most others specialized in a single genre, or became known for their accomplishments in one, even if they had tried others from time to time. But Agee was unclassifiable, neither fish nor fowl. In some circles he was known primarily as a distinguished film reviewer; in others, an inspired journalist. His college friends persisted in seeing him as a poet gone wrong. The wonder of Agee's multifaceted career was that he managed to make a noteworthy contribution in each medium he tried, with the exception of poetry.

By nurturing multiple ambitions he spread himself dangerously thin, but he remained among the most gifted and daring writers of his day. Approaching his mid-forties, he was of an age when other prominent American writers had burned out. But no matter how much Agee abused himself or his gift, he never ceased to improve as a writer. It was as though his talent had a life of its own and continued to grow over the years, independent of the often irrational demands he made on it.

Now that his family had joined him in California, Agee established a life on the West Coast that was separate but equal to his life in New York. He relished dining regularly at the Chaplins with Mia —usually on Thursdays, the servants' night off. He took great pleasure in playing tennis whenever he liked—in defiance of doctor's orders. And he continued to spend hedonistic weekends in San Francisco with Pat.

By the end of 1951 he had become accepted by the principal Hollywood salon of the era. It was run by the doyenne of show business society, Salka Viertel, a close friend of Greta Garbo and a former screenwriter. (She was, incidentally, the mother of Peter Viertel, who had helped Huston finish the script of *The African Queen* in Agee's absence.) Nearly every expatriate or intellectual of repute in Los Angeles found his or her way to one of Salka's Sunday brunches: Elsa Lanchester and her husband, Charles Laughton; Bertolt Brecht; Aldous Huxley; Arnold Schoenberg; and Christopher Isherwood, to name but a few. They were, many of them, the spoiled children of Hollywood, in the thrall of a medium that they all (with the exception of Agee) treated with the utmost condescension. They were essentially serious-minded people adrift in a baffling New World that valued play more than work, money more than honor. Agee thought them all geniuses, and he was delighted to take a pleasant, one-way trip to oblivion amid such stimulating company.

He took an instant liking to Isherwood, in particular, assuring the English writer that his homosexuality should pose no obstacle to their friendship. Isherwood found Agee's repeated declarations in this regard annoying and unnecessary but liked Agee nonetheless. Another English writer with whom Agee became acquainted was Ivan Moffat. Born in Cuba, Moffat's mother was Iris Tree, a member of a prominent English dramatic family and a society figure in her own right. After attending the London School of Economics, Moffat had worked his way into the British and later the American motion-picture industry. At the time they met, he was writing the script of the Hollywood spectacular of the moment, a screen version of Edna Ferber's sprawling novel *Giant.* Later they often socialized at Iris Tree's Santa Monica home, which was perched above a picturesque pier equipped with a carousel whose music filled the air. As the keenly observant Moffat recalled years later, Agee displayed a charming and generous nature.

> He had a wonderful sense of laughter—at himself and at all the people around him. And he possessed an extraordinary spontaneity in the reception of someone else's idea. It was as if before you had completed it, he had understood it, with a gasp

of pleasure, recognition, and sympathy, and changed it and given it back to you in a more benign form. . . .

He was a man of girth and size, a biggish man who seemed to occupy an even bigger space: big shoulders, bulging stomach, rolled up sleeves, sometimes a jacket, seldom a tie. He exulted in friendships and would place himself totally at the disposal of anyone in a state of tension or distress. There was something in this voluble and generous personality that nevertheless had an ambiguity about it, as if he was misplaced, androgynous, elusive.

Agee soon had occasion to demonstrate his generosity to Moffat. As the two walked along the beach in Santa Monica, Agee proposed going to a bar for a drink. Having no money on him, Moffat asked, "Jim, you couldn't lend me a five or ten, could you?"

Agee replied, uncharacteristically, it seemed, "I couldn't possibly have this back by Tuesday, could I?" Whereupon he pulled out a wad and peeled off not five but five hundred dollars, a fortune to the young Moffat, who hastened to explain that he needed only a fraction of the amount. To Moffat, the gesture epitomized Agee's "clumsy gallantry."

The English screenwriter marveled as well at Agee's capacity for alcohol, heart attack or not. Often he would "pour and swiftly consume a triple Scotch as an afterthought to a long night's drinking." As a result, what seemed to Moffat to be an unmistakable air of dissipation hovered about Agee; in fact, he looked like an unfrocked priest, his face unnaturally white with the talcum powder he applied after shaving. Agee ascribed this pallor not to talcum powder or drinking but to sex. "Even with someone you love to make love with most," he explained, "there's such a thing as fucking too much. Not physically but morally. Doing it too much depletes the both of you—wrings you out." At that moment, he reminded Moffat of the Byron who wrote:

> For the sword outwears its sheath,
> And the heart wears out the breast.

As for the hard-pressed wife of this latter-day Byron, Moffat thought Mia "rather beautiful, like a broken statue." Her reserve and slow rhythms contrasted sharply with Agee's constant animation and excess. Moffat discovered that Agee was in a constant state of anxiety over her unspoken disapproval of his antics, for which he assumed full responsibility while acknowledging he was incapable of changing his ways. If he did, he explained, he might live longer, but then he risked becoming the kind of prissy, rigid personality he detested. Better a sick artist than a healthy eunuch.

Walking the beach at Santa Monica with Moffat or other friends had a restorative effect on Agee. Beside it, he forgot about the jaded children of Paradise with whom he associated and rediscovered his inner voice. Schoenfeld had given up hope that Agee would ever return to serious writing until one night when they trod the warm sand together. "Over the screech of gulls and the fizz of the surf, he began to talk hopefully, challengingly, like a call in the darkness," Schoenfeld remembered. "It was startling to me, aware of his poor health and weariness, that, seemingly oblivious to weeks of waste, he could speak as sharp as the salty air. It was as if his innocence was never sullied." Agee talked about his novel-in-progress, *A Death in the Family,* work of an entirely different order from trivial screenplays. Although he had no sense of writing a great, significant, or even popular novel, Schoenfeld realized the book's importance would far exceed that of *The Morning Watch*—if Agee lived to finish it.

16

SAINTS

The African Queen opened in February 1952 to instant critical acclaim and popular success. Reviewers took a shine to Huston's sense of playfulness—a welcome departure from the director's recent turgid efforts—and to the tongue-in-cheek performances of Bogart and Hepburn, whose hijinks drew endless chuckles from the audience. The movie, in short, was a crowd pleaser. No one claimed the hastily contrived ending made much sense, but the film's general gaiety triumphed over its shortcomings.

The African Queen garnered three Oscar nominations: best picture, best actor (Humphrey Bogart), and, most important from Agee's point of view, best screenplay. While only Bogart actually won an Academy Award, the nominations, together with the picture's commercial success, caused Agee's reputation as a screen-writer to soar. Only four months before, he had been in the hospital, broke, and out of work. Now new offers flooded him and forced him to make agonizing decisions about what to do next. The period of doubt came to an end in March, when he received a telephone call from his Harvard roommate, Robert Saudek.

In the twenty years that had elapsed since he had seen Agee lope across the Eliot House courtyard, Saudek had become a television producer of considerable distinction. He began his career in broadcasting with the country's first radio station, KDKA, in Pittsburgh, and for a number of years had been a vice-president for public affairs of the Blue Network, predecessor of the American Broadcasting Company. At the time he telephoned Agee, he was in the midst of organizing a new and, by the rather conservative standards of television, daring series called "Omnibus," devoted to presenting the best cultural events and artifacts he could find. The framework of "Omnibus" was so loose and all-encompassing that even Agee, who regarded the advent of the medium with fear and loathing, approved. Almost anything was grist to the "Omnibus" mill, as long as it was in some way distinguished; the program made few concessions to mass taste. To survive in the highly commercial atmosphere of network television, it was produced not by a network but by the Radio and Television Workshop of the Ford Foundation. To signal its high-mindedness, the host was the British Broadcasting Corporation's American correspondent, Alistair Cooke. The series did operate under one handicap, however. CBS scheduled it in a time slot normally considered suicidal: Sunday afternoon. But "Omnibus" was to confound the experts and make its time period surprisingly popular.

When casting about for intriguing material to include in the series' first season, Saudek remembered well his late-night discussions with Agee about Abraham Lincoln. Over the phone, he made his pitch. Would Agee be interested in writing a five-part series about Lincoln's early years for "Omnibus"? Given his lifelong fascination with Lincoln, Agee instantly committed himself to the project. Since he was, by now, a reputable screenwriter, Saudek arranged generous financial terms, especially by the standards of "Omnibus." On April 22, Agee signed a contract specifying that he would receive $1,200 for each of the five half-hour scripts, in addition to $1,000 for a rewrite and a $250-a-week consultation fee.

From the outset, Agee decided that his Lincoln would be a poet's Lincoln, not a historian's. As his primary source of biographical information, he turned to the first volume of Carl Sandburg's majestic but suspect work on the subject, *Abraham Lincoln: The Prairie Years.* In particular, Agee wished to explore the tricky subject of Lincoln's relationship with women. He had heard of a supposed romance between the president-to-be and a young woman named Ann Rutledge. Scholars were inclined to regard the matter as myth, but Agee took it at face value.

In addition to his highly personal approach to the material, Agee had specific notions about the production itself. He demanded location shooting whenever possible. Even though his story contained a certain amount of fabrication, he wanted the actual places Lincoln had lived in and visited to serve as settings. And he had an actor in mind for the leading role, Royal Dano. The tall, gangly young man had been prominently featured in Huston's *Red Badge of Courage,* and Agee had been struck by his wide-set, sympathetic eyes. Finally, he chose to write a part for himself, once again as an alcoholic who comments perceptively on events.

Agee devoted most of his working hours in 1952 to the five Lincoln scripts, taking time out solely to write narration for a French documentary *White Mane,* directed by Albert Lamorisse. He began work in Malibu in the spring and continued in New York when he returned in the summer with Mia and the children. The abrupt change in his place of residence took a heavy toll. In his weakened condition, he found the five-flight climb to his Bleecker Street apartment hellishly difficult. At the suggestion of a doctor, Mia began looking for a house with few stairs and enough space to hold their family.

Agee badly missed California, its eternal sunshine, his glamorous friends, and, of course, Pat. He stayed away from most of his *Time* colleagues and literary acquaintances. They now belonged to a different world. One of the few friends he did see, however, was Whittaker Chambers, who was staying in a hotel in the city. A survivor of several recent heart attacks himself, Chambers was shocked to see how Agee had deteriorated over the last four years.

They walked along Fifth Avenue an inch at a time, the fastest pace Agee could manage. When they stopped before a store window filled with extravagantly dressed mannequins, Agee snorted, "It's a pansy's world." Chambers knew that his revered friend did not have long to live. Later, at home, he imagined Agee walking toward him, clutching his stomach in pain, then laughing it off.

Despite his failing health, Agee did a superb job with the Lincoln scripts, turning what might have been a civics lesson into a rhapsodic evocation of nineteenth-century America. His vision of Lincoln was undeniably sentimental, portraying him as a great, tragically flawed national hero who had accomplished his mission at the price, ultimately, of his life. To Agee, Lincoln was a modern saint; therefore, he portrayed Lincoln in moral and religious terms rather than psychological ones. Nuances yielded to bold emblems of good and evil, sin and virtue. He had written hagiography of the highest order, but hagiography nonetheless.

The opening sequences revealed Agee at his most inspired. In a brief tableau, the assassinated president breathes his last and is pronounced dead. Then the narrator, Martin Gabel, reads one of Agee's favorite poems, Whitman's "When Lilacs Last in the Dooryard Bloom'd." Whitman wrote of Lincoln's funeral train crossing "the large unconscious scenery of my land," and trains had always been a powerful symbol for Agee as well, ever since the days he had watched them leave the L&N depot in Knoxville. Thus his screenplay featured the funeral train chugging in cadence with Whitman's verse. At one point, a boy, intended to represent the young Agee, if he had lived in Lincoln's time, chases the train as it moves relentlessly through fields and towns. Even more than the imagery, the rhythm of the shots gave the sequence a hypnotic power. Agee made a studied and successful attempt to revive D. W. Griffith's method of dramatizing events embedded in the national unconscious, a category to which Lincoln's funeral train undoubtedly belonged.

After this captivating opening, the story flashed back to Lincoln's birth. Not much is known of actual events, and Agee chose to portray the birth Tennessee style, that is to say, with the savagery of his youthful poem "Ann Garner." Again, he sought to fuse two disparate forms, the screenplay and the poem.

NARRATOR. *(O.S.)* One hard night in February, 1809, they
   looked down on a little cabin in a fold of
   the Kentucky hills; and they saw how it all began:
   a very humble and obscure event; as ordinary as
   death. . . .

   CUT TO: CLOSE SHOT. *(Past the opaque rawhide window; past
   the shut door of ax-hewn planks with rawhide latchstring; and
   along black clay-chinked logs to an extreme close shot of a broken
   chink which lets through weak, shaky light.)* . . .

MIDWIFE. *(Almost crooning; also straining in sympathy.)* Bear
   down, honey; bear down, bear down, me lady . . . *(With
   sudden terrifying intensity.)* Bring him now!

At this point, Agee specified that the camera lunge toward the bed,
then drop *"as a primitive ploughshare, grating on the floor, is thrust
violently beneath the foot of the bed."* This graphic display of mountain
folkways caused concern at CBS, where an executive overseeing
the program, Hubbell Robinson, demanded it be excised. It was.

After the birth, the story skipped ahead to Lincoln's boyhood, emphasizing its bucolic simplicity, and came to rest in
1831, when the twenty-two-year-old Lincoln arrived in New
Salem, Illinois. One hundred and twenty-one years later, the
"Omnibus" film crew descended on the town and drafted local
citizens, some of them descendants of figures in the script, into
minor speaking roles. At this point in the story, Agee went to
considerable lengths to dramatize the presumed romance between
Ann Rutledge and the ambitious young politician Abe Lincoln.
Soon a conflict develops, for Ann wants Abe to remain in New
Salem and marry her, while he feels driven to move on to bigger
and better things. Surely his destiny cannot lie here, in this tiny
wilderness hamlet.

Agee now made his appearance in the story as Jack Kelso, a
mild-mannered, hard-drinking local given to quoting Shakespeare
beside a fishing hole. Abandoning all pretense of historical accuracy, the plot has Kelso meeting Lincoln; the two establish a rapport, and their conversation contains thinly disguised references to
what Agee thought of those who would try to stop him from
drinking.

KELSO. I can't make you out, Abe. You're the only temperance
man I can stand the sight of.

ABE. I'm not a temperance man. I just don't drink.

KELSO. You go to temperance meetings.

ABE. I sort of like people that take a thing so much to heart.

KELSO. A lot of busy bodies.

Whereupon Kelso takes to reciting Shakespeare, while Lincoln
watches in fascination. In the next scene, Lincoln comes to the
defense of drunks at a town meeting. "A drinkin' man compares
favorably with a teetotaler," he declares. And later in the story he
muses, "You know, Jack Kelso thinks what I really am is a poet."

In subsequent episodes Lincoln becomes ever more deeply
attached to the lovely Ann (played by Joanne Woodward). The
climax comes with Ann's fatal illness, over which Agee lingered
with inordinate fondness. The script specifies that the dying woman
has a "fierce, unearthly beauty" that she lacked when healthy. In
the very last scene of the series, Lincoln, riding a horse, slowly
passes the headstone of Ann's grave. Eventually he wanders out of
sight and into history.

This was a Lincoln in Agee's image. The writer stressed his
hero's warmth and sympathy, his perseverance and humility. At the
same time, Agee used the device of the romance with Ann Rutledge to establish Lincoln's ruthlessness. The story implied that in
order to accomplish anything of note, a man had to sacrifice whatever was dearest to him. Implicitly, Agee justified his flagrant infi-
delity on the same grounds; he believed his philandering necessary
to his growth as an artist. Like Lincoln, he had a higher destiny to
fulfill than was permitted under conventional codes of behavior.
They were both poets, one of action, the other in language.

In October, with the script finished, Agee joined the "Omnibus" crew in Illinois to film the scenes in which he appeared as
Kelso. To play the role he donned a fake mustache and rumpled
clothes. On paper, Kelso came off as a fire-breathing poet, but as
Agee played him, he was a sad, brooding drunk whose words had
no sting.

On returning to New York, Agee made a determined effort

to break the vicious cycle of dependence on alcohol and tobacco. "I'm staying short of any severe drunkenness and have brought cigarets down to about 8–9 a day," he reported to Father Flye, but he found that alcohol, "of itself relatively harmless, multiplied by 5 my craving for tobacco, and by roughly the same ratio, lessens my power of resisting temptation." Temptation was all the harder to resist because he suffered bouts of anxiety over the reception of his daring Lincoln scripts. Months of work on them had left him exhausted and "heartsick about my effort on this job, its possibilities, its failures . . . and, as I feel, my nearly ended life." Depression cast its shadow over every waking moment. He had no desire to see old friends, "let alone make new ones." Left to his own devices, he sought solace in more work, more alcohol. He despaired of ever finding his way back to health.

On November 16, "Abraham Lincoln—The Early Years," began running on "Omnibus," appearing every other week until February 8, 1953. From the first, the series elicited a positive response from viewers and critics alike. Although each of the five installments had its peaks and valleys, Agee demonstrated his mastery of the episodic format. The storyline's suspense, however fanciful, worked its habitual magic. Even *Variety* applauded this "superb vidpic." The publication commented, "It was a piece of pure film poetry. . . . The shooting of [the] 'Lonesome train' passing through the countryside, through fields of grain and grieving citizens, used all the resources of the camera to make the train itself come alive."

But one influential voice clamored in protest. The respected historian Allan Nevins of Columbia University took strenuous exception to Agee's flagrant abuse of poetic license. "Omnibus" 's Lincoln, Nevins believed, bore slight resemblance to the actual man and could cause widespread harm to Lincoln's reputation with its willfully distorted view. In response to the complaint, Saudek arranged a debate between Nevins and Agee to take place on the "Omnibus" of March 29.

The occasion marked Agee's first appearance on television. The camera was cruelly revealing of his fragile condition at the time. He was obviously nervous, chain-smoking, and cowed by Nevins' crusty professorial manner. Of Agee's portrayal of Lincoln's purported love affair with Ann Rutledge, Nevins declared,

"He has tampered with the truth. He has taken a myth . . . and presented it to a great American audience as if it were verified truth." As Nevins fulminated against him, Agee, wearing a somber suit, writhed uncomfortably in his chair and occasionally gazed upward, as if imploring a Superior Being—the producer, perhaps —to come to his rescue.

At last it was his turn to speak. Swallowing his words, he began with this proposition: "It has been definitely proved that there is no Santa Claus, but of course there is a Santa Claus. There are two kinds of truths." Gaining confidence, he described his vision of Lincoln, a "very young, very poor, and very gifted man" in the awkward position of realizing "the size of his vocation and his immense responsibility towards it." Nevins would have none of it and continued to attack while Agee retreated into dignified silence. In the end, he pleaded "entirely guilty" to the charge of inventing aspects of Lincoln's early life. The confrontation left him shaken. His voice shriveled to a whisper, tears filled his eyes, and he appeared pathetically vulnerable to Nevins' taunts. Saudek paid Agee $500 for the appearance.

By the time of the debate, Agee's physical condition had taken another turn for the worse. To combat Agee's myriad dependencies, Father Flye proposed that the two of them enter a Trappist monastery in Kentucky, where they would neither smoke nor drink nor even talk. "I think it is a fine and may be even an inspired idea, and I hope and in a degree pray, that we will do it," Agee wrote the priest, but privately he conceded that the regimen would amount to hell on earth for him. At the last minute he reluctantly refused the invitation.

Other friends suggested he reenter some form of psychoanalysis, but Agee adamantly rejected the "prevailing puritanical fanaticism of most modern Psychotherapists—the idea that the patient must *face everything.*" By *"everything,"* Agee meant his affair with Pat. First the doctors would be telling him not to drink; then they would be telling him not to have sex. The thought was intolerable. To friends he scored off Freud as a "dirty masturbator" spouting nonsense about penis envy and castration complexes. He would not be emasculated by psychiatry.

In his agitation, he drank ever more heavily and openly. No

longer was he ashamed to be an alcoholic; he adopted a belligerent attitude toward those who commented on his consumption. He boasted that he spent $3,000 a year on liquor at home, not including the money he drank away in bars and restaurants. And when he met another inebriated writer, Dylan Thomas, at a New York cocktail party, he shocked those in attendance by plying the Welsh poet with alcohol. There were many things these two literary confreres might have said to each other. The conversation might have turned to Thomas' prophetic utterance, "After the first death, there is no other." They might have gone on about poetry and rebellion and all manner of important topics, but Agee was drunk and determined that Thomas join him in that condition.

Abruptly, Agee abandoned his defiant attitude in February, submitting to a complete physical examination by a Dr. Arthur Sutherland. On seeing the results, the physician ordered Agee to Memorial Hospital (now Memorial Sloan-Kettering Cancer Center) on York Avenue for rest and observation. The patient quickly turned the occasion into a literary workshop. Given the run of the hospital by Dr. Sutherland, he befriended and interviewed patients and nurses about the ordeal of terminal illness, especially cancer. He found their experiences so interesting that he planned to write a movie on the subject, but after his release he forgot all about the provocative idea.

Home again, he wrote to Father Flye on February 12 to ease the priest's concern.

> I learned in the hospital that I am in good general health, but that my liver is more of a hazard than my heart. The liver condition is not bad—slow on detoxication and on converting cholesterol into cholesterol esters, if you follow me (I don't) —and is regarded as reversible. . . . I am to drink a minimal 2 highballs per day, and must absorb huge quantities (you may be happy to hear) of brewers yeast, and of various vitamins— mainly variants of B; about 4 times the normal dosage of vitamins.

All this attention to his body's chemistry struck Agee as mildly amusing and vaguely effeminate. The truth was, he continued, "I am by now much more deeply addicted to alcohol than at any time

I can remember. Yes, I am supposed to drink 2 drinks a day at most, but I have yet to succeed in that, except maybe once every 3 or 4 days. The effects of sobriety are intoxicatingly rewarding, but that is beside the point."

Chief among the rewards was a compelling new idea for a novel or screenplay—he was not sure which. In either case, it would be a "story about love, the way it really happens." In the manner of his other "fiction," the story would tell, with absolute faithfulness to the facts, of his breakup with Via, pursuit of Alma, and eventual marriage to Mia. Initially he envisioned the tale as a merry bed-hopping farce. He chose the sardonic title *Bigger Than We Are,* intended to refer to the irresistible power of love, or what Agee casually called his "cunt troubles."

Working on the story during the late winter, he realized the events he discussed were, in fact, no laughing matter. He became so involved with re-creating his romantic quandaries that he discovered anew his passion for Alma. No one had ever excited him quite the same way as his second wife, not even Pat. Deep in his cups, he wrote one love letter after another to Alma, never mailed. On the evening of March 20, his friend Helen Levitt happened to show him a photograph she had taken fourteen years earlier at Monk's Farm in New Jersey, where Agee and Alma had lived while he was struggling to complete *Let Us Now Praise Famous Men.* Overcome with emotion, Agee wrote that night to Alma to describe how, on seeing the photograph, "fourteen years dropped out from under me, and I knew just where we were then, and where we really belong, and where we always ought to." He continued:

> I am still in love with you, Alma. This is different from adding, "I always will be." I don't know or care whether I always will be—but I know I still am—and after all this time, and all the things between, that means a terrible amount to me. Whether it means that I would break up my life with Mia and two children (any more than you might with Bodo and Joel and Stefan [another son, whom she had had with Bodo]) I don't know. I at least have learned, since I last knew you, that life can get too thick to solve. But I do know that that question is as powerful in my life as anything I know: whether you and I can ever live again as man and woman. . . .

Alma—I have two children. I love them both, very dearly.
I also love their mother, very dearly. Since knowing you, I
have also fallen in love, once, very hard, with an Irish girl [Pat
Scallon] who possibly moved me even more, sexually, than
you did. But the more I know of everything, the more I know
. . . how hopeless my life is, compared with life with you. I gave
the Irish girl up, for the sake of everything I feel about Mia and
our children. I at least believe I might give everything else up,
to be with you again. . . .

I know you were my natural wife, forever—and I believe
I was your natural husband. And seeing this . . . snapshot
. . . I knew it again, instantaneously. Just seeing your face, I
knew both things: "I love this girl" and "you are my wife"—
and—"we should have so many children."

Oh, come back to me, my beloved.

This letter Agee intended to mail, but he lacked Alma's current
address. The words, along with their powerful implications, remained hidden in his desk drawer, away from Mia's eyes.

Unable to reclaim, or find, Alma, Agee displayed an alarming
willingness to initiate an affair with someone nearby. He soon
became involved with a new woman whose name he dared not
mention to anyone. As he explained in a letter to Schoenfeld,
written October 18, "the girl too is married & a mother, so that in
our quiet way we had hoped to preside in privacy and what pleasure
we could milk out of it, over what we inevitably knew to be our
own deathbed rites."

By the time Agee wrote, Mia had gotten wind of the affair, and
he faced yet another domestic crisis. "It is bringing her to perhaps
the ultimate showdown of her life," Agee confided to Schoenfeld,
"and that in turn is raising hell with me. . . . So round the dizzy
whirl we go." Unlike his affairs with Alma and Pat, Agee remained
cynical about the prospect of achieving true romantic happiness this
time. He had been this way once too often to grow more than
moderately alarmed at the emotional chaos he created. He joked
with friends that around home he had become known as "Old
Unfaithful."

In a more reflective mood, Agee surmised that a sense of
impending death drove him to grasp at what slender straws of
pleasure he might find. "I'm the kind of man who evidently always

needs 2 women of opposite kinds," he speculated. "Mia is the kind of woman (is there any other kind) who, equally as a matter of life & death, needs one man who needs just *one* woman." As a result of this incompatibility, Agee found himself in a perpetual state of "pain, disgust, despair, a sense of the needlessness and foolishness of getting so wrought up . . . over what peg fits in what hole."

Drinking only aggravated the problem by dulling his judgment. "You can imagine what kind of alcoholic I've become," he admitted to Schoenfeld, and went on to sketch a pathetic self-portrait.

> Nearly all the time, I am incompetent for work, or for thinking of work, or of anything except crawling around in a whiskey-logged blur, clarified only occasionally by the rare moments during which Mia and I reach understanding (a different matter from agreement) or the girl and I climb out of our misery sufficiently to know what we have got and what we have got to lose.

Even while his personal life disintegrated beyond recovery, his screenwriting career continued to prosper. In January 1953 RKO released *The Bride Comes to Yellow Sky* as the bottom half of a double bill topped by an adaptation of Joseph Conrad's "The Secret Sharer." Agee's straightforward screenplay earned high critical marks. "The barbed pungency that flavors every minute of 'The Bride Comes to Yellow Sky' . . . must be attributed largely to James Agee who, in transcribing a group of village diehards, clearly enjoyed the time of his life," said the *New York Times*. Agee's performance as the town drunk was every bit as confident and fluent as those of the leads, Robert Preston and Marjorie Steele. Slim and trim at the time of the shooting, he radiated star quality on the screen; his blue eyes flashed as he recited his lines in a resonant voice. Even Agee was pleasantly surprised by his acting ability, and he decided to continue writing roles for himself in his screenplays.

In March another important opportunity came Agee's way when Huston asked him to write a screen version of Herman Melville's *Moby Dick*. The task of bringing the long and intricate novel to the screen was just the sort of assignment that challenged Agee to outdo himself. He badly wanted to accept the assignment, but he had previously committed himself to another project for the Filipino director Emmanuel Conde, with whom he had worked briefly. But the new project Conde had in mind was vague; at one point Agee described it as "one of the most insanely large spectacular spectacles that you could ever imagine," with a budget of at least $3 million. It was to be shot on location in the Philippines, and Agee himself would both write and direct it. He dickered with Conde over the precise nature of the movie for months, yet by September plans were no further along than they had been in March.

In the meantime Huston took offense at Agee's refusal to commit himself to *Moby Dick*. Far better than the writer, Huston knew the difficulties of getting a film off the ground, and he considered Agee foolish to trust the evasive Conde. To entice Agee to work with him, Huston dangled the prospect of weeks of luxurious living in Ireland and the south of France, Mia and the children included. But, to the keen disappointment of both Huston and his wife, Agee insisted that he had a prior arrangement with Conde, and though it was merely a verbal one, a gentleman's word was his honor. Relations between Huston and Agee cooled, and the director began looking for another, more responsive collaborator. Months later, Agee realized he had made a dreadful mistake in casting his lot with Conde. He wrote to Huston to apologize for his disloyalty. "I knew it was the job of a lifetime," he said of the *Moby Dick* assignment. "And so I gradually came to realize that that is the one thing which . . . requires getting out of any conflicting commitments. . . . Well, I sweated around trying to be 'honorable' just too damned long; and within literally hours after I made myself sufficiently 'dishonorable,' I learned the Moby Dick job was lost." Worse than that, Agee had lost the chance to make the movie with Conde as well. "Now the place you're supposed to laugh is here: Within weeks . . . the project to which I was committed collapsed with nary a word from Conde. So much for that kind of Honor."

In fact, honor had not been Agee's prime motivation for turning down Huston's offer. The truth was that a third project had captured his attention. On April 2 he signed a contract to write a screenplay about the life of Paul Gauguin, the French Impressionist. Under the terms of the agreement, Agee received a modest recompense: $4,000 for the first draft, $3,000 for the rewrite.

However, he was willing to undertake it because he believed that he, the screenwriter, would be the driving force rather than a well-known director.

The choice of topic was, to say the least, curious. However, to a limited extent Agee identified with Gauguin as a rebellious romantic artist, and after reading up on the subject, Agee decided to portray Gauguin "not as the criminal romantic he's often set up to be, but as a man whose vocation was like a lure set out by God." Reflecting his own disillusionment, Agee supposed that Gauguin spent his entire life in art only to find it "was not the real thing, even, but only a lure . . . to teach him . . . to be as absolutely faithful to his own soul and being as he could, and he would find the price of that as he went along."

Agee wrote himself into the script, but this time he would portray not an alcoholic but a priest, Pastor Vernier. As Agee conceived him, the clergyman was a "tall, rather intelligent, melancholic man" given to intoning the film's message in a heavy-handed fashion. In a prologue depicting the death of the artist, Vernier proclaims, "He makes me think of Christ." Pressed to explain, he says that in death Gauguin has the appearance of "a man who has endured great suffering, with great courage, for a great purpose; and who has won a great victory. . . . And that's the one thing nobody can take away from him, ever, whether in heaven or hell." As if the lines were not stiff enough as they were, Agee planned to deliver them with a French accent.

The prologue set the tone for the rest of this heavy-handed exercise. Throughout, a scarcely believable Gauguin delivers saintly edicts on the role of the artist ("Civilization nauseates me. To make it a little better is only to make it a little worse. All I want is to be free of it") while his friend Vincent van Gogh gushes in admiration ("You're so much I've never been . . . never could be"). Attempting to combine an attack on society with pontification about the artist as revolutionary, Agee wound up with an embarrassing apologia for his own shortcomings. He gave the script an awkward title as well, *Noa Noa,* the Tahitian word for fragrance.

Constantly aware of the proximity of death, he acted as though determined to write his epitaph before anyone else got the chance. He seemed hell-bent on living up to his reputation as, in the words of one young admirer, a "whiskey listless and excessive saint." For instance, he added this biblical epigraph to the script: "Except a grain of wheat fall into the ground and die, it abideth alone: but if it die, it bringeth forth much fruit" (John 12: 24). In doing so, he implied that he would never be fully appreciated until after his death. All his life was merely preparation for a great posthumous reputation. The intuition revealed a mixture of self-pity, self-justification, and prophecy.

Seeking to retain the upper hand in the production of this highly personal movie, Agee decided to work with a director he could dominate. He selected the young and relatively inexperienced David Bradley. At thirty-one, Bradley's claim to fame was a 16-millimeter version of *Julius Caesar* he had directed. At his request, Frank Taylor, the producer, arranged a screening of the movie for a number of Hollywood luminaries. "Nothing in the film suggested he was a gifted director," Taylor recalled, but the movie's unknown star, Charlton Heston, made a considerable impact on the audience. Taylor later introduced Bradley to Agee.

In June Agee retreated to Hillsdale, where he added elaborate flourishes to the *Noa Noa* screenplay. At one point he paused to make casting suggestions for Bradley's benefit. While he reserved the role of Vernier for himself, there remained the question of who would play Gauguin: Heston? Anthony Quinn? Michael Redgrave? Marlon Brando? Agee tried and failed to interest any of these actors in the part. He was equally impractical about the crucial matter of financing. When Huntington Hartford expressed interest, Agee wrote Bradley, "Sure, if he wants to put his dough in, fine; but if he wants to mess around in it, to hell with him: he is an exceptionally stupid guy, it seems to me." Hartford withdrew.

The script's burgeoning length posed still more problems. By midsummer, Agee's draft was twice as long as required. "I am of course appalled to realize that I have already exceeded the rule-of-length of a Hollywood script," he explained to Bradley. "On the other hand, I know I go into an excessive and unconventional amount of stage direction; so that playing time is considerably shorter than would be indicated by the page-a-minute convention." Although Agee ruthlessly cut the script's 330 pages to 170, he retained an extravagant funeral sequence depicting the last rites of a Tahitian king. As always, he reserved his greatest literary passion for the subject of death. In this instance, he imagined an editing tour de force welding music, language, and image into a montage inspired by the great Russian silent film epics.

> The funeral sequence is to be cut rigidly to the music of Chopin's funeral march. I will indicate the cuts and shots exactly, but serve warning that without the melody to key it to, it will be hard to read, or to imagine the effectiveness of. I will write out and enclose the melody, as a key; the scoring, and performance, should be those of a French deep provincial military band of the period: rather shrill and squeaky, and not well-played; yet with genuine solemnity.

Thereafter Agee described in detail no less than fifty-eight shots, ending with dirt being shoveled on the coffin of the king. Unfortunately, the scene's grandeur is matched by its self-consciousness. Listening to a native dirge, Agee's Gauguin declares, "If only Beethoven could hear it!" Agee lavished attention on this never-to-be-filmed sequence as if he were rehearsing his own death.

Upon finishing the script, he immediately showed the result to Schoenfeld, who warned that it was "too 'literary' for production." By summer's end, Agee himself lost confidence in the project, confessing, "I can no longer stand to look at it or even to think of it." Nonetheless, he perceived some redeeming virtue in the script; at the very least, it had afforded him personal satisfaction, as he explained to Schoenfeld. "It's incomparably easier to do the 'hardest' kinds of writing—those you can put at least some voting minority of your heart and soul in and therefore half-kill yourself doing your best with—than to do those 'easy' kinds in which you can imagine nothing except your craftsmanship and some few relics of purely technical integrity." As Agee expected, backing for the movie proved elusive, and copies of the script languished unread in the vaults of the movie studios.

In September Agee departed Hillsdale for a new home in New York City. After months of looking, Mia had found a house that fulfilled her requirements: a modest, two-story dwelling at 17 King Street, a brief walk from the Bleecker Street apartment where they had lived for over ten years. Mia liked the neighborhood because it reminded her of an Italian village. Children played in the streets under the watchful eyes of grandparents. Agee took ghoulish pride in the knowledge that the house had been built by Aaron Burr, "who is reputed to have hidden out in it after killing Hamilton."

Soon after moving to King Street he received a letter from Alma, much to his relief, for he had grown concerned about the highly publicized rise of anti-Semitism in East Germany. He wrote her two letters of reply, lost both, but managed to keep the third long enough to mail it at the end of September. He had given up trying to woo Alma back to his side by now and was solely concerned with trying to establish a relationship with Joel. "I thoroughly understand and sympathize, as you do, with Joel's inability to write to someone he scarcely knows; I'm only glad he would even like to," Agee wrote to Alma. "Very much interested, needless to say, to hear that he would like to compose music—and likewise needless to say, as interested in anything about him. Please do send his picture."

As the letter rambled on, Agee inevitably came to dwell on himself. He glossed over the severity of the heart attacks that had "necessitated the ruinously drastic move of buying the house; but, back at the time, the doctor urged as a matter of life & death, that I must climb a minimum of stairs." And he summarized his wildly uneven career as a Hollywood screenwriter.

> If you are choosy about what jobs you accept, it is a great deal of pleasure and interest; but the only reliable security would be to sign a long term contract, which would eliminate or greatly reduce choice. So it isn't really very lucrative, year by year, nor is there time for much non-profit work of my own, so much is consumed in study, thought, & negotiation over new job possibilities. However, I like the work much better than any money-earning work I've done to date, so relatively speaking I feel very lucky.

Since Alma had inquired after the children Agee and Mia had had, their father went on to describe them in a few telling phrases. Teresa he termed "very subtle-minded and gentle," Andrea "very fierce, with murderous red hair." They were both, he said, "the greatest delights in life, and among the greatest pains in the ass." Though he did not tell Alma, Andrea in particular was adept at provoking him. He once went so far as to hit the child, an incident he could neither forgive himself nor forget. When he told a friend of his accidental cruelty, tears filled his eyes, and he wheezed, "Here I am, this great huge creature, threatening this tiny little thing."

In fact, Agee had come to detest his penchant for violent outbursts, no matter what the circumstances. His successor as *Time*'s film critic, Brad Darrach, witnessed a revealing incident in a bar at this time. Learning that the bar was about to close and had stopped serving liquor, Agee impulsively brought his glass down on the table. The glass did not break. Agee tried again, harder, this time smashing it and cutting his hand. Suddenly there was blood all over the table. Bystanders lifted Agee out of his chair and escorted him to the back, where the bartender wrapped the injured hand in a bandage. To Darrach, Agee now seemed a remorseful, overgrown child, as he softly moaned, "Oh, God, I've done it again."

Although he recognized that he lacked self-control, he was determined to prove himself a responsible parent. Acutely aware that he had repeatedly failed Mia as a husband, he sincerely wished to be worthy of their children. By the year's end Mia was again pregnant, and this time Agee hoped that fate would grant him a son. Of course, the expense of having children and maintaining the new house placed an increased financial burden on him. Once more he postponed work on *A Death in the Family* in favor of lucrative or at least reliable screenwriting assignments.

In November he contracted to write a brief adaptation of the Book of Ruth for "Omnibus." "My idea is, I think, a rather good one: i.e. not to dramatize it at all, but merely to have a now and then visible Old Testament 'Chronicler' read it aloud . . . while a cast . . . mimes the rest in some extreme simplified emblematic style which (roughly) blends illustration, dancing, and silent mime acting." Agee received $750 for the work, but the script was never used. Believing now that he was sidetracked in New York, he gave serious thought to returning to Hollywood.

At the last minute an entirely unexpected opportunity came his way, thanks to Howard Taubman, then a music critic for the *New York Times*. Taubman had long wanted to combine classical music with film to reach a larger audience than concerts normally did. With this idea in mind, he approached Agee, whom he knew solely by reputation. With his long-standing love of music, Agee naturally responded with the greatest of enthusiasm, and Taubman arranged for the writer to meet a prospective director, Fred Zinnemann, at the Drake Hotel in New York. At the time, Zinnemann was fresh from the success of *From Here to Eternity* and one of the hottest directors in Hollywood. At the meeting, Taubman and he found Agee a willing collaborator but under great stress and obviously in need of money. Although they suspected that Agee's drinking would impair his ability to write on demand, they formed a production company and offered Agee a contract to write a screenplay for them. Dated January 4, 1954, it specified that he was to receive $4,250 for the effort.

Agee immediately went to work on a detailed treatment. No longer on his own recognizance, as he had been with *Noa Noa,* he had to win Taubman's and Zinnemann's approval every step of the way. They instructed him to write a story about aspiring young musicians at the Tanglewood Music Festival in Lenox, Massachusetts. Agee made the pivotal figure of the story an ambitious conductor, whom he modeled on his younger self. He possessed an "absolute, all but maniacal devotion to music" and "capacities for intensity and for violence." He was also, Agee warned in his outline, a "devourer" and "destroyer" of those around him. To make this point, the story called for the conductor to jilt his girl friend to further his career. On seeing the outline, Zinnemann and Taubman put aside their reservations about Agee's fitness and showered the screenwriter with praise. The next step, they decided, was for Agee to visit Tanglewood in the summer, meet the musicians, gather impressions, and write a full-length script.

During the intervening months, Agee all but forgot about the Tanglewood movie. An army of new ideas marched through his imagination: a screenplay of Norman Mailer's *The Naked and the Dead,* a television series about crime, a film version of Kafka's *The Trial,* movies about John Wilkes Booth and Heinrich Heine. Then unforeseen events precluded work on any of these projects. In February, Father Flye's wife died, and Agee journeyed to St. Andrew's to attend the funeral. On returning to New York he reflected on the misfortunes that had recently befallen the beloved priest. "He's 70; forcibly retired after 35-odd years of wholly frustrated teaching; good for another 20 years; a tiny, minimal, just-feasible pension . . . ; nothing to do; no prospects." Agee's concern, though well intended, was misplaced, for Father Flye was irrepressible. After finishing the school year at St. Andrew's, he moved to Wichita, Kansas, where he spent winters assisting at a local church. In the summers, he assumed clerical responsibilities at St. Luke's Church on Hudson Street, only a ten-minute walk from Agee's home on King Street.

Later in February, Agee faced a major domestic challenge and opportunity to demonstrate his abilities as a parent. Mia told him that she very much wanted to go abroad on a *Fortune* assignment. She would be able to visit Switzerland and Germany and to look up family and friends in her home town of Vienna. She even volunteered to pay a call on Alma and Joel in East Germany for Agee's sake. Yet she doubted his ability to contend with their two children in her absence. Agee insisted that he would remain on his best behavior and that he could cope with any crisis that arose. Reassured, Mia left at the end of the month while Agee assumed responsibility for running the household.

He expected that taking care of Andrea and Teresa, now six and eight, respectively, would be "just a matter of getting them up and off for school, and to bed at the end of the day," as he put it, but he was in for a surprise. One of the girls came down with a fever, and soon all three of them were suffering from "an unusually long and hard series of virus attacks, bronchial and gastro-intestinal." Enfeebled by the stubborn illness, he found it difficult to discharge all his responsibilities. His writing inevitably fell by the wayside, but he scarcely minded, now that he had acquired a passion for playing the role of a full-time parent. He proudly noted, "The combination of aging, and living closely with children, has made me a good deal more responsible than I used to be, and a good deal more skeptical of a lot of ideas about how to raise children; and both the children and the aging . . . have combined to give me an awareness of death."

When Mia returned to New York after ten weeks in Europe, she was delighted to find the family healthy and happy. Her trip, in comparison, had been a great disappointment. She had been so preoccupied with research for *Fortune* that she had failed to make the excursions she had planned. When the articles later appeared in the magazine, they seemed so shallow to her that she thought she might just as well have researched them in New York.

Agee's enthusiasm for fatherhood continued unabated. He brooded endlessly on Joel's welfare. Many a time he had assembled a parcel of books to mail to the boy, but he never got around to making a trip to the post office. On April 26 he received a letter from Alma; this time she complained of Joel's lack of discipline. In a flash Agee imagined Joel repeating the sins of the father, and he was determined that this eventuality would not come to pass. He wrote to Alma, "It's curious how often this lack of self-discipline seems to go with talent: it's perfect hell, what it can play *against* talent: as bad or worse than rigid censorship, or a rigid religion, or dipsomania, or misused sex, or extreme neurosis." Inevitably, he thought of his own failings. "In my own way, I'm a hard and, in general, fairly effective worker, but I'm horrified every time I reflect on the amount of life and gift I have wasted, or not used well enough."

To instill discipline in Joel, Agee recommended Alma send the boy to a good American boarding school, since "this is the country and part of the world he was born of, and so in certain ways will always remain." Not that Agee had any great fondness for the American scene. In 1952 he had registered and voted in a presidential election for the first time, only to see his candidate, Adlai Stevenson, go down to defeat. Now he feared Senator Joseph McCarthy might become the next President. Still, he insisted, "one's *source* is of very profound importance . . . and . . . to come into maturity wholly deprived of living contact with [that] source, is to be deprived of all but indispensable resources within one's self."

Agee's recommendations concerning Joel contained equal parts of common sense and self-interest. With the boy in an American school, Agee hoped to be able to see him regularly, to function as a father rather than his mother's "friend." He went so far as to try to persuade Alma to permit Joel to live with him for a year. To this end, he painted a picture of himself as a thoroughly upright, responsible, mature adult—not at all the radical Alma remembered. He was non-Communist to the point of being anti-Communist; a staunch advocate of democracy; and almost, but not quite, a believer in God. His "faith," in general, consisted of a tenacious belief in the individual "and in whatever I suppose is best for the concept and growth of the individual." As such, he considered himself a member of a tiny but significant minority.

> I feel essentially I am of a dying and almost extinct species which may never become quite extinct and which almost certainly won't come to power again (and I'm not sure that matters) for centuries: a kind of semi-civilized descendant of the Greeks, through the Renaissance. I feel that my kind has had its time, and that the future (and for that matter the present) is in other hands, and on the whole I want no part of it, but believe in continuing to do my best for, and in, what I value, supposing that the best I can do is help keep alive, and to help pass on, dying and discredited ideas which I value above all others.

But Agee's bid to assume responsibility for Joel's welfare met with a crushing lack of response. Agee had shown precious little interest in the boy until now, and Alma and Bodo were not about to let Joel loose in a strange land in the care of an estranged father.

17

FULL CIRCLE

One by one, Agee's reasons for remaining in New York were vanishing. Joel would remain in East Germany. Mia was again looking after the children. His health had improved to the point where he was able to travel. The Tanglewood movie hung fire until the summer, and there were no other screenwriting jobs available to him in the East.

It was at this impasse that his enterprising agent, Ilse Lahn, snared for him an assignment of great interest. Charles Laughton, renowned as an actor, was to make his directorial debut with an adaptation of a popular novel by Davis Grubb, *The Night of the Hunter,* and he wanted his friend James Agee to write the screenplay. The financial terms were the most generous Agee had ever encountered: $30,000 for ten weeks' work.

He needed the money, of course; at the same time, he knew the novel would be a natural for him to adapt. The reclusive Grubb had written a Gothic tale of a psychotic Southern preacher who marries and kills wealthy widows for their money. Its theme bore a strong resemblance to that of *Monsieur Verdoux,* Agee's favorite movie, and children played a key role in the action. Nothing could be more calculated to appeal to a man of Agee's background and temperament. In the certain knowledge that his career had taken a dramatic upswing, Agee flew to California in May to begin work on the script. He installed himself at the Chateau Marmont hotel on Sunset Boulevard to await further developments.

Within days, Agee was once again socializing with Hollywood's expatriate elite; it was as though he had never been gone. At a gathering on May 14 he met a tall, lanky, highly articulate woman calling herself Tamara Comstock. Her given name was Gloria, but as a child in Mount Vernon, New York, she had fallen under the spell of the great Russian novelists and taken the name Tamara. She was thirty-three, worked at a psychiatric clinic in Beverly Hills, wrote poetry, and, she confided to Agee, was getting over an unhappy love affair. At the end of the evening Agee offered to drive her to her home in West Los Angeles. She accepted, and while en route they established a rapport Tamara found astonishing. They were so much alike, she decided, that they might have been brother and sister, not two strangers who had met hours before at a party. As they neared her home, they witnessed an apparition: buildings lit up like Christmas trees seemed to be moving along the street. On further exploration, they realized the buildings were being towed to a new location. Against this surrealistic backdrop, Agee told Tamara he wanted to spend the night with her. "I thought for a moment, and then it felt perfectly right," she remembered. However, they agreed at once not to fall in love. Agee explained his situation: He would be in Los Angeles for only a few weeks, and he had two children and a pregnant wife back in New York. The best they could hope for was a brief, painless affair, and on that note they went to bed.

The next day Agee appeared at Tamara's house with a peacock feather, which she took to be an ominous symbol. Sensing her concern, Agee asked, "Are you superstitious? Do you think peacocks mean death?" Though she answered no to both questions, she knew Agee carried death with him as surely as he carried the peacock feather.

The affair flourished in California's eternal summer. From May until August, Tamara was Agee's constant companion. They slept late, read poetry aloud until daybreak, and discussed literature endlessly. There was little of the obsessiveness that had marked Agee's affair with Pat. Tamara was older, more responsible, and did not drink, but she realized that Agee had a serious drinking problem and was in poor health. Though he refused to see a doctor, he always kept a bottle of nitroglycerin tablets beside the bed they shared in case of a heart attack. Insomnia plagued him. On waking, he often vomited: the result of liver damage. When she got home from work, she would pray that his car would be gone, a sign that he had not suffered an attack and died in her absence.

Tamara decided it would be futile to try to save Agee from himself. He needed alcohol so badly that he carried a bottle of Jack Daniel's wherever he went, even to the home of a friend. She marveled both at his tolerance for alcohol and its effect on him. The more he drank, it seemed to her, the more animated and brilliant he became; that is, until he arrived at what she termed the "fourth stage of drinking—the hate women stage" in which he spewed out long-suppressed resentments against his mother.

Furthermore, Agee refused to allow Tamara or, for that matter, anyone to lecture him about his health. When she reminded him to take the vitamin B required to counteract the effects of alcohol on his system, he became so infuriated that he lifted his ever-present bottle into the air and for a heart-stopping moment threatened to smash it against her. Shuddering, he lowered the bottle and regained control of himself. On another occasion she tried to moderate his consumption by surreptitiously watering down his drink. Agee took one sip, held out the glass, and boomed, "What is that?" Ultimately, Tamara resigned herself to living under the tyranny of alcohol.

Agee's determination to drink affected his writing as well as his relationship with Tamara. He spent most of his days working on the script for *The Night of the Hunter* beside Laughton's swimming pool, but he refused to show the results to anyone until he was finished. If scenes he had written were too long or complex to film, he did not want to hear about it. When Laughton finally got his hands on the complete script, he was greatly disappointed. Agee had not adapted the book; he had re-created a cinematic version of it in extraordinary detail. He specified use of newsreel footage to document the story's setting and added any number of elaborate, impractical montages.

With shooting scheduled to start in a matter of weeks, Laughton discarded Agee's 350-page script and wrote his own, occasionally incorporating some of Agee's simpler ideas. The final shooting script was far more Laughton's than Agee's. Nonetheless, it has since been (wrongly) attributed to Agee and reprinted in a well-known collection of his screenplays.

While Laughton hurriedly rewrote the script for *The Night of the Hunter,* Agee drank himself into a two-week-long stupor at the home of Paul Gregory, the film's producer. From time to time he roused himself to complain that Laughton was "killing" him by tampering with the script. Finally, Tamara collected Agee and returned him to the Chateau Marmont. By then he had earned enormous ill-will on the part of Laughton and Gregory, who held him responsible for delaying the movie, writing an unusable script, and, in the process, collecting his $30,000—more than even Laughton received for his work on the project.

Eventually Agee came to his senses and concluded that if he could not function responsibly as a screenwriter, he would turn his attention to his neglected novel, *A Death in the Family.* As he resumed work he briefly entered into therapy with a new analyst, again a Jungian. The therapy helped to restore his damaged self-esteem and stimulate his imagination and memory. He took keen pleasure in reading newly completed sections of the novel to Tamara, Bernard Schoenfeld, and Schoenfeld's wife, Ethel. "Under his California tan, his face looked drawn and his eyes falsely bright," Schoenfeld recalled of one reading. "After dinner and a few drinks, Jim asked us to listen to a chapter he had just finished writing. He sat cross-legged on the floor of our living room, a drink beside him, and started to read. He had always argued that the best writing was meant to be read aloud, and he was a fine reader." Agee began with the novel's opening scene, in which he, as a young boy, accompanies his father to the Majestic Theatre in Knoxville to see a Charlie Chaplin short.

At supper that night, as many times before, his father said, "Well, spose we go to the picture show."

"Oh, Jay!" his mother said. "That horrid little man!"

"What's wrong with him?" his father asked, not because he didn't know what she would say, but so she would say it.

"He's so *nasty!*" she said, as she always did. "So *vulgar!* With that nasty little cane; hooking up skirts and things, and that nasty little walk!"

His father laughed, as he always did, and Rufus felt that it had become rather an empty joke; but as always the laughter also cheered him; he felt that the laughter enclosed him with his father.

In writing the novel, Agee came full circle. Nearing what he knew to be the end of his life, he was determined to fathom and re-create its origins.

"When Jim finished reading," Schoenfeld remembered, "my wife gave a small sob and then bent down to embrace him, whispering her feelings. I held back my tears. . . . Suddenly I feared for him. No one knew better than I how seldom he had been able to . . . discipline his complex life." To Schoenfeld, this new evidence of Agee's having at last fulfilled his gift almost but not quite redeemed the years of dissipation.

By now it was August and time for Agee to return to New York. With the moment of departure at hand, Tamara began to weep in spite of herself. She had vowed to conduct a painless affair, but the leavetaking was hard to bear. She dreaded that she would never see Agee again, that he would not live long enough to return to California. He assured her that nothing evil would befall him, and he promised to write regularly.

In New York once again, Agee found Mia exhausted from the travails of her pregnancy, but he had no time to stay with her. The season at the Tanglewood Festival was nearly over, and he had yet to conduct his on-site research. Only a day after his arrival he drove with Howard Taubman to Massachusetts. There he spent the next several days, as he noted, "mainly wandering among the students, listening to them, watching them, and talking with them." One of the students who made the greatest impression on him was the jazz pianist Joe Bushkin, who was studying composition at the festival. One evening Taubman and he went to Bushkin's home, where they were up half the night drinking, talking, and playing music. By the time Taubman dragged Agee way, the writer and musician were both roaring drunk and vowing eternal love for one another.

The next day Taubman introduced Agee to the conductor Charles Munch, but Agee was far more fascinated by a woman cellist with whom he carried on an enthusiastic flirtation. He subsequently observed that he enjoyed a "beautiful, concentrated experience" at Tanglewood, "in which I saw—outside of what I was supposed to for my job—all the good reasons why I'm thankful I never became a teacher." He lightheartedly admitted that he "fell in love with at least a half-dozen students of both sexes, and with a couple of excellent teachers." Amid Tanglewood's pastoral setting, he imagined himself a middle-aged Pan cavorting with wood nymphs.

After ten days in Massachusetts, he returned to New York on August 19, exhausted but compelled to begin work on the Tanglewood script. Visiting his studio on Cornelia Street, he found several letters from Tamara awaiting him. They had agreed she would write to this address to keep their relationship a secret, but Agee took the letters home to King Street and inadvertently left them lying in full view of Mia. Belatedly, he realized he had made a serious error. The last thing he wanted was for her to learn of another affair. "I think it is quite possible . . . that Mia found them," he wrote to Tamara on August 23. "I can't be sure of her demeanor since, and I sure as hell won't ask her. I have since hidden them." The situation made him extremely nervous, but there was nothing he could do about it. "I find it hard to write—as I am doing now —a letter in my own home, feeling a betrayal of Mia, asleep downstairs, and feeling I may at any moment be interrupted."

In spite of his guilt, he assured Tamara that he wished to continue their "painless" affair. "May be you can know it by the fact that though there was much else I might have wished to do in Los Angeles, I was drowned in the present with you." Yet even to think of Tamara now was an effort. He was drunk, he told her, the hour was late, and it was all he could do to write, "My dearest, I love you, and I am deeply thankful for you. Please learn to accept my words with as little grief as possible—Jim."

Over the course of the next several days he tried to work on the Tanglewood script, but he was so distracted by concern over Tamara ("I . . . realize that you are suffering like hell, and that I am the cause or agent of that'') and the imminent birth of his child that he found himself incapable of concentration. "I'm getting paralyzed by the whole thing, and badly worried about it," he admitted to Tamara. Meanwhile, "Mia still waits for the child to get born. It's getting tiresome for her; but not for the doctor, who isn't worried at all. Doctors are so very brave; sometimes it's hard to see how they bear up under it all." He was as nervous as a caged animal around the house, unable to remain at his desk for more than brief periods.

On September 2 he fled New York and its myriad pressures to stay at Taubman's home in Danbury, Connecticut, about seventy miles north of the city—close enough to be at hand, should Mia require him. In Danbury, Taubman and Agee discussed the Tanglewood movie at length, but even there the writer was too restless to stay put. He suddenly decided to visit his mother at her home in Kent, Connecticut, where she had moved following the death of Father Wright. After paying his respects, Agee then drove to Hillsdale, ostensibly to visit Teresa, who was staying with neighbors. On the way, the car's battery failed, and he was forced to endure an anxiety-ridden night at a hotel before continuing his journey in the morning.

Returning to the Taubmans', he proceeded to embarrass his host by drinking all the bourbon in the house. At night, he insisted on sleeping in a shed in the backyard, taking the last bottle with him. He did not reappear until the following afternoon, in no shape to work or think coherently. When Taubman informed him that there was no more bourbon to be had, Agee dashed out of the house on an anonymous errand; he returned with a large brown paper bag filled with clinking bottles.

Finally, about noon on September 6, he received a call from Mia. She was in labor. Several days later he stealthily supplied Tamara with a full account of the events surrounding the birth.

> I drove down from Connecticut and took her to the hospital; he was born by a little after 5. Ten pounds; 23 inches; in case I've neglected these vital statistics. Calling-name—first name— rather quickly and easily settled on, as John (it has always been easy, with boys, to get a name); middle name still unsettled; both of us would like something to remind him, in case he ever

cares, that he is half Austrian; but it's hard to find one. Quite possibly Stefan will be it; I've always liked him as the first martyr, in this spelling he's far enough removed from one of my heroes, Stephen Dedalus (I don't believe in naming after one's heroes, including oneself), and he is the patron saint of Vienna, let alone one of the Cathedrals I like best. When he was 3 or 4 days old I dreamed he was talking to me fluently, but I forget what he said. I like him more than well and he evidently wonders, in a fairly friendly way, who the hell I am. . . .

The moment I heard he was a boy, I felt a leaping of joy inside me. Whereas with Andrea's birth which I looked forward to with equal delusions of equanimity, when I heard she was a girl, my heart sank for a fraction of a second—until, in other words, I could say to myself, "Why, you son of a bitch! *That's* a fine welcome into this world." From then on I felt fine about that, too.

Following the excitement of the birth, Agee was thrown into a domestic maelstrom. Although he did his level best to act responsibly, the ordeal of caring for the newborn child tried his patience to the utmost. In the midst of the confusion, he stole a moment to write to Tamara of his hectic schedule. It was three o'clock in the morning, and he was "waiting out the overdue effects of a sleeping pill." He looked forward to "waking to feed the baby at 5 (so I can leave it to Mia to get the children up for school at 8), and hoping to God I sooner or later can get a good enough night's sleep to start a good day's work sometime earlier than 2 in the afternoon." To make matters worse, Mia came down with phlebitis and had to take to her bed to recover. He bitterly lamented not being able to afford " 'round-the-clock servants" to assist with the feedings, changings, baths, diapers, and bottles.

The Tanglewood movie, when he did find the time to work on it, remained a continual source of frustration. In secret, to Tamara on September 21:

Another glorious day has ebbed. I'm still nosing along through the Tanglewood story. I'm puzzled. Scene by scene I rather like it; over-all I think it's sound, honest, reasonably "searching" and "revealing" of what it's supposed to "search" and "reveal"; here and there I think it's really good fun, or brilliant, or both; yet I can't work up the level of momentum, and enthusiasm, which would be indispensable to making it really good, or more than a pleasant and gradually depressing kind of drudgery. It lacks what every good dramatic story has got to have: a core of poetry, no matter how concealed—or all the better, if concealed, so long as it is continuously alive and resonant through the surface material.

Anxiety over the reaction of Zinnemann and Taubman was largely responsible for depriving Agee of the "poetry" he demanded. In the past, collaborators such as Huston and Evans had brought out the best in him, but he had revered these men. In contrast, he merely liked and respected Taubman and Zinnemann. In fact, he knew so much more about writing in general and screenwriting in particular that he could easily fool them with a show of technique. He warned Zinnemann, "I feel sure you will forgive me if . . . I infringe on other territories, including those of the director. I can no more conceive of a writer's not trying to imagine the film as a whole, and finished, then your not entering as deeply as you might wish to, into the writing stage of it."

At the same time, he labored under the nagging suspicion that he had outgrown the craft of screenwriting, as he had earlier outgrown journalism. At his age, nearly forty-five, he was too old and too expert to be doing it for the money. He considered his poor health a blessing in disguise, for it would force him to concentrate on the essential task of serious writing. He would withdraw into a Proustian shell and at last create the works he had endlessly postponed. On November 8, he discussed his embryonic plans in a letter to Tamara.

> I'm very tempted to leave off every kind of remunerative writing I've ever done, and thus to force myself to see whether I can make a living out of the few kinds of writing I most want to do. I'm very much afraid to, for some obvious reason: I've never yet allowed the thought of money to enter this work. . . . It could lead me into anxieties and confusions beyond what I'm competent to carry, let alone master; and it could be the destruction of me and my talent. But it could also, just conceivably, bring just the opposite—like finally growing up and using

your own face, instead of a set of semi-masks, and exposing
your own face wherever you go, rather than giving it the over
protected child treatment.

Few, if any, of Agee's exercises in self-analysis approached the
insight of that last remark. If his intuitions were correct, he was
about to enter an important new phase in his career in which he
would be able to support himself by and therefore devote himself
solely to serious writing. No longer would he have to endure a
painfully divided career as a novelist-journalist or novelist-screen-
writer. It seemed to him that he had at last come to the end of years
of "wretched spade-work"; now the wellspring of his imagination
would "flow up clear." In this optimistic mood, he dallied with the
idea of returning to poetry, his native discipline, but discovered
"the very effort to write a line [is] like signing your name, with a
fingertip, on a hot stove-lid. I simply lack the courage and the
stamina." No, if he was to "use his own face," he would reveal
himself as a supremely autobiographical novelist.

And yet he sensed that death stalked his every move, mocked
his brave little resolves. Confined to his home at the end of the year,
he brooded on a "constant awareness of death, and the shortness
of time, and of time wasted." He was dying in a manner befitting
a Romantic poet: a lingering, exquisite death, hastened and rendered painless by alcohol. So fascinated with the process of dying
did he become that he courted it as his next lover, and meditated
on it in all his subsequent writing.

A notable instance of his attempt to come to terms with death
was his contribution to a musical adaptation of Voltaire's *Candide*.
Lillian Hellman, the playwright, and Leonard Bernstein, the conductor and composer, invited Agee to contribute lyrics to the play.
The request set his liquor-sodden imagination whirling. He envisioned an afterworld ruled by a king whose power derives from
genius rather than heritage. A fantastic version of Father Flye, this
king is mild and saintly; he grants his citizens whatever they wish.
For example, an old farmer comes before the king, declaring, "I
have loved God; and the poets; and my wives; and their children;
and theirs; and I have loved the soil, and have dealt with it rever-
ently. Now, I declare my wish to die."

Like Agee, the farmer longs for the "unknown, whatever it may be; and to tire in his faculties. He can foresee an ever saddening decline, which he does not wish to inflict either on those who love him, or upon himself." The king allows the farmer to drink a fatal potion, and the farmer dies as Agee would have wished: "quickly and without pain, surrounded by his family." Afterward, a "sublime and serene celebration of death begins—all white, silver, gold, and peaceful joy." *Exeunt Omnes. Finis.*

Thus Agee imagined his own death, but in reality the prospect aroused his anxieties. One night he dreamed he was back at St. Andrew's, attending the funeral of Father Flye's wife. The corpse emerged from her coffin, walked up the aisle, and embraced him. They kissed "as we always have, after a long time apart." He was so shaken by the premonition that he was unable to work effectively on lyrics for *Candide,* and he was soon replaced.

During the waning days of 1954, he began to suffer painful attacks of angina—an inflammation of the lining surrounding the heart. The attacks were alarmingly frequent, as many as twelve a day. He took what he called "home-hospital care": heavy sedation and about ten hours' sleep in a twenty-four-hour period. He alternated nitroglycerin for his heart with doses of chloral hydrate to induce sleep. Drugged, he lost track of time, dozing away the days and reading through the nights. At the moment, he favored "early Raymond Chandler," but he wished he might have "some late Tamara Comstock, or even some upper high middle James Agee."

During this trying and indecisive period, he received a visitor in his home on King Street: Howard Taubman, hoping to prod the writer into finishing the Tanglewood script. With effort, Agee rose from his bed, came downstairs, and asked, "Would you like a drink?" Taubman refused. "I'm not supposed to drink," Agee said, "but if you'll have a tiny one, I'll have a tiny one." With that, he brought out a bottle. There was an element of teasing and provocation in the gesture. "Tell me frankly," he said. "Do you think I'm a lush?" Taubman could not bring himself to reply.

When the conversation turned to the Tanglewood movie, Agee revealed that in spite of all the obstacles he had faced, he had completed a 250-page script. On reading it, Taubman found a cinematic paean to God, nature, love, and music. Though many of the scenes were exciting, Taubman realized the script required much revision and cutting, and he was reluctant to push the enfee-bled Agee. It was miraculous that he had managed to accomplish this much. Having heard stories that Huston had pushed Agee to the breaking point during the writing of *The African Queen*, Taub-man concluded that he "didn't care enough about the project to kill a man."

Against his better judgment, he sent the script to Zinnemann as it stood, but by then it was too late to engage the director's interest. Having tired of waiting for Agee, Zinnemann had recently accepted a lucrative offer to direct the filmed version of the musical *Oklahoma*. Despite Taubman's best efforts to interest Hollywood in the script, *A Tanglewood Story*, as Agee called it, never again came so close to production. The circumstance was indeed a shame, because of all Agee's unfilmed screenplays, this was the most suc-cessful. In it he forsook the compulsion to describe scenes in out-landish detail, concentrating instead on dramatic development. From the vantage point of middle age he spun a tale of youth's eternal struggle to reconcile romance with vocation. In one speech, the conductor-protagonist, Jubal King, sums up the theme: "If you've got it—even if you think you *may* have it—then you give it every minute and breath and ounce of strength and every drop of blood you've got. It boils down to this: can *anybody* serve *two masters?* I doubt it. I doubt you can serve even one, halfway well enough. All I know is until you know an awful lot better than I do, now, you've got to travel light."

Though it is not clear what role Agee reserved for himself in this instance, he did work in a character modeled on Father Flye. He ministers to Jubal's girl friend, Mary, and, like the original, is given to exclaiming, "I don't know *when* I've had such a *splendid* time! Or stayed up so outrageously late!" By the time the story has worked its way to an exhausting conclusion, the priest has not managed to mediate a resolution between Jubal and Mary. When the conductor finally proposes, she gently refuses him. They are hopelessly in love, but destined to be torn asunder.

Freed of the burden of grinding out scenes for *A Tanglewood Story*, Agee took a decided turn for the better. By the middle of January he felt well enough to accept a commission to write a thirty-minute orientation film about Colonial Williamsburg. He took on the assignment out of a sense of nostalgia, for, as a young *Fortune* writer not long out of Harvard, he had written caustically about the restoration. It was a measure of his transformation over the years that he now regarded it in a sentimental, patriotic light. It was no longer a monument to national vanity, but a shrine of civic religion. The past, Agee acknowledged, was worth preserving, even when it was less than perfect.

Although Agee was excited by the prospect of abandoning his bed for a plane to Virginia, where he planned to spend several days doing research for the movie, he feared the trip would be his last. "I'm afraid I may collapse," he confided to Tamara, "unless . . . I learn to guarantee myself 8 hours' heavy sleep, ending at 8 a.m. In the same interest I go, tomorrow, for an electrocardiograph and a fluoroscope reading."

On Monday, January 19, he caught an early plane to Virginia, where he spent two wearying days crisscrossing the restoration on foot. With every step he tried to conserve his energy and, if possible, his life, but there was work to do: interviews, surveys, tours. Despite the exertion, he returned to a cold, blustery New York feeling invigorated and supplied with enough ideas to flesh out not a half-hour documentary but two full-length feature films. One would concern Tories versus Loyalists, the other the Age of Revolution. Both would be "mystical," "Virgilian" poems of a "prenatal nation."

Judging from his newly acquired vigor, travel served him well. He concluded that the sedentary life, with its temptation to drink and brood in isolation, had been contributing to his deterioration. Rest killed; work cured. But just as he began work on the Williamsburg movie at the end of February, the angina attacks returned with an ever increasing ferocity. He spent two weeks in bed. Death had disillusioned him. It was not sweet and forgiving, as the Romantic poet in him imagined; it was a cruel invasion of his life. Deprived of stimulation, he spent the hours monitoring the decay of his body with morbid fascination.

> Friday [February 25], midnight-to-midnight, 17 attacks, one of them 2-[nitroglycerin] tablet (medium painful), one 3-tablet (very), 2 quite light (just barely worth a tablet), the rest above average (unpleasant, but one tablet disposes of it). Saturday

Feb 26: 15 attacks, one of 2 tablets, 5 light. Sunday: 16; 2 of
2 tablets; 4 light. Monday: 14; of 2 tblts; 5 light. Tuesday: 13;
9 light; 1 of 2 NG; 1 of 3. Since Midnight of this Wednesday;
none so far; it's almost five. They are most frequent during my
first hours lying down and my first hours asleep.

Fear of a fatal heart attack plagued his dreams as well as his
waking hours. By early March he was lapsing into a hallucinatory
state of mind. Dreams took on more specificity and meaning than
reality. On the morning of March 2 he dreamed a blowtorch was
searing the inside of his chest. Suddenly he is confronted by a
nameless woman dressed in gold and azure. "She is evidently
my girl friend and my employer or associate in jewel-making,"
Agee noted, "and neither relationship has been very good." In
despair he tells her, "I've come to where I can no longer bear to
use pity. I back out." He awoke with his most painful attack in
days.

There seemed to be no clear-cut boundary between death and
life, no end to the physical torment he endured. He awaited an
illumination, the magical appearance of a forgiving king who would
pardon his sins and lift him toward the light, but no savior came to
the rescue. He withdrew behind a silken web of self-absorption.
Occasionally Andrea and Teresa intruded on his private domain,
but he could not tolerate their exuberance and cacophony. Yet the
worst part of dying was the enforced loneliness. How much he
would have liked to take Tamara and Mia and his mother with him
on the voyage.

By the middle of March the immediate crisis had passed. The
number of angina attacks fell to six a day, "nearly all of them mild."
He rallied and made plans as if he were going to live forever: finish
A Death in the Family, write the Williamsburg documentary, adapt
Kipling's "The Man Who Would Be King" for Huston. "I'm less
at a loss for work than for choice and for time, and the question
. . . of what I can afford to do for little or no money," he wrote
Father Flye on March 17. He took time as well to counsel Schoenfeld on how a screenwriter should go about writing a novel. He
suggested that his friend tell himself, " 'I am writing a novel but
only because it would be impossible to make it as a movie. . . . I'm
writing a movie in print.' "

These precepts had served Agee well in the writing of *A Death in the Family*, yet it galled him not to be able to write poetry on his deathbed. He resorted to the oldest of excuses for this failing: "I value it too highly, relative to other kinds of writing. I reverence it too much. And this brings fear. And fear is *the* enemy of good work." Instead he typed letters to Tamara and Schoenfeld and Father Flye until he was too tired and drugged to strike the keys accurately. The letters' coherence demonstrated to him that although his body was dying, his mind remained as lively as ever. He reacted with a show of impatience to premature eulogizing on the part of his friends. He still held out the hope of recovery, if only he could discover the emotional basis of his afflictions. "There is indeed some still unknown element of deep trouble, which I expect is at the root of the illness and of my failure to use the weeks of pain and stillness well enough," he wrote Tamara on March 25. Habitually self-critical, he could not bring himself to approve even of the manner of his dying.

In his impatience, he grew nostalgic for the days of wine and roses he had spent with Pat Scallon. He had been given to thinking of her as a harlot, an object, but now he rehabilitated her. He confided to Schoenfeld that Pat was "the last girl I'll ever be in love with. So the missing is awful every time I speak of her." And he took offense that Schoenfeld should chide him for being "as free with my life as a Greek deity." The very phrase gave Agee "a spiritual erection" and made him "feel fine, and deeply honored." In the same breath, however, he despaired at the "mess" he had made out of his life through allegiance to his desires. "You must not overrate anything about me," he warned Schoenfeld, "for if you do, you'll find out how wrong you were and, wise as you are, you'll then tend to be bound to blame me for having deceived you."

Easter found Agee in better health than he had enjoyed for months. But now the rest of the household, swollen with Mia's mother and stepfather, came down with a persistent virus. Agee reeled in contempt at the omnipresence of illness. To Father Flye he complained, "At moments I wonder whether those who go, as I do, for a Full Life, don't get their exact reward, which is that The Full Life is full of crap." Once Agee thought of the phrase "The Full Life" he became enamored of it and repeated it to anyone willing to listen. Yes, he had lived The Full Life—wine, women, and song—every species of literary endeavor under the sun—only to recognize at the last moment that it all added up to much less than it had seemed when he was in the midst of one of his mad pursuits. His life had come to resemble an incomplete poem. Here and there sections were brilliantly realized; many others were vague and sketchy. It was obvious he had not completed what he had set out to accomplish. He had explored only a fraction of the ideas he had had, and of the ideas he had explored, he had put only a fraction on paper, and of those on paper, he had completed an even smaller fraction.

In this mood of self-censure he resumed work on the novel about his three marriages. So involved with the task did he become that for brief, blissful periods he forgot all about his dying. By re-creating this turbulent part of his past he hoped to uncover the hidden "roots" of his illness.

Then, abruptly, he planned to return to California in May to look for fresh film work. It seemed that Ilse Lahn had an endless supply of diverting new projects up her sleeve. The latest was an offer of work on a script about Billy Mitchell, father of the modern Air Force. It was not exactly Agee's cup of tea, but it would help pay the mortgage and mounting medical bills.

Thinking that he would soon depart for Hollywood, Agee put aside the novel about marriage to complete the Williamsburg script. Agee deliberately worked to refine the approach he had employed in his Lincoln biography. Though portraying traditional, patriotic themes, he embraced innovative techniques. He specified use of a new wide-screen photographic process to enhance visual details and sowed the script with humble childhood memories of rural life. In stark contrast to his grim daily life, sunlight flooded his re-creation of Colonial Williamsburg. Inspired, Agee worked steadily on the movie throughout April. Stray pages littered the floor of his house on King Street. The gentle, timeless events he depicted steadied his nerves more effectively than any sedative.

He held death at arm's length, but no farther. In reflective moments he discussed his burial with Mia. He preferred that he be laid to rest at his farm in Hillsdale on a grassy knoll. He even gave thought to what should be engraved on his tombstone. After discarding many possibilities, he told Mia he wanted a simple representation of a bird, the Egyptian symbol of the afterlife.

Early in May, when he felt death closing in on him once again, he interrupted work on the Williamsburg script long enough to concoct a fable about his destiny. It had to do with elephants. In a May 11 letter to Father Flye—never mailed—Agee described the cruel end of an elephant in the Tennessee of 1916. The animal goes berserk and kills three men. As a result, the populace decides that she should be hanged. They string her to a railroad derrick, but it collapses under her weight. They get a stronger derrick, and after two hours the elephant dies, while "5,000 oafs" look on. So Agee was dying, while family and friends looked on.

The elephant continued to haunt his imagination. He next envisioned the choreographer George Balanchine teaching a corps de ballet composed entirely of the ungainly beasts. As they dance to the music of Stravinsky, a fire consumes them all, and "their huge souls, light as clouds, settle like doves, in the great secret cemetery back in Africa." Agee thought this fable would make a splendid movie, but when he told his friends about it, they decided he was losing his mind. On further reflection, he decided it would not be satisfying as a film after all; like so many of his ideas, it was nothing more than the merest wisp of a dream.

On Friday, May 13, Agee felt well enough to leave the house to attend a small party in the Village given by socialite Gloria Vanderbilt. Surrounded by friends and immersed in conversation, he felt his old self again and stayed up until five o'clock in the morning talking with David McDowell about *A Death in the Family.* Agee said he planned to return to Hillsdale in the summer and finish the novel within a month or two.

Monday, May 16, dawned pleasantly fair and cool. In the afternoon, Agee left the house and hailed a taxi to take him to Dr. Sutherland's office for another examination. During the ride, he suffered an attack of angina, the worst he had ever experienced. The pain mounted until he lost consciousness. Alarmed, the cabbie raced across town to Roosevelt Hospital. By the time he arrived, James Agee, forty-five, had died of a coronary occlusion. He left no will, life insurance, or other indemnification. There was $450 in his savings account at the time.

Mia received a call from the hospital. When she reached the

emergency room, the hospital staff, afraid that she would have hysterics, refused to let her see her husband's body. But they did not know Mia Fritsch Agee. She demanded to see her husband until, finally, a doctor escorted her into a room where he lay in utter repose. Mia made an identification for the staff. Later she looked for the cabbie who had taken her husband to the hospital, but he was nowhere to be found.

Later in the day, McDowell called Father Flye in Wichita with the sad news of Agee's death. Within hours the priest was on a plane to New York, where he arrived at dawn the following morning to make funeral arrangements. Soon after, a representative of the Williamsburg Foundation, having learned of Agee's death, arrived at King Street to retrieve the script. He walked around the house, picking up pages as he went. He snatched a last page from the typewriter and left with the papers under his arm.

Obituaries appeared in the principal New York papers on May 18. The *New York Times* called Agee a "poet, critic, and sensitive writer in many media." Next to the obituary there appeared a small photograph of the writer, looking very somber and wearing a wrinkled work shirt.

Tamara accidentally came across the photograph at work the following day. She suffered "incredible shock" to learn that her friend and lover had died. That night she got together with the Schoenfelds and Ivan Moffat to hold an informal wake in Agee's honor. Moffat announced, "It was the death of a lifetime." Not everyone in California reacted with sorrow to Agee's death. Laughton and Gregory, whose *Night of the Hunter* was about to open, felt an enormous sense of relief that they would not have to put up with him anymore. The movie, incidentally, was a commercial disaster, and Laughton never again had the chance to direct, though today the film enjoys cult status.

In East Germany, Joel learned of his father's death by phone. Over crackling long-distance wires, an unknown male voice said, "I have to tell you some sad news. Your father died yesterday. He had a heart attack. Please tell your mom." Joel conveyed the news to Alma, as instructed.

"Jim? It can't be! He can't be dead," she exclaimed. She sat down and held her head in her hands.

Joel had been looking forward to visiting his father in the

United States. "I guess there's no reason for me to go to the States now, is there?" he asked. Alma burst into tears.

On the morning of May 19, Father Flye conducted the funeral at St. Luke's Chapel. Agee's body lay in a simple, black, closed coffin. The priest read the Burial Office and conducted a Requiem Mass before about a hundred family members and friends. In closing, Father Flye remarked, "It is not the custom of this church to eulogize its dead. I can only say that those who knew James Agee will never forget him."

After the ceremony, a group of mourners drove the two hundred miles to the farm in Hillsdale, where the burial took place in the afternoon. The site, located a hundred yards from the farmhouse, overlooked the rolling hills, now tinted with green. A simple stone marked the grave, but there was no carving on it. It was a beautiful spring day. Agee's favorite flower, the lilac, bloomed everywhere, filling the soft air with its sweet scent. His children broke off several sprays and threw them on the coffin.

POSTMORTEM

As he predicted, James Agee won greater acclaim in death than he had in life.

David McDowell set up a publishing company in partnership with Yvonne Obolensky. In 1957, McDowell, Obolensky published *A Death in the Family.* Though not quite complete, the novel met with great critical and commercial success and won the 1957 Pulitzer Prize for fiction.

In 1958, McDowell, Obolensky published *Agee on Film: Reviews and Comments,* volume 1, a collection of his film reviews and articles for *Time, Life,* and *The Nation.* It was immediately recognized as a classic of the genre, and remains required reading for anyone interested in film.

In 1960, McDowell, Obolensky published *Agee on Film: Five Film Scripts by James Agee,* volume 2, a collection of five screenplays —*Noa Noa, The African Queen, The Bride Comes to Yellow Sky, The Blue Hotel,* and Laughton's version of *The Night of the Hunter.* John Huston contributed a brief Foreword.

In the same year, Houghton Mifflin reissued the long-forgotten *Let Us Now Praise Famous Men,* complete with Walker Evans' photographs. In hardcover and paperback editions, the book has since sold nearly half a million copies.

Late in 1960, Tad Mosel's theatrical adaptation of *A Death in the Family* became a Broadway hit. *All the Way Home,* as the play was called, won a Pulitzer Prize.

In 1962 the publishing firm of George Braziller issued *James Agee's Letters to Father Flye,* a collection of Agee's thirty-year-long correspondence with the priest. It, too, won critical acclaim.

In the fall of 1963 the film version of *All the Way Home,* based on Agee's novel, had its world premiere in Knoxville, Tennessee. Produced by David Susskind and directed by Alex Segal, the movie starred Jean Simmons as Agee's mother and Robert Preston (with whom Agee had appeared in *The Bride Comes to Yellow Sky*) as his father.

NOTES

I have generally relied on primary sources: letters and manuscripts, both published and unpublished; and interviews with friends, colleagues, and family members. Because original editions of Agee's published works are scarce, citations refer to more commonly available versions. Abbreviations for frequently cited sources are as follows:

BOOKS

AOF1   *Agee on Film: Reviews and Comments,* vol. 1. New York: Perigee Books, 1983. (Originally published by McDowell, Obolensky, New York, 1958.)

NOTES

AOF2   *Agee on Film: Five Film Scripts by James Agee,* vol. 2. New York: Perigee Books, 1983. (Originally published by McDowell, Obolensky, New York, 1960.)

Poems   *The Collected Poems of James Agee.* Edited by Robert Fitzgerald. Boston: Houghton Mifflin, 1962.

Prose   *The Collected Short Prose of James Agee.* Edited by Robert Fitzgerald. Boston: Houghton Mifflin, 1962.

ADIF   *A Death in the Family.* New York: Bantam Books, 1969. (Originally published by McDowell, Obolensky, New York, 1957.)

FF   *The Letters of James Agee to Father Flye.* 2d ed. Boston: Houghton Mifflin, 1971. (Originally published by George Braziller, New York, 1962.)

LUFM   *Let Us Now Praise Famous Men.* Boston: Houghton Mifflin, 1960. (Originally published by Houghton Mifflin, Boston, 1941.)

MW   *The Morning Watch.* New York: Ballantine Books, 1966. (Originally published by Houghton Mifflin, Boston, 1951.)

PMV   *Permit Me Voyage.* New Haven: Yale University Press, 1934.

RJA   *Remembering James Agee.* Edited by David Madden. Baton Rouge: Louisiana State University Press, 1974.

PERIODICALS

HA   *Harvard Advocate.* Cambridge, Massachusetts.
NYT   *New York Times.*
PEA   *Phillips Exeter Monthly.* Exeter, New Hampshire.
PR   *Partisan Review.* New York.
TN   *The Nation.* New York.

INDIVIDUALS

TC   Tamara Comstock
WE   Walker Evans

411

RF   Robert Fitzgerald

JH   John Huston

AM   Archibald MacLeish

DM   Dwight Macdonald

BS   Bernard Schoenfeld

JS   James Stern

LS   Louise Saunders

FT   Frank Taylor

COLLECTIONS

Academy   John Huston papers, Margaret Herrick Library, Academy of Motion Picture Arts and Sciences, Los Angeles, California.

Columbia   Rare Book and Manuscript Library, Columbia University, New York.

Exeter   The Library, Phillips Exeter Academy, Exeter, New Hampshire.

Hamilton   Saunders Family papers, The Library, Hamilton College, Clinton, New York.

Harvard   Harvard University Alumni Records Office, Cambridge, Massachusetts.

Houghton   The Houghton Library, Harvard University, Cambridge, Massachusetts.

Indiana   Frank Taylor papers, Lilly Library, Indiana University, Bloomington, Indiana.

LC   Manuscript Division, Library of Congress, Washington, D.C.

NYPL   Robert Fitzgerald papers, Berg Collection, New York Public Library.

Princeton   Allen Tate papers, R. P. Blackmur papers, Firestone Library, Princeton University, Princeton, New Jersey.

St. Andrew's   James Agee Memorial Library, St. Andrew's-Sewanee, Sewanee, Tennessee.

Texas   James Agee papers, Humanities Research Center, University of Texas at Austin.

Time Time Inc. archives, New York.

Twentieth Archives, Twentieth Century-Fox Pictures, Beverly Hills, California.

Wesleyan Saudek-Omnibus Collection, Wesleyan University Department of Archives and Records, Middletown, Connecticut.

Williamsburg The Colonial Williamsburg Foundation, Williamsburg, Virginia.

Yale Dwight Macdonald papers, Yale University, Sterling Library, New Haven, Connecticut.

CHAPTER 1: A DEATH IN THE FAMILY

3. *"We are talking":* ADIF, 11.
4. Mathieu Agee: *A Record of the Agee Family* (Independence, Mo.: privately printed, 1937).
5. Hugh James Agee: Mark Doty, *Tell Me Who I Am* (Baton Rouge: Louisiana State University Press, 1981), 2.
6. she contracted syphilis: W. M. Frohock, interview with the author, Cambridge, Massachusetts, June 1982.
6. contemplative order: *Tell Me Who I Am,* 2.
7. "white man's climate": *St. Andrew's.*
8. *"Uh-Rufus":* ADIF, 205.
8. "gave his words": *ibid.,* 280.
9. "too trusting": *ibid.,* 231–32.
9. shiny new black Ford: Unpublished scene intended for inclusion in *ADIF, Texas.*
9. *"Ughgh-Ughgh":* ADIF, 46.
9. "dry grass": *ibid.,* 99.
9. "If I ever get drunk": *ibid.,* 94.
10. "tasting the mean goodness": *ibid.,* 13.
10. "All my people": *ibid.,* 15.
10. local landmarks: *ibid.,* 24.
10. Majestic Theatre: *ibid.,* 19–21.
10. On the way home: *ibid.,* 24.
11. *"I got a gallon":* ibid., 90.

12. "But O Lord": *ibid.,* 31.

12. "faint skeins of steel": *ibid.,* 48.

13. "This was the real": *ibid.,* 52.

13. "crazy drunk": *ibid.,* 152.

13. "terrifying noise": *ibid.,* 153.

13. Tinsley sent for help: Knoxville *Journal and Tribune,* May 19, 1916.

14. "tight, set": *ADIF,* 140.

14. "He wasn't a *Christian*": *ibid.,* 144.

15f. In the morning: *ibid.,* 246–48.

16. "tasted of darkness": *ibid.,* 265.

17. "The arm was bent": *ibid.,* 289–90.

17. "downright incestuous": *ibid.,* 174.

17. "stumbling, sobbing rush": Notes for *ADIF, Texas.*

18. "almost wholly without emphasis": *ADIF,* 280.

18. "repeatedly saw himself": *ibid.,* 278.

18. "In His Strength": *ibid.,* 166.

19. "perfectly magnificent butterfly": *ibid.,* 314.

19. Three weeks later: *St. Andrew's.*

CHAPTER 2: STRANGE RITES

21. *"That branch is thick":* "Widow," *PEA* 30 (May 1926), 180.

21. streaked with blood: Genevieve Moreau, *The Restless Journey of James Agee* (New York: Morrow, 1977), 52.

21. "Why does God": *ADIF,* 60–61.

22. "Why do they": *RJA,* 17.

22. "taken at the pit": *LUFM,* 124.

23. "half-shaped child": *ibid.*

23. she insisted he be circumcised: Alma Mailman Neuman, interview with the author, New York, New York, September 1982; Tamara Comstock, interview with the author, San Marcos, California, October 1982.

23. *"Mumsy you were so genteel":* Poems, 145.

24. "I used as a child": *LUFM,* 84.

24. serving God: Doty, *Tell Me Who I Am*, 13.

24. "all one wall": *MW*, 47.

24. long black dress: *St. Andrew's*.

25. The students' life: *RJA*, 18; Moreau, *The Restless Journey of James Agee*, 44–45; Doty, *Tell Me Who I Am*, 14.

25. "Father, have you read": Father James Harold Flye, interview with the author, New York, New York, November 1981.

26. "There were no signs": Recorded interview with Father Flye on *James Agee: A Portrait*. New York: Caedmon Records TC 2042. (Hereafter referred to as "recorded interview.")

26. "traumatized": Flye interview with author.

26. His family: *ibid*.

26. they talked endlessly: *RJA*, 16.

26. James expressed confusion: *MW*, 53–54.

27. "prostrate head": *ibid.*, 48.

27. "the one place": *ibid.*, 64.

27. In his anger: *ibid.*, 62.

27. He resumed hunting: "Boys Will Be Brutes," *HA* 116 (April 1930), 29–33.

27f. "vigil over his": *MW*, 69.

28. STRANGE RITES: *ibid.*, 76.

28. "not that you *mean* it": *ibid.*, 66.

29. "Morning had not yet begun": *ibid.*, 121.

29. "found a locust shell": *ibid.*, 129.

29. "lashed about his fist": *ibid.*, 143.

29. "pretty well anaesthetized": Agee to JH, September 14, 1950, *Academy*.

30. *Songs of the Way*: Doty, *Tell Me Who I Am*, 14.

30. He was exceedingly proper: Frohock interview.

31. He became a semi-invalid: *ibid*.

31. "virgin before me": *LUFM*, 340.

32. They sailed for Boulogne: "The Bell Tower of Amiens," *PEA* 30 (December 1925), 48–51; "The Scar," *PEA* 30 (January 1926), 77–78; Moreau, *The Restless Journey of James Agee*, 56.

32f. "I stood knee-deep": "The Bell Tower of Amiens."

CHAPTER 3: FIRST LOVES

34. "tough and definite": *Bulletin of The Phillips Exeter Academy* 30 (April 1929), 5.

35. Soon after entering: Impressions of Agee drawn from Myron Williams, "James Rufus Agee: 1909–1915," August 20, 1961, *Exeter.*

35. One of the few friends: *FF,* 17.

36. "overwhelming passion": Moreau, *The Restless Journey of James Agee,* 62.

36. He undertook: "Notes on James Rufus Agee," *Exeter.*

36. "I have been snowed under": *FF,* 17.

36. "Minerva Farmer": *PEA* 30 (November 1925), 39–42.

36f. "The Circle": *PEA* 30 (April 1926), 143–51.

37. "In the first place": "The Moving Picture," *PEA* 30 (March 1926), 115–17.

38. "I'm going to spend": *FF,* 19.

39. final examinations: Agee's final grades for the academic year 1925/26 were: Latin, D; Math, D; English, A; French, C; History, C; Declamation, C. "Notes on James Rufus Agee," *Exeter.*

39. hitched up their robes: Frohock interview.

39f. "pointedly ill at ease": Untitled manuscript, *Texas.* Probably late 1940s. The events Agee portrayed clearly refer to those he described in letters to Father Flye during the summer and fall of 1926.

41. "Jenkinsville": "Jenkinsville I," *PEA* 31 (December 1926), 71–72; "Jenkinsville II," *PEA* 31 (January 1927), 81–82.

41. "This morning": *FF,* 22.

42. "All I did": *ibid.,* 23–24.

42. Fred Lowenstein: Frohock interview. Lowenstein died of influenza in 1933.

43. Macdonald had written: Dwight Macdonald, interview with the author, New York, New York, April 1982.

43. "Where Lewis should have used": *"Elmer Gantry," PEA* 31 (May 1927), 189–91.

43. "I'd become terribly mad": Agee to DM, June 26, 1927, *Yale.*

44. "disgusted at myself": *FF,* 27–28.

44. "filthy book": *FF,* 28–29.

44. Night after night: *ibid.,* 29–30.

45f. "became very unhappy": Agee to DM, June 26, 1927, *Yale.*

47. "Pygmalion": *Yale.*

47. At the last minute: Agee to DM, June 26, 1927, *Yale.*

48. "Last September": Agee to DM, June 16, 1927, *Yale.*

48. "As for Potemkin": Agee to DM, June 26, 1927, *Yale.*

48f. "Jim could always": Dwight Macdonald, *On Movies* (New York: Da Capo Press, 1981), 7.

49. "I have a wild desire": Agee to DM, June 26, 1927, *Yale.*

49f. "Our generation": *RJA,* 119.

50. "As for my feelings now": Agee to DM, July 21, 1927, *Yale.*

50. a local friend: Frohock interview; *FF,* 37; Agee to DM, July 21, 1927, *Yale.*

50f. Dorothy Carr: Frohock interview; letter from Malcolm Cowley to the author, March 29, 1982.

51f. Ann Garner: "Ann Garner," *PEA* 32 (May 1928), 77–86.

52. S. Foster Damon: Frohock interview; *FF,* 37.

53. Exeter faculty members recommended: "Notes on James Rufus Agee," *Exeter.*

53. "His one deep enthusiasm": Laura Tyler Wright to Dean Hanford, August 14, 1928, *Harvard.*

53. "give to the world": "Class History," *PEA* 32 (June 1928), 207–11.

54. "I'm much fonder": *FF,* 36.

54f. "so tired that several times": "1928 Story," *Texas Quarterly* 11 (Spring 1968), 23–37.

CHAPTER FOUR: OF HARVARD AND HOBOES

56. "The door burst open": *RJA,* 23.

57. The Harvard Agee came to: Samuel Eliot Morison, *Three Centu-*

ries of Harvard: 1636–1936 (Cambridge: Harvard University Press, 1965), 420–81.

57. Every few weeks: Robert Saudek, interviews with the author, Bronxville, New York, January and October 1982.

57. "incredible mirror maze": quoted in *The Restless Journey of James Agee,* 84.

58. "An intellectual aristocrat": Morison, *Three Centuries of Harvard,* 441.

58. "Cook's tour": *FF,* 39.

58. In the numerous libraries: *ibid.,* 58.

59. the word *genius:* Saudek interviews, *RJA,* 25.

59. That Prohibition was in full force: Saudek interviews.

59f. "fearful and wonderful": *FF,* 39.

60. wickedly effective parodist: Saudek interviews, *RJA,* 25.

60. "He went over": *ibid.*

61. He told Saudek: Saudek interviews.

61. This premonition: Frohock interview.

62. "I've felt rather petrified": *ibid.,* 40.

62. "Ann Garner": *Hound and Horn* 2 (Spring 1929), 223–35.

63. Since graduating from Yale: Macdonald interview.

63. "What sort of work": Agee to DM, April 24, 1929, *Yale.*

63. career in Hollywood: *FF,* 46.

63. "A fellow in my dormitory": Agee to DM, April 24, 1929, *Yale.*

64. "did my soul good": Agee to DM, May 10, 1929, *Yale.*

64. "He seems generally": *ibid.*

65. "A Walk Before Mass": *HA* 116 (December 1929), 18–20.

65. "Near the Tracks": *HA* 116 (June 1930), 9–20.

65f. "I'm going to spend": Agee to DM, May 10, 1929, *Yale.*

66. He hitched rides: Agee to DM, August 1929, *Yale;* "Death in the Desert," *HA* 117 (October 1930), 16–24.

66f. "Maybe August 1st": Agee to DM, August 1929, *Yale.*

67. mediocre grades: Agee's record for the academic year 1928/29: Greek, B; Geology, C; German, E; History, C; Latin, B. *Harvard.*

67. an anxious letter: Laura Tyler Wright to Richard Wierum, June 30, 1929, *Harvard.*

67. "The form which was sent": W. I. Nichols to Laura Tyler Wright, *Harvard.*

67f. He came to a boardinghouse: "They That in Sorrow Shall Reap," *HA* 117 (May 1931), 9–23.

69f. The return trip: "Death in the Desert," *HA* 117 (October 1930), 16–24.

70f. Saudek was thrilled: Saudek interviews.

71. "drove off a mountain curve": Agee to DM, December 1929, *Yale.*

71. "I feel more and more": *FF,* 42.

72. "On the whole": *ibid.,* 44–45.

72. "the most powerful and poisonous": Agee to DM, December 1929, *Yale.*

72f. "Oh, God damn": Agee to DM, January 17, 1930, *Yale.*

73. "I can't write": Agee to DM, March 1930, *Yale.*

73. "It needs condensation": Agee to DM, January 17, 1930, *Yale.*

73. *"Even now, a serpent swells my living skull":* "Sonnet," *HA* 116 (June 1931), 19.

74. "Epithalamium": *PMV,* 38–45.

74. "redolent of mothballs": Agee to DM, March 1930, *Yale.*

74. "I feel as though he had stolen": letter from Irvine Upham to the author, July 15, 1982.

75. Irvine Upham: Upham's impressions of Agee, *ibid.*

75. Franklin Miner: "Irvine Upham on James Agee," ed. George Wead, transcript of a recorded interview, 1968. (Hereafter referred to as "Upham transcript.")

76. "Because I automatically": Agee to DM, January 17, 1930, *Yale.*

76. "On a Wednesday afternoon": *RJA,* 38.

77. "turgid and technically flawed": *ibid.*

77. "sympathy with innocent living nature": *ibid.,* 40.

78. "unquestionably more poetic talent": Theodore Spencer to Dean Hanford, May 27, 1930, *Harvard.*

CHAPTER 5: ONE GRAND TIME TO BE MAUDLIN

79f. "The Saunders family": Elsie Pomeroy, *William Saunders and His Five Sons: The Story of the Marquis Wheat Family* (Toronto: The Ryerson Press, 1956), 156–67; Explanatory Matter, *Hamilton;* B. F. Skinner, *Particulars of My Life* (New York: Alfred A. Knopf, 1976); Neuman interview.

80. "I don't know": *FF,* 52.

80. *"O that my boat might be shipwrecked":* Pomeroy, *William Saunders and His Five Sons,* 165.

81. "high-strung and intense": *FF,* 52.

81. Before marrying: Explanatory Matter, *Hamilton.*

82. "fine and lovable": *FF,* 51–52.

83. "When he spoke": *RJA,* 44.

83. "It's perfectly impossible": *FF,* 53.

84. "great program of reading": Agee to LS, July 7, 1930, *Hamilton.*

84. CONFIDENT THAT DESPITE YOUTH: Agee to LS, June 22, 1930, *Hamilton.*

84. "more and more convinced": Agee to LS, July 7, 1930, *Hamilton.*

84f. "I've been homesick": *ibid.*

85. At the end of August: Agee to LS, September 1, 1930, *Hamilton.*

85. "We began to sit": *FF,* 54.

85. "glory": Agee to LS, September 22, 1930, *Hamilton.*

86. "stridently happy": *FF,* 54.

86. treasurer for the Signet Society: Agee to LS, September 22, 1930, *Hamilton.*

86. Tom Raywood: Saudek interviews; *RJA,* 25–26; Agee to LS, September 22, 1930, *Hamilton.*

87. Surrounded by a few sticks: *RJA,* 43; Agee to LS, March 17, 1931, *Hamilton.*

87. "poems that ride halfway": Agee to LS, probably late 1930, *Hamilton.*

87. *"I have been fashioned on a chain of flesh":* HA 117 (Christmas 1930), 22; *PMV,* 47.

88. "I've gone through": Agee to LS, probably late 1930, *Hamilton.*

88. "monstrous series of charts": *ibid.*

89. "rich enjoyment in the drama": Upham transcript.

89. "I'd do anything": *FF,* 45–48.

90. He began dating: Agee to BS, probably late 1930, *Texas.*

90. "teen-age innocence": Reminiscence by BS, 1983.

91f. "There are a lot of reasons": Agee to Dorothy Carr, December 29, 1930, *Texas.*

93. On New Year's Eve: Agee to LS, January 4, 1931, *Hamilton.*

93. "paper in front of him": Agee to LS, March 17, 1931, *Hamilton.*

93. "it was one grand time": Agee to LS, January 4, 1931, *Hamilton.*

94. "mellow, tired Cambridge": "Summer Is Come, and Evening Spreads Its Gold," unpublished poem by Agee, *Hamilton.*

95. "creative flabbiness": Agee to BS, July 21, 1931, *Texas.*

95. "Your remarks *re* Dorothy Carr": *ibid.*

95. August tally: Agee to LS, August 31, 1931, *Hamilton.*

96. "set fire": *FF,* 53.

96. "spectacularly happy": Agee to LS, October 16, 1931, *Hamilton.*

97. "for every breath": *ibid.*

97. Skinner observed: B. F. Skinner interview with the author, Cambridge, Massachusetts, July 1982.

98. "fairly successful death-dance": Agee to LS, October 16, 1931, *Hamilton.*

98. "everything going *continuously*": *FF,* 54–55.

98f. "It's still on me": Agee to LS, October 16, 1931, *Hamilton.*

100. Louise was ill: Agee to LS, November 3, 1931, *Hamilton.*

100. "Almost everyone seems": *ibid.*

101. *"Like Byron, I'll begin at the beginning": Poems,* 81.

101f. "Spiritually speaking": *ibid.,* 79–81.

103. "Backward ran sentences": Robert Elson, *Time Inc.: The Intimate History of a Publishing Enterprise, 1923–1941* (New York: Atheneum, 1968), 266.

103. "Sirs: Imagine your staff": Agee to *Time,* March 6, 1931, *Time.*

104. David Weir: Weir to Roy Larsen, November 25, 1931, *Time.*

104. Larsen requested: Larsen to Weir, December 1, 1931, *Time.*

104. One wintry Saturday: *RJA,* 29–30.

105. *"Advocate's* cover": Boston *Herald,* March 18, 1932.

105. "too much like TIME's": Larsen to Weir: March 30, 1932, *Time.*

105f. "scribbles a good deal": *HA* 118 (March 1932), 18.

106. "latest nerve-shatterer": *ibid.,* 22.

106. Macdonald harbored serious doubts: *RJA,* 127.

107. "generous and evil intentioned": Agee to DM, probably spring 1932, *Yale.*

108. obstacles faced by a serious American writer: *RJA,* 45.

109. "I didn't do him a favor": *ibid.,* 127.

109. On the night before: *ibid.,* 30–31; Saudek interviews.

109. *"Now the snows are withdrawn": Poems,* 140–41.

110. "I remember looking down": *RJA,* 31.

CHAPTER 6: EMPIRE

114ff. The publishing empire: *Time Inc.: The Intimate History of a Publishing Enterprise, 1923–1941; Luce and His Empire.*

116. *"Time is* a re-write sheet": *Time Inc.: The Intimate History of a Publishing Enterprise,* 197.

117. "Business is, essentially": *ibid.,* 127.

117. "kittenish as a Victorian": *ibid.*

117. "as a journalistic inspiration": Dwight Macdonald, " 'Fortune' Magazine," *TN* 144 (May 8, 1937), 527.

117. "At the end of 1931": *ibid.*

118. In the lobby: *RJA,* 35.

118. "A desk, for Godsake": *Writing for Fortune: Nineteen Authors Remember Life on the Staff of a Remarkable Magazine* (New York: Time Inc., 1980), 150–51.

118. The Last Judgment: *Luce and His Empire,* 146.

119. "Fundamentally we don't": *Time Inc.: The Intimate History of a Publishing Enterprise,* 212.

119. Macdonald, for one: Macdonald, " 'Fortune' Magazine," 529.

119. "booming little capitalist culture": Dwight Macdonald, "Time, Fortune, Life," *TN* 144 (May 22, 1937), 586.

120. "strictly from hunger": *Writing for Fortune,* 153–54.

120. "If the articles": Macdonald, " 'Fortune' Magazine," 530.

120. "How can you": *Writing for Fortune,* 151.

121. "You can work": *ibid.,* 10.

121. "The most efficient male": Macdonald, " 'Fortune' Magazine," 530.

122. "Just put all the material": *Writing for Fortune,* 153–54.

122. "For about 3 weeks": Agee to Howard Doughty, summer 1932, in possession of Mrs. Doughty.

122. *"The aristocracy of wealth and talents":* Archibald MacLeish, *Collected Poems, 1917–1952* (Boston: Houghton Mifflin, 1952), 337.

123. "Something attracts me": *FF,* 60–61.

123. "gruesome sense": Agee to E. Talbot Donaldson, July 1932, quoted in Doty, *Tell Me Who I Am,* 31.

123f. He found a bleak: *ibid.*

124. she displayed symptoms: Skinner interview.

124. "very little advantage": Agee to Olivia Saunders, August 1, 1932, quoted in Moreau, *The Restless Journey of James Agee,* 107.

124. "I take this off moment": Agee to Olivia Saunders, summer 1932, *ibid.,* 109.

124. "poetry is the product": *FF,* 56.

125. "I've been used to bad spells": *ibid.*

125. *"epidemic* of despair": *ibid.,* 58.

125. "pretty well out": *ibid.*

125. "the *foul* results": *ibid.,* 59.

126. "Let Us Now Praise Famous Men": *RJA,* 46.

126. "I expect I would live": *ibid.,* 47.

126. "see a glimpse": Moreau, *The Restless Journey of James Agee,* 111.

127. "trying as never before": *FF,* 63.

127. *Symposium: ibid.,* 62.

127. "When I'm with your family": Agee to LS, December 5, 1932, *Hamilton.*

127. "A very beautiful": Agee to LS, November 24, 1932, *Hamilton.*

128. "no more subject": *FF,* 64.

128. "I don't think": Agee to LS, December 5, 1932, *Hamilton.*

129. "I never saw": Doty, *Tell Me Who I Am,* 58.

129. matching holes: Frohock interview.

130. one of the guests: Neuman interview.

CHAPTER 7: VOYAGE

132. "Now it is competent, our common heart": Agee to LS, April 1933, *Hamilton.*

133. "a vocation": *RJA,* 50; Saudek interviews.

133. "I'm so tied up": *RJA,* 54.

134. "I know there is a character": Agee to LS, June 21, 1933, *Hamilton.*

134. *"John Carter"* was doomed: for extant verses of the poem, see *Poems,* 81–82.

135. They batted around: Agee to LS, July 16, 1933, *Hamilton.*

135. "Joyce I think": Agee to LS, August 3, 1933, *Hamilton.*

135. "too long, too feeble": Agee to RF, August 29, 1933, *NYPL.*

136. "ever born in Tennessee": Agee to LS, June 21, 1933, *Hamilton.*

136. "Near Knoxville the streams": "The Project Is Important," *Fortune* 8 (October 1933), 81–97.

137. Harvard Business School: Moreau, *The Restless Journey of James Agee,* 117.

137. "He will feed me": *FF,* 66–67.

137. "immoral that a writer": *RJA,* 124.

138. "Now, Jim, don't you see": *ibid.*

138. "The trouble with Agee": *ibid.*

138. "It varies with me": Agee to RF, August 29, 1933, *NYPL.*

138. "fast, loose, long-legged walk": *RJA,* 52.

138. "Ivy League journalistic delving": Robert Fitzgerald, interview with the author, New York, New York, July 1982.

139. "extraordinary promise": Stephen Vincent Benét to Eugene Davidson, June 22, 1934, quoted in Moreau, *The Restless Journey of James Agee*, 122.

139. "Equally obviously": *PMV*, 5–7.

140. "Invocation to the Social Muse": *Collected Poems, 1917–1952*, 93–95.

140. *"Forbear, forbear to look at me with joy"*: *PMV*, 50.

140. *"Not of good will my mother's flesh was wrought"*: ibid., 52.

141. "My heart and mind": ibid., 59.

141f. "Dedication": *ibid.*, 16–23.

142. "Why I am . . . writing this": Agee to Allen Tate, no date, *Princeton*.

142f. "Though I have badly failed": Agee to John Livingston Lowes, no date, *Houghton*.

143. "deepest namable interests": Agee to Louis Untermeyer, July 3, 1935, *Indiana*.

143. "I hate promise": Agee to LS, summer 1934, *Hamilton*.

144. "gentle, sensitive": *FF,* 171.

144. "in most possible kinds of pain": *ibid.,* 68–69.

144. On entering Agee's office: Moreau, *The Restless Journey of James Agee*, 119–20.

144. "apathy, or a sort": *FF*, 68.

144. "attracted to teaching": *ibid.,* 70.

145. "Great American Roadside": *Fortune* 10 (September 1934), 53–63, 172–77.

145f. "Very much like the subject": Agee to LS, summer 1934, *Hamilton*.

146. "nationalist propaganda": Agee to DM, spring 1935, *Yale*.

146. "Get a radio": *LUFM*, 14–15.

147. "trouble in the bowels": Agee to DM, spring 1935, *Yale*.

147. "kick in the ass": Agee to RF, probably summer 1934, *NYPL*.

147. "picture caption-chapter head": *FF*, 75.

147. "The Supreme Effort": Agee to DM, July 1, 1935, *Yale*.

147. "Probably shall go somewhere": Agee to DM, spring 1935, *Yale*.

147f. Via favored: *FF*, 80; Agee to LS, September 3, 1935, *Hamilton.*

148. "much the hardest": Agee to DM, spring 1935 and July 1, 1935, *Yale.*

149. "clear & inescapable": *FF*, 77.

149. "the Largest, the Loudest": *ibid.*, 81.

149. "People's reactions to it": *ibid.*, 77.

149. "cheerfully remember": *Time Inc.: The Intimate History of a Publishing Enterprise*, 222.

150. possibility of shooting him: *RJA*, 36.

150. "You may return": Agee to DM, July 1, 1935, *Yale.*

150. jacket was on fire: Saudek interviews.

151. "edges on shallow sand": *RJA*, 65.

151. "full and 'relevant' ": Agee to LS, December 26, 1935, *Indiana.*

151. "New Orleans is stirring": *LUFM*, 43.

151. "really married": *Tell Me Who I Am*, 58.

151. He imagined mothers: Agee to LS, April 14, 1936, *Indiana.*

151. They had shouting matches: Doty, *Tell Me Who I Am*, 58.

152. "a great writer": *ibid.*

152. quantities of current magazines: Agee to LS, December 26, 1935, *Indiana;* Agee to Silvia Saunders, December 2, 1935, *Indiana.*

152. "However many heels": Agee to LS, December 27, 1935, *Hamilton.*

152. "some Jung-disciple": Agee to LS, December 26, 1935, *Indiana.*

153. Five times he tried: *ibid.*

153. "On the rough wet grass": *ADIF*, 15.

153. "Have been working": *RJA*, 64.

154. *"Parents on porches":* *ADIF*, 15.

154. "twinges of homesickness": Agee to LS, December 26, 1935, *Indiana.*

154. "Got quite a fair slug": Agee to DM, early 1936, *Yale.*

155. "Pleasantest event in weeks": Agee to LS, April 14, 1936, *Indiana.*

155. "I guess it is unfailingly wrong": Agee to DM, 1936, *Yale.*

155. "I know there are two things": *FF*, 86–87.

155. "The weather wonderful": *ibid.*, 90.
156. "catching up the threads": Flye, recorded interview.
156. "as likable and moving": *FF*, 78–79.
156f. "He made no comment": *RJA*, 96.
157. "No time or visit": *ibid.*

CHAPTER 8: SPIES

159. "swallowing with excitement": *RJA*, 37.
159. "Best break": *FF*, 92.
161. "Harvard and Exeter": *LUFM*, ix–xi.
162. "is certainly showing": Agee to WE, 1936, *Texas*.
162. *Greed: RJA*, 66.
162. "in flight from Greenwich Village": *LUFM*, xi.
163. "The very blood": *ibid.*, 212.
163. "It seems to me curious": *ibid.*, 7.
164. *"Against time and the damages of the brain": ibid.*, 5.
164. "in a perversion": *ibid.*, 30.
164f. Loitering by the courthouse: *ibid.*, 329–37.
165. "[Tingle] went $400 into debt": *ibid.*, 108.
166. They spent two days: *ibid.*, 339.
166ff. "narrow and twisted concrete": *ibid.*, 341–81.
170. "His people": Flye, recorded interview.
171. "sweated and scratched": *LUFM*, xi.
171. "It is late": *ibid.*, 47–52.
171. "In all this house": *ibid.*, 130–31.
172. "One is the steaming": *ibid.*, 132.
172. "The odor of pine": *ibid.*, 139–40.
172f. "a clutter of obese": *ibid.*, 191.
173. "I was on the porch": *ibid.*, 60–61.
174. "a word to suspect": *ibid.*, 215.
174. "fragments of cloth": *ibid.*, 12.
174f. "Freshly laundered cotton": *ibid.*, 233–34.
175. "And on this façade": *ibid.*, 241–43.

175. "It is simple": *ibid.*, 306.

176. "The family exists": *ibid.*, 291.

176. "Oh, I do *hate*": *ibid.*, 188.

177. "with one broken": *ibid.*, 401–02.

177. "half-crazy with the heat": *FF*, 94.

178. Evans' pitiless photographs: In 1980 *New York Times* reporter Howell Raines returned to the scenes and some of the people Agee and Evans had visited in Alabama. In the resulting article, "Let Us Now Revisit Famous Folk," *NYT Magazine*, May 25, 1980, Raines discovered persistent resentment on the part of the original families and their children. "Those pictures are a scandal on the family," said one, speaking of Evans' photographs. Agee was remembered more favorably, though the reverence he felt for his subjects was clearly not returned.

178. "by scraping the very cervix": Agee to WE, 1936, *Texas.*

178. Wilder Hobson: *Writing for Fortune,* 9; Fitzgerald interview; Richard Harrison, interview with the author, New York, New York, May 1982.

178. He transferred Ingersoll: Ingersoll later left Time Inc. to found the avowedly leftist newspaper *PM.*

179. "Dwight," his mother exclaimed: *Writing for Fortune,* 155–57.

179. "impossible": *FF*, 94.

179f. "It appeared that the magazine": *RJA,* 66.

180. "I am giving myself": Agee to WE, probably late 1936, *Texas.*

180. "I seem to be lazy": *FF*, 96.

181. "He is a smart guy": Agee to WE, probably late 1936, *Texas.*

181. Edward Aswell: *RJA,* 67–68.

CHAPTER 9: PASSION

183ff. The early months of 1937: The following account is based on Agee's unpublished notes for *Bigger Than We Are: A Love Story* (1948–1955), in possession of Helen Levitt.

191. *"Mumsy told me not to play"*: *Poems,* 145–46.

191. "Even for a modern writer": Dwight Macdonald, *Against the American Grain* (New York: Random House, 1963), 152.

191. "I never intend to write": *FF*, 97.

192. "prim Arthur Treacher": "Six Days at Sea," *Fortune* 16 (September 1937), 117–20.

193. "by sympathy and conviction": *LUFM*, 225.

194. "I've got them in my head": Selden Rodman, interview with the author, Oakland, New Jersey, July 1982.

194. *"From now on kill America out of your mind"*: Poems, 155.

194. "His skill with traditional meters": *RJA*, 68–69.

195. "I have a fractional idea": Agee to LS, probably summer 1937, *Hamilton*.

195. "the great North American Agee": Rodman interview.

196. Walking through Sheridan Square: Frohock interview.

204. movie scenario: "Notes for a Moving Picture: The House," *Prose*, 151–73.

205. Guggenheim Fellowship: *RJA*, 70; *Prose*, 131–48.

208. "An excess of vitality": *FF*, 96.

208. When the creative mood: Brad Darrach, interview with the author, New York, New York, September 1983.

CHAPTER 10: THE RELUCTANT RADICAL

212. "small and charming": *Bigger Than We Are.*

212. "My father," she recalled: Alma Mailman Neuman, "Thoughts of Jim: A Memoir of Frenchtown and James Agee," *Shenandoah* 33 (1981–1982), 25–26. (Hereafter referred to as "Thoughts of Jim.")

213. One night: Neuman interview.

213. "resembled his way": "Thoughts of Jim."

213. In his mind's eye: *Bigger Than We Are.*

214. neither "journalistic": *Prose*, 133.

214. "should be as definitely": *ibid.*, 134.

215. "disintegrating and 'growing up' ": *FF*, 105.

215. "a rough yellow lump": "Thoughts of Jim."

215. "unable even to boil": Agee to WE, 1938, *Texas*.

215. Did Wilder Hobson need: Agee to Wilder Hobson, 1938, *Texas*.

215. "libellous": Agee to DM, 1938, *Yale*.

216. "who will not capitulate": *FF*, 106.

217. "A magazine unqualifiedly to be respected": Agee to DM, 1938, *Yale*.

217. midnight ride: "Thoughts of Jim."

217. August 1 deadline: Agee to WE, May 1938, *Texas*.

217f. "I have in general": *ibid.*

218. "long blind-streak": Agee to WE, June 20, 1938, *Texas*.

218. "Several times a day": Agee to WE, July 1, 1938, *Texas*.

219. Aswell extended the deadline: *ibid.*

219. "My trouble is": *FF*, 104–05.

219. "hours of sexual nightmare": Agee to WE, July 27, 1938, *Texas*.

219. he dreamed of William Faulkner: Agee to WE, August 24, 1938, *Texas*.

219f. "Poverty shall tear": Agee to WE, November 1938, *Texas*.

220. "My relief from stress": Agee to WE, August 12, 1938, *Texas*.

220. "The two main facts": *Prose*, 134.

220. "P. S. Abbie stept": Agee to WE, May 9, 1938, *Texas*.

220. "should be colorless": *Prose*, 136.

221. "I am wanting": Agee to WE, September 15, 1938, *Texas*.

221. "I think it would be very nice": *ibid.*

221. "twiddling": *ibid.*

221. "I am sufficiently superstitious": Agee to RF, September 2, 1938, *NYPL*.

221. "a bad boil": Agee to WE, September 25, 1938, *Texas*.

222. "None of it": Agee to WE, October 3, 1938, *Texas*.

222. "a round lump": Agee to WE, October 15, 1938, *Texas*.

222. "A fair way of indicating": Agee to WE, July 27, 1938, *Texas*.

222. "The world has not": Agee to WE, September 25, 1938, *Texas.*

223. "Not an inch": Agee to WE, October 15, 1938, *Texas.*

223. "always surprised": "Thoughts of Jim."

223. "I would never have known": *FF,* 115.

224. "We didn't think": "Thoughts of Jim."

224. $12.52: *RJA,* 71.

225. they were married: "Thoughts of Jim."

225. "I wish my book": Agee to LS, December 21, 1938, *Hamilton.*

225. "thoroughly to the good": Agee to WE, late 1938, *Texas.*

226. more precious gift: Agee to WE, December 1938, *Texas.*

226. "pleasure people claim": *ibid.*

226. "All these shifts": *ibid.*

227. "getting into the home stretch": Agee to DM, 1938, *Yale.*

227. The night they returned: "Thoughts of Jim."

228. "the collaborated creature": "Southeast of the Island: Travel Notes," *Prose,* 177–201.

228f. "I will admit": *Time Inc.: The Intimate History of a Publishing Enterprise,* 349–51.

229. *"It is one": Fortune* 20 (July 1939), 145.

229f. "It sounds like a meeting": *LUFM,* 318–25.

230. "It has been": *FF,* 116.

231. "Whenever we made love": Neuman interview.

231. Monk's Farm: *ibid.*

231. "Why, all God's outdoors": Saudek interviews.

232. "It's gospel": Eunice Jessup, interview with the author, Wilton, Connecticut, April 1982.

232. "I am essentially an anarchist": *FF,* 98–99.

233. "it is possible": *ibid.,* 120.

233. "falseness in his goodness": Neuman interview.

233. Accompanied by Father Flye: Flye, recorded interview.

233f. "More delay from Harpers": Agee to WE, September 8, 1939, *Texas.*

234. "I have organized": Agee to WE, probably late 1939, *Texas.*

234. "Though I am still": Agee to WE, September 1939, *Texas.*

234. wrote a memorandum: Paul Brooks, interview with the author, Lincoln, Massachusetts, July 1982.

234f. "I wish to call attention": *Texas.*

234. omitting unsightly flyspecks: Brooks interview.

234. With the ever helpful Hobson: Moreau, *The Restless Journey of James Agee,* 175.

234. "weak, sick, vindictive": *FF,* 121.

CHAPTER 11: THE CAPTIVE POET

238. 322 West 15th Street: Robert Phillips Russell to Leonard Rapport, September 23, 1940, in possession of Mrs. Robert Russell; Neuman interview.

238. When the time arrived: Neuman interview.

239. "I have caused": Agee to WE, late 1939, *Texas.*

239. Robert Fitzgerald: *RJA,* 76.

239. "the steady man": *ibid.,* 115.

241. "satanic naïveté": quoted in James Stern, "Walker Evans (1903–1975): A Memoir," *London Magazine* (August–September 1977), 9.

242. "Hush, the walls": Fitzgerald interview.

243. Eunice Clark: Jessup interview. Eunice Clark was briefly married to Agee's friend Selden Rodman. She later married Jack Jessup of Time Inc.

244. "Paul," he said: Brooks interview.

245. Mia Fritsch: Mia Fritsch Agee, interviews with the author, New York, New York, June and July 1982. (Hereafter referred to as Agee interviews.)

246. "clarity of mind": *FF,* 124.

246. "intensely satisfactory": *Bigger Than We Are.*

247. "I know these statistics": Agee to LS, March 1940, *Hamilton.*

247. To his fury: Brooks interview.

247. Alma's three-inch heels: Neuman interview.

248. Once she went flying: *ibid.*

248. at the Baldwin estate: Jessup interview.

248f. "I feel mainly two things": Agee to LS, December 1940, *Hamilton.*

249ff. "constantly in the bottom": *RJA,* 82–84.

251. *"Two years have passed, and made a perfect wheel": Poems,* 144.

252. Alice Morris: Alice Morris, interview with the author, New York, New York, September 1982.

252. "I am, thank God": Agee to RF, no date, *NYPL.*

253. "Please give my": Agee to Robert Linscott, no date, *Texas.*

253. "Why don't I continue": Agee to RF, June 1941; *RJA,* 84.

254. small amounts of money: Neuman interview.

254. "I feel the deepest kind of sympathy": Agee to RF, March 21, 1941, *NYPL.*

255. "It was impossible": Macdonald interview.

255f. "Nothing makes me more frantic": *FF,* 127.

256. "When I saw the picture": *ibid.,* 129.

258. "throw down the volume": Selden Rodman, "The Poetry of Poverty," *Saturday Review* 24 (August 23, 1941), 6.

258. "Mr. Agee does a good deal": Harvey Breit, "Cotton Tenantry," *The New Republic* 105 (September 15, 1941), 349–50.

259. "I'll gladly make the agreement": Agee to RF, 1941, *NYPL.*

259. "stiff and reverent": *RJA,* 86.

259. She told her son: Agee interviews.

260. "great book": Lionel Trilling, "Greatness with One Fault in It," *Kenyon Review* 4 (Winter 1942), 99–102.

260. six hundred copies: Brooks interview. In the November 16, 1957, issue of *The New Yorker,* Agee's friend Dwight Macdonald took Houghton Mifflin to task for failing to promote the book: "The publishers remaindered it as soon as they decently could, and they have not brought it back into print, although its reputation has grown by word of mouth, until copies fetch as much as twenty dollars." Houghton Mifflin took exception to the criticism, maintaining that it stocked the book for seven years. But the fact remains that the book was ignored during Agee's lifetime.

Three years after Macdonald's article Houghton Mifflin finally reissued *Let Us Now Praise Famous Men.*

260. "It is a sinful book": *FF,* 131.

261. "This is of course": Stern, "Walker Evans (1903–1975): A Memoir," 7.

261. The photographer inadvertently left it: James Thompson, interview with the author, Amenia, New York, November 1982.

CHAPTER 12: IN THE DARK

264. "To see and hear": *RJA,* 87.

264. magnifying glass: "Let Us Now Remember a Famous Man," *FYI* (in-house publication of Time Inc.) (February 3, 1975), 1–3.

264. He deliberately mispronounced: Winthrop Sargeant, *In Spite of Myself* (New York: Doubleday, 1970), 233.

265. "tank up on whiskey": *In Spite of Myself,* 234.

265f. "Not satisfied with this classification": Agee to Alden Grover, October 19, 1942, *Time.*

267. "I have not seen combat service": Agee to Edwin Westrate, October 1, 1942, *Texas.*

268. "Project X": Alfred Kazin, *New York Jew* (New York: Alfred A. Knopf, 1978), 59.

268f. "It is the business of journalism": "Notes and Suggestions of the Magazine Under Discussion," memorandum by Agee, 1942, *Time.*

271. "unrealized great writer": Clement Greenberg, interview with the author, North Salem, New York, June 1982.

272. "like shit through a goose": Archer Winsten, interview with the author, New York, New York, July 1982.

272. "in so far as a professional's preoccupation": *AOF1,* 23.

272. *Casablanca: ibid.,* 29.

272. *Citizen Kane:* Agee to Edwin Westrate, October 1, 1942, *Texas.* As Wells's reputation sank in later years, Agee came to value him not as a genius but as a genuinely talented director.

273. They spotted him lunching: Kazin, *New York Jew,* 57.

274. "Like so many Southern writers I knew": *ibid.*, 58.

274. "Dear Sirs": *AOF1*, i.

275. "Stalinism with New Dealism": *ibid.*, 37–39.

275. "uninformed superiority": Diana Trilling, interview with the author, New York, New York, September 1982.

276. "What kind of doubletalk": *TN* 156 (June 19, 1943), 873–74.

276. "I expect the worst": *FF*, 134.

276. "Our only really good films": *AOF1*, 65.

276. "The pressures of work": *FF*, 132.

277. "Pseudo-Folk": *PR* 11 (Spring 1944), 219–23.

277. He wrote the critic: AM to Agee, February 6, 1943, *LC;* AM to Agee, February 23, 1943, *LC.*

278. Leaving Florida: Agee interviews.

278. "I would be glad enough": *FF*, 132.

279f. dreadful nightmare: "Dreams, March–April, 1944," *Texas.*

280. To prod Agee: AM to Agee, July 4, 1944, *LC;* Agee to AM, July 26, 1944, *LC.*

280. "I'm grateful for your offer": Agee to AM, July 26, 1944, *LC.*

280. TERRIBLY SORRY: Agee to AM, August 4, 1944, *LC.*

281. "He had some pitiful": Agee to AM, August 6, 1944, *LC.*

282. "very encouraging": Agee to JS, September 12, 1944, in possession of JS.

282. "with conspicuous lack of valor": *ibid.*

283. In Los Angeles: Dwight Whitney, interview with the author, Los Angeles, California, July 1983.

284. "It was the fashion": Greenberg interview.

284. "Ever since I first saw": *AOF1*, 132.

284. "He is an extremely wise": *ibid.*, 133.

284f. "If you compare": *ibid.*, 136–39.

285. she got in touch: Neuman interview.

286. "I already had a father": Joel Agee, *Twelve Years* (New York: Farrar, Straus & Giroux, 1981), 90–91.

286f. The two of them: Neuman interview.

CHAPTER 13: A DANGEROUS MAN

288. "gotten fully around": Agee to James Stern, August 7, 1944, in possession of JS.

289. "It seems unlikely": *FF,* 139.

289. "vivid, sensitive intelligence": *AOF1,* 158–60.

289. "nothing on earth": *FF,* 144.

290. "Such a thing": *ibid.,* 138.

290. "I know . . . by personal experience": Unpublished manuscript, *Texas.* Agee referred to the *Sewanee Review* article in *FF,* 148.

290. "It is clear": *AOF1,* 162–64.

291. "I am forced": *ibid.,* 150.

291. "perfect liberty": *ibid.,* 188.

292. "The mere thought": Agee to James Stern, August 7, 1944, in possession of JS.

292. "Some of the best photographs": Helen Levitt, *A Way of Seeing: Photographs of New York* (New York: The Viking Press, 1965), 3–8, 73–78.

293. "There, unaware and unnoticed": Commentary in possession of Helen Levitt.

294. "I would suppose": Agee to JS, August 7, 1944, in possession of JS.

294f. "At the end of the next war": *FF,* 153.

295. "O my poor country": *Poems,* 157.

295f. "The greatest and most terrible": *Time* 44 (August 20, 1945), 19.

296. "*second* worst thing": *FYI* (December 12, 1980), 1.

296. "When people tell me": *RJA,* 116.

296. "My two great doubts": *FF,* 149.

296. two works about the bomb: *ibid.,* 152.

297. Flying to Maine: Moreau, *The Restless Journey of James Agee,* 214.

297. "I, who by chance walked safely past a war": *Poems,* 68.

297. "This is . . . half drunk": *FF,* 154.

298. Rorschach test: Agee interviews.

298. easygoing older woman: Darrach interview.

298. "You can either work this": Comstock interview.

298f. "I've started a short novel": *FF*, 152.

299. "Dave Mooney—*Hobe Gillum*": Doty, *Tell Me Who I Am*, 76–77.

300. "Julia Teresa Agee": *FF*, 197.

300. life and death: *ibid.*, 179.

301f. Beginning with the issue of May 31: *AOF1*, 252–62.

302. "How does it feel": Charles Chaplin, *My Autobiography* (New York: Simon & Schuster, 1964), 452.

303. "logical extension of business": *AOF1*, 370–72.

303. "It would violate": Henry Luce to Agee, July 28, 1947, *Time*.

303. "peculiar logic": Agee to Henry Luce, July 1947, *Time*.

304. "Civilization has come a long way": *AOF1*, 238.

304. "For the nothing": *ibid.*, 285.

305. "still nominally the germinal force": *ibid.*, 278–80.

305. "favorite stories": Agee to T. S. Matthews, June 1947, *Time*.

305. enormous green frog: Perrin Stryker, interview with the author, New York, New York, June 1982.

306. "Dream Sequence": *Texas*.

306. "It is Thanksgiving": *Prose*, 124.

307. "This book is chiefly": *Texas*.

307. "Week after week": *FF*, 170.

308. actual names: Some names were changed in the published version to protect the privacy of family members. Thus the writer's mother, Laura, became Mary, and the writer's sister, Emma, became Catherine.

308. "Theme: I worship him": *Texas*.

310. "a feast for the self-righteous": *AOF1*, 300.

310. "I have no doubt": *ibid.*, 290–93.

310. a letter of appreciation: John Huston, *An Open Book* (New York: Alfred A. Knopf, 1980), 188.

311. "any critic is a fool": Agee to JH, February 21, 1948, *Texas*.

311. friends of Agee: Jay Leyda, interview with the author, New York, New York, July 1983.

312. "It is a drastic thing": *FF*, 173.

313f.   A vaguely disappointed Matthews: *RJA*, 115.

314.   "Dear Tom": Agee to T. S. Matthews, June 1948, *Time*.

315.   "Perhaps he was torn apart": *RJA*, 118.

CHAPTER 14: THE OPPORTUNIST

319.   Christopher Gerould: Agee interviews.

320.   He fell in: *RJA*, 156; Agee interviews.

320.   "To watch his work": *AOF1*, 313–18.

321.   he required the writer: Agee interviews.

321f.   In three days: *ibid.*

322.   "It is not snowing": *AOF2*, 394.

322ff.   *Scientists and Tramp: Texas.*

325f.   Frank Taylor: Frank Taylor, interview with the author, New York, New York, June 1982; Nan Abell (formerly Taylor), interview with the author, New York, New York, May 1982.

326.   "The way things are going": Agee to FT, December 29, 1948, *Indiana*.

327.   "It was one of the things": *RJA*, 157.

327.   "This has certainly been": *FF*, 178–79.

328.   deathbed reconciliation: Doty, *Tell Me Who I Am*, 70–71.

328.   "I don't see": *FF*, 176.

328f.   National Institute of Arts: *NYT*, May 13, 1949.

329.   "Comedy's Greatest Era": *AOF1*, 2–19.

330.   "It was a deeply melancholy day": *FF*, 180.

330.   "Religion and the Intellectuals": *PR* 17 (February 1950), 106–13.

330f.   "Any expression of religion": *FF*, 184.

331.   "The book will be finished": Agee to JH, February 6, 1950, *Academy*.

332.   "What time": *FF*, 181.

332.   "I'd give anything": Agee to JH, July 6, 1950, *Academy*.

333.   the editor concluded: *RJA*, 157.

333. "with a one-to-hundred expectation": Agee to David McDowell, September 20, 1950, *Columbia.*

333. Two literary journals: *Botteghe Oscure* 6 (1950), 339–409; *PR* 18 (March 1951), 137–66.

334. Cerf represented: Upham transcript.

334. "In every objective way": Agee to David McDowell, September 20, 1950, *Columbia.*

335. "long, very slow": Agee to JH, September 14, 1950, *Academy.*

335f. *Life* profile: *AOF1*, 320–31.

337. "What irks and sickens": Agee to JH, September 14, 1950, *Academy.*

337. Bitterroot Range: Huston, *An Open Book,* 188; John Huston, interview with the author, New York, New York, June 1982.

337. "great good": *FF,* 182.

337f. "She's been a lovely": *ibid.,* 183.

CHAPTER 15: THE GIRL WITH THE GOLDEN EYES

339. For two weeks: Huston, *An Open Book,* 188–89; Huston interview.

339ff. "He loved to talk": *ibid.*

342. "Oh, Christ, Jim": Lillian Ross, "Picture," *The New Yorker* (June 7, 1952), 68–69.

342. "If everything works": *FF,* 185–86.

343. One evening he found himself: Leyda interview.

343ff. Patricia Scallon: Abell interview; Taylor interview.

345. "I was all": Huston interview.

345f. "sense of hope": Agee to JS, January 3, 1951, in possession of JS.

346. "Jim was a willing collaborator": Huston, *An Open Book,* 189; Huston interview.

346f. "All of a sudden": *AOF2*, 157.

347. "The singing of most": *ibid.,* 152.

348. "a series of attacks": *FF,* 186.

348. Joseph Cotten: Abell interview.
348. They believed he had escaped: *FF,* 186.
349. "My God, no, Jim": Huston interview.
349. he bribed nurses: Abell interview.
349. "This whole thing": *FF,* 186–87.
349f. "I'm in a hospital": Agee to WE, January 21, 1951, *Texas.*
351. "Tobacco—with or without": Unpublished manuscript, *Texas.*
352. "I am supposed": Agee to JS, January 24, 1950, in possession of JS.
352. terrible mistake: Upham transcript.
353. "A Mother's Tale": *Prose,* 221–43.
354. "We're going to the Santa Barbara": Abell interview.
354. "dark poem": *NYT Book Review,* April 8, 1951, 4.
354. "He has fraternized": *TN* 172 (April 28, 1951), 400–401.
355. Robert Fitzgerald's heart: *RJA,* 92.
355. stranded in England: Agee to RF, November 8, 1951, *NYPL.*
355. " 'African Queen,' 1st draft": Agee to David Bradley, June 26, 1953, *Texas.*
356. he disapproved: Huston interview.
356. Agee paid a surprise call: Upham transcript.
356. Frank Taylor's turn: Taylor interview.
357. *Bloodline: Twentieth.*
357. Agee pursued Pat: Taylor interview.
357. "pressing," she explained: Abell interview.
358. Each day he wore: Taylor interview.
358. "hellishly bored": *FF,* 189.
358f. "She really isn't a saint": *ibid.,* 188.
359. "depressed at being broke": *ibid.,* 194.
360. "In another 3 weeks": *ibid.,* 195.
360. "a long, anguished love-letter": *ibid.,* 199–200.
361. Dust and magazines: Abell interview; letter from Bernard Schoenfeld to the author.
361. the hapless young woman: Abell interview.

362. *The Bride Comes to Yellow Sky: AOF 2,* 357–90.

362. Hartford sponsored: Agee interviews.

363. "my dear friend": Reminiscence by BS, 1983.

364. assuring the English writer: Christopher Isherwood, interview with the author, Los Angeles, California, October 1982.

364f. "He had a wonderful sense": Ivan Moffat, interview with the author, Beverly Hills, California, October 1982.

366. "Over the screech": Reminiscence by BS, 1983.

CHAPTER 16: SAINTS

368. In the twenty years: Saudek interviews.

368. On April 22: *Wesleyan.*

370. "It's a pansy's world": Whittaker Chambers, *Cold Friday* (New York: Random House, 1964), 269.

371. "NARRATOR": *Abraham Lincoln: The Early Years,* 385–86.

372. "KELSO": *ibid.,* 397.

373. "I'm staying short": *FF,* 102.

373. "superb vidpic": *Variety,* November 20, 1952.

374. Saudek paid Agee: *Wesleyan.*

374. "I think it is a fine": *FF,* 205.

374. "prevailing puritanical fanaticism": *ibid.,* 203.

375f. "I learned in the hospital": *ibid.,* 209–10.

376f. "fourteen years dropped": Agee to Alma Mailman Neuman, March 20, 1953, in possession of Neuman. Twenty years later a friend finally gave her the letter.

377. "the girl too is married": Agee to BS, October 18, 1953, *Texas.*

378. "The barbed pungency": *NYT,* January 14, 1953.

379. "one of the most insanely large": Flye, recorded interview.

379. he considered Agee foolish: Tom Dardis, *Some Time in the Sun* (New York: Scribner's, 1976), 219.

379. "I knew it was the job": Agee to JH, December 20, 1954, *Academy.*

380. "not as the criminal romantic": Flye, recorded interview.

380. "tall, rather intelligent": *AOF2*, 4.

380. "He makes me think": *ibid.*, 5–6.

380. Agee planned to deliver: Agee to David Bradley, July 13, 1953, *Texas.*

380. "Civilization nauseates me": *AOF2*, 18.

380. "whiskey listless": *RJA*, 92.

381. "Nothing in the film": Taylor interview.

381. "Sure, if he wants": Agee to David Bradley, June 26, 1953, *Texas.*

381. "I am of course appalled": *ibid.*

381. Agee ruthlessly cut: Agee to BS, October 18, 1953, *Texas.*

381f. "The funeral sequence": *AOF2*, 60.

382. "If only Beethoven": *ibid.*, 64.

382. "too 'literary' ": Reminiscence by BS, 1983.

382. "It's incomparably easier": Agee to BS, October 18, 1953, *Texas.*

382. Mia liked the neighborhood: Agee interviews.

383. "who is reputed": Agee to Alma Mailman Neuman, September 21, 1953, in possession of Neuman.

383f. "I thoroughly understand": *ibid.*

384. "Here I am": Comstock interview.

384. Agee had come to detest: Darrach interview.

384. "My idea is": Agee to BS, October 18, 1953, *Texas.*

384. Agee received $750: *Wesleyan.*

384. Taubman had long wanted: Howard Taubman, interview with the author, New York, New York, July 1982.

385. "absolute, all but maniacal": Unpublished manuscript, "Minimal Story Outline for the Tanglewood Film," *Texas.*

385. new ideas: *FF*, 213.

385. "He's 70": Agee to BS, August 25, 1954, *Texas.*

386. Mia told him: *RJA*, 159.

386. "just a matter of getting them up": Agee to Alma Mailman Neuman, April 26, 1954, in possession of Neuman.

CHAPTER 17: FULL CIRCLE

390. $30,000: Paul Gregory, interview with the author, Palm Springs, California, March 1983.

390f. At a gathering: Comstock interview.

391f. He spent most: Elsa Lanchester, *Elsa Lanchester: Herself* (New York: St. Martin's Press, 1983), 236; Gregory interview; Terry Sanders, interview with the author, Los Angeles, California, March 1983.

392. new analyst: Comstock interview.

392. "Under his California tan": Reminiscence by BS, 1983.

393. "At supper that night": *ADIF,* 19.

393. "When Jim finished reading": Reminiscence by BS, 1983.

393. Tamara began to weep: Comstock interview.

393. "mainly wandering": Agee to TC, August 23, 1954, in possession of TC.

393. One evening Taubman: Taubman interview.

394. "beautiful, concentrated experience": Agee to TC, August 23, 1954, in possession of TC.

394. "I think it is quite possible": *ibid.*

394f. "I . . . realize": Agee to TC, August 25, 1954, in possession of TC.

395. He suddenly decided: Agee to TC, September 1954, in possession of TC.

395. embarrass his host: Taubman interview.

395f. "I drove down": Agee to TC, October 1, 1954, in possession of TC.

396. "waiting out the overdue effects": *ibid.*

396f. "Another glorious day": Agee to TC, September 21, 1954, in possession of TC.

397. "I feel sure": Dardis, *Some Time in the Sun,* 218.

397f. "I'm very tempted": Agee to TC, November 8, 1954, in possession of TC.

398. "constant awareness": *FF,* 215–16.

398. "I have loved God": *ibid.,* 217.

399. "as we always have": *ibid.,* 220.

399. "early Raymond Chandler": Agee to TC, January 1955, in possession of TC.

399. "Would you like": Taubman interview.

400. "didn't care enough": *ibid.*

400. "If you've got it": James Agee and Howard Taubman, *A Tanglewood Story,* 1955, *Twentieth.*

401. "I'm afraid I may": Agee to TC, January 1955, in possession of TC.

401. interviews, surveys, tours: *FF,* 222.

401. "mystical": *ibid.,* 224.

401f. "Friday [February 25]": Agee to TC, March 2, 1955, in possession of TC.

402. "She is evidently": *ibid.*

402. "I'm less at a loss": *FF,* 226.

402. " 'I am writing . . .' ": Agee to BS, Spring 1955, *Texas.*

403. "I value it too highly": Agee to BS, March 21, 1955, *Texas.*

403. "There is indeed": Agee to TC, March 22, 1955, in possession of TC.

403. "the last girl": Agee to BS, April 1955, *Texas.*

403f. "At moments I wonder": *FF,* 227.

404. He specified use: "Some Notes on the Williamsburg Film," 1955, *Williamsburg.*

404f. engraved on his tombstone: "Light on a Small Boy in the Dark," *New York Post,* May 11, 1958.

405. In a May 11 letter: *FF,* 229–32.

405. On Friday, May 13: "Light on a Small Boy in the Dark."

405. Monday, May 16: Agee interviews.

406. McDowell called Father Flye: *FF,* 232.

406. representative of the Williamsburg Foundation: letter from John Goodbody to the author, March 24, 1982; Peter Brown, interview with the author, Williamsburg, Virginia, June 1982.

406. Tamara accidentally: Comstock interview.

406. "It was the death": Moffat interview.

406. Laughton and Gregory: Gregory interview.

406. In East Germany: Joel Agee, *Twelve Years,* 122.
407. "It is not the custom": Doty, *Tell Me Who I Am,* 128.
407. After the ceremony: Taylor interview.

BIBLIOGRAPHY

PRIMARY SOURCES

BOOKS

Agee on Film: Reviews and Comments, vol. 1. New York: Perigee Books, 1983. (Originally published by McDowell, Obolensky, New York, 1958.)

Agee on Film: Five Film Scripts by James Agee, vol 2. New York: Perigee Books, 1983. (Originally published by McDowell, Obolensky, New York, 1960.)

The Collected Poems of James Agee. Edited by Robert Fitzgerald. Boston: Houghton Mifflin, 1962.

The Collected Short Prose of James Agee. Edited by Robert Fitzgerald. Boston: Houghton Mifflin, 1962.

A Death in the Family. New York: Bantam Books, 1969. (Originally published by McDowell, Obolensky, New York, 1957.)

The Letters of James Agee to Father Flye. 2d ed. Boston: Houghton Mifflin, 1971. (Originally published by George Braziller, New York, 1962.)

Let Us Now Praise Famous Men. Boston: Houghton Mifflin, 1960. (Originally published by Houghton Mifflin, Boston, 1941.)

The Morning Watch. New York: Ballantine Books, 1966. (Originally published by Houghton Mifflin, Boston, 1951.)

Permit Me Voyage. New Haven: Yale University Press, 1934.

POEMS

"Ann Garner." *Phillips Exeter Monthly* 32 (May 1928), 77–86.

"Ann Garner" (new version). *Hound and Horn* 2 (Spring 1929), 223–35.

"Apotheosis." *Harvard Advocate* 115 (June 1929), 21.

"Beauvais." *Phillips Exeter Monthly* 30 (May 1926), 177.

"China." *Phillips Exeter Monthly* 30 (January 1926), 79.

"Class Ode." *Harvard Class Album* (1932), 204.

"Description of Elysium—with Reservations." *Harvard Advocate* 117 (March 1931), 18.

"Dixie Doodle." *Partisan Review* 4 (February 1938), 8.

"Ebb Tide." *Phillips Exeter Monthly* 30 (November 1925), 27.

"La Fille aux Cheveux de Lin." *Phillips Exeter Monthly* 30 (January 1926), 68.

"Good Friday." *Harvard Advocate* 116 (April 1930), 27.

"I Had a Little Child." *Scholastic Review* 34 (May 27, 1939), 27.

"In Heavy Mind." In Louis Untermeyer, ed., *Modern American Poetry* (New York: Harcourt, Brace, 1936).

"In Memory of My Father (Campbell County, Tennessee)." *transition* 26 (Spring 1937), 7.

"In Preparation." *Phillips Exeter Monthly* 30 (November 1925), 27.

"A Lovers' Dialogue." *Harvard Advocate* 116 (February 1930), 29.

"Lullaby." In Selden Rodman, ed., *100 Modern Poets* (New York: Mentor Books, 1949), 100.

"Lyric." *transition* 24 (June 1936), 7.

"Lyrics." *Partisan Review* 4 (December 1937), 40–43.

"Menalcas." *Phillips Exeter Monthly* 32 (December 1927), 59–65.

"Millions Are Learning How." *Common Sense* 7 (January 1938), 27.

"Opening of a Long Poem." *Harvard Advocate* 118 (June 1932), 12–20.

"Orbs Terrae." *Phillips Exeter Monthly* 31 (May 1927), 188.

"A Parable of Doors." *Harvard Advocate* 118 (Christmas 1931), 31.

"The Passionate Poet to His Love." *Harvard Advocate* 118 (February 1932), 21.

"A Poem of Poets." *Harvard Advocate* 118 (October 1931), 37.

"Rapid Transit." In Louis Untermeyer, ed., *Modern American Poetry* (New York: Harcourt, Brace, 1936).

"The Rendezvous." *Harvard Advocate* 116 (March 1930), 31.

"Resolution." *Harvard Advocate* 117 (May 1931), 77.

"Résumé." *Harvard Advocate* 116 (June 1930), 22.

"The Shadow." *Harvard Advocate* 116 (February 1930), 17.

"Six Sonnets." *Harvard Advocate* 118 (December 1931), 20–21.

"A Song." *transition* 24 (June 1936), 7.

"Song with Words." In Louis Untermeyer, ed., *Modern American Poetry* (New York: Harcourt, Brace, 1936).

"Sonnet: Death Never Swoops Us Around . . ." *Harvard Advocate* 116 (Commencement 1930), 19.

"Sonnet: I Have Been Fashioned on a Chain of Flesh . . ." *Harvard Advocate* 117 (Christmas 1930), 22.

"The Storm." *Harvard Advocate* 116 (December 1929), 15.

"Summer Evening." *Harper's Magazine* 176 (January 1938), 209.

"Sunday: Outskirts of Knoxville, Tenn." *New Masses* 24 (September 14, 1937), 22.

"Sun Our Father." *Forum* 97 (February 1937), 115.

"To Lydia." *Harvard Advocate* 115 (April 1929), 33.

"The Truce." *Harvard Advocate* 117 (May 1931), 58–59.

"Two Songs on the Economy of Abundance." In Louis Untermeyer, ed., *Modern American Poetry* (New York: Harcourt, Brace, 1936).

"Two Sonnets from a Dream." *Botteghe Oscure* 5 (1950), 336–37.

"Water." *Phillips Exeter Monthly* 31 (February 1927), 96.

"Widow." *Phillips Exeter Monthly* 30 (May 1926), 180.

STORIES

"The Bell Tower of Amiens." *Phillips Exeter Monthly* 30 (December 1925), 48–51.

"Between Trains." *Phillips Exeter Monthly* 31 (May 1927), 171–73.

"Bound for the Promised Land." *Phillips Exeter Monthly* 32 (January 1928), 85–88.

"Boys Will Be Brutes." *Harvard Advocate* 116 (April 1930), 29–33.

"Chivalry—An Allegory." *Phillips Exeter Monthly* 32 (November 1927), 25–40.

"The Circle." *Phillips Exeter Monthly* 30 (April 1926), 143–51.

"Death in the Desert." *Harvard Advocate* 117 (October 1930), 16–24.

"A Death in the Family—A Section." *Harper's Bazaar* (July 1956), 40.

"Jenkinsville I." *Phillips Exeter Monthly* 31 (December 1926), 71–72.

"Jenkinsville II." *Phillips Exeter Monthly* 31 (January 1927), 81–82.

"Knoxton High." *Phillips Exeter Monthly* 31 (April 1927), 161–66.

"Knoxville: Summer 1915." *Partisan Review* 5 (August–September 1938), 22–25.

"Minerva Farmer." *Phillips Exeter Monthly* 30 (November 1925), 39–42.

"A Mother's Tale." *Harper's Bazaar* (July 1952), 66–68.

"Mrs. Bruce and the Spider." *Phillips Exeter Monthly* 32 (February 1928), 113.

"Near the Tracks." *Harvard Advocate* 116 (June 1930), 9–20.

"1928 Story." *Texas Quarterly* 11 (Spring 1968), 23–37.

"Phogias and Meion." *Phillips Exeter Monthly* 30 (May 1926), 167–71.

"Revival." *Phillips Exeter Monthly* 30 (May 1926), 181.

"Rufus." *The New Yorker* 33 (November 2, 1957), 36–41.

"Sacre du Printemps." *Phillips Exeter Monthly* 32 (April 1928), 158–60.

"The Scar." *Phillips Exeter Monthly* 30 (January 1926), 77–78.

"A Sentimental Journey." *Phillips Exeter Monthly* 32 (March 1928), 133–37.

"They That in Sorrow Shall Reap." *Harvard Advocate* 117 (May 1931), 9–23.

"The Waiting." *The New Yorker* 33 (October 5, 1957), 41–62.

"A Walk Before Mass." *Harvard Advocate* 116 (Christmas 1929), 18–20.

"You, Andrew Volstead." *Harvard Advocate* 117 (March 1931), 22–29.

UNCOLLECTED DRAMAS AND SCREENPLAYS

PUBLISHED

Abraham Lincoln: The Early Years. In Rodney Sheratsky, ed., *The Lively Arts: Four Representative Types.* New York: Globe Books, 1964, 380–416.

Any Seventh Son. Phillips Exeter Monthly 31 (June 1927), 107–9.

Catched: A Play in Three Scenes. Phillips Exeter Monthly 30 (February 1926), 87–97.

Dedication Day. Politics 3 (April 1946), 121–25.

The House. In Horace Gregory, ed., *New Letters in America.* New York: Norton, 1937, 37–55.

Man's Fate. Films 1 (1939), 51–60.

In Vindication. Phillips Exeter Monthly 30 (March 1926), 122–26.

UNPUBLISHED

Bloodline (treatment), 1952.

Genghis Khan, 1952.

In the Street, 1945.

The Quiet One, 1949.

A Tanglewood Story (with Howard Taubman), 1955.

White Mane, 1953.

Williamsburg (incomplete) 1955.

ARTICLES

"Abysmal Ah Youth." *Harvard Advocate* 117 (December 1931), 28.

"Arbitrage." *Fortune* 9 (June 1934), 93–97, 150–60.

"Art for What's Sake?" *New Masses* 21 (December 15, 1936), 48.

"Average Man." *Time* 46 (November 26, 1945), 58–60, 64.

"Butler's Ball." *Fortune* 9 (March 1934), 68–69.

"Cabinet Changes." *Fortune* 10 (July 1934), 126–27.

"Class History." *Phillips Exeter Monthly* 32 (June 1928), 207–11.

"Cockfighting." *Fortune* 9 (March 1934), 90–95, 146.

"Colon." In James Laughlin, ed., *New Directions.* Norfolk, Conn.: New Directions, 1936, 181–92.

"Drought." *Fortune* 10 (October 1934), 76–83.

"Elmer Gantry." *Phillips Exeter Monthly* 31 (May 1927), 189–91.

"Europe: Autumn Story." *Time* 46 (October 15, 1945), 24–25.

"Extract from the Diary of a Disagreeable Young Man." *Phillips Exeter Monthly* 30 (December 1925), 62.

"Food—Harvest Home." *Time* 48 (September 23, 1946), 30.

"Gandhi." *Politics* 5 (Winter 1948), 4.

"Glass." *Fortune* 11 (January 1935), 48.

"Godless Götterdämmerung," *Time* 46 (October 15, 1945), 62–64.

"The Great American Roadside." *Fortune* 10 (September 1934), 53–63, 172–77.

"Great Britain." *Time* 48 (September 23, 1946), 32–33.

"Great Britain: Beyond Silence." *Time* 48 (October 7, 1946), 31.

"Hercules Powder." *Fortune* 12 (September 1935), 57–62, 110–25.

"Illuminated Manuscripts." *Fortune* 10 (December 1934), 90–98.

"In This Corner: The *Normandie.*" *Fortune* 11 (June 1935), 84–88.

"James Agee: By Himself." *Esquire* 60 (December 1963), 149.

"Jewel Spread." *Fortune* 14 (August 1936), 70.

"Largest Class in History of School Grades." *Phillips Exeter Monthly* 31 (November 1926), 48–52.

"Mr. Rockefeller's $14,000,000 Idyll." *Fortune* 12 (July 1935), 69–73.

"The Moving Picture." *Phillips Exeter Monthly* 30 (March 1926), 115–17.

"The Nation." *Time* 46 (November 5, 1945), 22–24.

"New York." *Time* 46 (October 1, 1945), 22–23.

"Notes on Portfolio of Photographs by Walker Evans." *Cambridge Review* 5 (1956), 25.

Parody of *Time. Harvard Advocate,* 118 (March 1932).

"Posters by Cassandra." *Fortune* 15 (May 1937), 120.

"The Project Is Important." *Fortune* 8 (October 1933), 81–97.

"Pseudo-Folk." *Partisan Review* 11 (Spring 1944), 219–23.

"Quinine to You." *Fortune* 9 (February 1934), 76–86.

"Religion and the Intellectuals." *Partisan Review* 17 (February 1950), 106–13.

"Roman Society." *Fortune* 10 (July 1934), 68–71, 144–50.

"Russia: Last Mile." *Time* 48 (September 9, 1946), 34.

"Saratoga." *Fortune* 12 (August 1935), 63–69, 96–100.

"Sharecropper Novels." *New Masses* 21 (June 8, 1937), 23.

"The Silver Sheet." *Harvard Advocate* 116 (April 1930), 42.

"Sins and Synonyms." *New Masses* 21 (November 17, 1938), 25.

"Six Days at Sea." *Fortune* 16 (September 1937), 117–20.

"Smoke." *Fortune* 15 (June 1937), 100–102, 130.

"A Star in the Darkness." *Time* 49 (April 7, 1947), 55–56.

"The Steel Rails." *Fortune* 8 (December 1933), 42–47, 153.

"Suburban Cawdor." *Harvard Advocate* 117 (May 1931), 86–88.

"Syria: Triumph of Civilization." *Time* 48 (September 9, 1946), 34.

"Three Tenant Families: A Selection." *Common Sense* 8 (October 1939), 9–12.

"To What Extent Do the Ramifications . . ." *Phillips Exeter Monthly* 31 (March 1927), 135–40.

"TVA I: Work in the Valley." *Fortune* 11 (May 1935), 93–98, 140–53.

"U.S. Ambassadors." *Fortune* 9 (April 1934), 108–22.

"U.S. Art: 1935." *Fortune* 12 (December 1935), 68–75.

"U.S. at War." *Time* 45 (April 23, 1945), 1.

"The U.S. Commercial Orchid." *Fortune* 12 (December 1935), 108–14, 126–29.

"Victory: The Peace," *Time* 46 (August 20, 1945), 19–21.

"Voice of Reason." *Time* 48 (August 26, 1946), 28.

"What D'You Mean, Modern?" *Fortune* 12 (November 1935), 97–103, 164.

SECONDARY SOURCES

BOOKS

AGEE, JOEL. *Twelve Years.* New York: Farrar, Straus & Giroux, 1981.

CHAMBERS, WHITTAKER. *Cold Friday.* New York: Random House, 1964.

————. *Witness.* New York: Random House, 1952.

CHAPLIN, CHARLES. *My Autobiography.* New York: Simon & Schuster, 1964.

COLES, ROBERT. *Irony in the Mind's Life.* Charlottesville: University Press of Virginia, 1973.

DARDIS, TOM. *Some Time in the Sun.* New York: Scribner's, 1976.

DOTY, MARK. *Tell Me Who I Am: James Agee's Search for Selfhood.* Baton Rouge: Louisiana State University Press, 1981.

DUPEE, F. W. *King of the Cats and Other Remarks on Writers and Writing.* New York: Farrar, Straus & Giroux, 1965.

ELSON, ROBERT. *Time Inc.: The Intimate History of a Publishing Enterprise, 1923–1941.* New York: Atheneum, 1968.

————. *The World of Time Inc.: The Intimate History of a Publishing Enterprise, 1941–1960.* New York: Atheneum, 1973.

FROHOCK, W. M. *The Novel of Violence in America.* Boston: Beacon Press, 1964.

HUSTON, JOHN. *An Open Book.* New York: Alfred A. Knopf, 1980.

KAZIN, ALFRED. *Contemporaries.* Boston: Little, Brown, 1962.

————. *New York Jew.* New York: Alfred A. Knopf, 1978.

KIRSTEIN, LINCOLN. *Rhymes of a Pfc.* Rev. ed. Boston: David R. Godine, 1981.

KRONENBERGER, LOUIS. *No Whippings, No Gold Watches.* Boston: Little, Brown, 1970.

LANCHESTER, ELSA. *Elsa Lanchester: Herself.* New York: St. Martin's Press, 1983.

MACDONALD, DWIGHT. *Against the American Grain.* New York: Random House, 1965.

————. *On Movies.* New York: Da Capo Press, 1981.

MACLEISH, ARCHIBALD. *Collected Poems, 1917–1952.* Boston: Houghton Mifflin, 1952.

MADDEN, DAVID, ed. *Remembering James Agee.* Baton Rouge: Louisiana State University Press, 1974.

MOREAU, GENEVIEVE. *The Restless Journey of James Agee.* New York: William Morrow, 1977.

MORISON, SAMUEL ELIOT. *Three Centuries of Harvard: 1636–1936.* Cambridge: Harvard University Press, 1965.

POMEROY, ELSIE. *William Saunders and His Five Sons: The Story of the Marquis Wheat Family.* Toronto: The Ryerson Press, 1956.

A Record of the Agee Family. Independence, Mo.: privately printed, 1937.

ROSS, LILLIAN. *Picture.* New York: Rinehart, 1953.

SARGEANT, WINTHROP. *In Spite of Myself.* New York: Doubleday, 1970.

SKINNER, B. F. *Particulars of My Life.* New York: Alfred A. Knopf, 1976.

SWANBERG, W. A. *Luce and His Empire.* New York: Scribner's, 1975.

WICKES, FRANCES. *The Inner World of Childhood: A Study in Analytical Psychology.* New York: Appleton-Century, 1927.

Writing for Fortune: Nineteen Authors Remember Life on the Staff of a Remarkable Magazine. New York: Time Inc., 1980.

ARTICLES

BREIT, HARVEY. "Cotton Tenantry." *The New Republic* 105 (September 15, 1941), 349–50.

DUPEE, F. W. "Pride of Maturity." *The Nation* 172 (April 28, 1951), 400–401.

FROHOCK, W. M. "James Agee: The Question of Unkept Promise." *Southwest Review* 42 (Summer 1957), 221–29.

KIRSTEIN, LINCOLN. "First Poems." *The New Republic* 72 (February 27, 1935), 80–81.

MACDONALD, DWIGHT. "James Agee: Some Memories and Letters." *Encounter* 19 (December 1962), 73–84.

———. "On Chaplin, Verdoux and Agee." *Esquire* 63 (April 1965), 18.

MATTHEWS, T. S. "James Agee—Strange and Wonderful." *Saturday Review* (April 16, 1966), 22–23.

NEUMAN, ALMA. "Thoughts of Jim: A Memoir of Frenchtown and James Agee." *Shenandoah* (Fall 1983), 25–36.

RAINES, HOWELL. "Let Us Now Revisit Famous Folk." *New York Times Magazine* (May 25, 1980).

STERN, JAMES. "Walker Evans (1903–1975): A Memoir." *London Magazine* (August–September 1977).

TRILLING, LIONEL. "Greatness with One Fault in It." *Kenyon Review* 4 (Winter 1942), 99–102.

INDEX

455